BATMAN

BLACK and WHITE

WRITERS

BRIAN **BOLLAND**
HOWARD **CHAYKIN**
CHUCK **DIXON**
NEIL **GAIMAN**
ARCHIE **GOODWIN**
ANDREW **HELFER**
KLAUS **JANSON**
JOE **KUBERT**
TED **MCKEEVER**
DENNIS **O'NEIL**
KATSUHIRO **OTOMO**
(TRANSLATED BY JO DUFFY)
BILL **SIENKIEWICZ**
WALTER **SIMONSON**
JAN **STRNAD**
BRUCE **TIMM**
MATT **WAGNER**
KENT **WILLIAMS**

ILLUSTRATORS

SIMON **BISLEY**
BRIAN **BOLLAND**
HOWARD **CHAYKIN**
RICHARD **CORBEN**
GARY **GIANNI**
KLAUS **JANSON**
TEDDY **KRISTIANSEN**
JOE **KUBERT**
LIBERATORE
TED **MCKEEVER**
JOSÉ **MUÑOZ**
KEVIN **NOWLAN**
KATSUHIRO **OTOMO**
BILL **SIENKIEWICZ**
WALTER **SIMONSON**
BRIAN **STELFREEZE**
BRUCE **TIMM**
MATT **WAGNER**
KENT **WILLIAMS**
JORGE **ZAFFINO**

LETTERERS

KEN **BRUZENAK**
JOHN **COSTANZA**
ELLIE **DE VILLE**
PHIL **FELIX**
TIM **HARKINS**
TODD **KLEIN**
BILL **OAKLEY**
JOHN **WORKMAN**

PINUPS/COVERS

MICHAEL **ALLRED**
MOEBIUS
MICHAEL WM. **KALUTA**
TONY **SALMONS**
P. CRAIG **RUSSELL**
MARC **SILVESTRI** AND **BATT**
ALEX **ROSS**
NEAL **ADAMS**
PINUPS

JIM **LEE** AND SCOTT **WILLIAMS**
FRANK **MILLER**
BARRY **WINDSOR-SMITH**
ALEX **TOTH**
COVERS

ALEX TOTH
FRONT COVER ILLUSTRATION

JEFF JONES
BACK COVER PAINTING

B A T M A N C R E

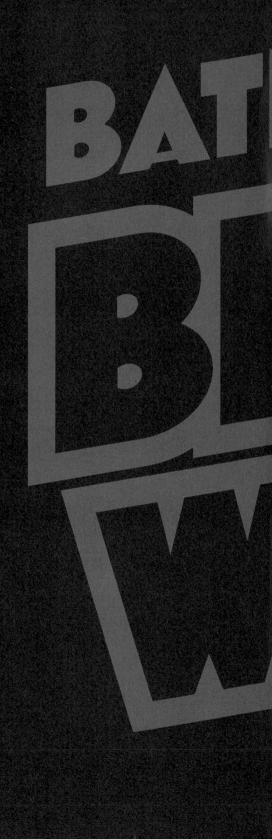

...MAN
...ACK and
...HITE

...TED BY BOB KANE

For Neal Pozner-

Who knew not everything was black and white

D E D I C A T I O N

JENETTE KAHN PRESIDENT & EDITOR-IN-CHIEF **PAUL LEVITZ** EXECUTIVE VICE PRESIDENT & PUBLISHER
DENNIS O'NEIL GROUP EDITOR **MARK CHIARELLO & SCOTT PETERSON** EDITORS-ORIGINAL MINISERIES
DALE CRAIN EDITOR-COLLECTED EDITION **DARREN VINCENZO** ASSOCIATE EDITOR-ORIGINAL MINISERIES
NICK J. NAPOLITANO ASSOCIATE EDITOR-COLLECTED EDITION **MICHAEL WRIGHT** ASSISTANT EDITOR-COLLECTED EDITION
GEORG BREWER DESIGN DIRECTOR **ROBBIN BROSTERMAN** ART DIRECTOR
RICHARD BRUNING VP-CREATIVE DIRECTOR **PATRICK CALDON** VP-FINANCE & OPERATIONS
DOROTHY CROUCH VP-LICENSED PUBLISHING **TERRI CUNNINGHAM** VP-MANAGING EDITOR
JOEL EHRLICH SENIOR VP-ADVERTISING & PROMOTIONS **ALISON GILL** EXEC. DIRECTOR-MANUFACTURING
LILLIAN LASERSON VP & GENERAL COUNSEL **JIM LEE** EDITORIAL DIRECTOR-WILDSTORM
JOHN NEE VP & GENERAL MANAGER-WILDSTORM **BOB WAYNE** VP-DIRECT SALES

B A T M A N   B L A C K   A N D   W H I T E

DC Comics, 1700 Broadway, New York, NY 10019
A division of Warner Bros. - A Time Warner Entertainment Company
Printed in Canada. First Printing.
ISBN: 1-56389-439-4

CONTENTS

7
FOREWORD BY
MARK CHIARELLO

10
COVER
BATMAN BLACK AND WHITE #1 BY
JIM LEE AND SCOTT WILLIAMS

11
PERPETUAL MOURNING
WRITTEN AND ILLUSTRATED BY
TED MCKEEVER
LETTERED BY
JOHN WORKMAN

21
TWO OF A KIND
WRITTEN AND ILLUSTRATED BY
BRUCE TIMM
LETTERED BY
TODD KLEIN

31
THE HUNT
WRITTEN AND ILLUSTRATED BY
JOE KUBERT

41
PETTY CRIMES
WRITTEN AND ILLUSTRATED BY
HOWARD CHAYKIN
LETTERED BY
KEN BRUZENAK

51
THE DEVIL'S TRUMPET
WRITTEN BY
ARCHIE GOODWIN
ILLUSTRATED BY
JOSÉ MUÑOZ

62-63
SKETCHES FROM
BATMAN BLACK AND WHITE 1
COMMENTS BY MARK CHIARELLO

64
COVER
BATMAN BLACK AND WHITE #2 BY
FRANK MILLER

65
LEGEND
WRITTEN AND ILLUSTRATED BY
WALTER SIMONSON
LETTERED BY
JOHN WORKMAN

75
MONSTER MAKER
WRITTEN BY
JAN STRNAD
ILLUSTRATED BY
RICHARD CORBEN
LETTERED BY
PHIL FELIX

85
DEAD BOYS EYES
WRITTEN AND ILLUSTRATED BY
KENT WILLIAMS

95
THE DEVIL'S CHILDREN
WRITTEN BY
CHUCK DIXON
ILLUSTRATED BY
JORGE ZAFFINO
LETTERED BY
JOHN COSTANZA

105
A BLACK AND WHITE WORLD
WRITTEN BY
NEIL GAIMAN
ILLUSTRATED BY
SIMON BISLEY
LETTERED BY
JOHN COSTANZA

116-117
SKETCHES FROM
BATMAN BLACK AND WHITE 2
COMMENTS BY MARK CHIARELLO

118
COVER
BATMAN BLACK AND WHITE #3 BY
BARRY WINDSOR-SMITH

119
GOOD EVENING, MIDNIGHT
WRITTEN AND ILLUSTRATED BY
KLAUS JANSON
LETTERED BY
BILL OAKLEY

CONTENTS

CONTENTS

129
IN DREAMS
WRITTEN BY
ANDREW HELFER
ILLUSTRATED BY
LIBERATORE
LETTERED BY
JOHN COSTANZA

139
HEIST
WRITTEN AND ILLUSTRATED BY
MATT WAGNER
LETTERED BY
TIM HARKINS

149
BENT TWIGS
WRITTEN AND ILLUSTRATED BY
BILL SIENKIEWICZ

159
A SLAYING SONG TONIGHT
WRITTEN BY
DENNIS O'NEIL
ILLUSTRATED BY
TEDDY KRISTIANSEN

170-171
SKETCHES FROM
BATMAN BLACK AND WHITE 3
COMMENTS BY MARK CHIARELLO

172
COVER
BATMAN BLACK AND WHITE #4 BY
ALEX TOTH

173
AN INNOCENT GUY
WRITTEN AND ILLUSTRATED BY
BRIAN BOLLAND
LETTERED BY
ELLIE DEVILLE

183
MONSTERS IN THE CLOSET
WRITTEN BY
JAN STRNAD
ILLUSTRATED BY
KEVIN NOWLAN

193
HEROES
WRITTEN BY
ARCHIE GOODWIN
ILLUSTRATED BY
GARY GIANNI
LETTERED BY
TODD KLEIN

203
LEAVETAKING
WRITTEN BY
DENNIS O'NEIL
ILLUSTRATED BY
BRIAN STELFREEZE
LETTERED BY
JOHN COSTANZA

213
THE THIRD MASK
WRITTEN AND ILLUSTRATED BY
KATSUHIRO OTOMO
TRANSLATED BY
JO DUFFY
LETTERED BY
BILL OAKLEY

224-225
SKETCHES FROM
BATMAN BLACK AND WHITE 4
COMMENTS BY MARK CHIARELLO

226
PINUP GALLERY

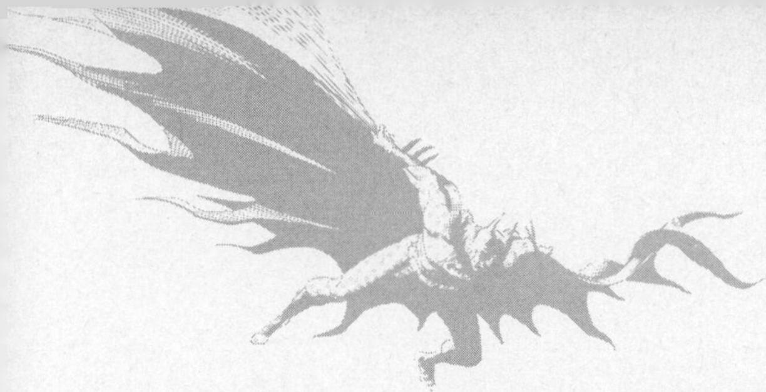

INTRODUCTION **BY MARK CHIARELLO**

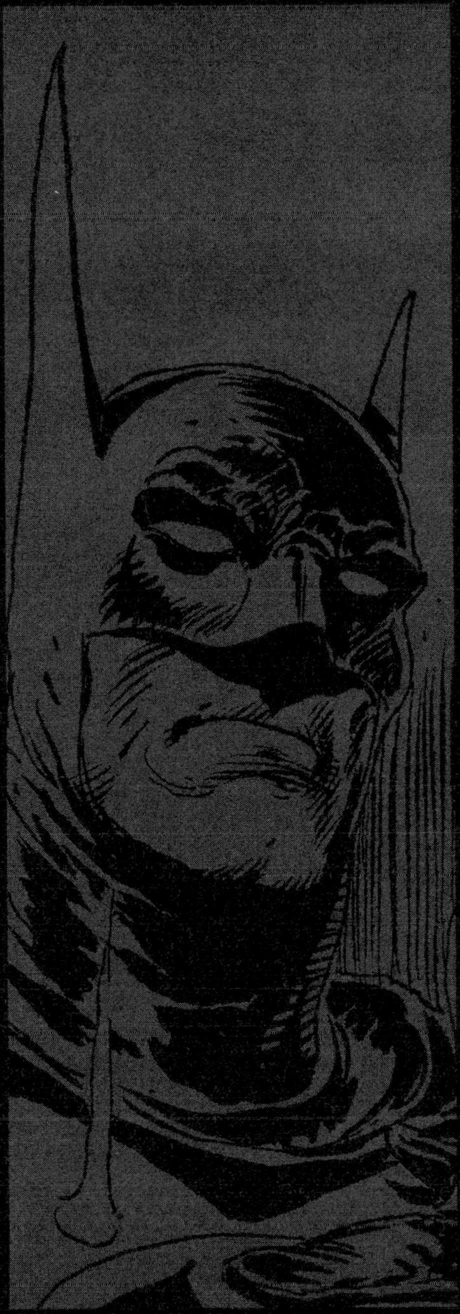

A few years back, I was sitting around a dinner table with a few famous comic-book artists.

It was late at night, after we had all put in a hard day at another long-since-forgotten comics convention. Being the diehard fanboys that we are forever cursed to be, we were of course talking about comic books.

Someone raised the inevitable "desert island" question: you're stranded, cut off from civilization —what complete run of *one* comics title would you want to have with you?

Well, we all pondered for half a minute. A big-time penciller piped up "*Creepy* or *Eerie*." One of those comics painter guys said "Yep, definitely *Creepy*." I agreed, no question about it. Amazingly, we all agreed, pound for pound, page for page, there has never been such a collection of stellar artists assembled under one banner publication. And they all did their careers' best work in those pages! Toth, Frazetta, Williamson, Torres, Colan, Ditko, Wrightson, Corben — the list goes on and on. Funny, spooky, corny, horrific stories, any kid's comic dream, any artist's dream comic.

Well, as we all know, comics are the synthesis of pictures *and* words. Someone had to write all (or most) of those stories. That guy's name was Archie Goodwin. Probably the very best editor ever to work in comics, probably the very best writer ever to work in comics. The work Archie did on the Warren books (*Creepy*, *Eerie* and *Blazing Combat*) was his homage to the favorite comics of his youth, the E.C. line.

Flash forward a whole bunch of years. For some unknown, godforsaken reason, I become an editor at DC Comics. I pitch the idea of a black and white anthology series featuring Batman. The key to the series' success, I figure, is to hire the very best artists in the business. Most everyone at DC tells me it won't sell. No one likes black and white comics. No one likes anthologies. Somehow the series gets the green light. In his infinite wisdom, Executive Editor Mike Carlin has Batman Editor Scott Peterson come on board to keep me honest and make sure I don't destroy the integrity of one of DC's flagship characters.

Over the course of the next eight months, Scott and I compile a list of the artists we'd like to work with, make a million phone calls, send out and receive a million faxes.

And then the art starts coming in. Holy moley! You can only imagine me and Scott running up and down the hallway, office to office, each time a package arrives. BRIAN BOLLAND'S PAGES ARE HERE!!! HEY LOOK, IT'S ALEX TOTH'S COVER!!! WOW! LOOK, GUYS, IT'S OTOMO'S STORY!!!

The series becomes a creative and financial success.

PERPETUAL **MOURNING**

TED McKEEVER

Ted McKeever's singular vision of mankind's inner turmoil has left an indelible impression on modern comics.

He is one of the few artist/writers of his generation not content with merely rehashing genre clichés. Ted's conscious decision to stay outside the world of mainstream comics allows his highly personal creations to defy being categorized.

McKeever's work on such creator-owned projects as *Eddy Current, Plastic Forks* and *Metropol* is as haunting as it is memorable.

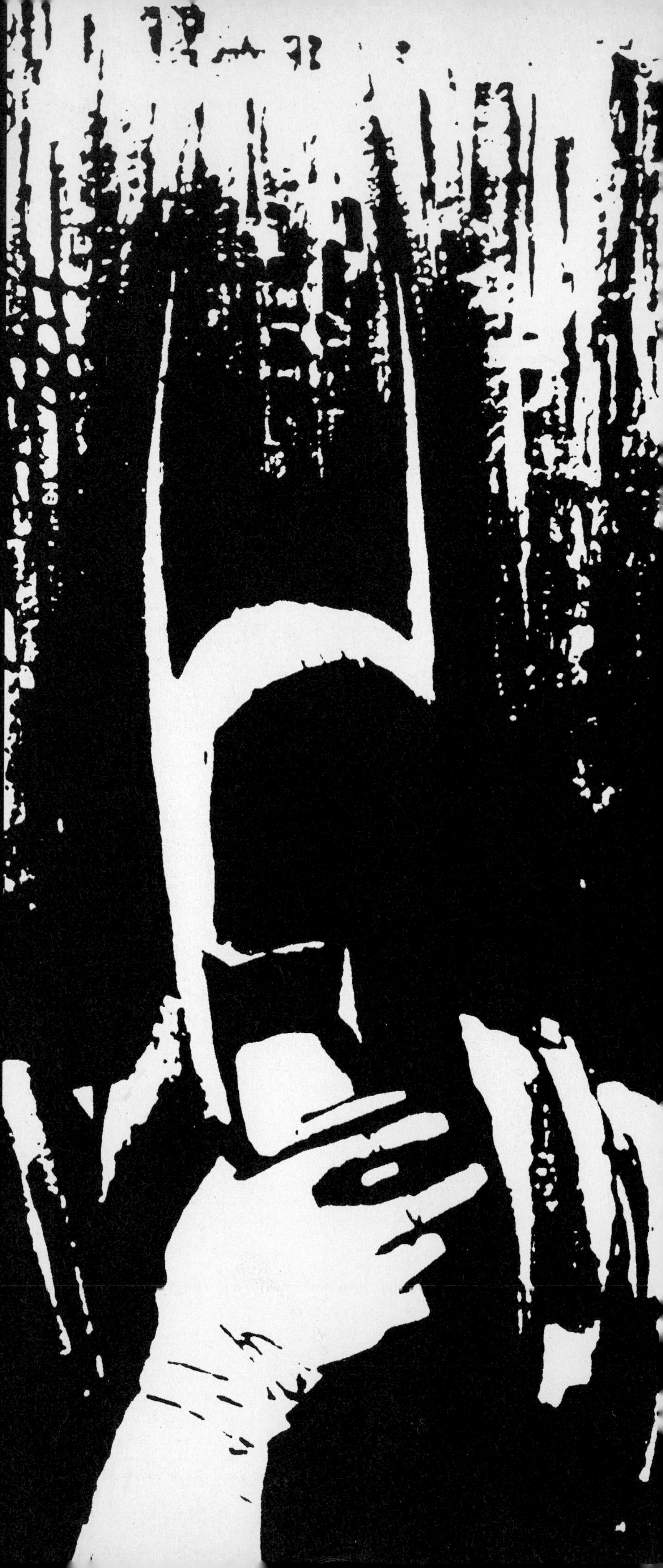

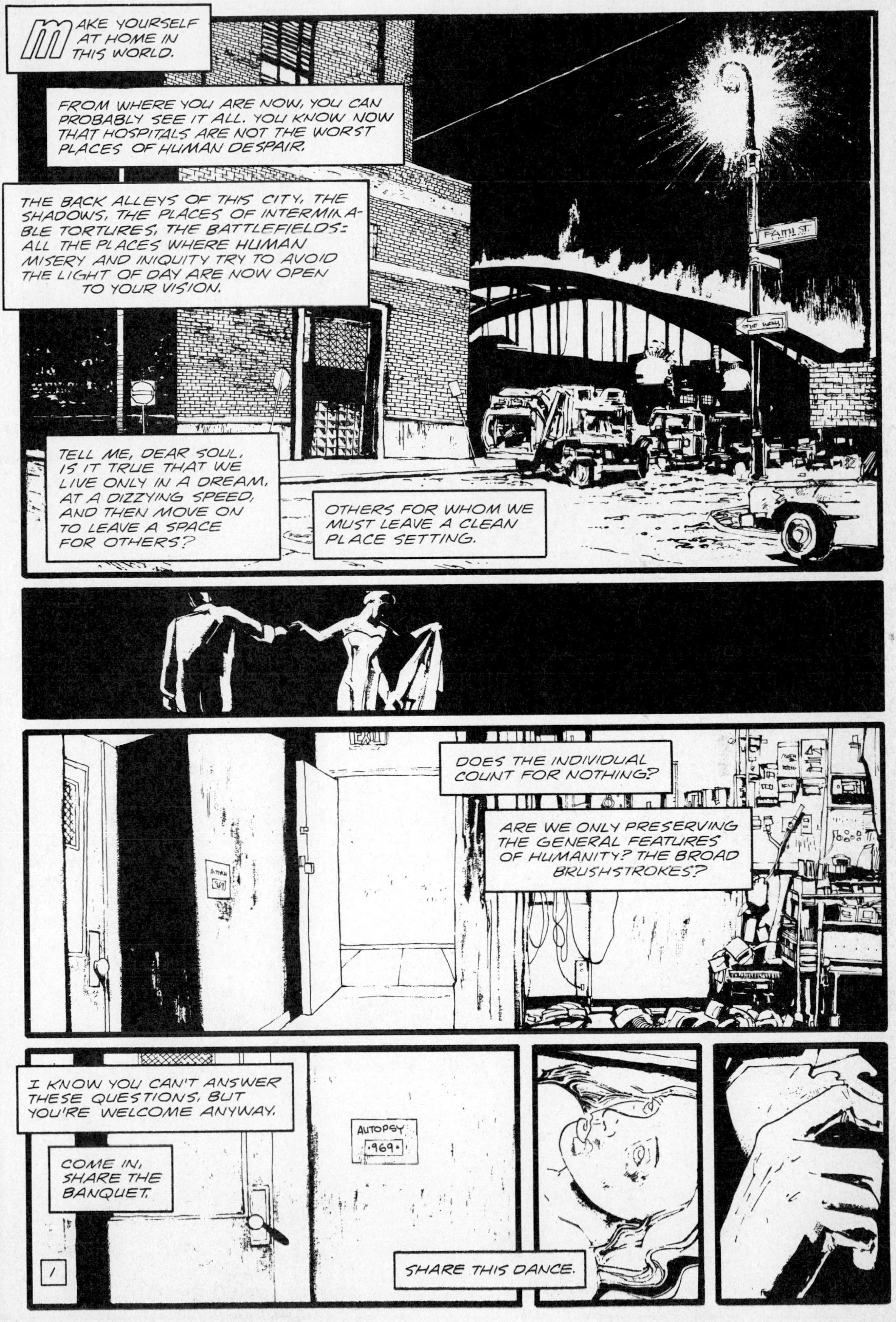
MAKE YOURSELF AT HOME IN THIS WORLD.
FROM WHERE YOU ARE NOW, YOU CAN PROBABLY SEE IT ALL. YOU KNOW NOW THAT HOSPITALS ARE NOT THE WORST PLACES OF HUMAN DESPAIR.
THE BACK ALLEYS OF THIS CITY, THE SHADOWS, THE PLACES OF INTERMINABLE TORTURES, THE BATTLEFIELDS: ALL THE PLACES WHERE HUMAN MISERY AND INIQUITY TRY TO AVOID THE LIGHT OF DAY ARE NOW OPEN TO YOUR VISION.
FAITH ST.
ONE WAY
TELL ME, DEAR SOUL, IS IT TRUE THAT WE LIVE ONLY IN A DREAM, AT A DIZZYING SPEED, AND THEN MOVE ON TO LEAVE A SPACE FOR OTHERS?
OTHERS FOR WHOM WE MUST LEAVE A CLEAN PLACE SETTING.
EXIT
DOES THE INDIVIDUAL COUNT FOR NOTHING?
ARE WE ONLY PRESERVING THE GENERAL FEATURES OF HUMANITY? THE BROAD BRUSHSTROKES?
I KNOW YOU CAN'T ANSWER THESE QUESTIONS, BUT YOU'RE WELCOME ANYWAY.
COME IN, SHARE THE BANQUET.
AUTOPSY
·969·
SHARE THIS DANCE.

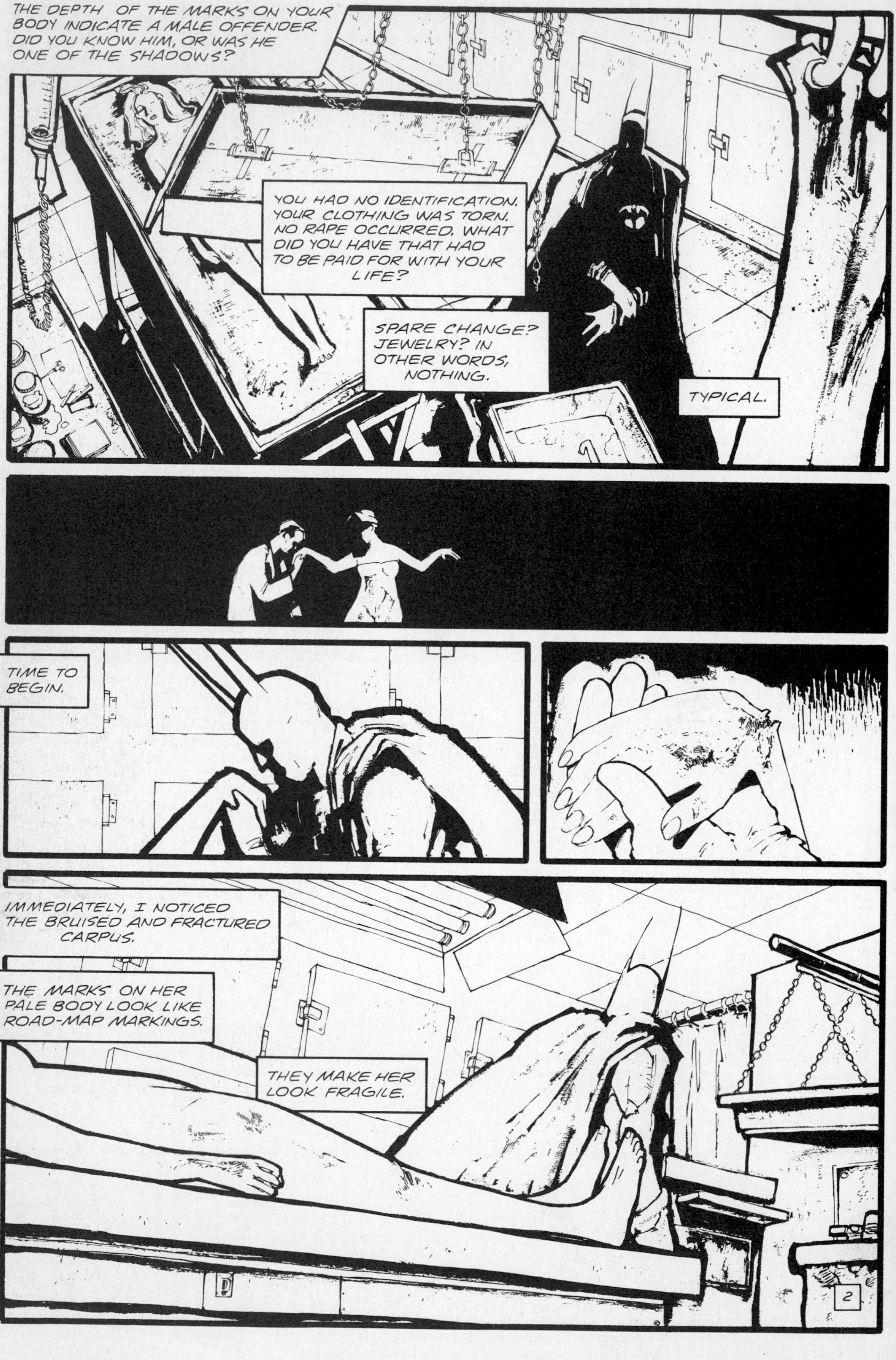
THE DEPTH OF THE MARKS ON YOUR BODY INDICATE A MALE OFFENDER. DID YOU KNOW HIM, OR WAS HE ONE OF THE SHADOWS?
YOU HAD NO IDENTIFICATION. YOUR CLOTHING WAS TORN. NO RAPE OCCURRED. WHAT DID YOU HAVE THAT HAD TO BE PAID FOR WITH YOUR LIFE?
SPARE CHANGE? JEWELRY? IN OTHER WORDS, NOTHING.
TYPICAL.
TIME TO BEGIN.
IMMEDIATELY, I NOTICED THE BRUISED AND FRACTURED CARPUS.
THE MARKS ON HER PALE BODY LOOK LIKE ROAD-MAP MARKINGS.
THEY MAKE HER LOOK FRAGILE.
2

THE BROKEN CARPUS COULD'VE COME FROM A BLOW BY A BLUNT OBJECT. A PIPE, A STICK.

THE BASTARD.

DISLOCATED CLAVICLE. PROBABLY FROM HITTING THE GROUND.

BRUISED PLATYSMA. THE SPACES INDICATE SHE WAS EITHER BEING STRANGLED ...OR AN UNINTENTIONAL LEVERAGE POINT.

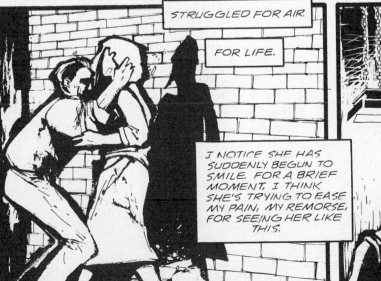

STRUGGLED FOR AIR.

FOR LIFE.

I NOTICE SHE HAS SUDDENLY BEGUN TO SMILE. FOR A BRIEF MOMENT, I THINK SHE'S TRYING TO EASE MY PAIN, MY REMORSE, FOR SEEING HER LIKE THIS.

3

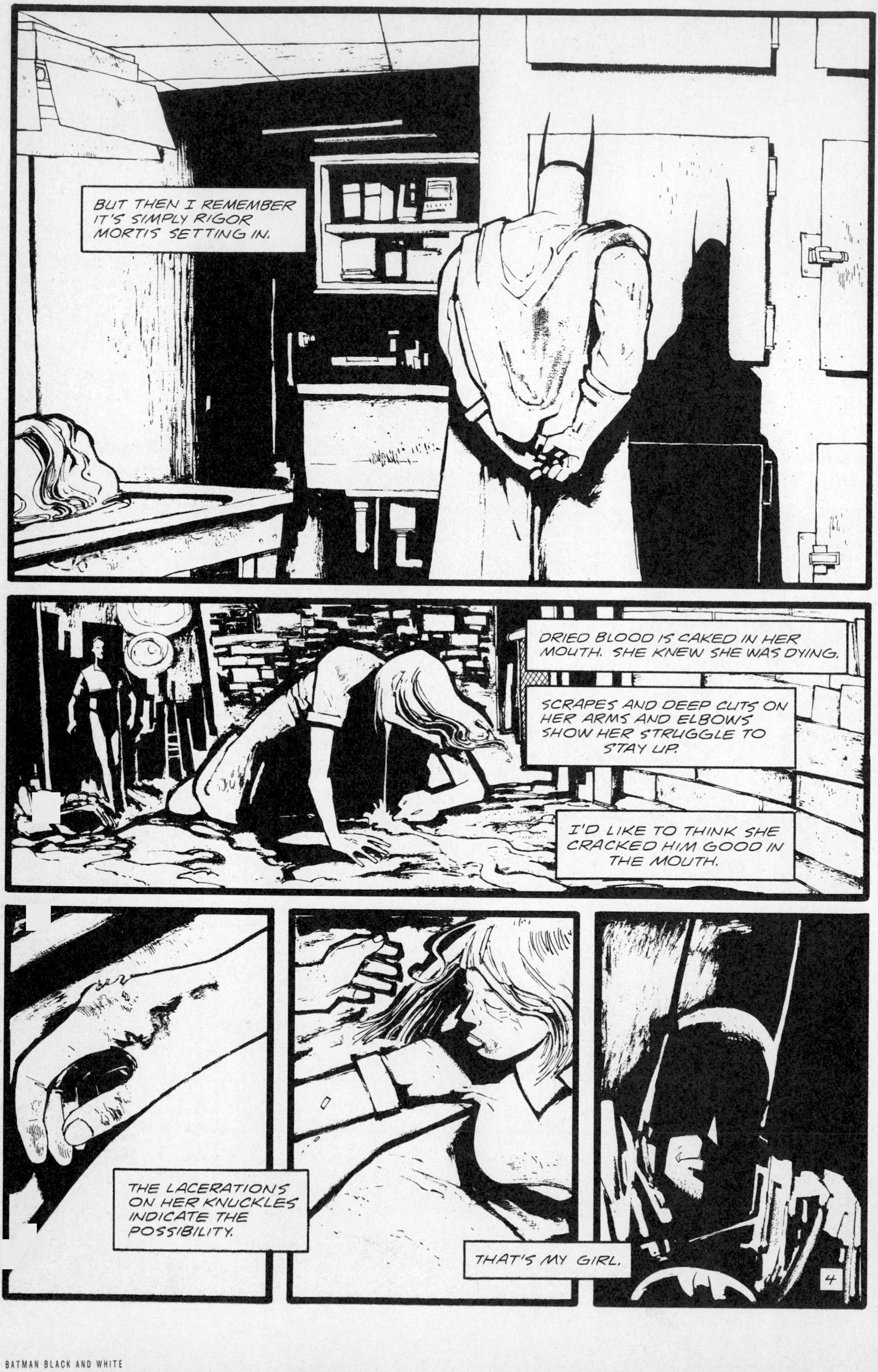
BUT THEN I REMEMBER IT'S SIMPLY RIGOR MORTIS SETTING IN.
DRIED BLOOD IS CAKED IN HER MOUTH. SHE KNEW SHE WAS DYING.
SCRAPES AND DEEP CUTS ON HER ARMS AND ELBOWS SHOW HER STRUGGLE TO STAY UP.
I'D LIKE TO THINK SHE CRACKED HIM GOOD IN THE MOUTH.
THE LACERATIONS ON HER KNUCKLES INDICATE THE POSSIBILITY.
THAT'S MY GIRL.
4

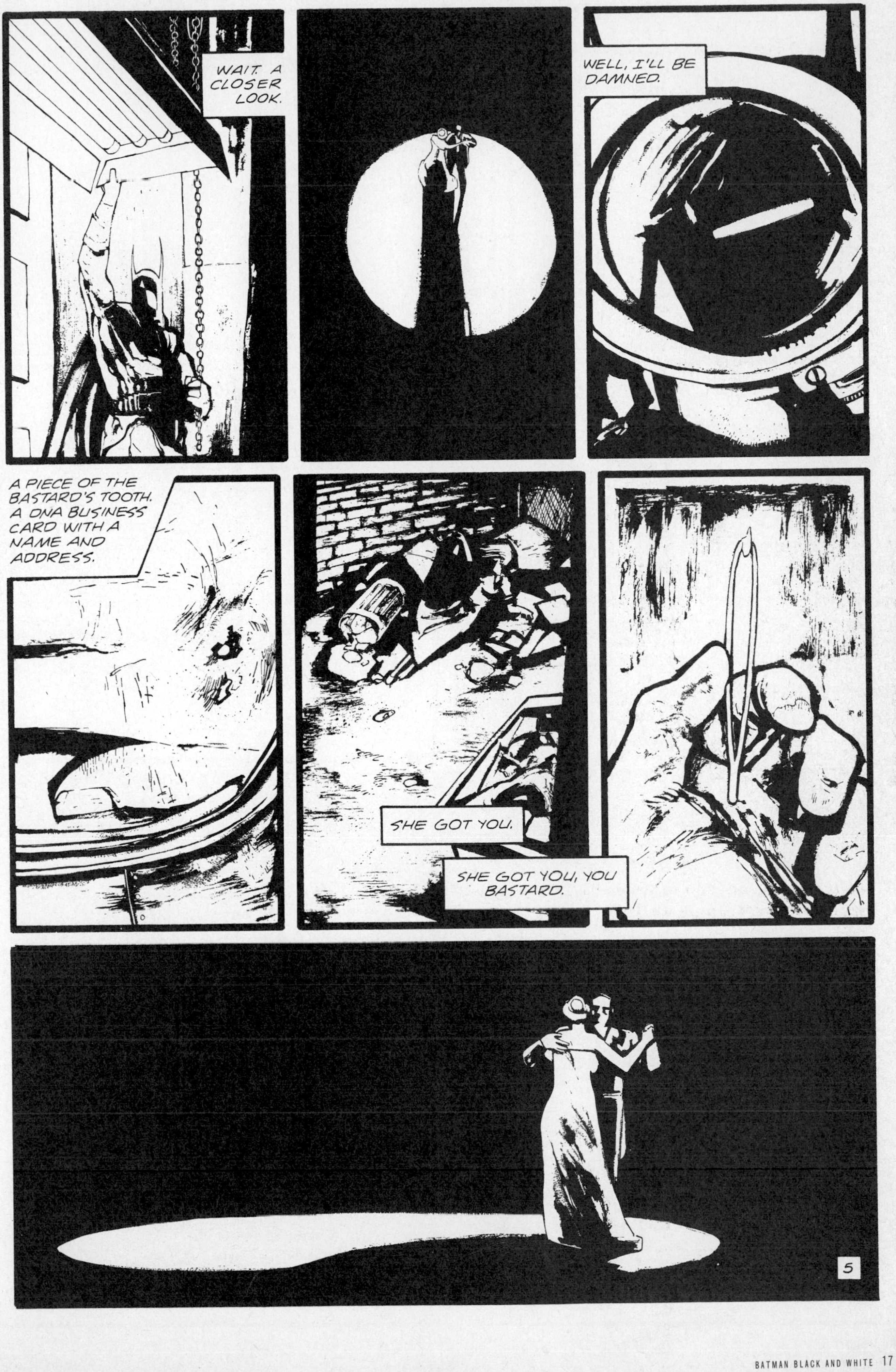

WAIT. A CLOSER LOOK.
WELL, I'LL BE DAMNED.
A PIECE OF THE BASTARD'S TOOTH. A DNA BUSINESS CARD WITH A NAME AND ADDRESS.
SHE GOT YOU.
SHE GOT YOU, YOU BASTARD.
5

THERE'S STILL ONE MORE THING LEFT FOR YOU TO DO.
YOU'VE ALLOWED ME TO STEP INSIDE YOUR CIRCLE, ALLOWED ME TO SEARCH YOUR BODY FOR ANSWERS. NOW LET ME REACH INTO YOUR SOUL.
I NEED YOUR NAME.
HOME COOKIN EAT HERE TAKE-OUT
OPEN 24 hrs
BROADWAY DINER
6

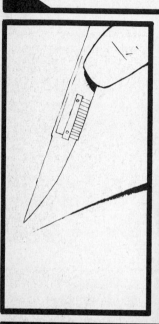

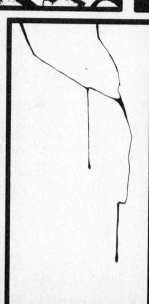

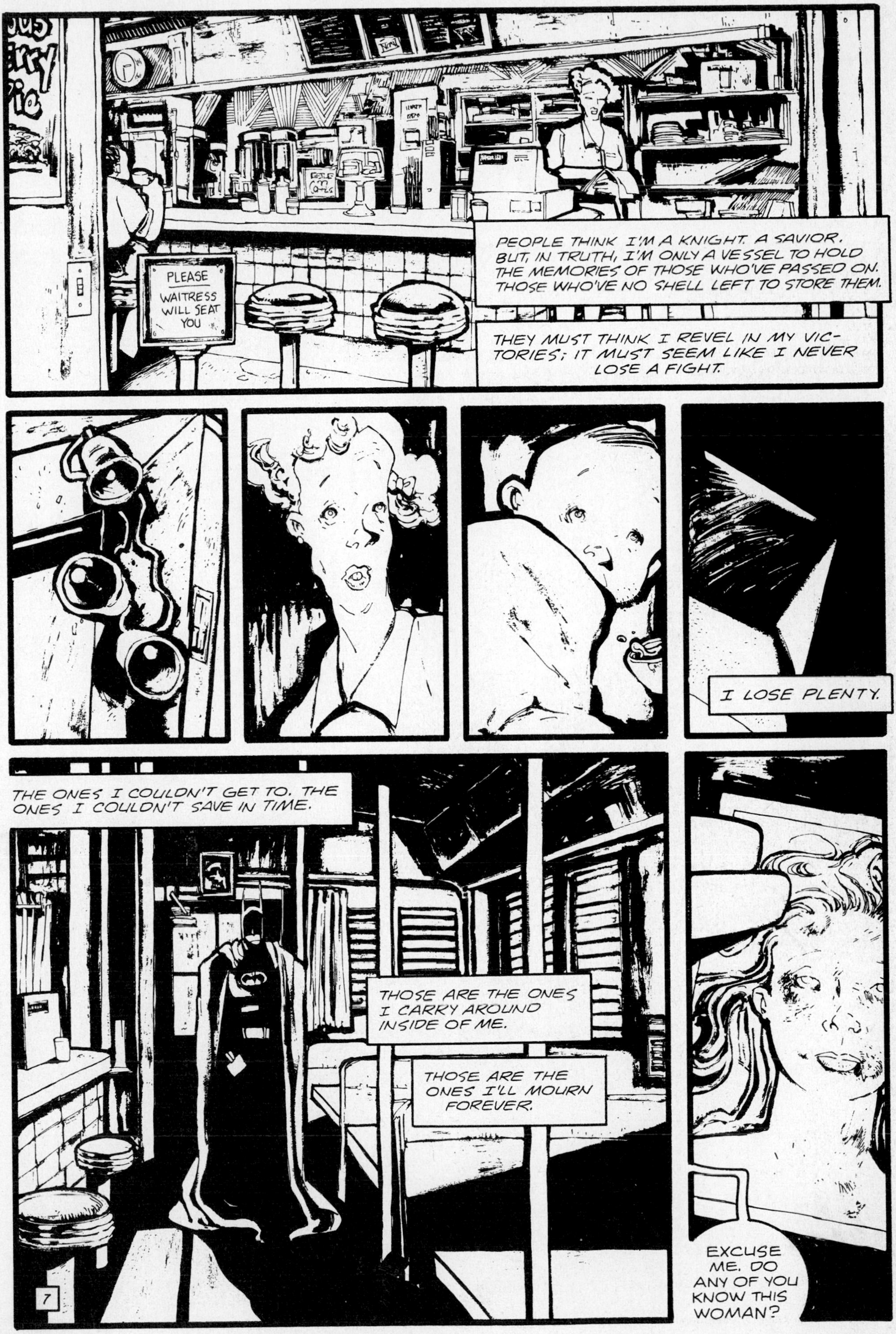
PLEASE
WAITRESS WILL SEAT YOU
PEOPLE THINK I'M A KNIGHT. A SAVIOR. BUT, IN TRUTH, I'M ONLY A VESSEL TO HOLD THE MEMORIES OF THOSE WHO'VE PASSED ON. THOSE WHO'VE NO SHELL LEFT TO STORE THEM.
THEY MUST THINK I REVEL IN MY VICTORIES; IT MUST SEEM LIKE I NEVER LOSE A FIGHT.
I LOSE PLENTY.
THE ONES I COULDN'T GET TO. THE ONES I COULDN'T SAVE IN TIME.
THOSE ARE THE ONES I CARRY AROUND INSIDE OF ME.
THOSE ARE THE ONES I'LL MOURN FOREVER.
7
EXCUSE ME. DO ANY OF YOU KNOW THIS WOMAN?

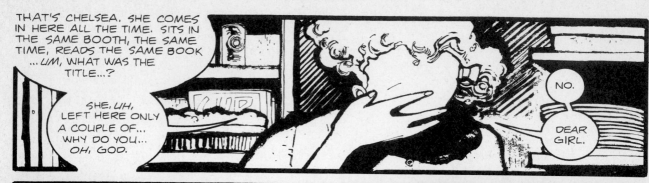

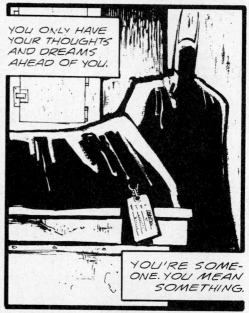

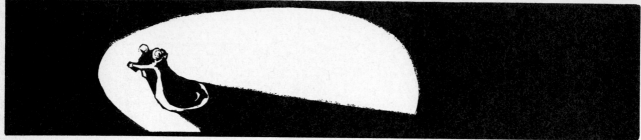

THAT'S CHELSEA. SHE COMES IN HERE ALL THE TIME. SITS IN THE SAME BOOTH, THE SAME TIME, READS THE SAME BOOK ...UM, WHAT WAS THE TITLE...?
SHE, UH, LEFT HERE ONLY A COUPLE OF... WHY DO YOU... OH, GOD.
NO.
DEAR GIRL.
LUCKILY, YOU HADN'T DIGESTED YOUR LAST MEAL, CHELSEA. THERE'RE ONLY A FEW PLACES IN THE NEIGHBORHOOD WHERE YOU WERE FOUND THAT SERVE BLUEBERRY PIE AT THIS HOUR OF THE MORNING.
YOU ONLY HAVE YOUR THOUGHTS AND DREAMS AHEAD OF YOU.
YOU'RE SOMEONE. YOU MEAN SOMETHING.
Name: Chelsea Rain
Age: 30
Sex: Female
Race: Caucasian
I'LL REMEMBER. YOU'RE WITHIN ME NOW.
8
FOREVER.
END

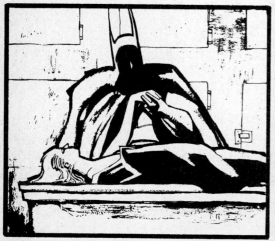

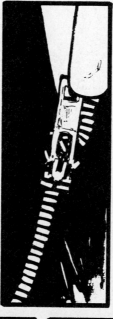

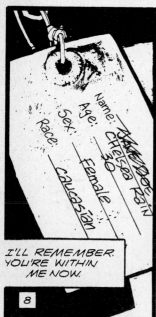

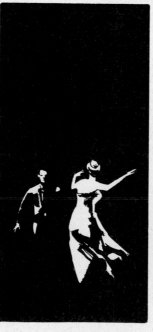

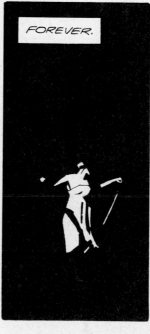

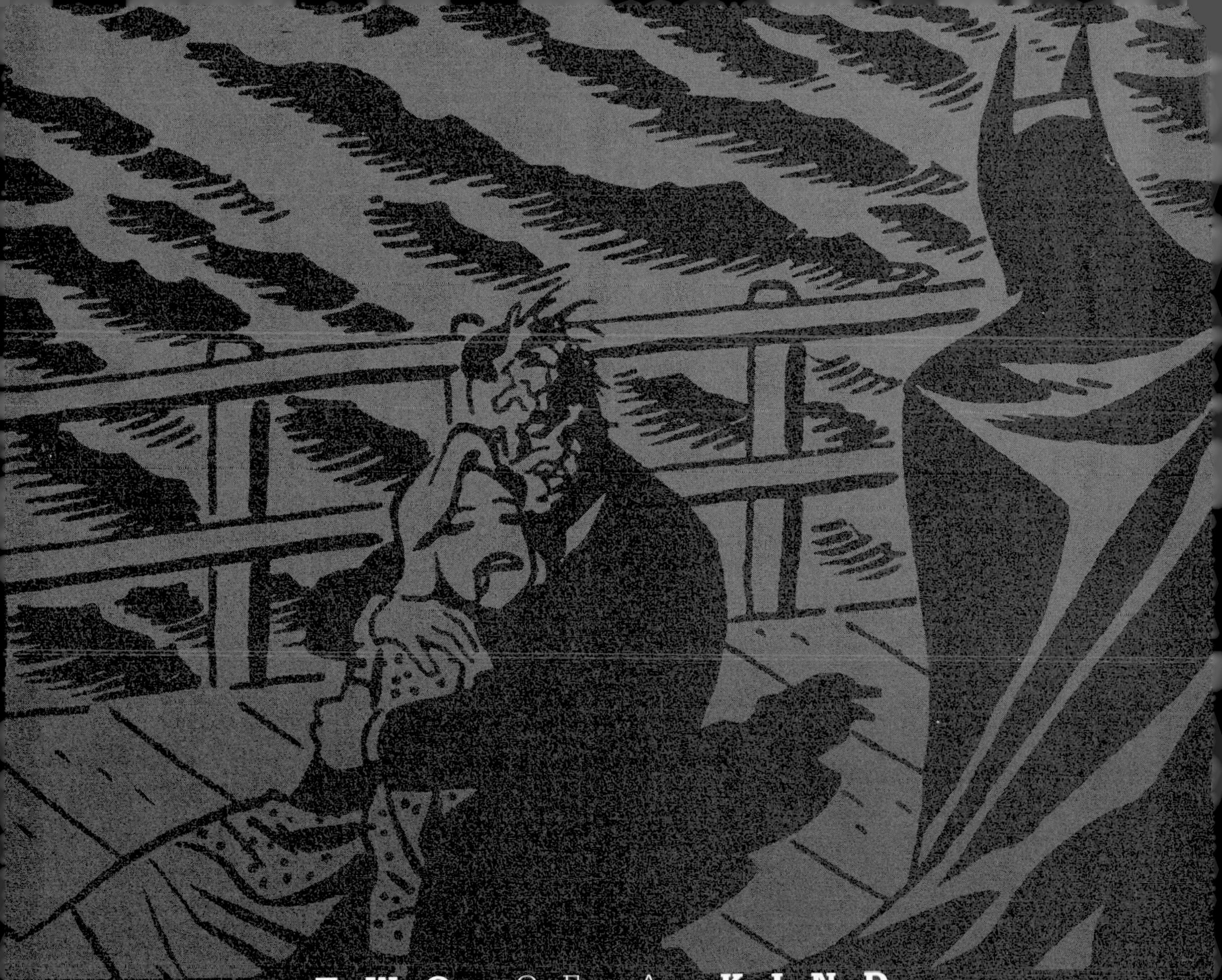

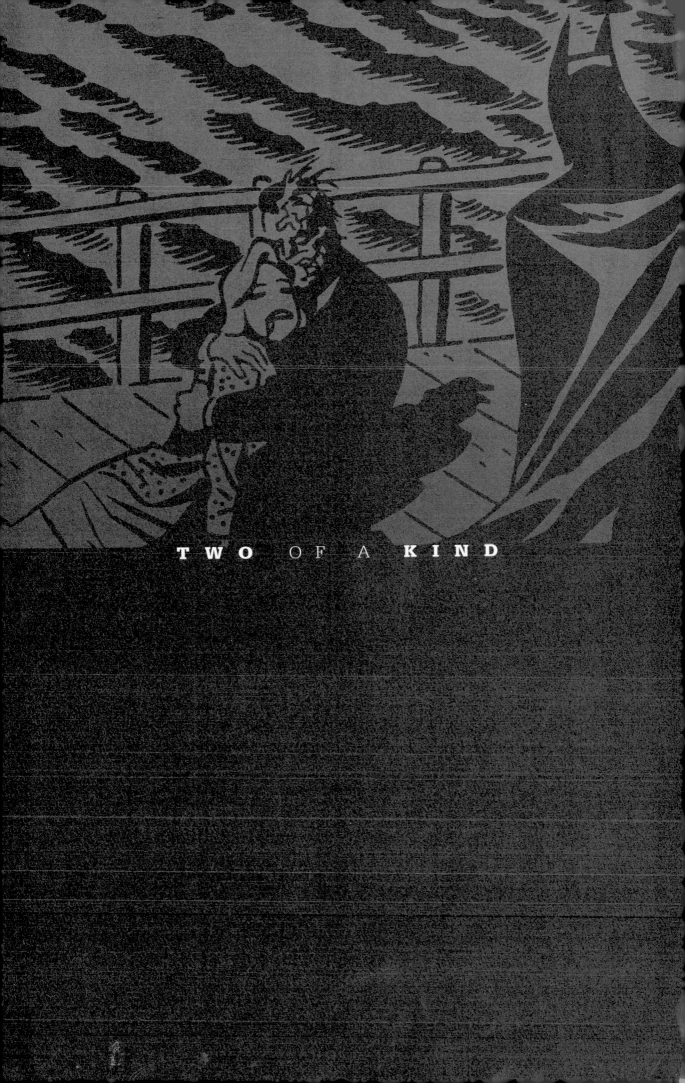

TWO OF A KIND

and his small body of comics work is equally respected and valued. In 1995, Bruce and writer Paul Dini won the coveted Eisner and Harvey awards for Best Single Issue with their comic book tour de force THE BATMAN ADVENTURES: MAD LOVE, the only super-hero comic ever to win both awards.

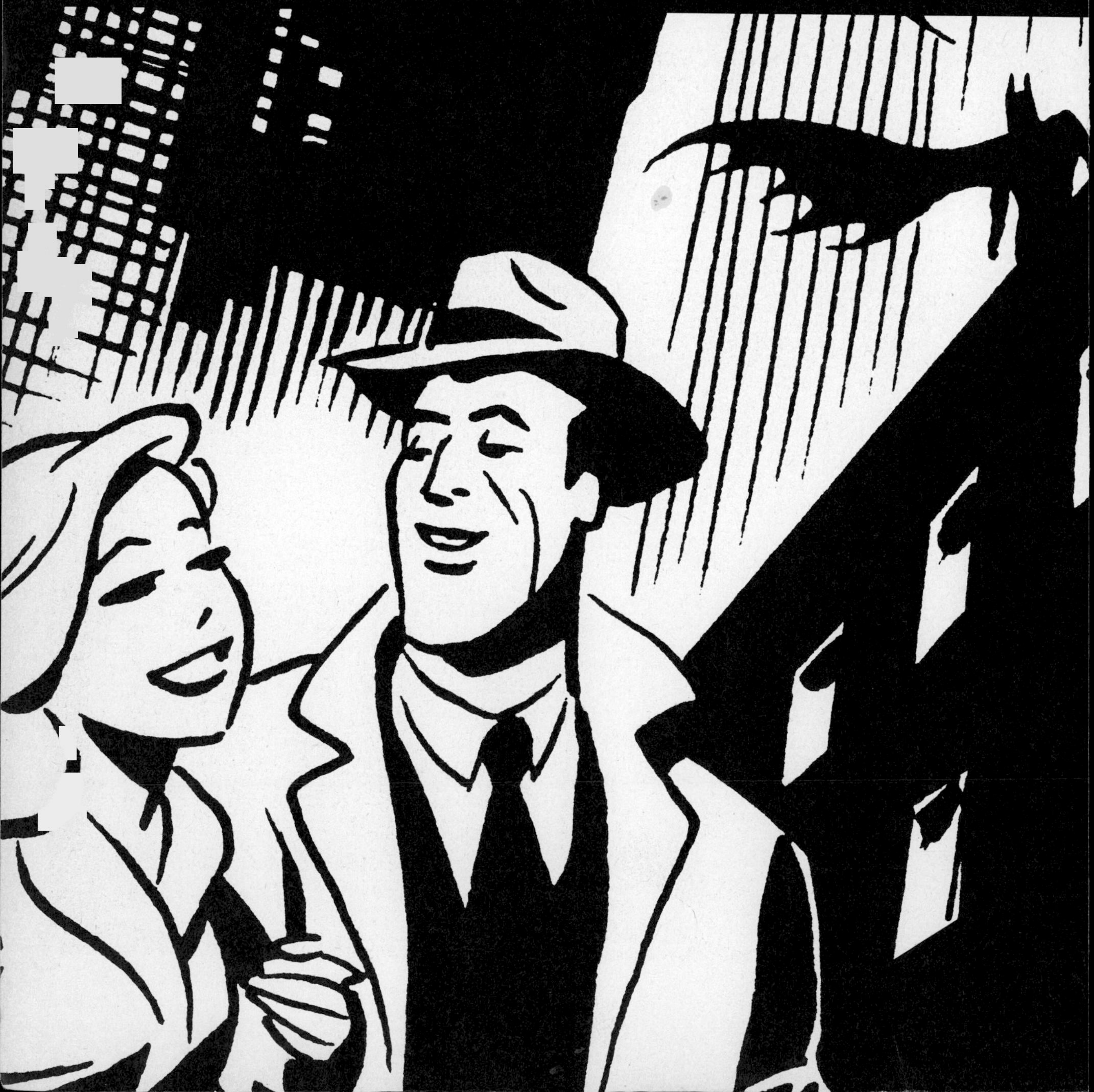

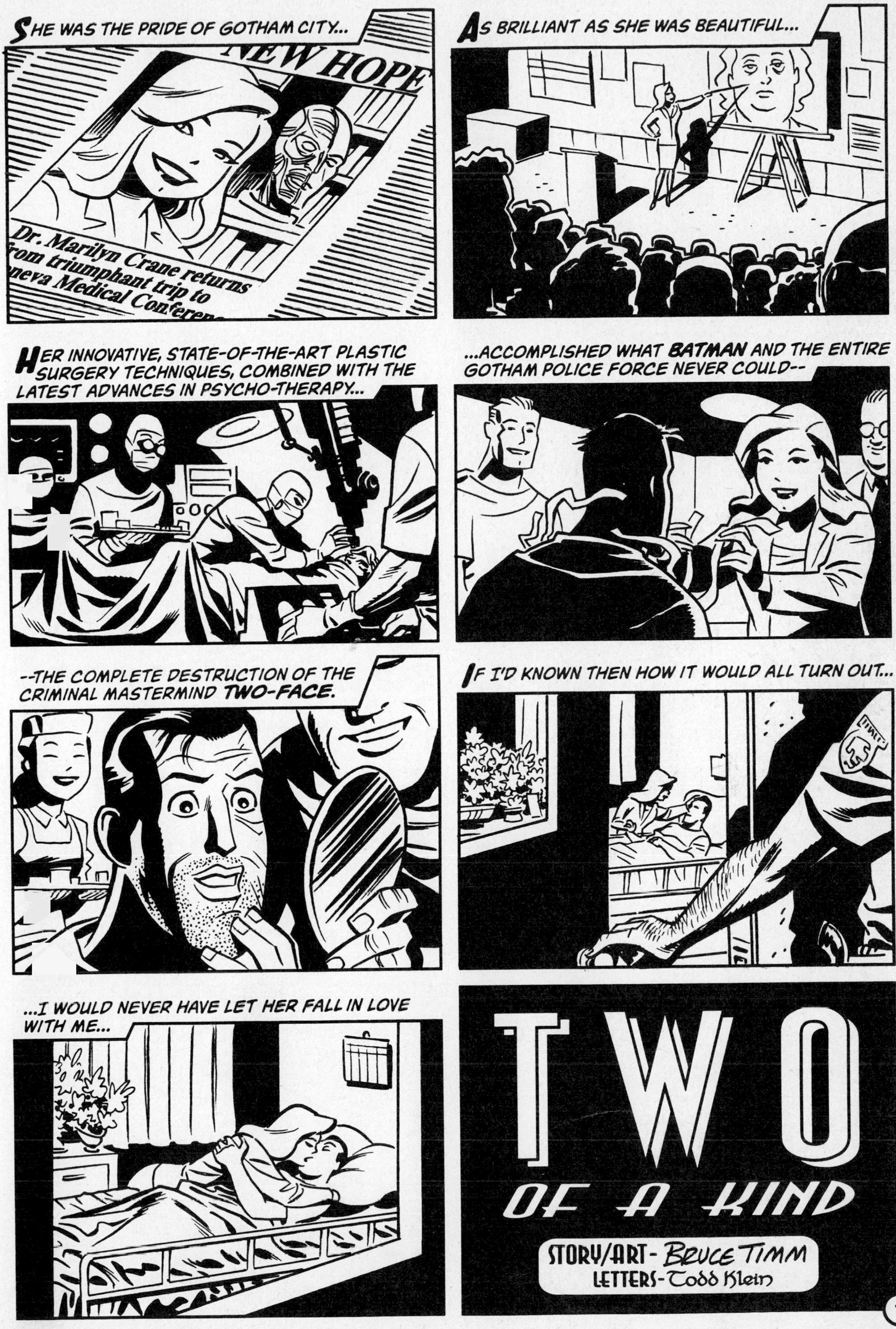
SHE WAS THE PRIDE OF GOTHAM CITY...
NEW HOPE
Dr. Marilyn Crane returns from triumphant trip to neva Medical Conferen
AS BRILLIANT AS SHE WAS BEAUTIFUL...
HER INNOVATIVE, STATE-OF-THE-ART PLASTIC SURGERY TECHNIQUES, COMBINED WITH THE LATEST ADVANCES IN PSYCHO-THERAPY...
...ACCOMPLISHED WHAT BATMAN AND THE ENTIRE GOTHAM POLICE FORCE NEVER COULD--
--THE COMPLETE DESTRUCTION OF THE CRIMINAL MASTERMIND TWO-FACE.
IF I'D KNOWN THEN HOW IT WOULD ALL TURN OUT...
...I WOULD NEVER HAVE LET HER FALL IN LOVE WITH ME...
TWO OF A KIND
STORY/ART- BRUCE TIMM
LETTERS- Todd Klein

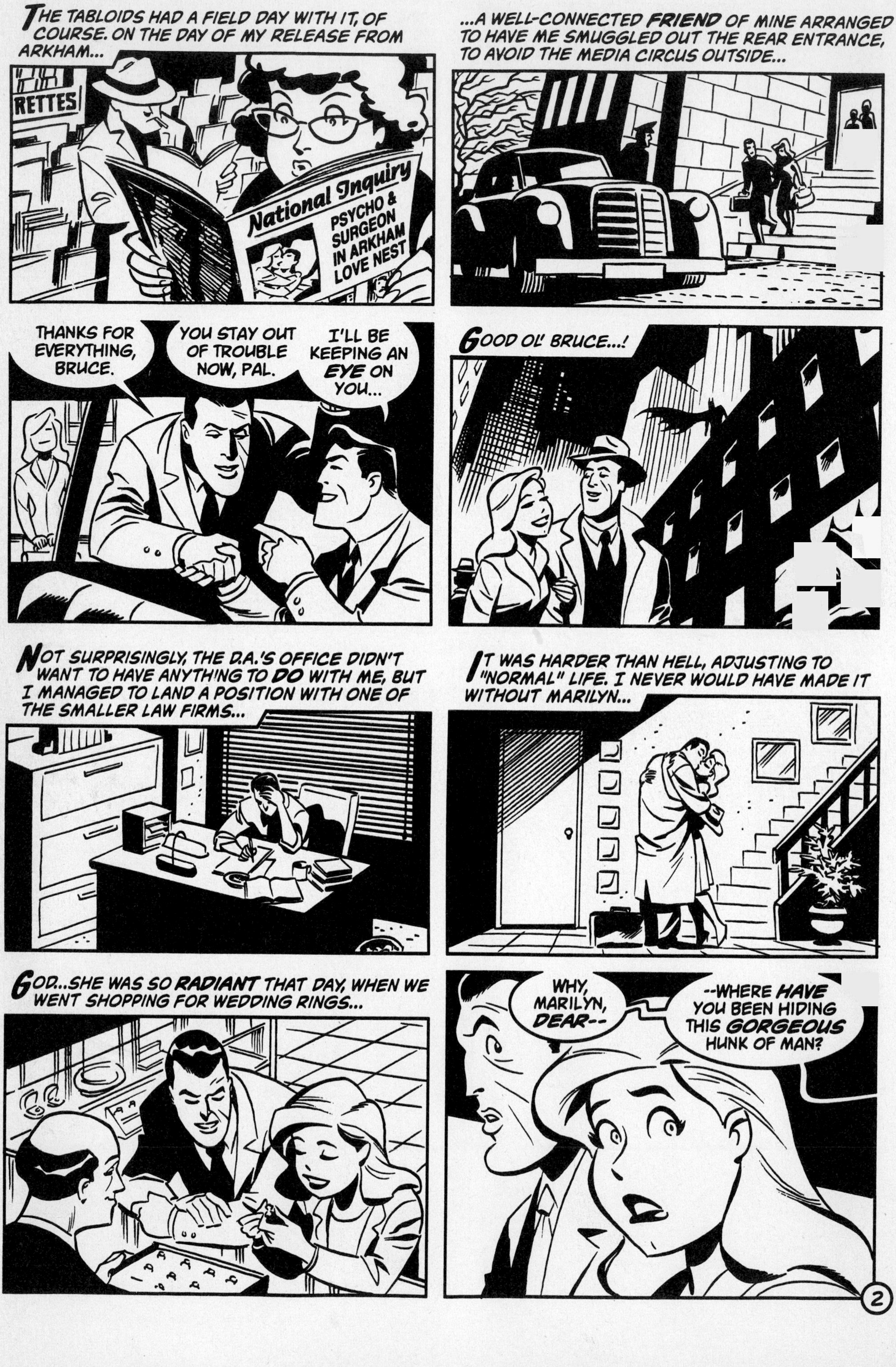
THE TABLOIDS HAD A FIELD DAY WITH IT, OF COURSE. ON THE DAY OF MY RELEASE FROM ARKHAM...
RETTES
National Inquiry
PSYCHO & SURGEON IN ARKHAM LOVE NEST
...A WELL-CONNECTED FRIEND OF MINE ARRANGED TO HAVE ME SMUGGLED OUT THE REAR ENTRANCE, TO AVOID THE MEDIA CIRCUS OUTSIDE...
THANKS FOR EVERYTHING, BRUCE.
YOU STAY OUT OF TROUBLE NOW, PAL.
I'LL BE KEEPING AN EYE ON YOU...
GOOD OL' BRUCE...!
NOT SURPRISINGLY, THE D.A.'S OFFICE DIDN'T WANT TO HAVE ANYTHING TO DO WITH ME, BUT I MANAGED TO LAND A POSITION WITH ONE OF THE SMALLER LAW FIRMS...
IT WAS HARDER THAN HELL, ADJUSTING TO "NORMAL" LIFE. I NEVER WOULD HAVE MADE IT WITHOUT MARILYN...
GOD...SHE WAS SO RADIANT THAT DAY, WHEN WE WENT SHOPPING FOR WEDDING RINGS...
WHY, MARILYN, DEAR--
--WHERE HAVE YOU BEEN HIDING THIS GORGEOUS HUNK OF MAN?
2

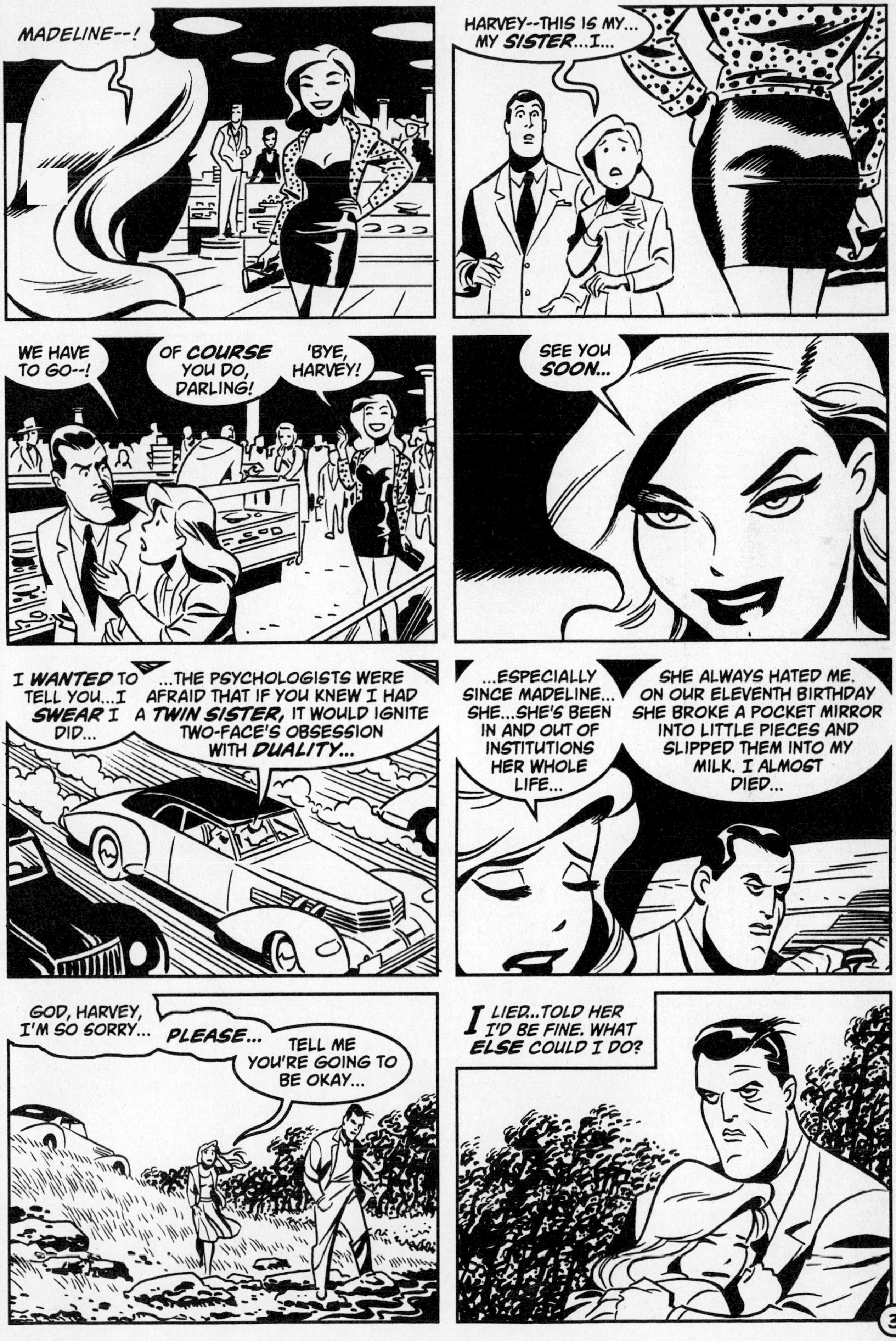
MADELINE--!
HARVEY--THIS IS MY... MY SISTER...I...
WE HAVE TO GO--!
OF COURSE YOU DO, DARLING!
'BYE, HARVEY!
SEE YOU SOON...
I WANTED TO TELL YOU...I SWEAR I DID...
...THE PSYCHOLOGISTS WERE AFRAID THAT IF YOU KNEW I HAD A TWIN SISTER, IT WOULD IGNITE TWO-FACE'S OBSESSION WITH DUALITY...
...ESPECIALLY SINCE MADELINE... SHE...SHE'S BEEN IN AND OUT OF INSTITUTIONS HER WHOLE LIFE...
SHE ALWAYS HATED ME. ON OUR ELEVENTH BIRTHDAY SHE BROKE A POCKET MIRROR INTO LITTLE PIECES AND SLIPPED THEM INTO MY MILK. I ALMOST DIED...
GOD, HARVEY, I'M SO SORRY...
PLEASE...
TELL ME YOU'RE GOING TO BE OKAY...
I LIED...TOLD HER I'D BE FINE. WHAT ELSE COULD I DO?
3

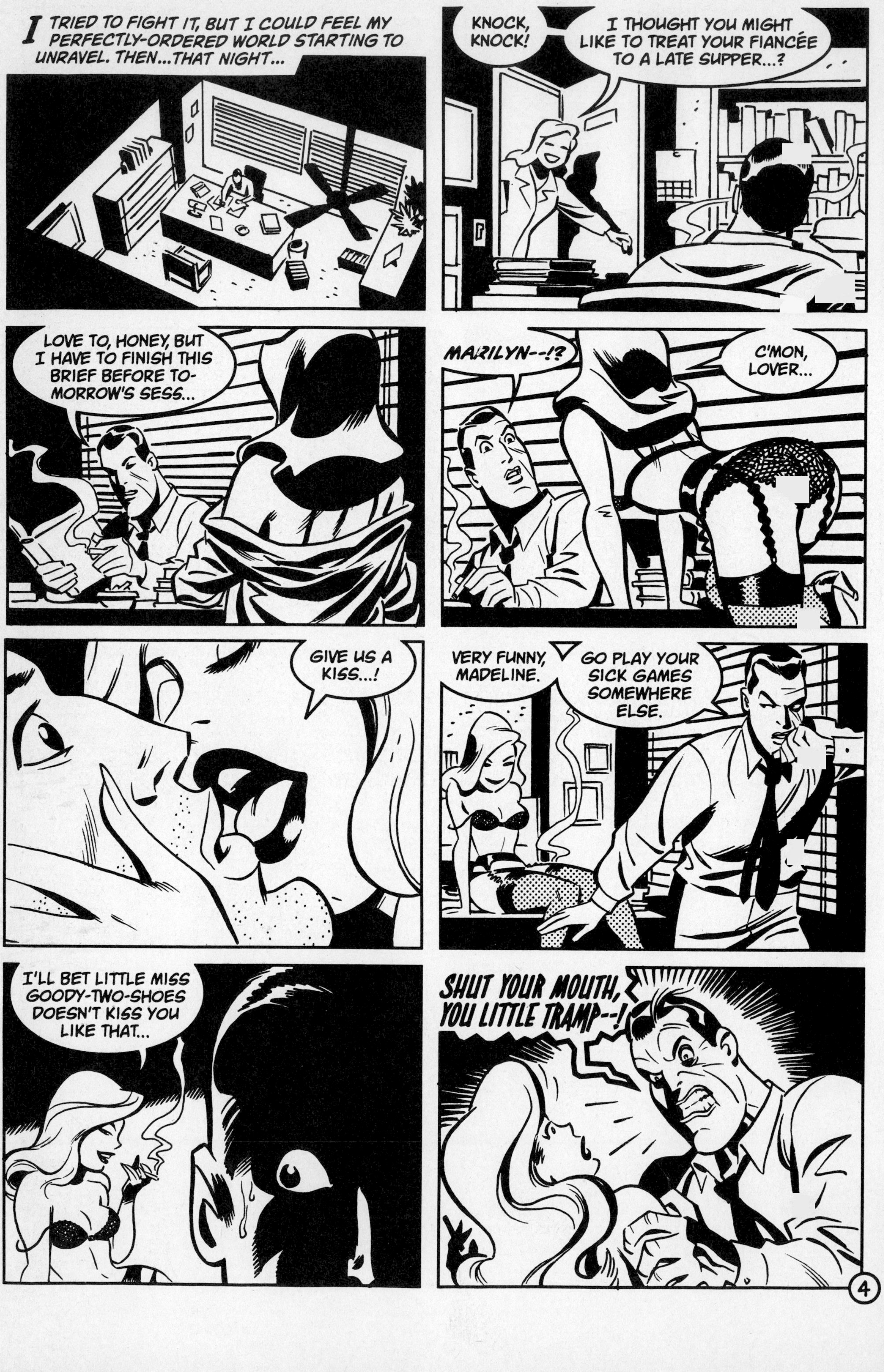
I TRIED TO FIGHT IT, BUT I COULD FEEL MY PERFECTLY-ORDERED WORLD STARTING TO UNRAVEL. THEN...THAT NIGHT...
KNOCK, KNOCK!
I THOUGHT YOU MIGHT LIKE TO TREAT YOUR FIANCÉE TO A LATE SUPPER...?
LOVE TO, HONEY, BUT I HAVE TO FINISH THIS BRIEF BEFORE TO-MORROW'S SESS...
MARILYN--!?
C'MON, LOVER...
GIVE US A KISS...!
VERY FUNNY, MADELINE.
GO PLAY YOUR SICK GAMES SOMEWHERE ELSE.
I'LL BET LITTLE MISS GOODY-TWO-SHOES DOESN'T KISS YOU LIKE THAT...
SHUT YOUR MOUTH, YOU LITTLE TRAMP--!
4

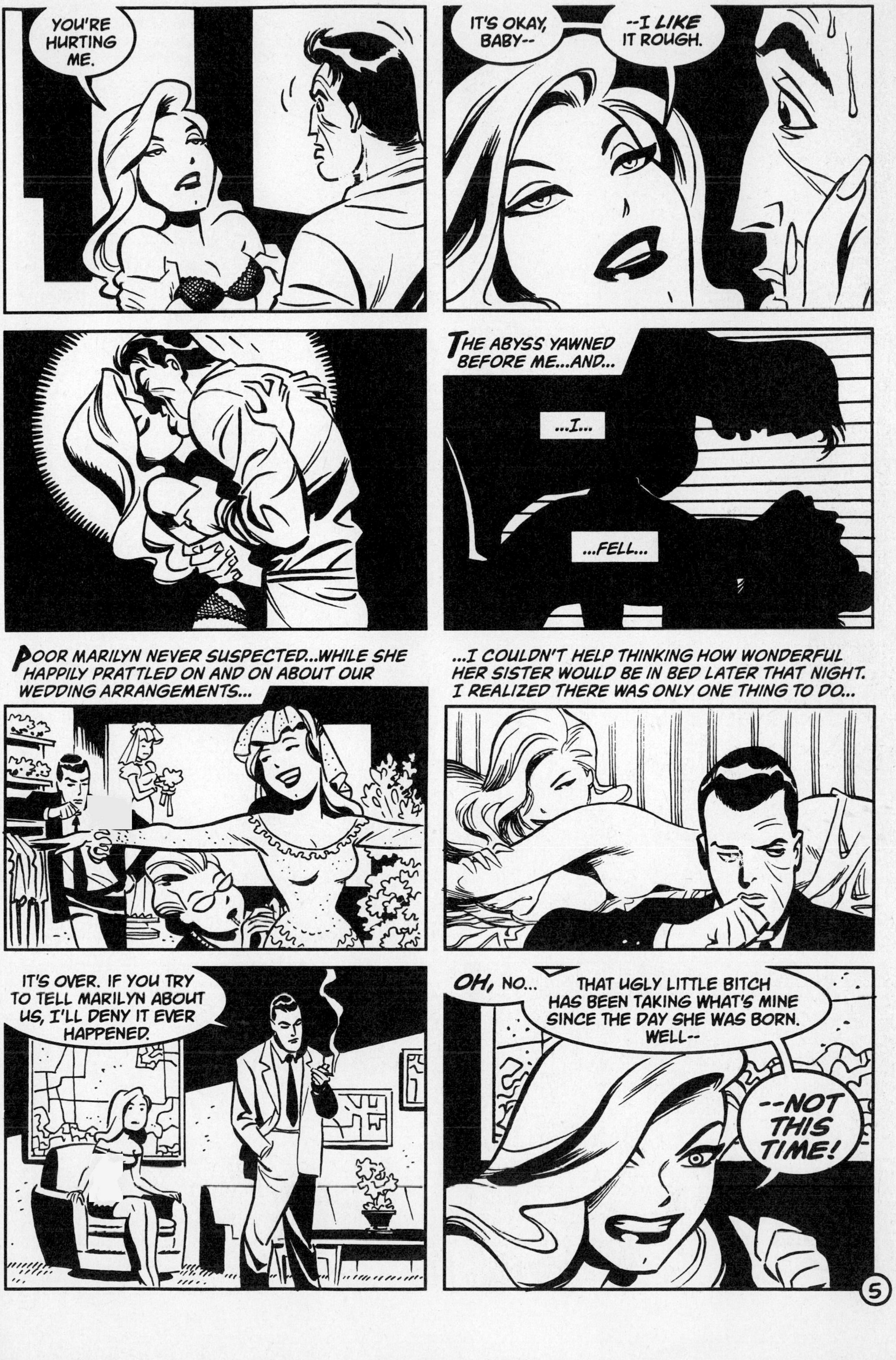
YOU'RE HURTING ME.
IT'S OKAY, BABY--
--I LIKE IT ROUGH.
THE ABYSS YAWNED BEFORE ME...AND...
...I...
...FELL...
POOR MARILYN NEVER SUSPECTED...WHILE SHE HAPPILY PRATTLED ON AND ON ABOUT OUR WEDDING ARRANGEMENTS...
...I COULDN'T HELP THINKING HOW WONDERFUL HER SISTER WOULD BE IN BED LATER THAT NIGHT. I REALIZED THERE WAS ONLY ONE THING TO DO...
IT'S OVER. IF YOU TRY TO TELL MARILYN ABOUT US, I'LL DENY IT EVER HAPPENED.
OH, NO...
THAT UGLY LITTLE BITCH HAS BEEN TAKING WHAT'S MINE SINCE THE DAY SHE WAS BORN. WELL--
--NOT THIS TIME!
5

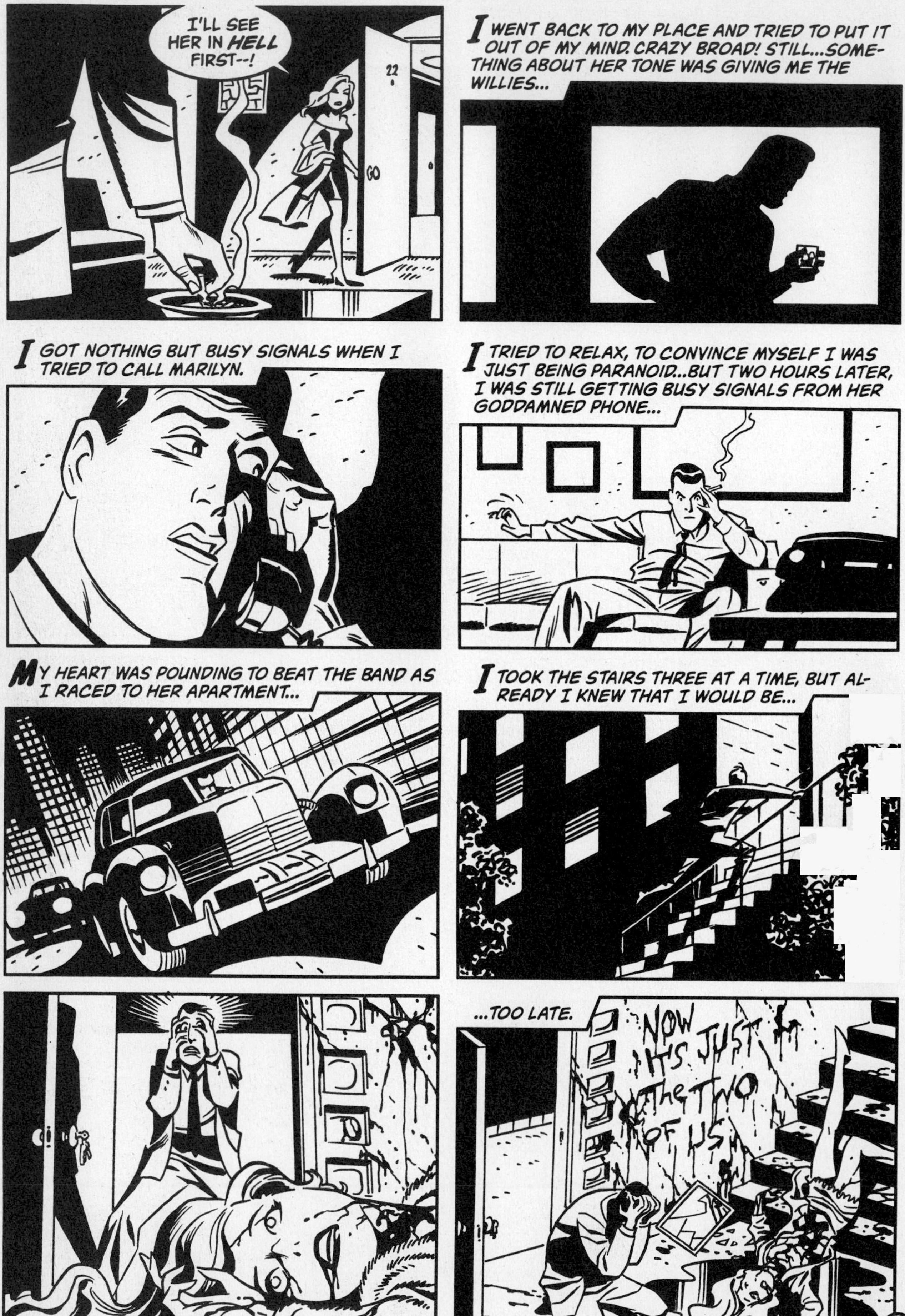
I'LL SEE HER IN HELL FIRST--!
22
GO
I WENT BACK TO MY PLACE AND TRIED TO PUT IT OUT OF MY MIND. CRAZY BROAD! STILL...SOMETHING ABOUT HER TONE WAS GIVING ME THE WILLIES...
I GOT NOTHING BUT BUSY SIGNALS WHEN I TRIED TO CALL MARILYN.
I TRIED TO RELAX, TO CONVINCE MYSELF I WAS JUST BEING PARANOID...BUT TWO HOURS LATER, I WAS STILL GETTING BUSY SIGNALS FROM HER GODDAMNED PHONE...
MY HEART WAS POUNDING TO BEAT THE BAND AS I RACED TO HER APARTMENT...
I TOOK THE STAIRS THREE AT A TIME, BUT ALREADY I KNEW THAT I WOULD BE...
...TOO LATE.
NOW IT'S JUST THE TWO OF US
6

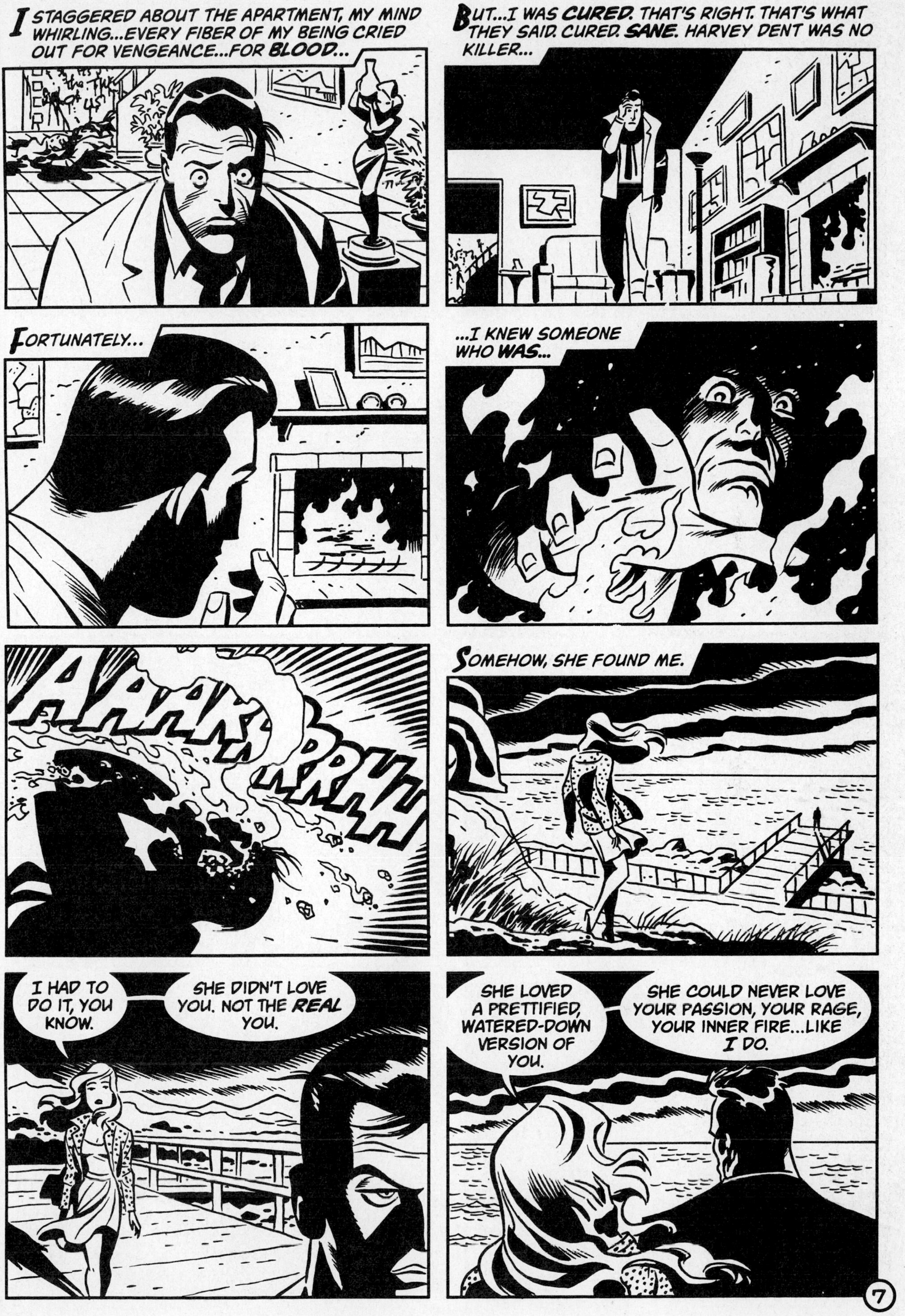
I STAGGERED ABOUT THE APARTMENT, MY MIND WHIRLING...EVERY FIBER OF MY BEING CRIED OUT FOR VENGEANCE...FOR BLOOD...
BUT...I WAS CURED. THAT'S RIGHT. THAT'S WHAT THEY SAID. CURED. SANE. HARVEY DENT WAS NO KILLER...
FORTUNATELY...
...I KNEW SOMEONE WHO WAS...
AAAAK! RRRH!
SOMEHOW, SHE FOUND ME.
I HAD TO DO IT, YOU KNOW.
SHE DIDN'T LOVE YOU. NOT THE REAL YOU.
SHE LOVED A PRETTIFIED, WATERED-DOWN VERSION OF YOU.
SHE COULD NEVER LOVE YOUR PASSION, YOUR RAGE, YOUR INNER FIRE...LIKE I DO.
7

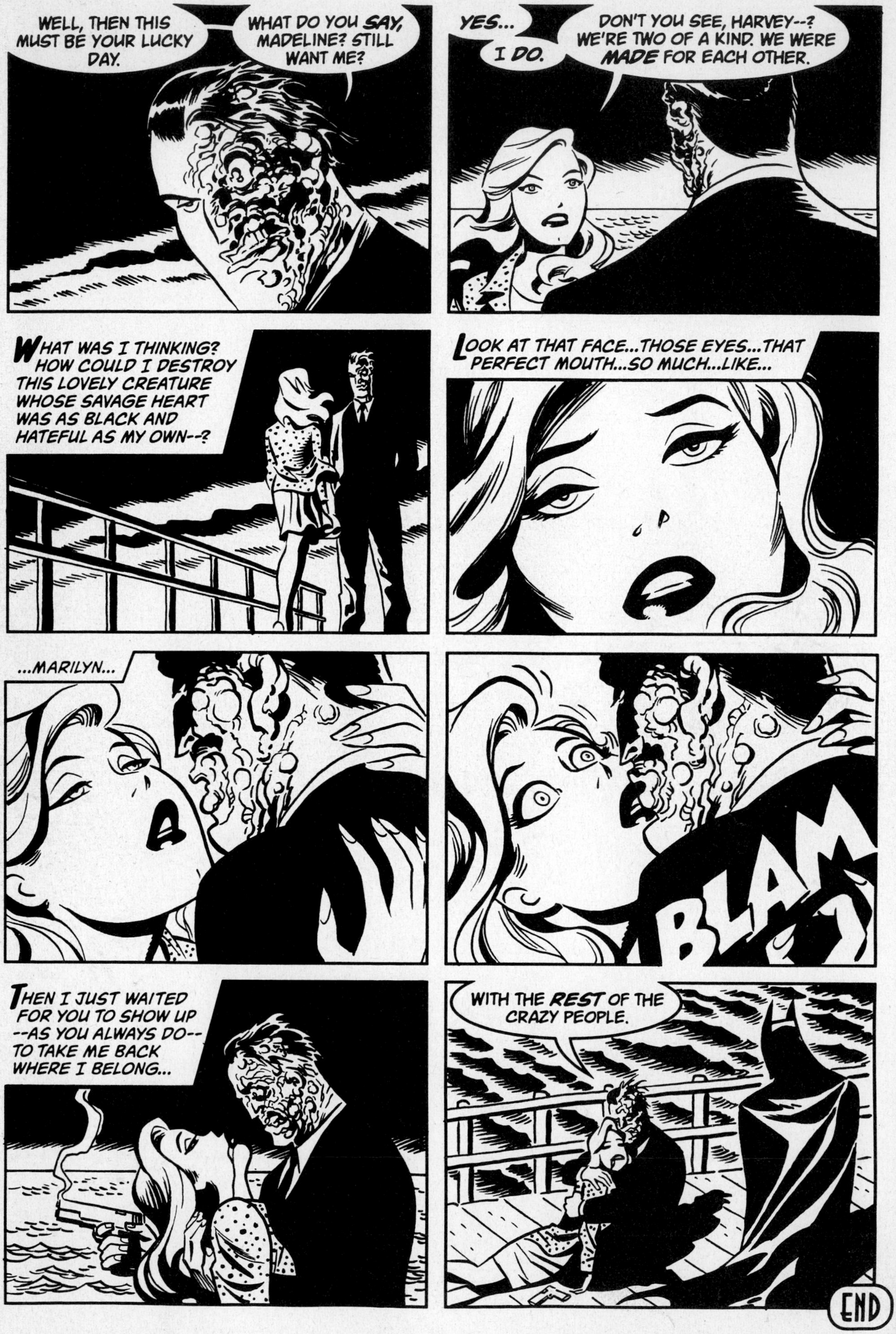
WELL, THEN THIS MUST BE YOUR LUCKY DAY.
WHAT DO YOU SAY, MADELINE? STILL WANT ME?
YES...
I DO.
DON'T YOU SEE, HARVEY--? WE'RE TWO OF A KIND. WE WERE MADE FOR EACH OTHER.
WHAT WAS I THINKING? HOW COULD I DESTROY THIS LOVELY CREATURE WHOSE SAVAGE HEART WAS AS BLACK AND HATEFUL AS MY OWN--?
LOOK AT THAT FACE...THOSE EYES...THAT PERFECT MOUTH...SO MUCH...LIKE...
...MARILYN...
BLAM
THEN I JUST WAITED FOR YOU TO SHOW UP --AS YOU ALWAYS DO-- TO TAKE ME BACK WHERE I BELONG...
WITH THE REST OF THE CRAZY PEOPLE.
END

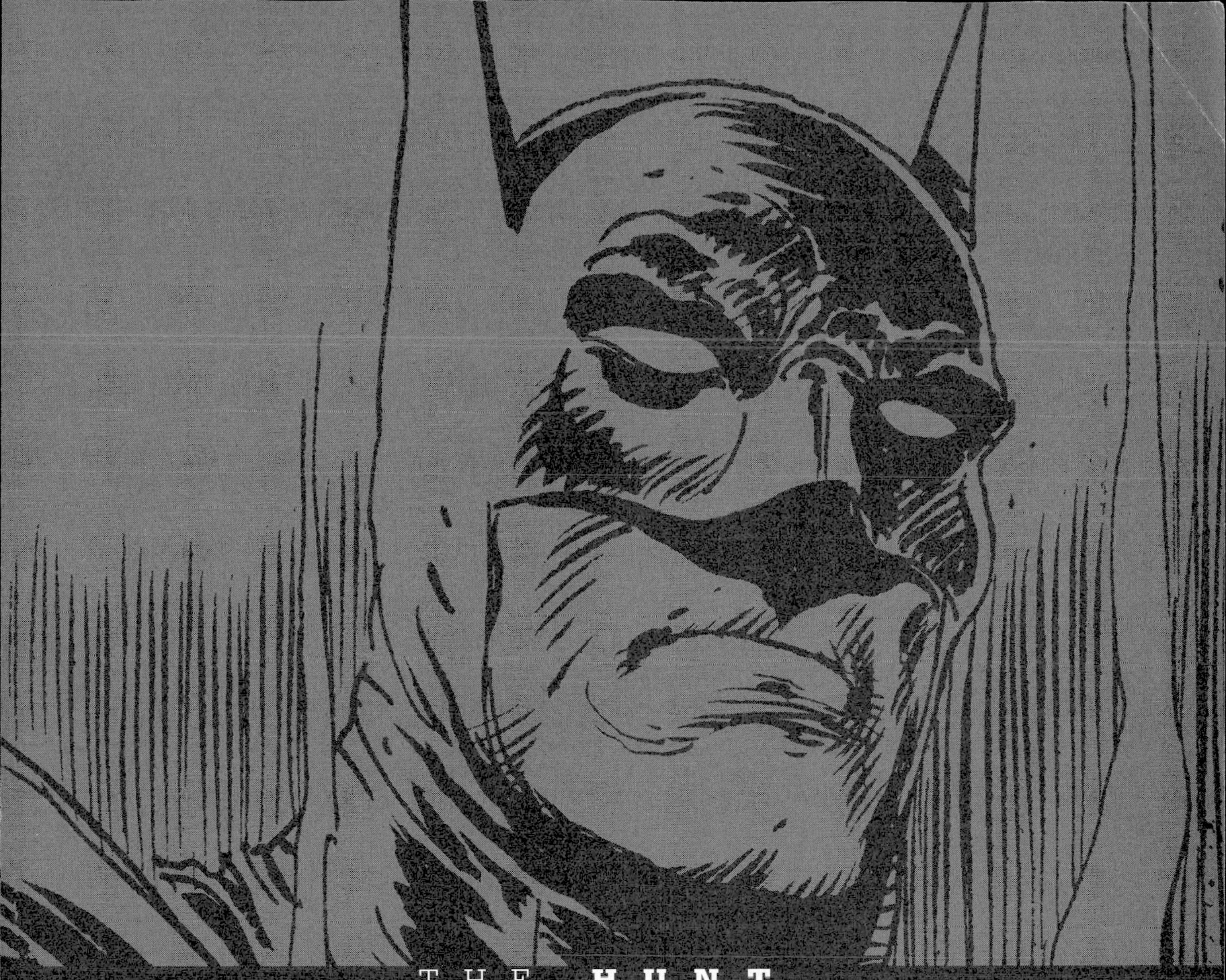

THE **HUNT**

JOE **KUBERT**

Not content with simply being one of the greatest draftsmen in comics history, comics legend Joe Kubert has also embraced the role of teacher and mentor. Over the past 40 years he has acted as artist, editor, and art director, and in 1976 opened the Joe Kubert School of Cartoon Art, the only school of its kind in the country.

For young artists looking to break into the comics business, thank God there's Joe Kubert to teach them the ropes. For all of us wretched fanboys looking to relive the golden moments of our youth, thank God there is Kubert's ENEMY ACE, TOR, TARZAN and SGT. ROCK.

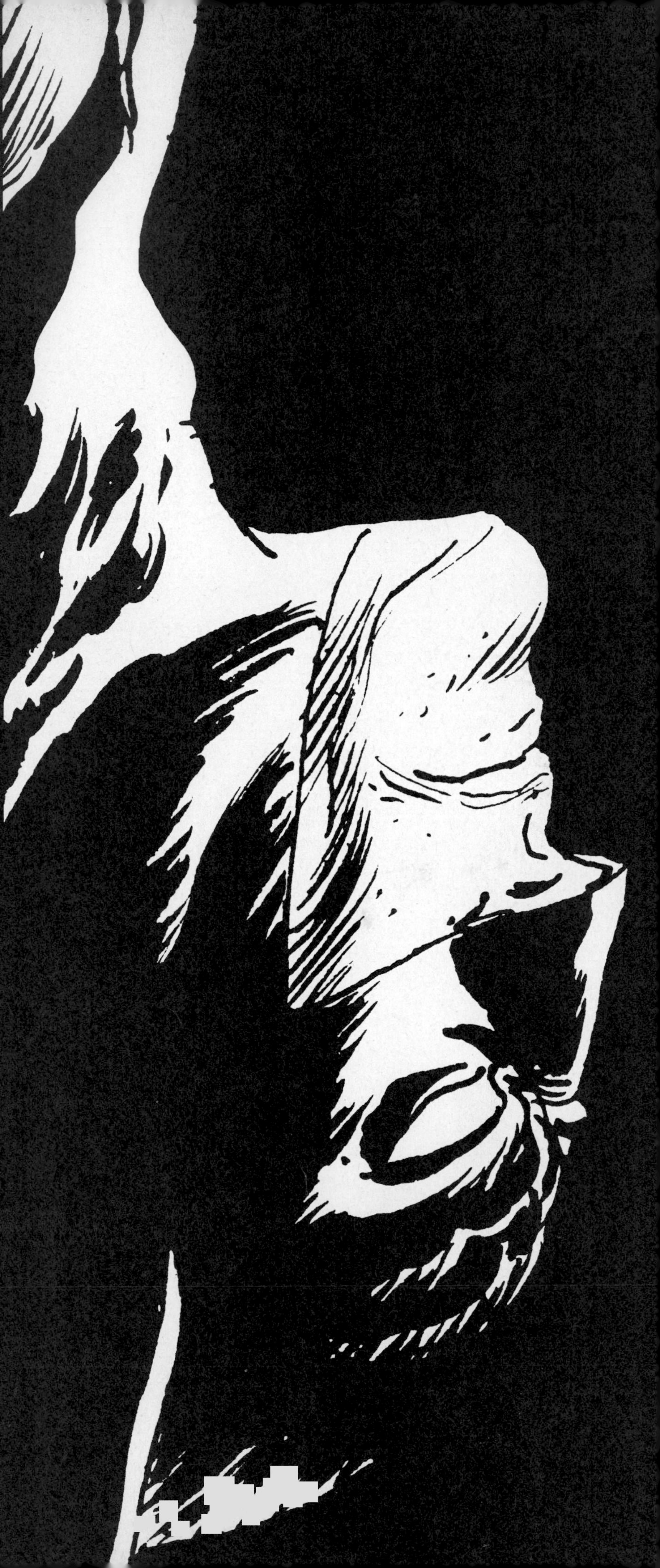

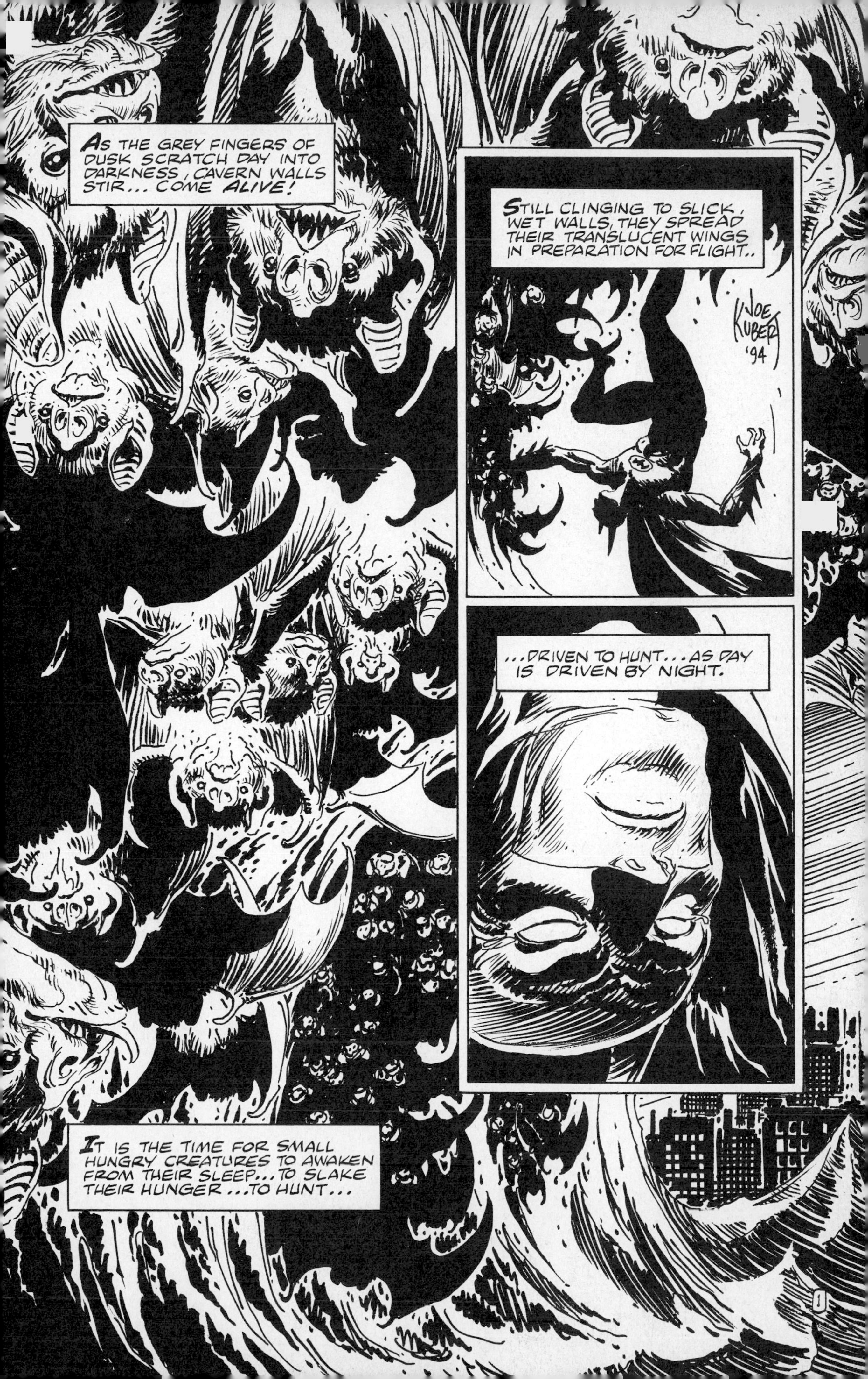
AS THE GREY FINGERS OF DUSK SCRATCH DAY INTO DARKNESS, CAVERN WALLS STIR... COME ALIVE!
STILL CLINGING TO SLICK, WET WALLS, THEY SPREAD THEIR TRANSLUCENT WINGS IN PREPARATION FOR FLIGHT..
JOE KUBERT '94
...DRIVEN TO HUNT...AS DAY IS DRIVEN BY NIGHT.
IT IS THE TIME FOR SMALL HUNGRY CREATURES TO AWAKEN FROM THEIR SLEEP...TO SLAKE THEIR HUNGER...TO HUNT...

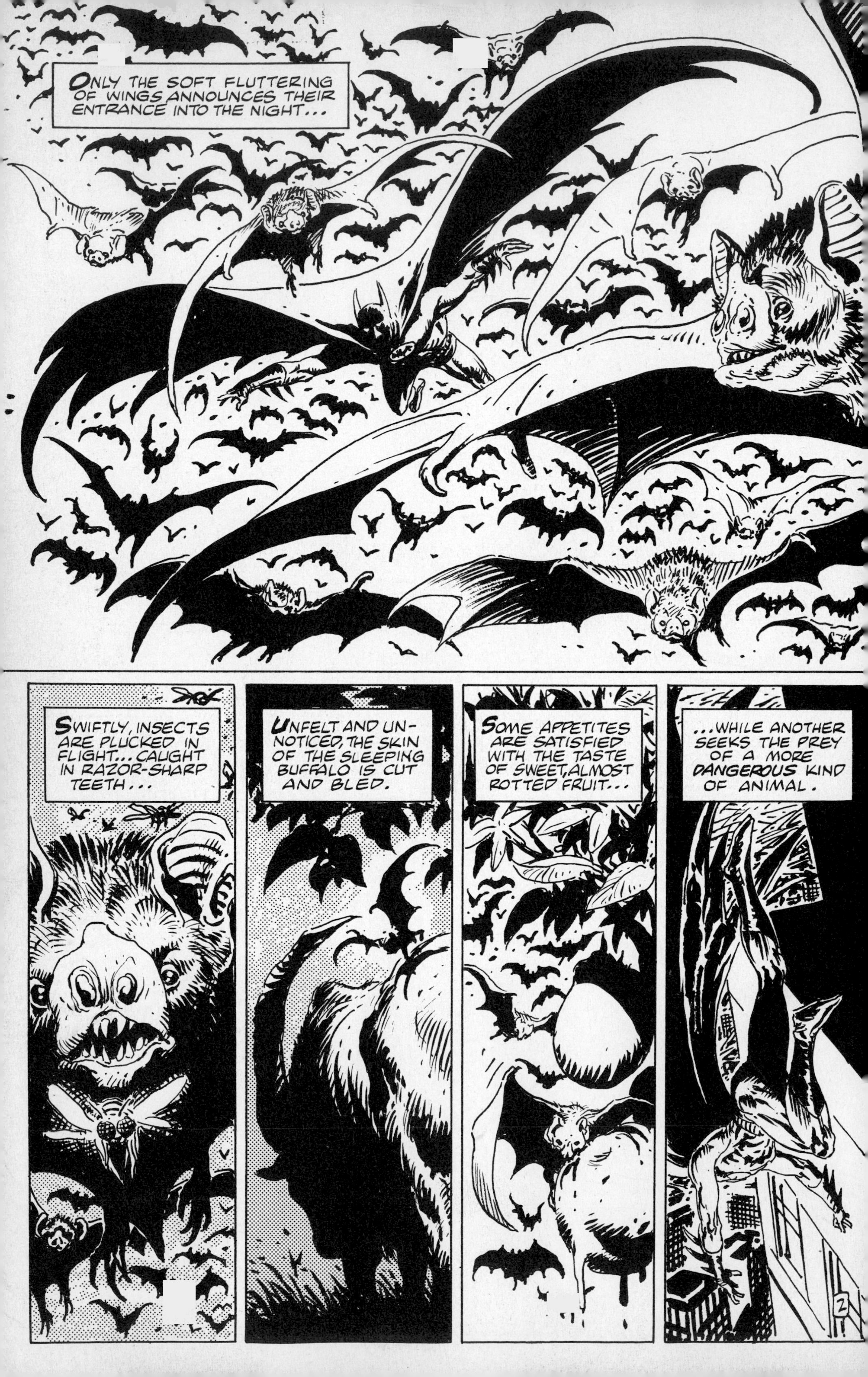
ONLY THE SOFT FLUTTERING OF WINGS ANNOUNCES THEIR ENTRANCE INTO THE NIGHT...
SWIFTLY, INSECTS ARE PLUCKED IN FLIGHT... CAUGHT IN RAZOR-SHARP TEETH...
UNFELT AND UNNOTICED, THE SKIN OF THE SLEEPING BUFFALO IS CUT AND BLED.
SOME APPETITES ARE SATISFIED WITH THE TASTE OF SWEET, ALMOST ROTTED FRUIT...
...WHILE ANOTHER SEEKS THE PREY OF A MORE DANGEROUS KIND OF ANIMAL.
2

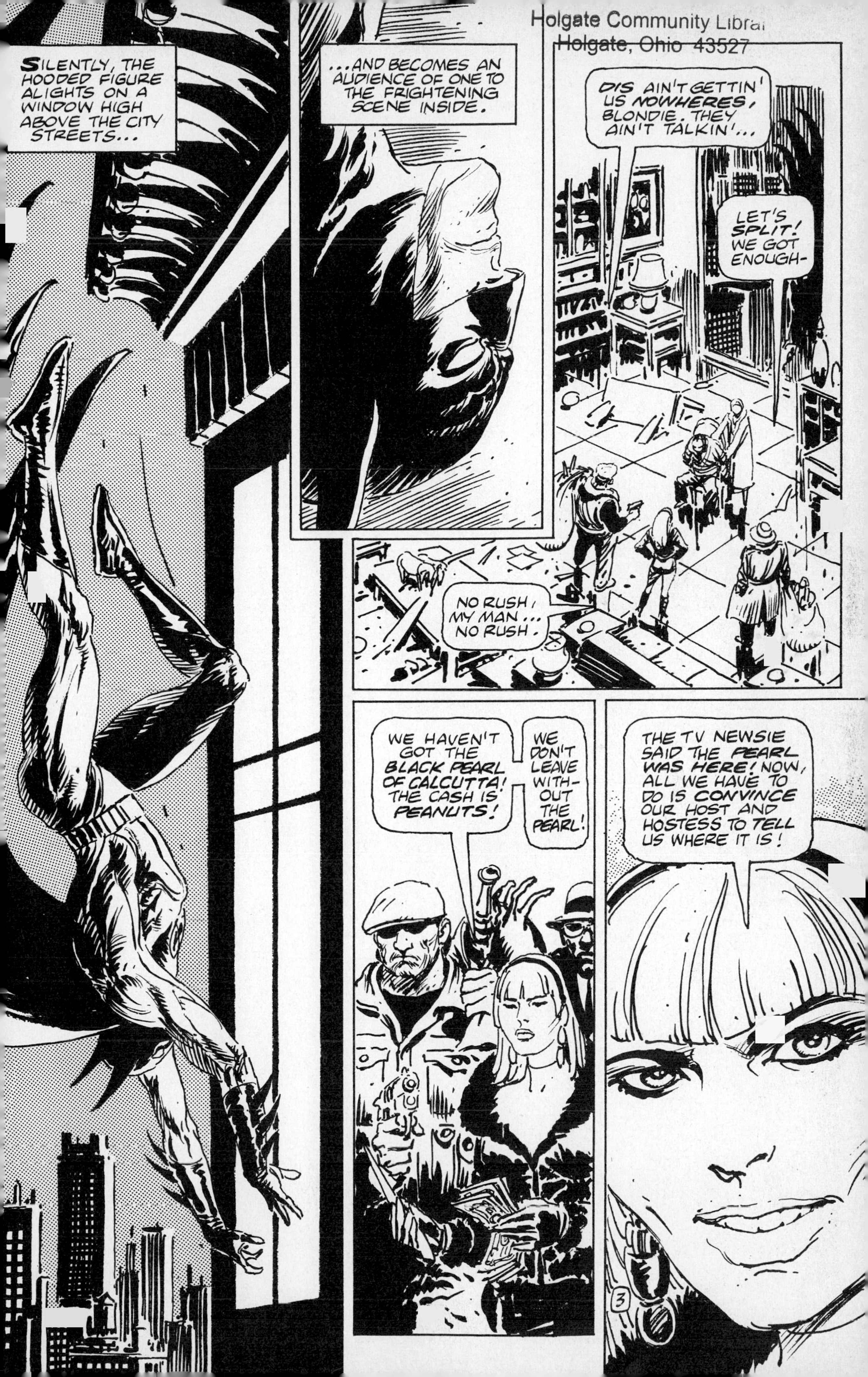
SILENTLY, THE HOODED FIGURE ALIGHTS ON A WINDOW HIGH ABOVE THE CITY STREETS...
...AND BECOMES AN AUDIENCE OF ONE TO THE FRIGHTENING SCENE INSIDE.
DIS AIN'T GETTIN' US NOWHERES, BLONDIE. THEY AIN'T TALKIN'...
LET'S SPLIT! WE GOT ENOUGH-
NO RUSH, MY MAN... NO RUSH.
WE HAVEN'T GOT THE BLACK PEARL OF CALCUTTA! THE CASH IS PEANUTS!
WE DON'T LEAVE WITH-OUT THE PEARL!
THE TV NEWSIE SAID THE PEARL WAS HERE! NOW, ALL WE HAVE TO DO IS CONVINCE OUR HOST AND HOSTESS TO TELL US WHERE IT IS!
3

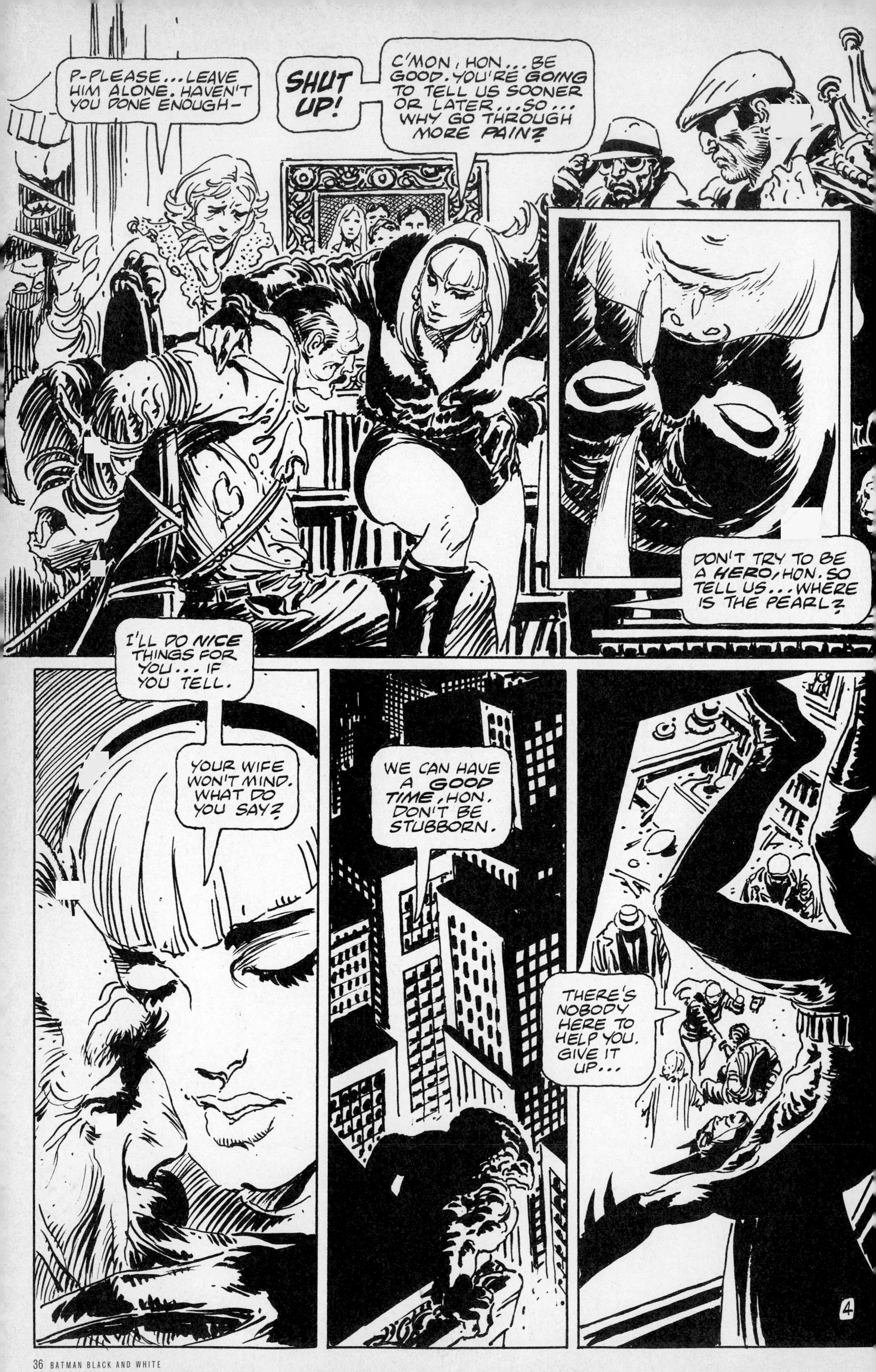
P-PLEASE...LEAVE HIM ALONE. HAVEN'T YOU DONE ENOUGH-
SHUT UP!
C'MON, HON...BE GOOD. YOU'RE GOING TO TELL US SOONER OR LATER...SO...WHY GO THROUGH MORE PAIN?
DON'T TRY TO BE A HERO, HON. SO TELL US...WHERE IS THE PEARL?
I'LL DO NICE THINGS FOR YOU...IF YOU TELL.
YOUR WIFE WON'T MIND. WHAT DO YOU SAY?
WE CAN HAVE A GOOD TIME, HON. DON'T BE STUBBORN.
THERE'S NOBODY HERE TO HELP YOU. GIVE IT UP...
4

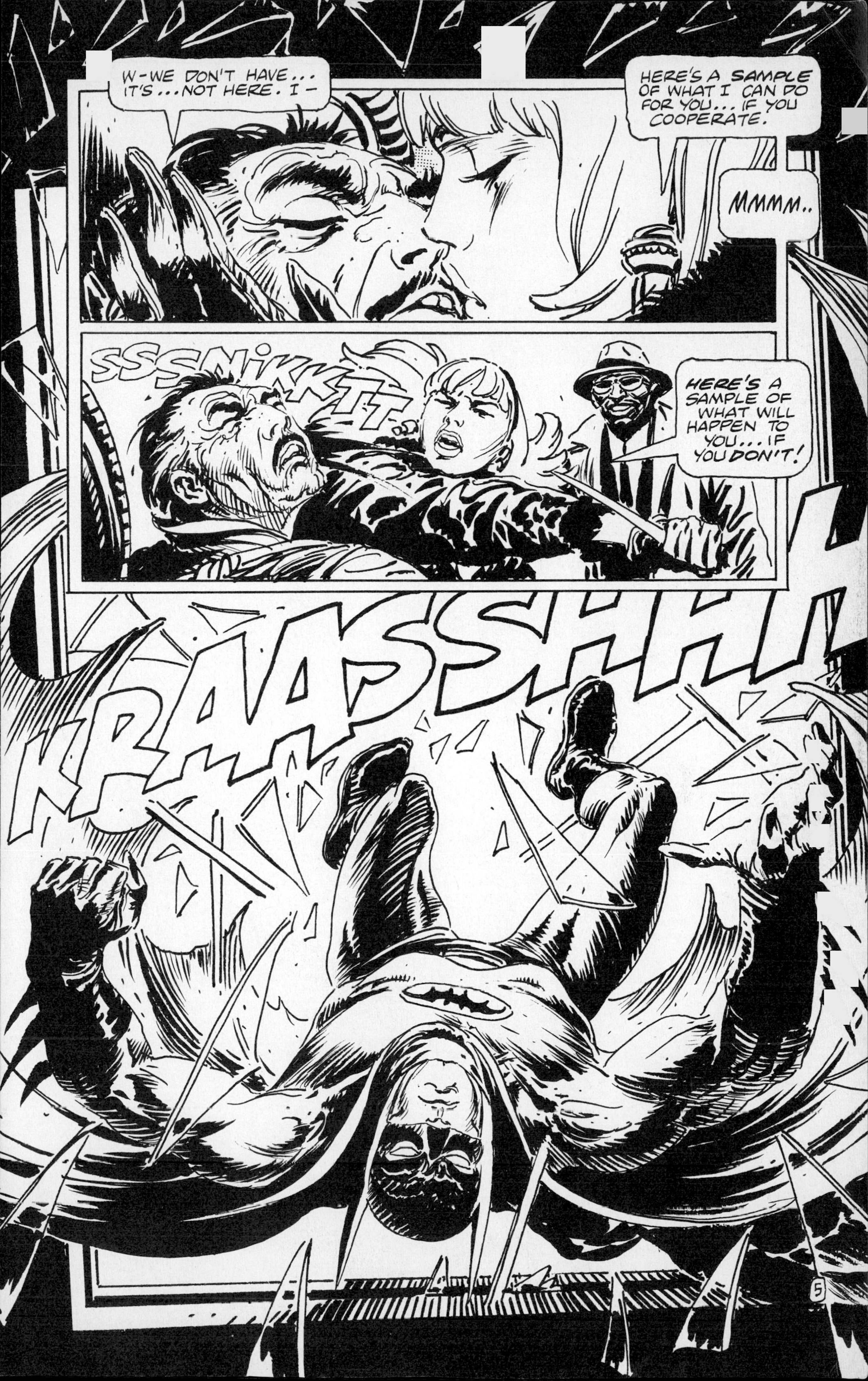
W-WE DON'T HAVE... IT'S...NOT HERE. I -
HERE'S A SAMPLE OF WHAT I CAN DO FOR YOU... IF YOU COOPERATE.
MMMM..
SSSNIKKTT
HERE'S A SAMPLE OF WHAT WILL HAPPEN TO YOU... IF YOU DON'T!
KRAASSHH!
5

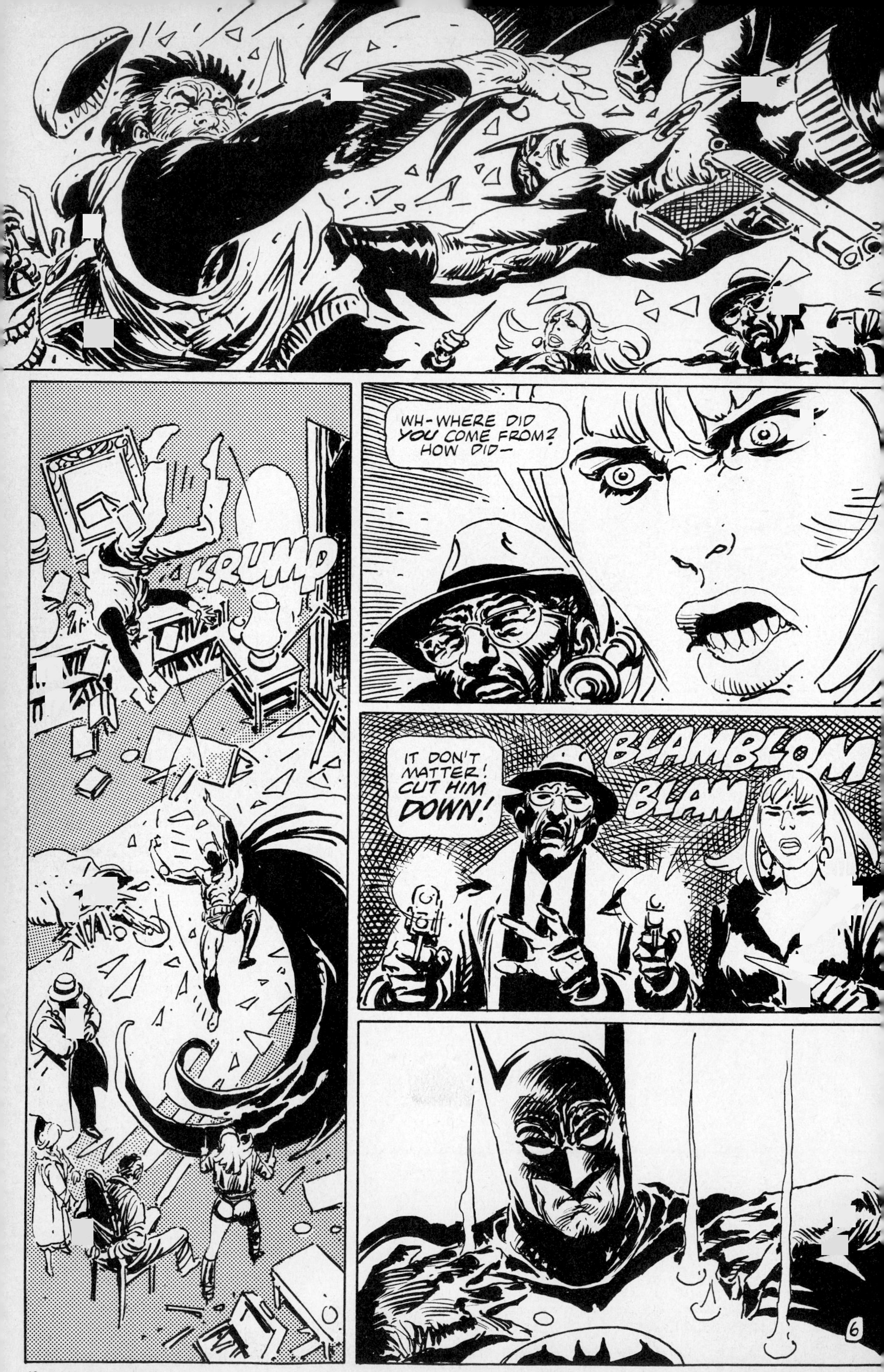
KRUMP
WH-WHERE DID YOU COME FROM? HOW DID-
IT DON'T MATTER! CUT HIM DOWN!
BLAMBLOM
BLAM
6

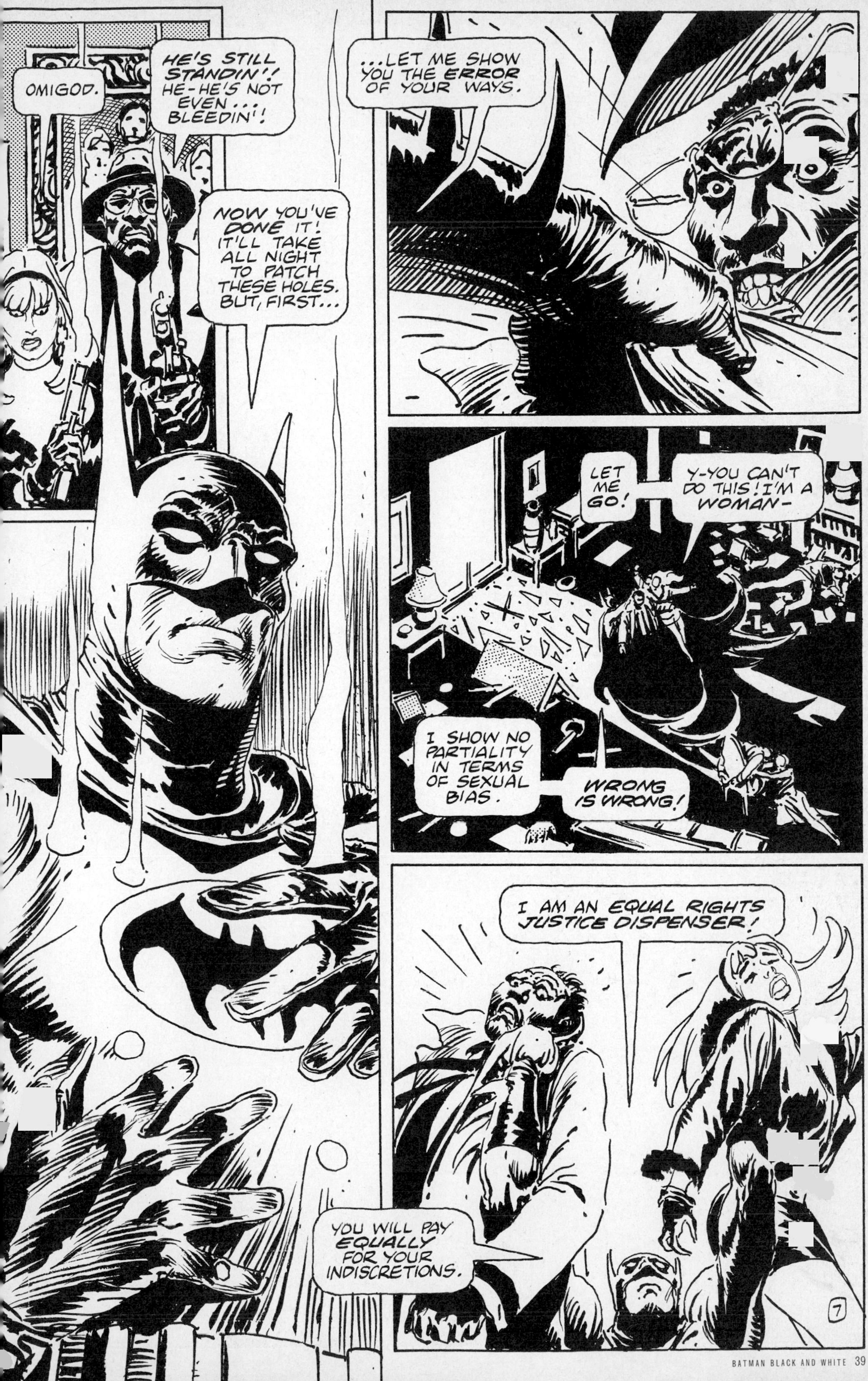
OMIGOD.
HE'S STILL STANDIN'! HE-HE'S NOT EVEN... BLEEDIN'!
NOW YOU'VE DONE IT! IT'LL TAKE ALL NIGHT TO PATCH THESE HOLES. BUT, FIRST...
...LET ME SHOW YOU THE ERROR OF YOUR WAYS.
LET ME GO!
Y-YOU CAN'T DO THIS! I'M A WOMAN-
I SHOW NO PARTIALITY IN TERMS OF SEXUAL BIAS.
WRONG IS WRONG!
I AM AN EQUAL RIGHTS JUSTICE DISPENSER!
YOU WILL PAY EQUALLY FOR YOUR INDISCRETIONS.
7

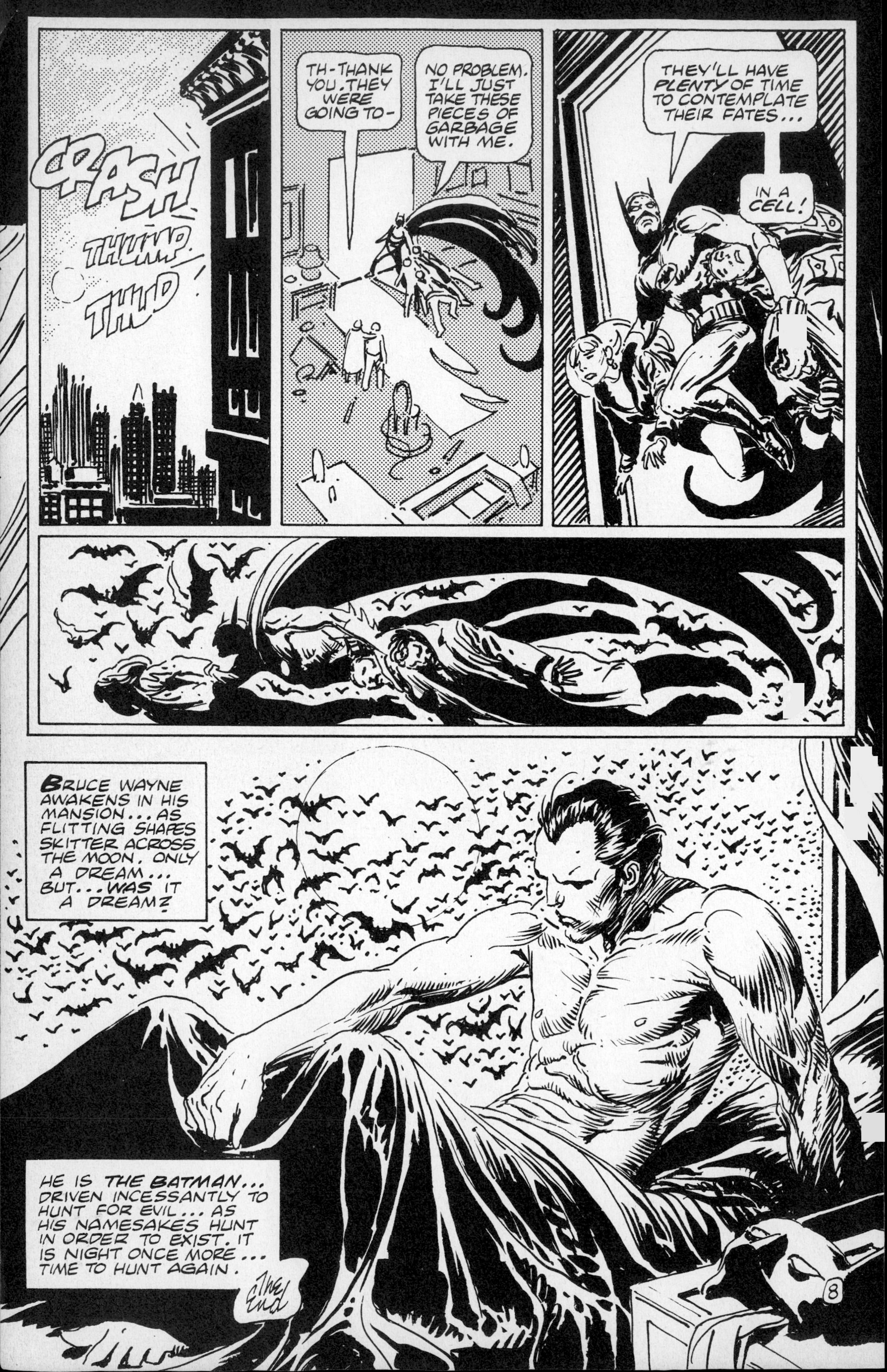
CRASH
THUMP
THUD
TH-THANK YOU. THEY WERE GOING TO-
NO PROBLEM. I'LL JUST TAKE THESE PIECES OF GARBAGE WITH ME.
THEY'LL HAVE PLENTY OF TIME TO CONTEMPLATE THEIR FATES...
IN A CELL!
BRUCE WAYNE AWAKENS IN HIS MANSION... AS FLITTING SHAPES SKITTER ACROSS THE MOON. ONLY A DREAM... BUT... WAS IT A DREAM?
HE IS THE BATMAN... DRIVEN INCESSANTLY TO HUNT FOR EVIL... AS HIS NAMESAKES HUNT IN ORDER TO EXIST. IT IS NIGHT ONCE MORE... TIME TO HUNT AGAIN.
The End
8

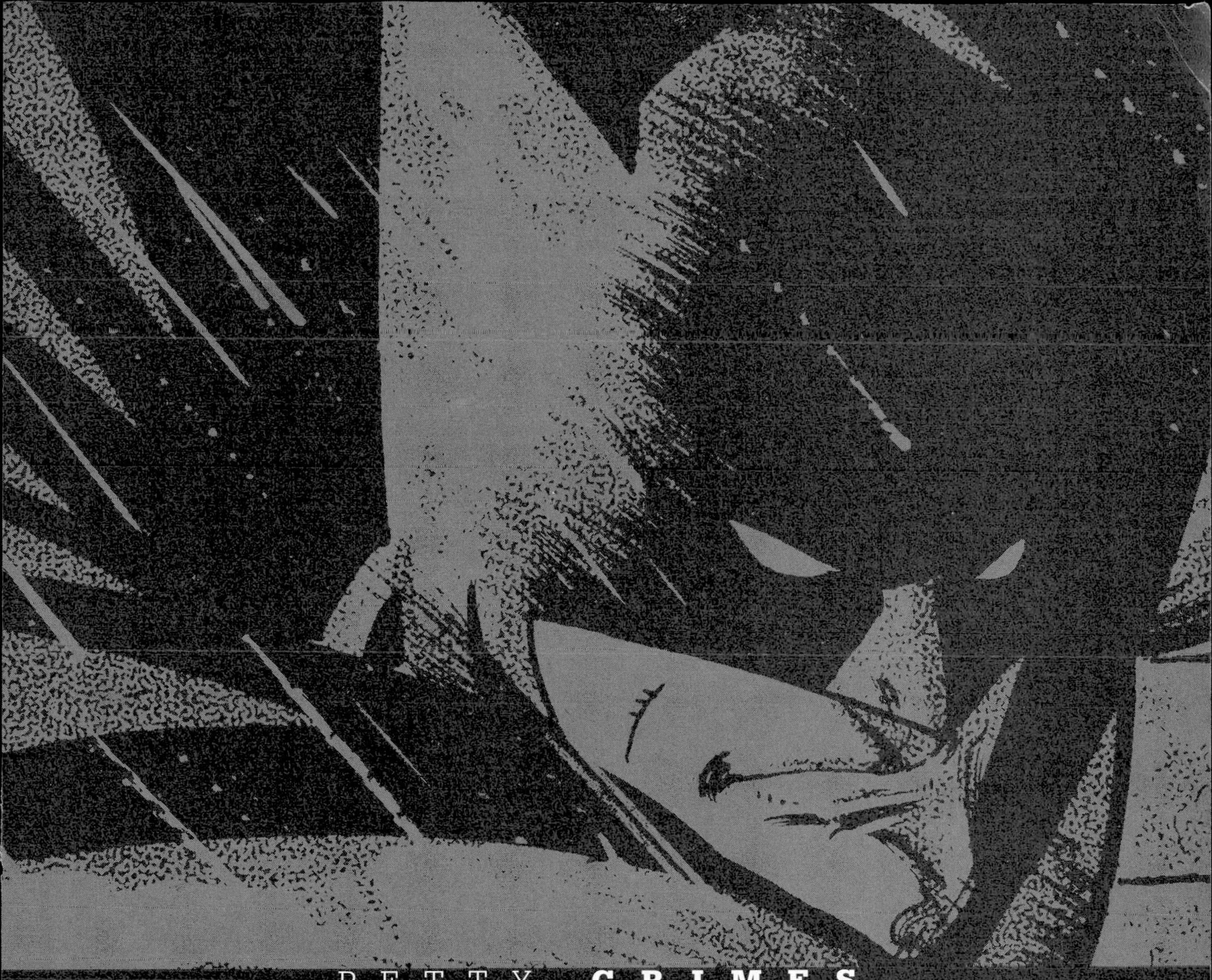

PETTY **CRIMES**

HOWARD **CHAYKIN**

Howard Chaykin has been one of comics' superstars since he began work in the medium in the '70s.

Always stretching the boundaries of comics, Howard was one of the first artists to bring the aesthetic influences of classic American illustrators and designers to the medium.

He created the groundbreaking series *American Flagg,* which combined a striking graphic sense with a complex narrative and a strong satirical look at popular culture. It is considered a high watermark of the past decade.

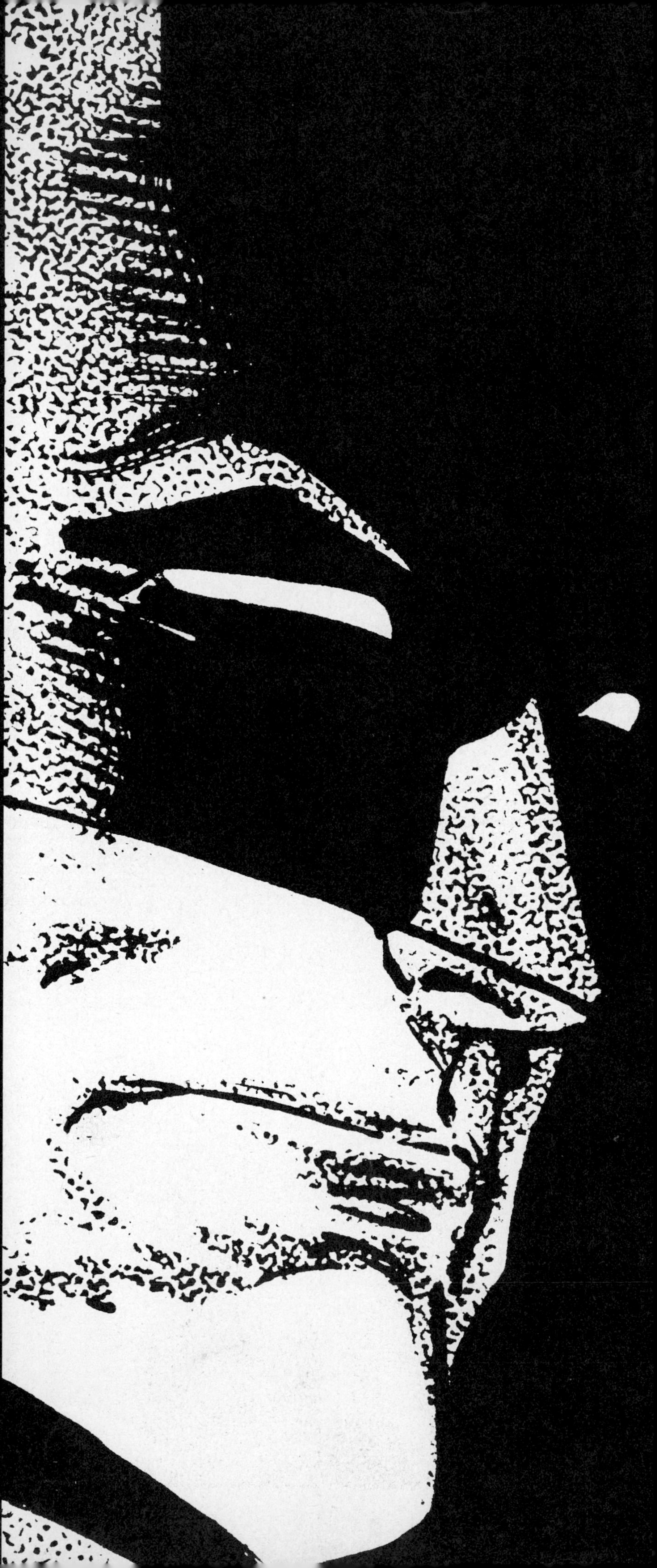

It has been a long, viciously hot *summer*--and an equally cruel *autumn.* Steam rose from Gotham's sidewalks like waves of *frustration.* The dank humidity and the blinding sunshine seemed to fray *everyone's* nerves--but no one more than *CIVIC VIRTUE*-- a serial *killer* out to put an end to--

PETTY CRIMES

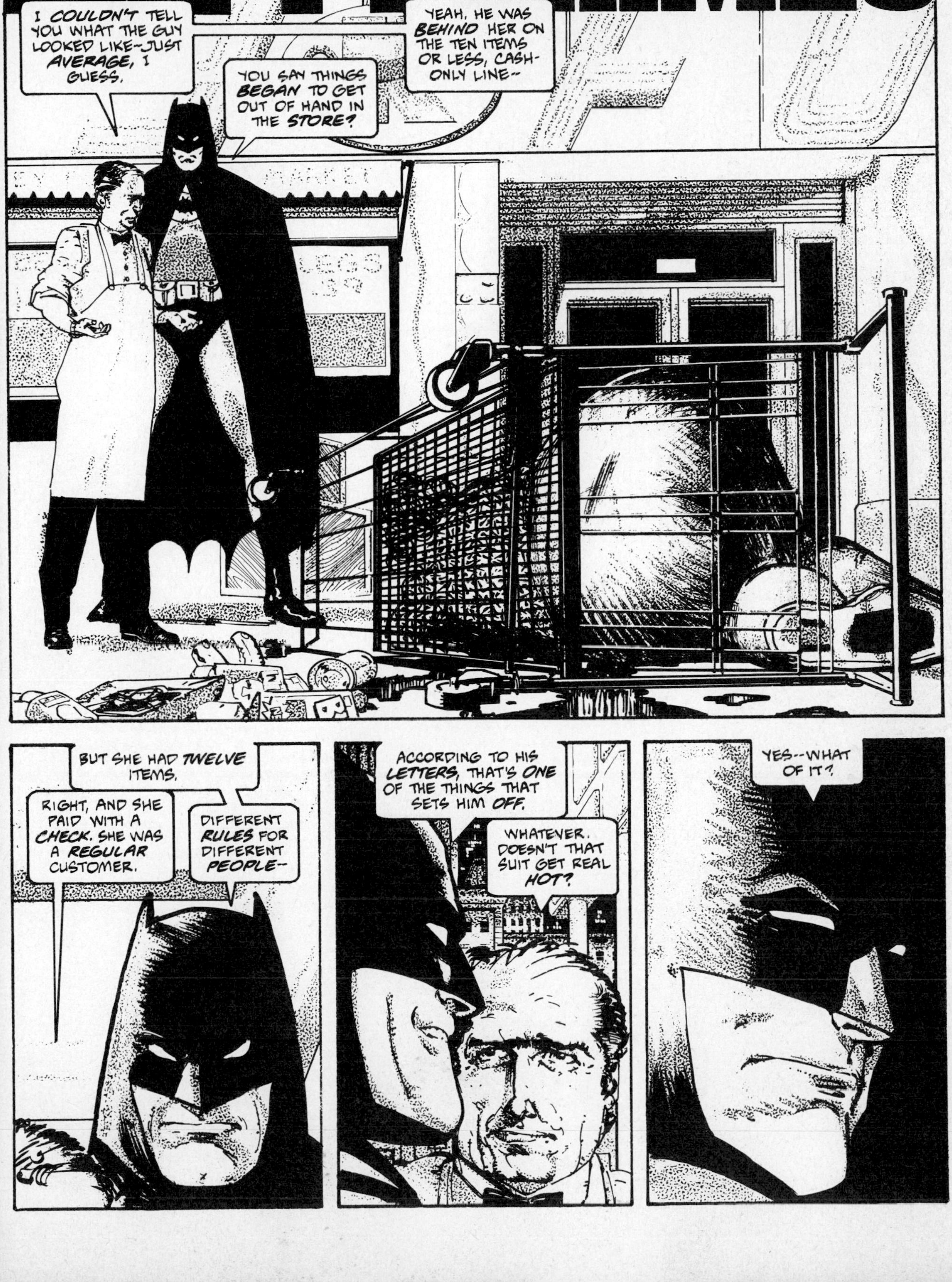
I *COULDN'T* TELL YOU WHAT THE GUY LOOKED LIKE--JUST *AVERAGE,* I GUESS.
YOU SAY THINGS *BEGAN* TO GET OUT OF HAND IN THE *STORE?*
YEAH, HE WAS *BEHIND* HER ON THE TEN ITEMS OR LESS, CASH-ONLY LINE--
BUT SHE HAD *TWELVE* ITEMS.
RIGHT, AND SHE PAID WITH A *CHECK.* SHE WAS A *REGULAR* CUSTOMER.
DIFFERENT *RULES* FOR DIFFERENT *PEOPLE*--
ACCORDING TO HIS *LETTERS,* THAT'S *ONE* OF THE THINGS THAT SETS HIM *OFF.*
WHATEVER. DOESN'T THAT SUIT GET REAL *HOT?*
YES--WHAT OF IT?

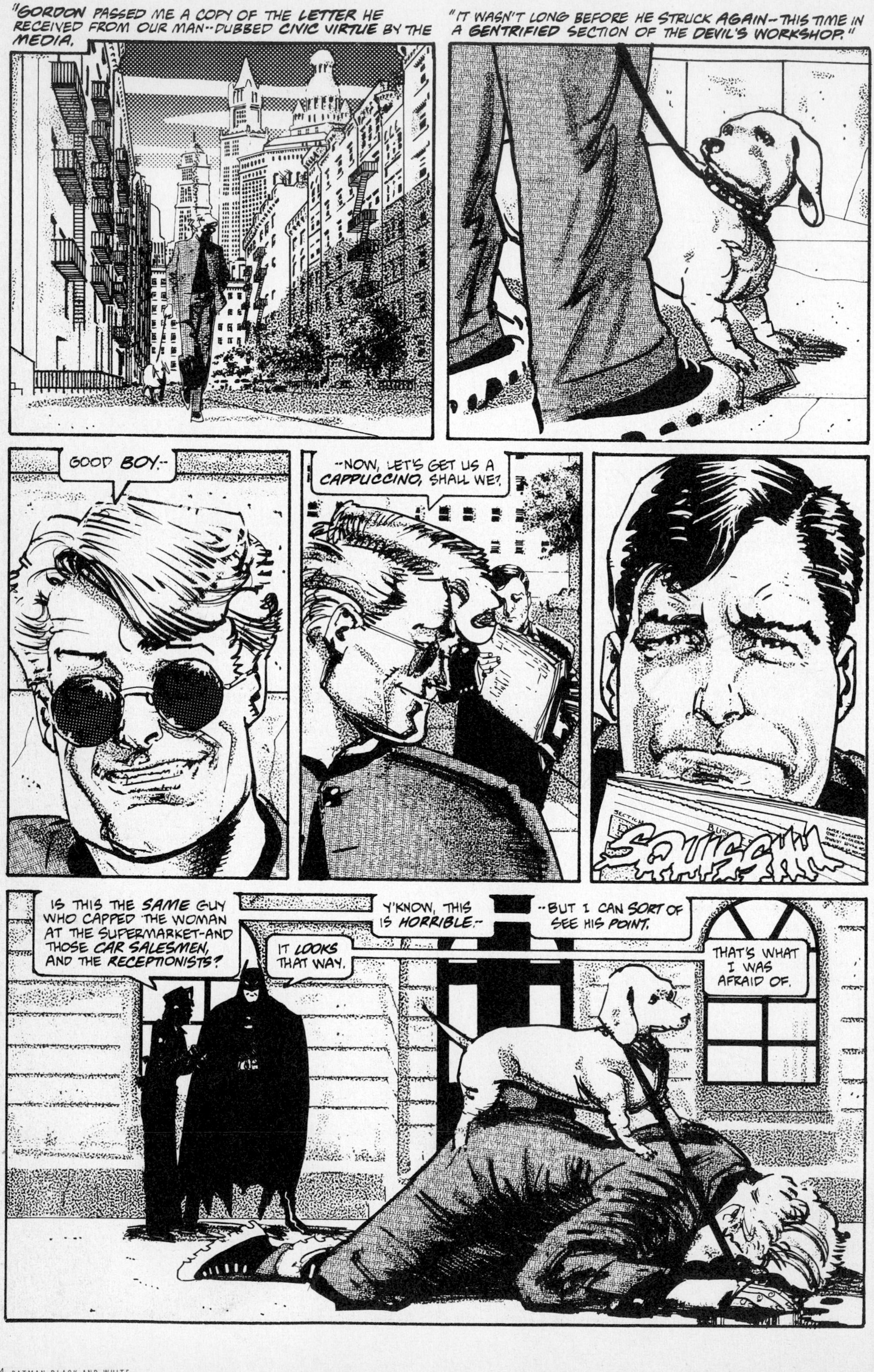
"GORDON PASSED ME A COPY OF THE LETTER HE RECEIVED FROM OUR MAN--DUBBED CIVIC VIRTUE BY THE MEDIA.
"IT WASN'T LONG BEFORE HE STRUCK AGAIN--THIS TIME IN A GENTRIFIED SECTION OF THE DEVIL'S WORKSHOP."
GOOD BOY.-
--NOW, LET'S GET US A CAPPUCCINO, SHALL WE?
SQUISSH
IS THIS THE SAME GUY WHO CAPPED THE WOMAN AT THE SUPERMARKET-AND THOSE CAR SALESMEN, AND THE RECEPTIONISTS?
IT LOOKS THAT WAY.
Y'KNOW, THIS IS HORRIBLE.-
--BUT I CAN SORT OF SEE HIS POINT.
THAT'S WHAT I WAS AFRAID OF.

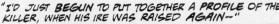

"CIVIC VIRTUE'S LETTERS WERE THOUGHTFUL, REASONABLE, AND LOGICAL--EVEN THOUGH HE CONSISTENTLY USED 'INFER' WHEN HE MEANT 'IMPLY.'"

"I'D JUST BEGUN TO PUT TOGETHER A PROFILE OF THE KILLER, WHEN HIS IRE WAS RAISED AGAIN--"

HEY, LADY-- GET OVER!!

IT SAYS MAXIMUM SPEED--NOT MINIMUM!

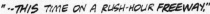

"--THIS TIME ON A RUSH-HOUR FREEWAY."

THIS IS THE FAST LANE, LADY--

--AND THIS JERK BEHIND ME IS TAILGATING--

--LADY-- YOU'RE GOING TO CAUSE AN--

--ACCIDENT.

KWARR-RUNNCH!!

THE MIDDLE OF RUSH HOUR--FOR GOD'S SAKE-- AND THIS BROAD'S DOING FIFTY IN THE LEFT-HAND LANE. YOU ASK ME--

WELL....

SO YOU THINK SHE HAD IT COMING, HUH?

"AND *THAT* SEEMED TO BE THE WAY THINGS WERE HEADING. THE KILLINGS WERE UTTERLY *HEINOUS*--"

"--BUT IN THE WORST *POSSIBLE* WAY, UTTERLY *COMPREHENSIBLE*."

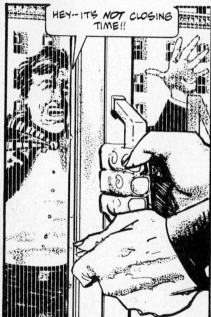

HEY-- IT'S *NOT* CLOSING TIME!!

KLIK!

HE WAS NEAR *DEAF* AND *TERRIBLY* NEAR-SIGHTED,

SO THIS HAS HAPPENED *BEFORE?*

SURE, HE CLOSED A LITTLE *EARLY* ONCE OR TWICE A MONTH-- NO *HARM* DONE--

'TIL NOW.

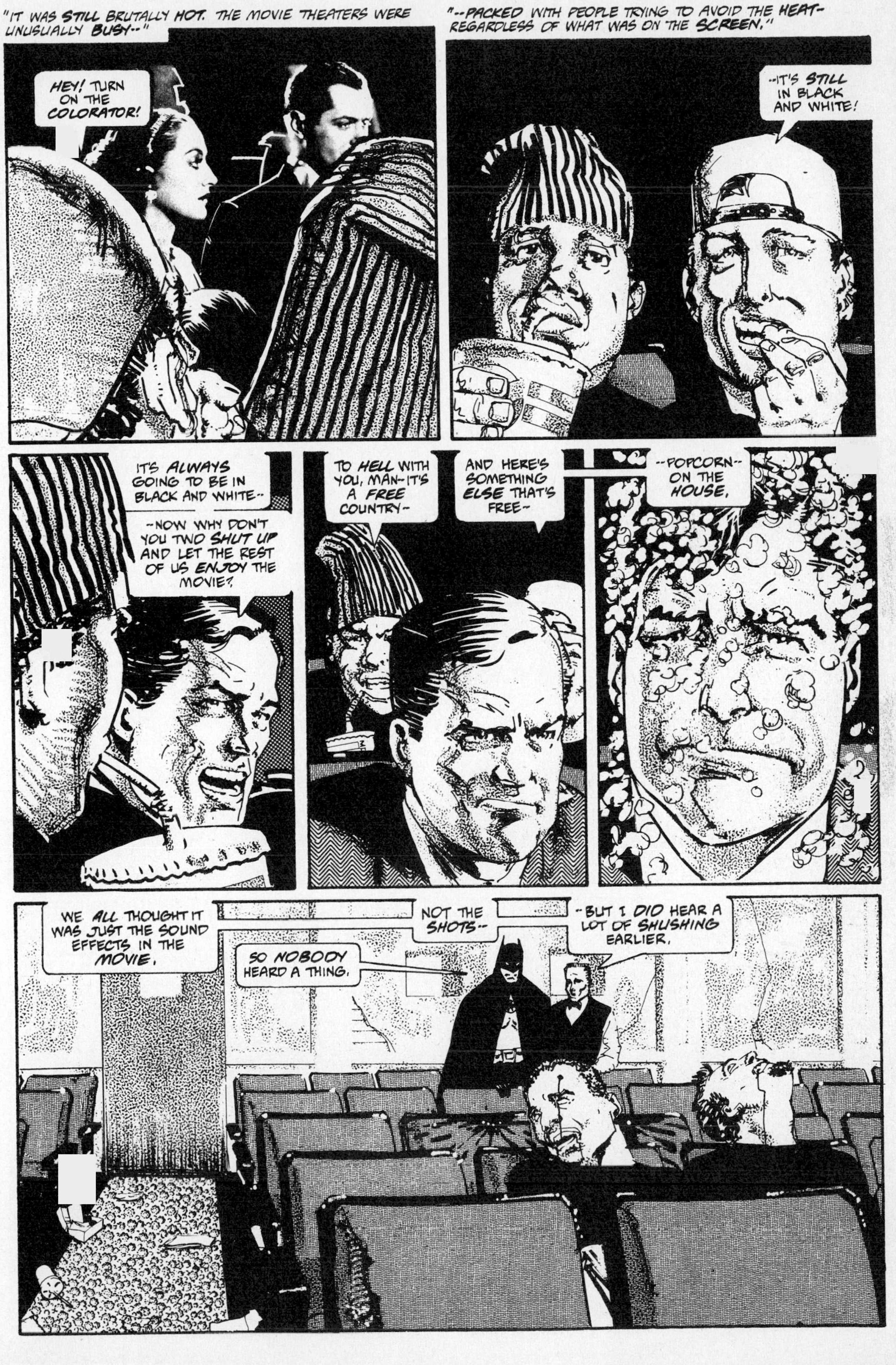
"IT WAS STILL BRUTALLY HOT. THE MOVIE THEATERS WERE UNUSUALLY BUSY--"
"--PACKED WITH PEOPLE TRYING TO AVOID THE HEAT--REGARDLESS OF WHAT WAS ON THE SCREEN."
HEY! TURN ON THE COLORATOR!
--IT'S STILL IN BLACK AND WHITE!
IT'S ALWAYS GOING TO BE IN BLACK AND WHITE--
--NOW WHY DON'T YOU TWO SHUT UP AND LET THE REST OF US ENJOY THE MOVIE?
TO HELL WITH YOU, MAN--IT'S A FREE COUNTRY--
AND HERE'S SOMETHING ELSE THAT'S FREE--
--POPCORN--ON THE HOUSE.
WE ALL THOUGHT IT WAS JUST THE SOUND EFFECTS IN THE MOVIE.
SO NOBODY HEARD A THING.
NOT THE SHOTS--
--BUT I DID HEAR A LOT OF SHUSHING EARLIER.

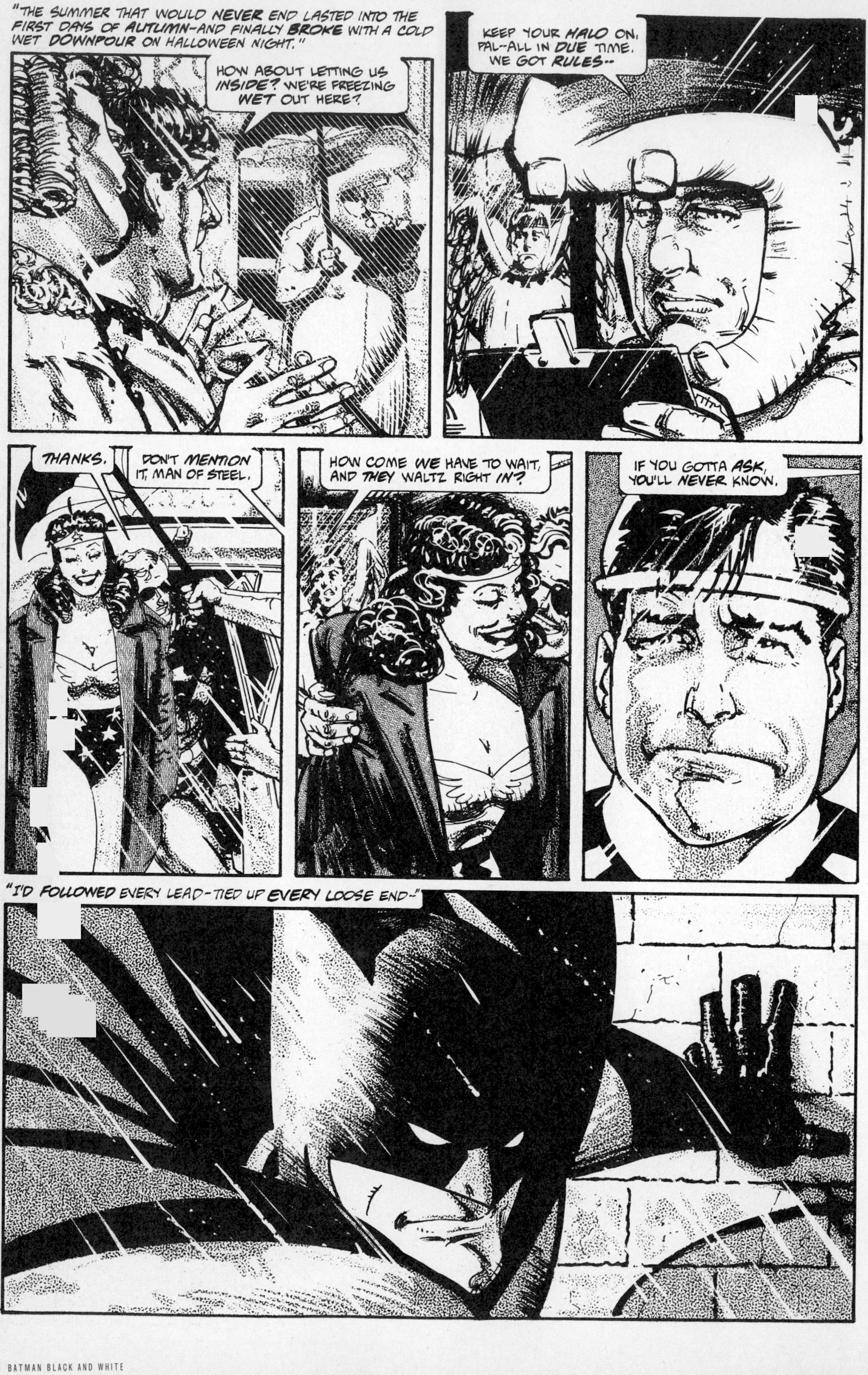
"THE SUMMER THAT WOULD NEVER END LASTED INTO THE FIRST DAYS OF AUTUMN--AND FINALLY BROKE WITH A COLD WET DOWNPOUR ON HALLOWEEN NIGHT."
HOW ABOUT LETTING US INSIDE? WE'RE FREEZING WET OUT HERE?
KEEP YOUR HALO ON, PAL--ALL IN DUE TIME. WE GOT RULES--
THANKS.
DON'T MENTION IT, MAN OF STEEL.
HOW COME WE HAVE TO WAIT, AND THEY WALTZ RIGHT IN?
IF YOU GOTTA ASK, YOU'LL NEVER KNOW.
"I'D FOLLOWED EVERY LEAD--TIED UP EVERY LOOSE END--"

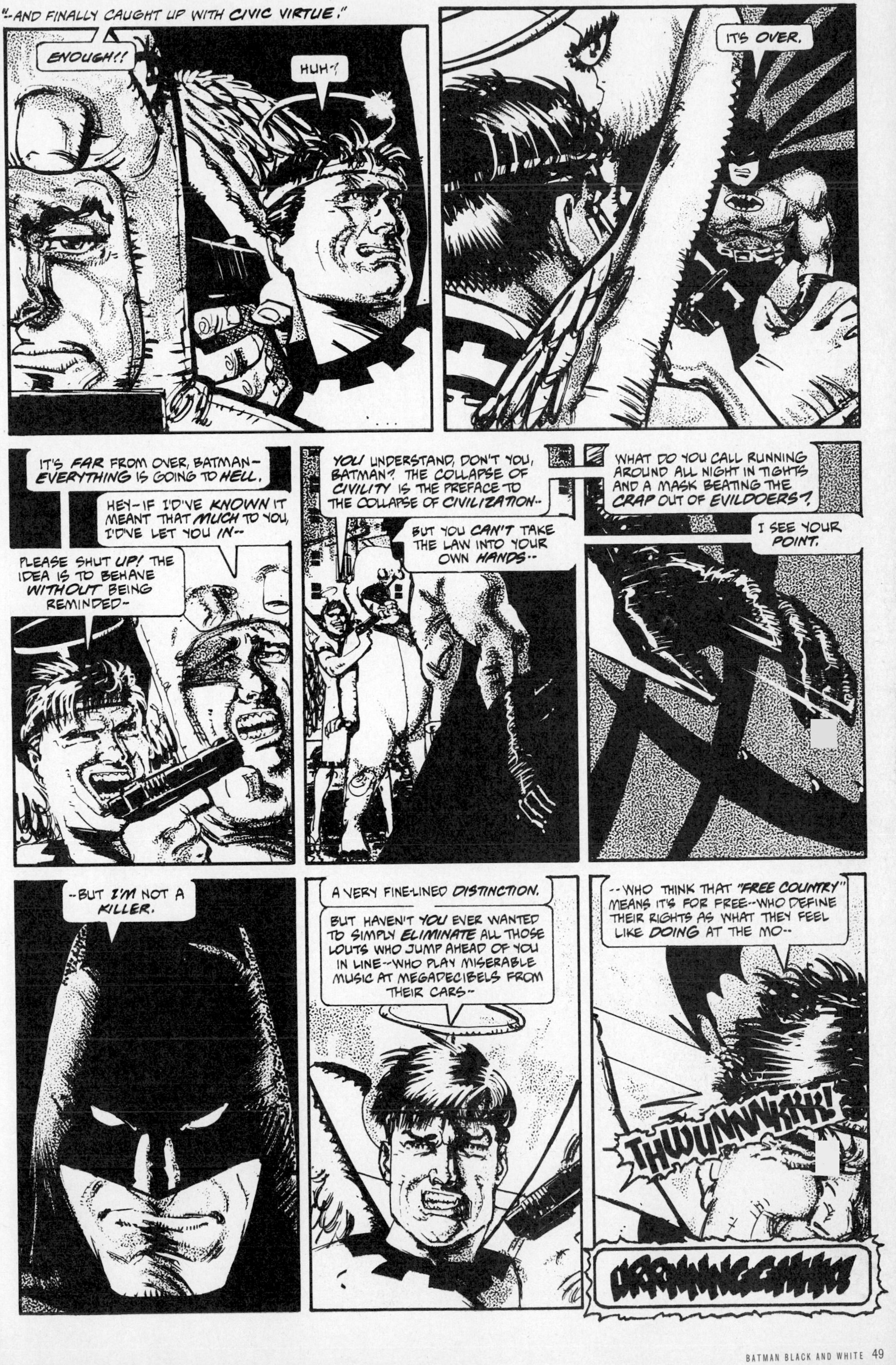
"--AND FINALLY CAUGHT UP WITH CIVIC VIRTUE."
ENOUGH!!
HUH-?
IT'S OVER.
IT'S FAR FROM OVER, BATMAN-- EVERYTHING IS GOING TO HELL.
HEY--IF I'D'VE KNOWN IT MEANT THAT MUCH TO YOU, I'D'VE LET YOU IN--
PLEASE SHUT UP! THE IDEA IS TO BEHAVE WITHOUT BEING REMINDED--
YOU UNDERSTAND, DON'T YOU, BATMAN? THE COLLAPSE OF CIVILITY IS THE PREFACE TO THE COLLAPSE OF CIVILIZATION--
BUT YOU CAN'T TAKE THE LAW INTO YOUR OWN HANDS--
WHAT DO YOU CALL RUNNING AROUND ALL NIGHT IN TIGHTS AND A MASK BEATING THE CRAP OUT OF EVILDOERS?
I SEE YOUR POINT.
--BUT I'M NOT A KILLER.
A VERY FINE-LINED DISTINCTION.
BUT HAVEN'T YOU EVER WANTED TO SIMPLY ELIMINATE ALL THOSE LOUTS WHO JUMP AHEAD OF YOU IN LINE--WHO PLAY MISERABLE MUSIC AT MEGADECIBELS FROM THEIR CARS--
--WHO THINK THAT "FREE COUNTRY" MEANS IT'S FOR FREE--WHO DEFINE THEIR RIGHTS AS WHAT THEY FEEL LIKE DOING AT THE MO--
THWUNNNKKK!

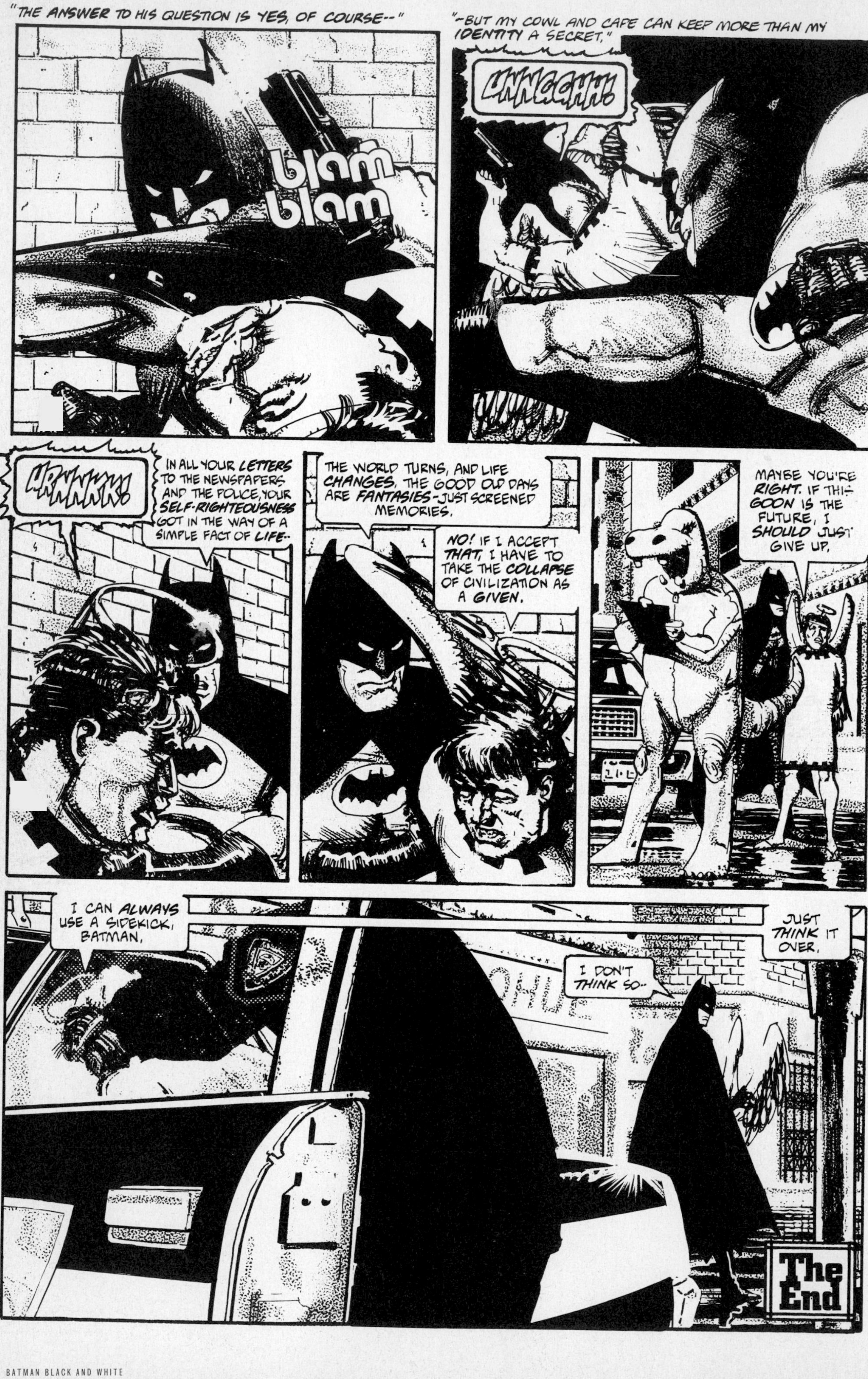
"THE ANSWER TO HIS QUESTION IS YES, OF COURSE--"
BLAM BLAM
"--BUT MY COWL AND CAPE CAN KEEP MORE THAN MY IDENTITY A SECRET."
UNNGGHH!
URNNKK!
IN ALL YOUR LETTERS TO THE NEWSPAPERS AND THE POLICE, YOUR SELF-RIGHTEOUSNESS GOT IN THE WAY OF A SIMPLE FACT OF LIFE..
THE WORLD TURNS, AND LIFE CHANGES. THE GOOD OLD DAYS ARE FANTASIES--JUST SCREENED MEMORIES.
NO! IF I ACCEPT THAT, I HAVE TO TAKE THE COLLAPSE OF CIVILIZATION AS A GIVEN.
MAYBE YOU'RE RIGHT. IF THIS GOON IS THE FUTURE, I SHOULD JUST GIVE UP.
I CAN ALWAYS USE A SIDEKICK, BATMAN.
I DON'T THINK SO--
JUST THINK IT OVER.
The End

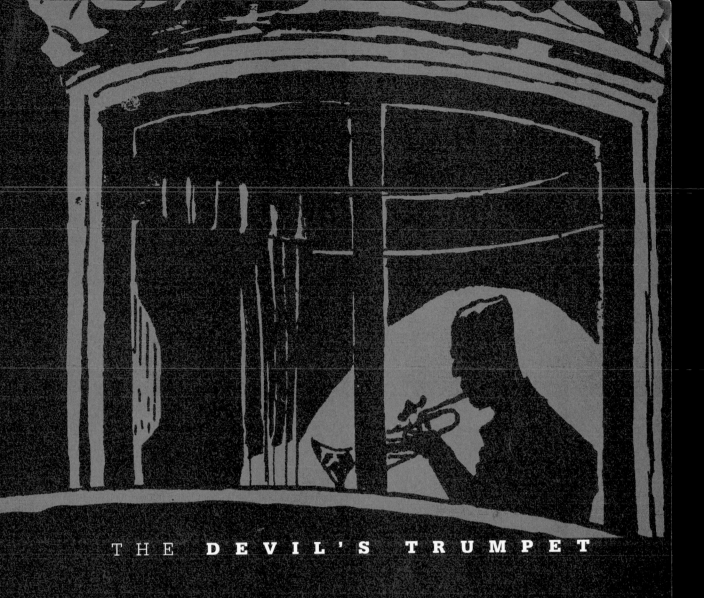

THE **DEVIL'S** TRUMPET

JOSÉ**MUÑOZ**

Born in Argentina in 1942, José Muñoz has become one of the world's most respected and admired artists. A true original in his approach to draftsmanship and storytelling, his work on the graphic novels *Sinner* and *Joe's Bar* are classics of the medium. To say that José's unique, unrestrained drawing style has been influential to many well-known American artists over the years would be an understatement.

His work with longtime collaborator Carlos Sampayo on the 1993 graphic biography *Billie Holiday* remains a touchstone for dozens of comics' leading illustrators.

ARCHIE**GOODWIN**

Often hailed as the most respected writer in the industry, Archie Goodwin is a thirty-year veteran in the comics field. He has written most of the major characters for DC and Marvel, has written syndicated newspaper strips such as *Star Wars* and *Tarzan*, and was once Editor-in-Chief at Marvel Comics.

Archie's astounding writing and editing stints on *Creepy*, *Eerie* and *Blazing Combat* are a creative feat that is still held in awe. He is currently a group editor at DC Comics.

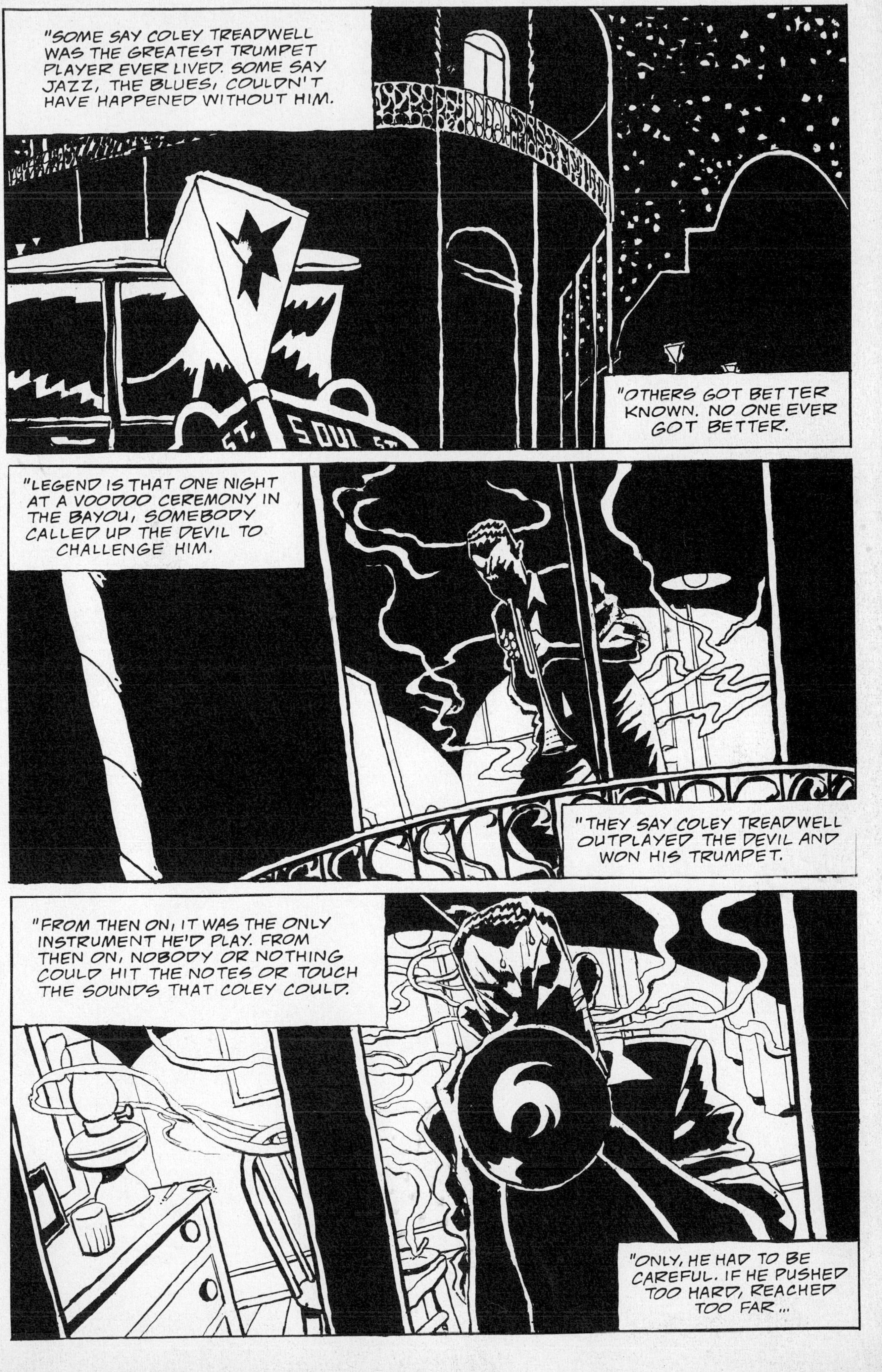
"SOME SAY COLEY TREADWELL WAS THE GREATEST TRUMPET PLAYER EVER LIVED. SOME SAY JAZZ, THE BLUES, COULDN'T HAVE HAPPENED WITHOUT HIM.
"OTHERS GOT BETTER KNOWN. NO ONE EVER GOT BETTER.
"LEGEND IS THAT ONE NIGHT AT A VOODOO CEREMONY IN THE BAYOU, SOMEBODY CALLED UP THE DEVIL TO CHALLENGE HIM.
"THEY SAY COLEY TREADWELL OUTPLAYED THE DEVIL AND WON HIS TRUMPET.
"FROM THEN ON, IT WAS THE ONLY INSTRUMENT HE'D PLAY. FROM THEN ON, NOBODY OR NOTHING COULD HIT THE NOTES OR TOUCH THE SOUNDS THAT COLEY COULD.
"ONLY, HE HAD TO BE CAREFUL. IF HE PUSHED TOO HARD, REACHED TOO FAR...

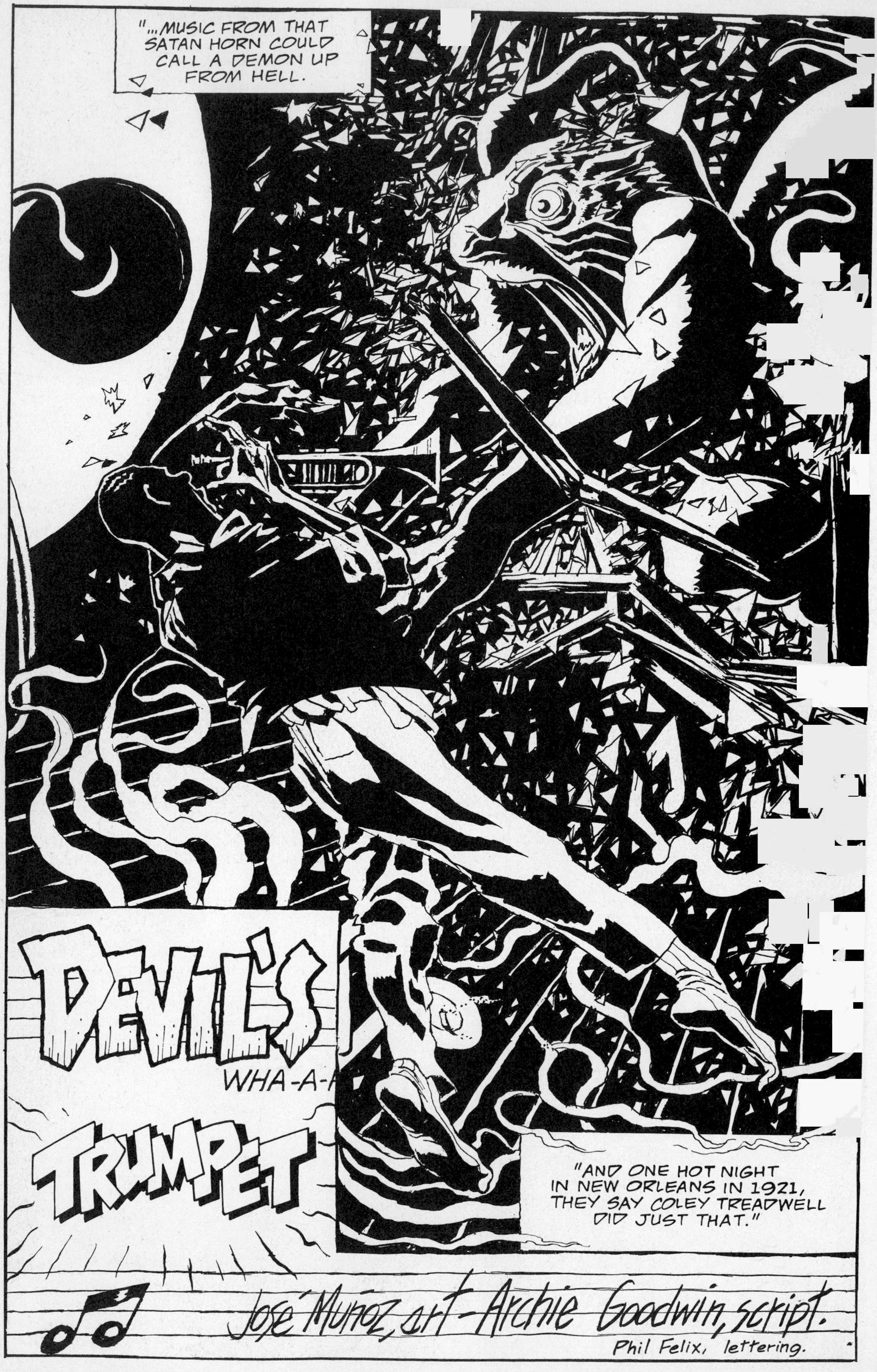
"...MUSIC FROM THAT SATAN HORN COULD CALL A DEMON UP FROM HELL.
DEVIL'S
WHA-A-
TRUMPET
"AND ONE HOT NIGHT IN NEW ORLEANS IN 1921, THEY SAY COLEY TREADWELL DID JUST THAT."
José Muñoz, art - Archie Goodwin, script.
Phil Felix, lettering.

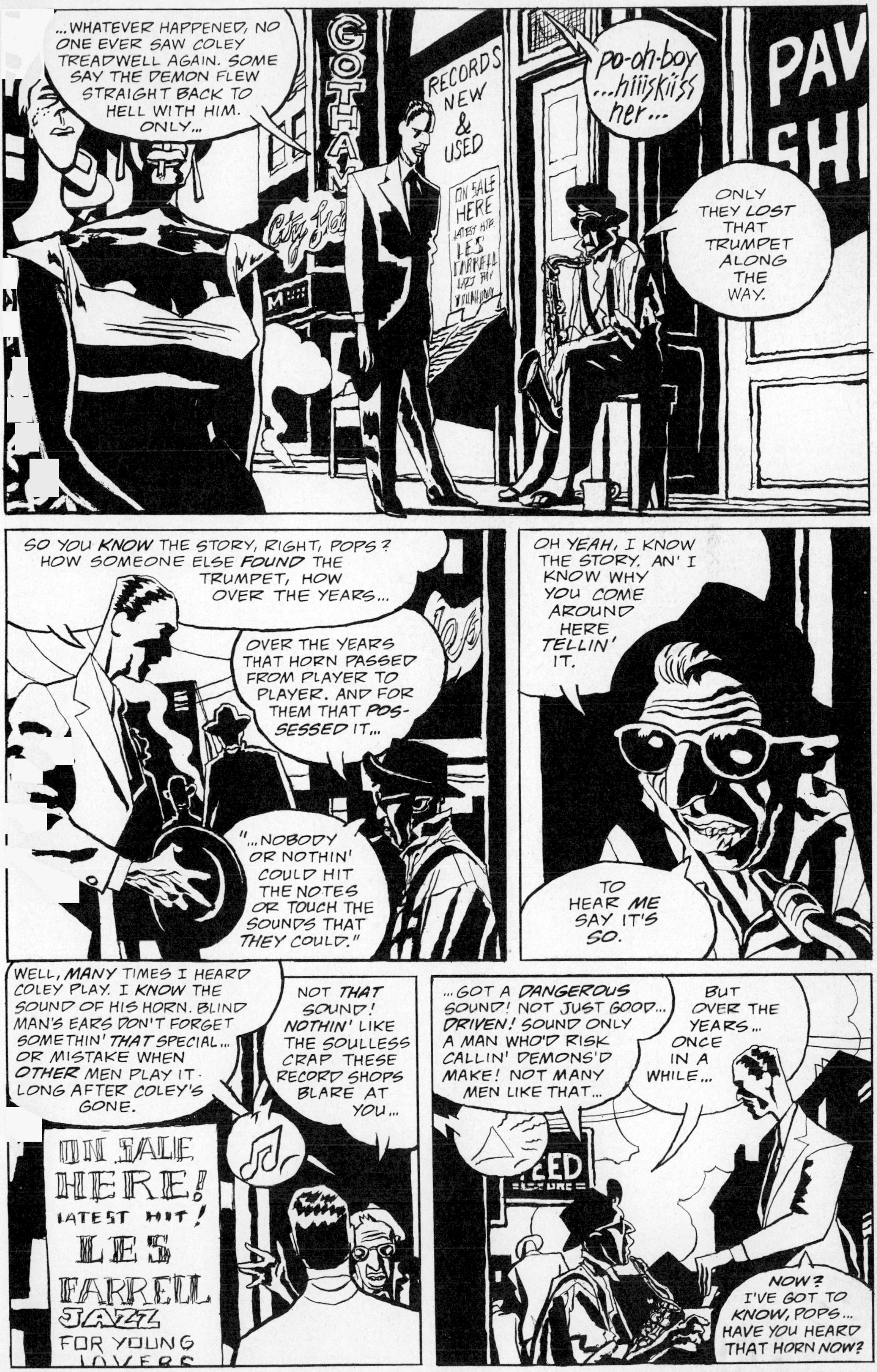

...WHATEVER HAPPENED, NO ONE EVER SAW COLEY TREADWELL AGAIN. SOME SAY THE DEMON FLEW STRAIGHT BACK TO HELL WITH HIM. ONLY...
GOTHAM
RECORDS NEW & USED
po-oh-boy ...hiiiskiiss her...
PAV SH
ON SALE HERE
ONLY THEY LOST THAT TRUMPET ALONG THE WAY.
SO YOU KNOW THE STORY, RIGHT, POPS? HOW SOMEONE ELSE FOUND THE TRUMPET, HOW OVER THE YEARS...
OVER THE YEARS THAT HORN PASSED FROM PLAYER TO PLAYER. AND FOR THEM THAT POSSESSED IT...
"...NOBODY OR NOTHIN' COULD HIT THE NOTES OR TOUCH THE SOUNDS THAT THEY COULD."
OH YEAH, I KNOW THE STORY. AN' I KNOW WHY YOU COME AROUND HERE TELLIN' IT.
TO HEAR ME SAY IT'S SO.
WELL, MANY TIMES I HEARD COLEY PLAY. I KNOW THE SOUND OF HIS HORN. BLIND MAN'S EARS DON'T FORGET SOMETHIN' THAT SPECIAL... OR MISTAKE WHEN OTHER MEN PLAY IT LONG AFTER COLEY'S GONE.
NOT THAT SOUND! NOTHIN' LIKE THE SOULLESS CRAP THESE RECORD SHOPS BLARE AT YOU...
ON SALE HERE! LATEST HIT! LES FARRELL JAZZ FOR YOUNG LOVERS
...GOT A DANGEROUS SOUND! NOT JUST GOOD... DRIVEN! SOUND ONLY A MAN WHO'D RISK CALLIN' DEMONS'D MAKE! NOT MANY MEN LIKE THAT...
BUT OVER THE YEARS... ONCE IN A WHILE...
NOW? I'VE GOT TO KNOW, POPS... HAVE YOU HEARD THAT HORN NOW?

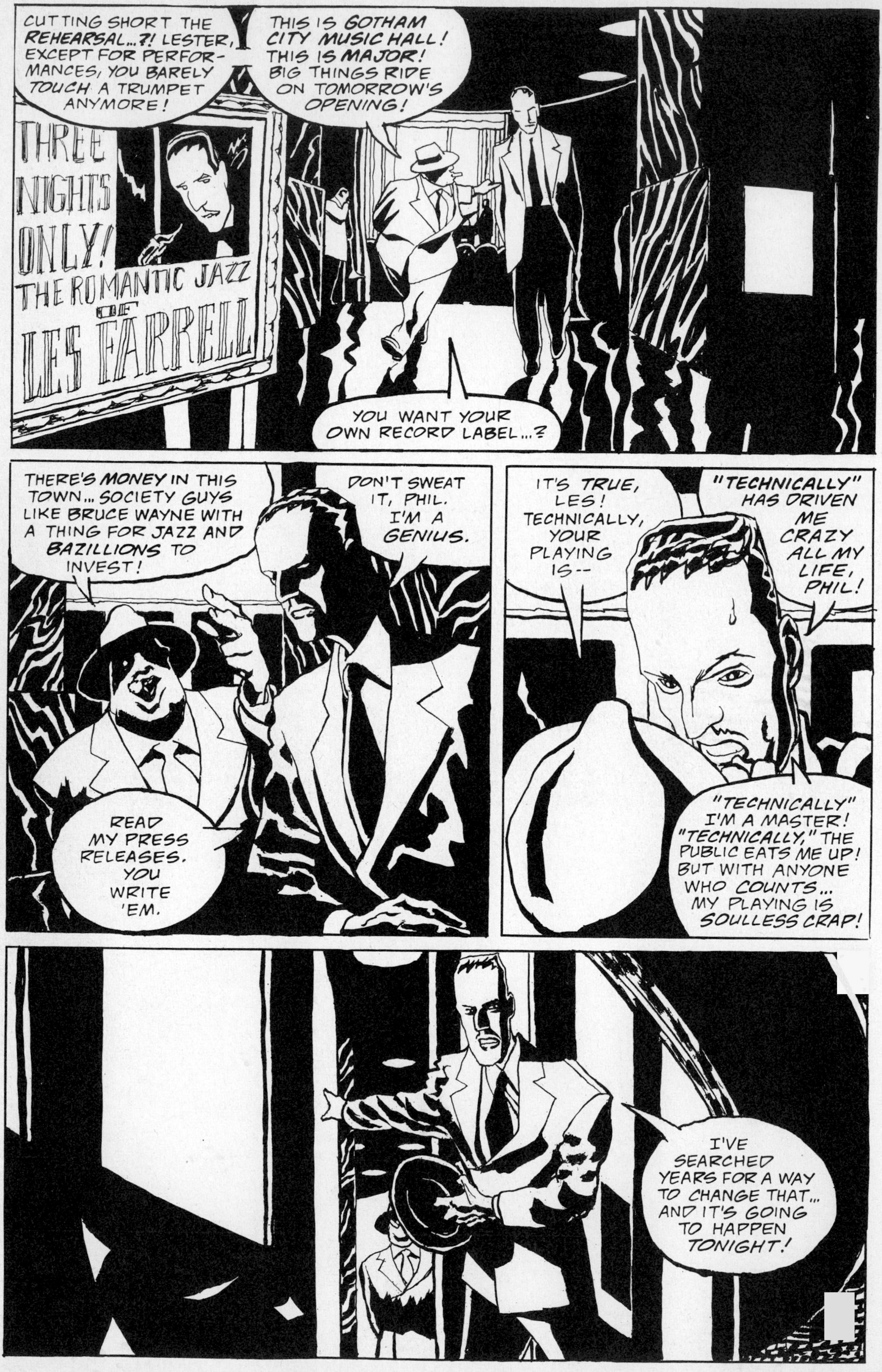
CUTTING SHORT THE REHEARSAL...?! LESTER, EXCEPT FOR PERFORMANCES, YOU BARELY TOUCH A TRUMPET ANYMORE!
THIS IS GOTHAM CITY MUSIC HALL! THIS IS MAJOR! BIG THINGS RIDE ON TOMORROW'S OPENING!
THREE NIGHTS ONLY! THE ROMANTIC JAZZ OF LES FARRELL
YOU WANT YOUR OWN RECORD LABEL...?
THERE'S MONEY IN THIS TOWN... SOCIETY GUYS LIKE BRUCE WAYNE WITH A THING FOR JAZZ AND BAZILLIONS TO INVEST!
DON'T SWEAT IT, PHIL. I'M A GENIUS.
READ MY PRESS RELEASES. YOU WRITE 'EM.
IT'S TRUE, LES! TECHNICALLY, YOUR PLAYING IS--
"TECHNICALLY" HAS DRIVEN ME CRAZY ALL MY LIFE, PHIL!
"TECHNICALLY" I'M A MASTER! "TECHNICALLY," THE PUBLIC EATS ME UP! BUT WITH ANYONE WHO COUNTS... MY PLAYING IS SOULLESS CRAP!
I'VE SEARCHED YEARS FOR A WAY TO CHANGE THAT... AND IT'S GOING TO HAPPEN TONIGHT!

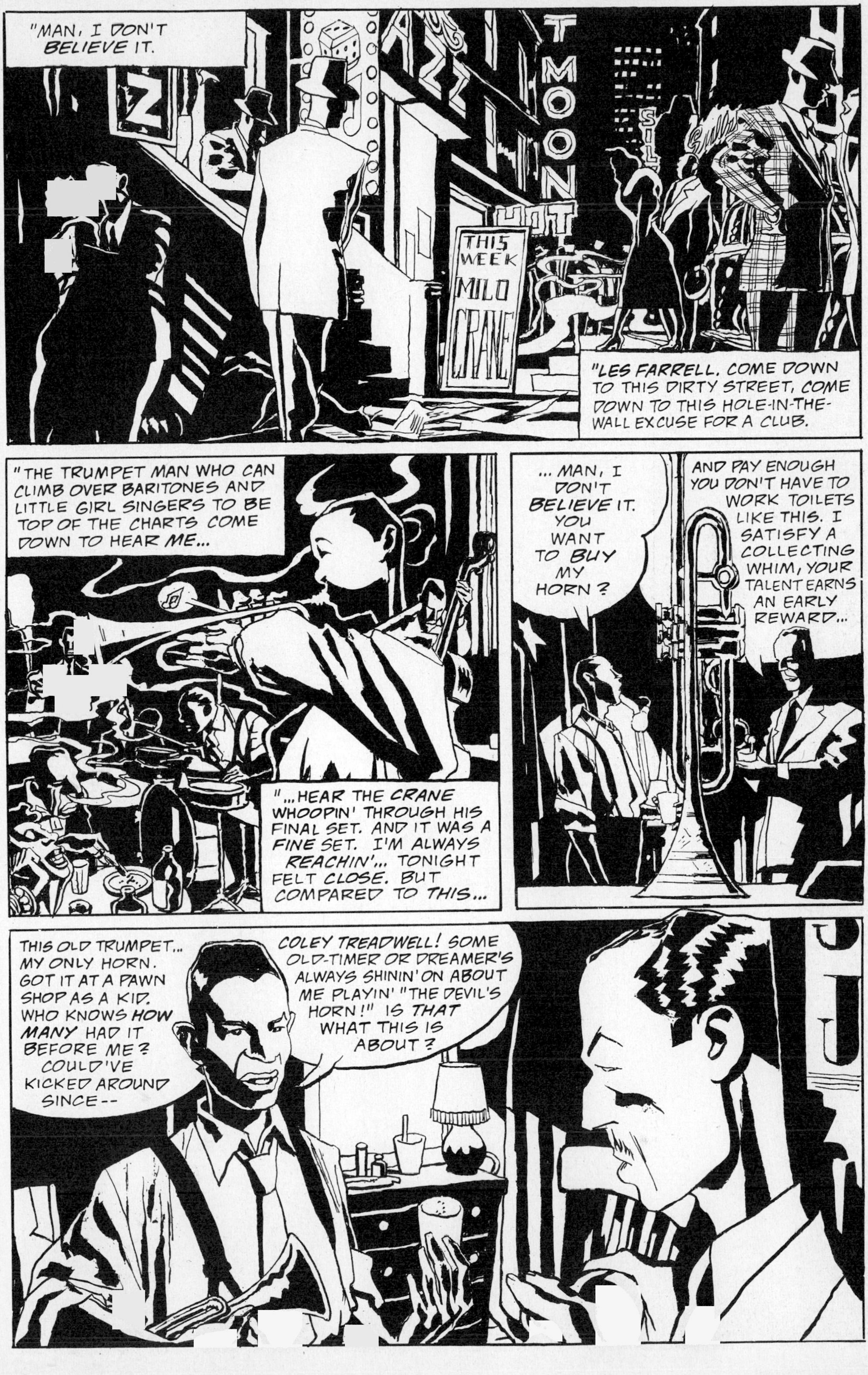
"MAN, I DON'T BELIEVE IT.
"LES FARRELL. COME DOWN TO THIS DIRTY STREET, COME DOWN TO THIS HOLE-IN-THE-WALL EXCUSE FOR A CLUB.
THIS WEEK MILO CRANE
"THE TRUMPET MAN WHO CAN CLIMB OVER BARITONES AND LITTLE GIRL SINGERS TO BE TOP OF THE CHARTS COME DOWN TO HEAR ME...
"...HEAR THE CRANE WHOOPIN' THROUGH HIS FINAL SET. AND IT WAS A FINE SET. I'M ALWAYS REACHIN'... TONIGHT FELT CLOSE. BUT COMPARED TO THIS...
... MAN, I DON'T BELIEVE IT. YOU WANT TO BUY MY HORN ?
AND PAY ENOUGH YOU DON'T HAVE TO WORK TOILETS LIKE THIS. I SATISFY A COLLECTING WHIM, YOUR TALENT EARNS AN EARLY REWARD...
THIS OLD TRUMPET... MY ONLY HORN. GOT IT AT A PAWN SHOP AS A KID. WHO KNOWS HOW MANY HAD IT BEFORE ME ? COULD'VE KICKED AROUND SINCE--
COLEY TREADWELL! SOME OLD-TIMER OR DREAMER'S ALWAYS SHININ' ON ABOUT ME PLAYIN' "THE DEVIL'S HORN!" IS THAT WHAT THIS IS ABOUT ?

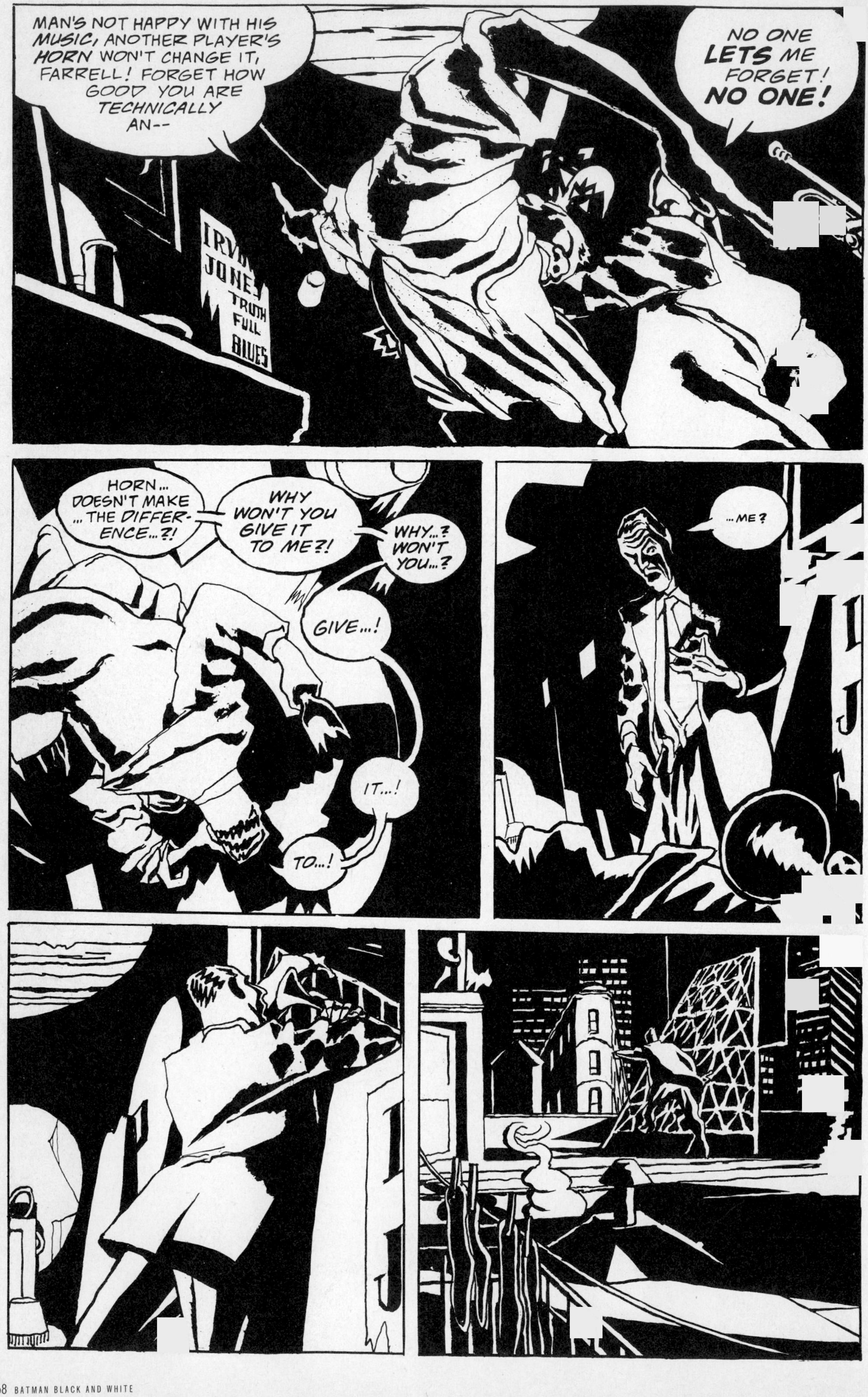
MAN'S NOT HAPPY WITH HIS *MUSIC*, ANOTHER PLAYER'S *HORN* WON'T CHANGE IT, FARRELL! FORGET HOW GOOD YOU ARE TECHNICALLY AN--
NO ONE **LETS** ME FORGET! **NO ONE!**
TRUTH FULL BLUES
HORN... DOESN'T MAKE ...THE *DIFFER-ENCE*...?!
WHY WON'T YOU GIVE IT TO ME?!
WHY...? WON'T YOU...?
GIVE...!
IT...!
TO...!
...ME?

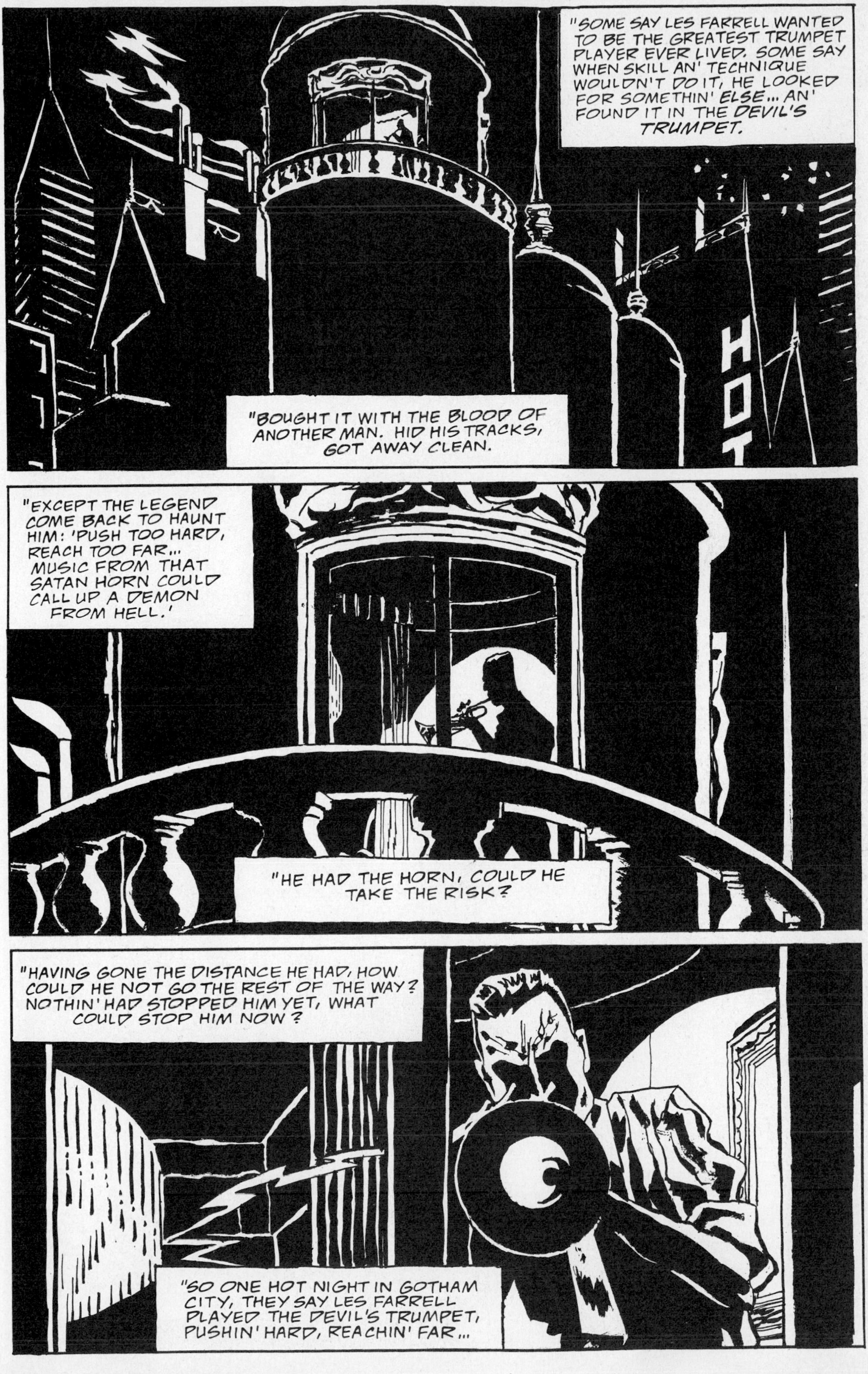
"SOME SAY LES FARRELL WANTED TO BE THE GREATEST TRUMPET PLAYER EVER LIVED. SOME SAY WHEN SKILL AN' TECHNIQUE WOULDN'T DO IT, HE LOOKED FOR SOMETHIN' ELSE... AN' FOUND IT IN THE DEVIL'S TRUMPET.
"BOUGHT IT WITH THE BLOOD OF ANOTHER MAN. HID HIS TRACKS, GOT AWAY CLEAN.
HOT
"EXCEPT THE LEGEND COME BACK TO HAUNT HIM: 'PUSH TOO HARD, REACH TOO FAR... MUSIC FROM THAT SATAN HORN COULD CALL UP A DEMON FROM HELL.'
"HE HAD THE HORN, COULD HE TAKE THE RISK?
"HAVING GONE THE DISTANCE HE HAD, HOW COULD HE NOT GO THE REST OF THE WAY? NOTHIN' HAD STOPPED HIM YET, WHAT COULD STOP HIM NOW?
"SO ONE HOT NIGHT IN GOTHAM CITY, THEY SAY LES FARRELL PLAYED THE DEVIL'S TRUMPET, PUSHIN' HARD, REACHIN' FAR...

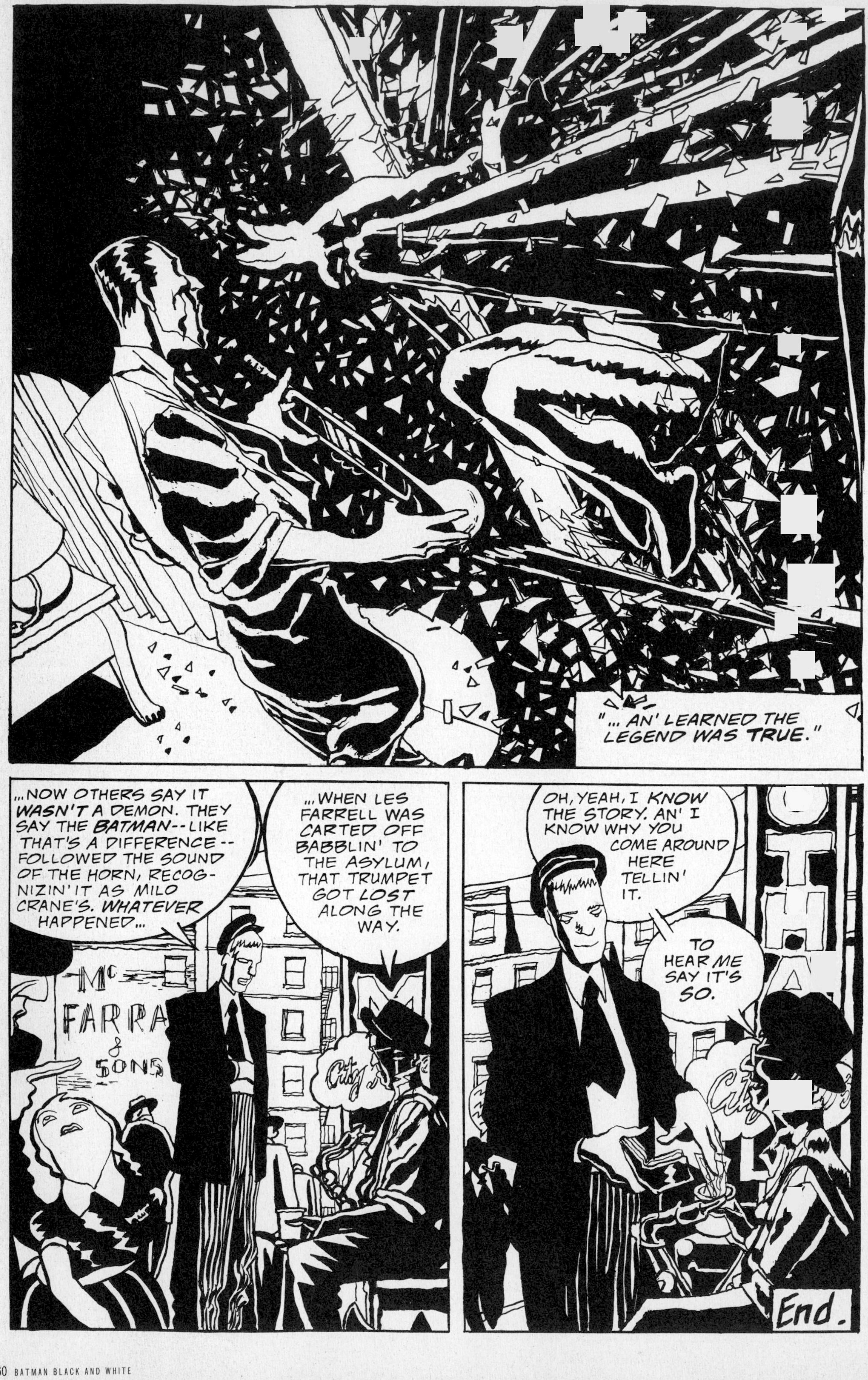
"...AN' LEARNED THE LEGEND WAS TRUE."
...NOW OTHERS SAY IT WASN'T A DEMON. THEY SAY THE BATMAN--LIKE THAT'S A DIFFERENCE--FOLLOWED THE SOUND OF THE HORN, RECOGNIZIN' IT AS MILO CRANE'S. WHATEVER HAPPENED...
...WHEN LES FARRELL WAS CARTED OFF BABBLIN' TO THE ASYLUM, THAT TRUMPET GOT LOST ALONG THE WAY.
Mc FARRA & SONS
OH, YEAH, I KNOW THE STORY. AN' I KNOW WHY YOU COME AROUND HERE TELLIN' IT.
TO HEAR ME SAY IT'S SO.
End.

JIM LEE COVER SKETCH

The most influential comics artist of the '90s, Jim Lee agreed to try his hand at the cover of our first issue. His original sketch fully captures the character's dark, brooding nature.

TED McKEEVER PENCILS

For someone who's known for his obsessively frenetic artwork, Ted McKeever's pencils give the appearance of a well thought-out road map. It's in the inking stage that Ted transforms his calm and orderly pencils into the high-contrast world of nightmare and noir.

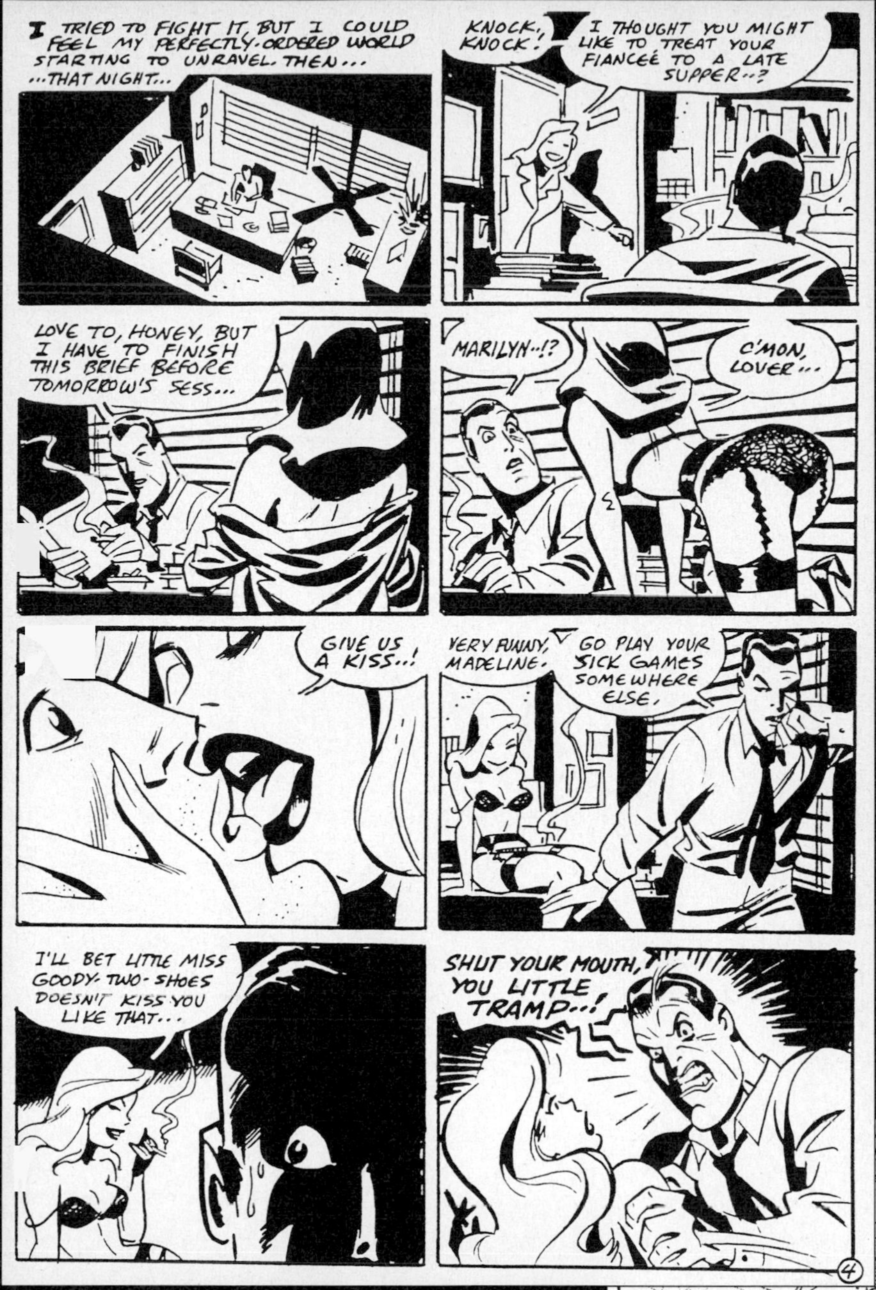
I TRIED TO FIGHT IT, BUT I COULD FEEL MY PERFECTLY-ORDERED WORLD STARTING TO UNRAVEL. THEN...
...THAT NIGHT...
KNOCK, KNOCK!
I THOUGHT YOU MIGHT LIKE TO TREAT YOUR FIANCEÉ TO A LATE SUPPER..?
LOVE TO, HONEY, BUT I HAVE TO FINISH THIS BRIEF BEFORE TOMORROW'S SESS...
MARILYN..!?
C'MON, LOVER...
GIVE US A KISS..!
VERY FUNNY, MADELINE.
GO PLAY YOUR SICK GAMES SOMEWHERE ELSE.
I'LL BET LITTLE MISS GOODY-TWO-SHOES DOESN'T KISS YOU LIKE THAT...
SHUT YOUR MOUTH, YOU LITTLE TRAMP..!
4

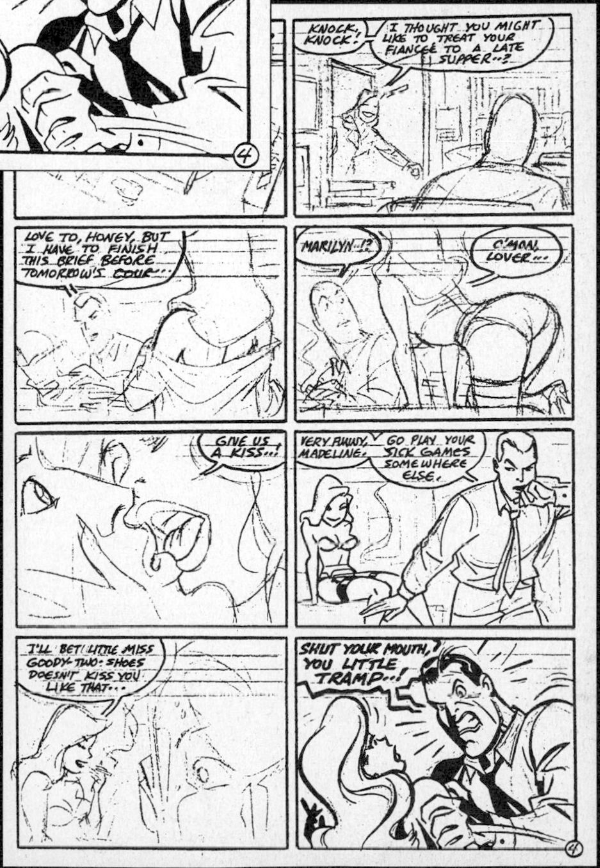
KNOCK, KNOCK!
I THOUGHT YOU MIGHT LIKE TO TREAT YOUR FIANCEÉ TO A LATE SUPPER..?
MARILYN..!?
C'MON, LOVER...
GIVE US A KISS..!
VERY FUNNY, MADELINE.
GO PLAY YOUR SICK GAMES SOMEWHERE ELSE.
I'LL BET LITTLE MISS GOODY-TWO-SHOES DOESN'T KISS YOU LIKE THAT...
SHUT YOUR MOUTH, YOU LITTLE TRAMP..!
4

BRUCE TIMM LAYOUTS

Although most comic artists work in a fairly straightforward manner (thumbnail layouts first, followed by tight pencils and then inks), some choose to work in strange and mysterious ways. Bruce Timm, for instance, does his loose layouts on typing paper and then blows them up to large original art size then inks them (with a magic marker). The inks are pretty tight and could at this point be reproduced from, but Bruce chooses to add another step. Using a lightbox, he completely traces the page onto another sheet of paper, refining the images to the point where he's satisfied with the end result. If you compare this "layout" page with the finished page, you'll notice subtle alterations and additions.

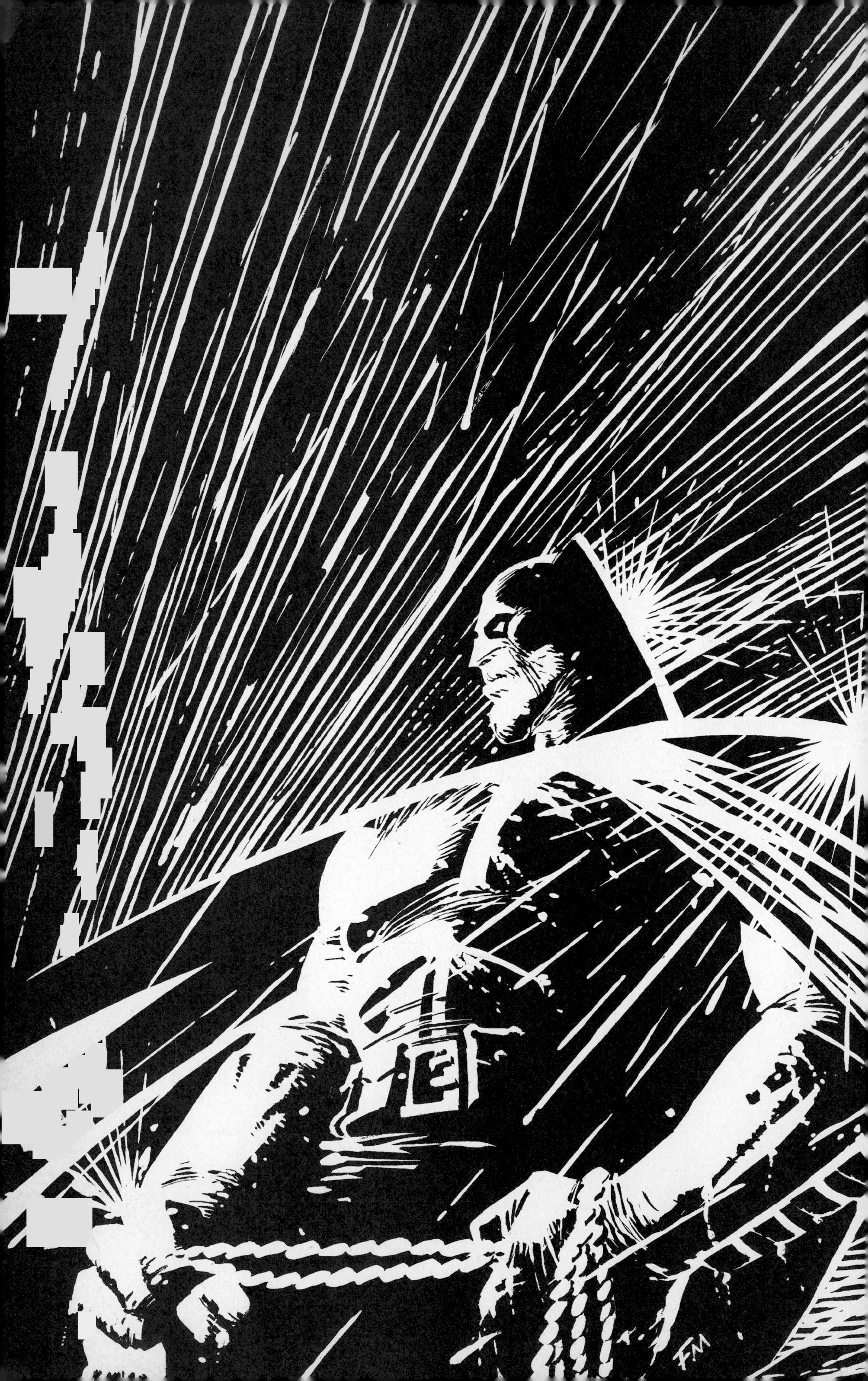
FM

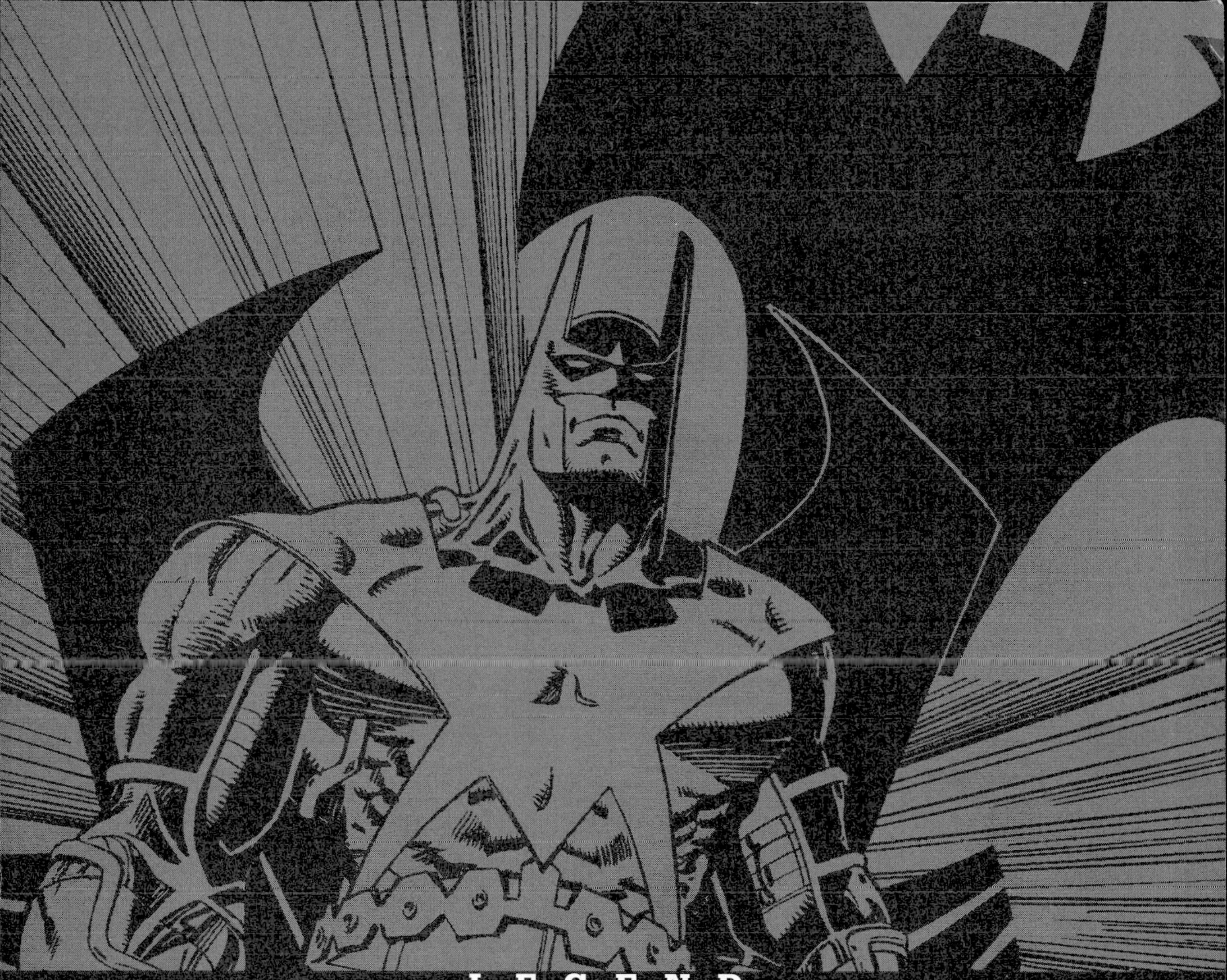

L E G E N D

WALTER**SIMONSON**

When it comes to raw power and pure energy, no living comic-book artist's work surpasses that of Walter Simonson. His dynamic graphic style and pioneering use of sound effects have kept him at the very top of the comics world since the 1970's.

Walt's personal interest in folklore, legends and mythology are a continuing thread in much of his work. He explored these themes in depth in his mid-1980's work on Marvel's *The Mighty Thor*, a stint that was as groundbreaking as it is memorable.

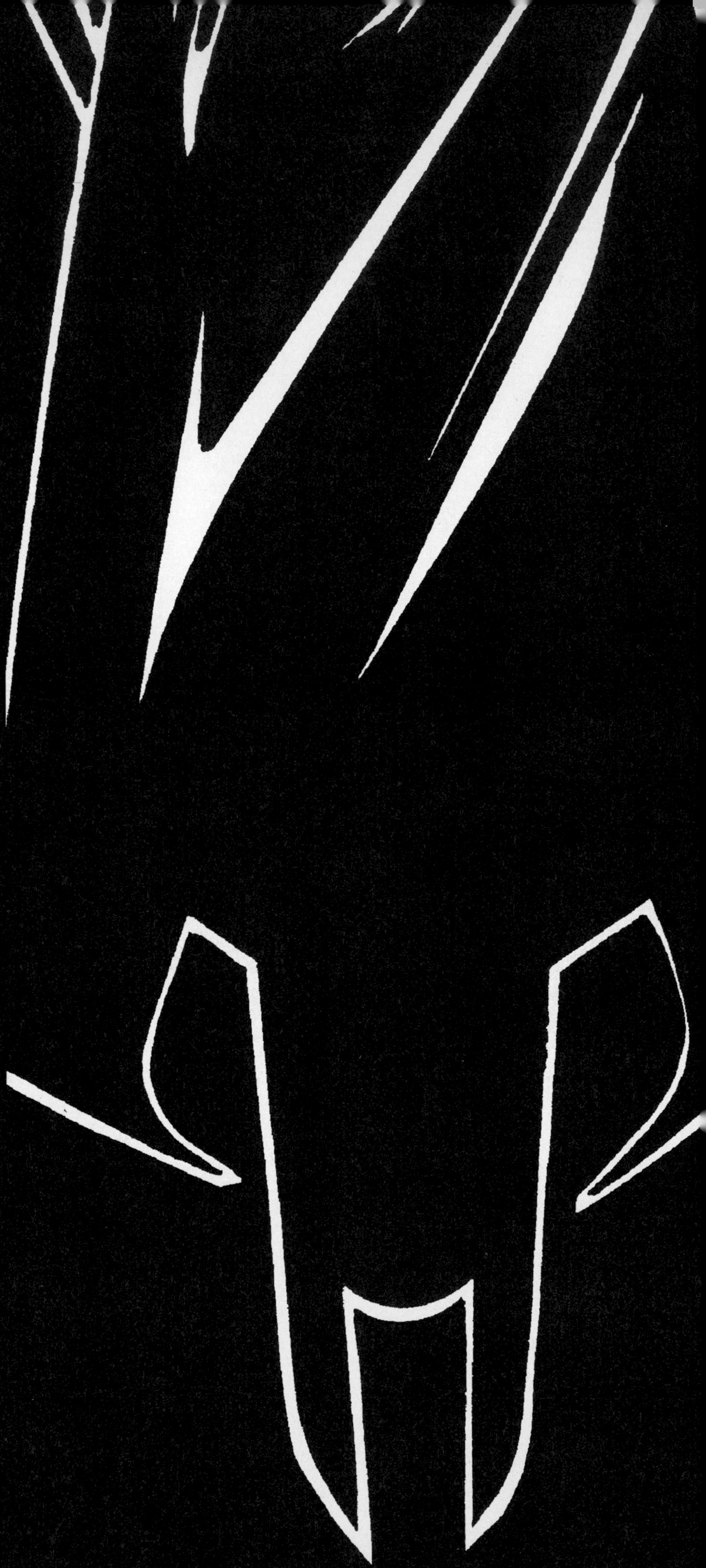

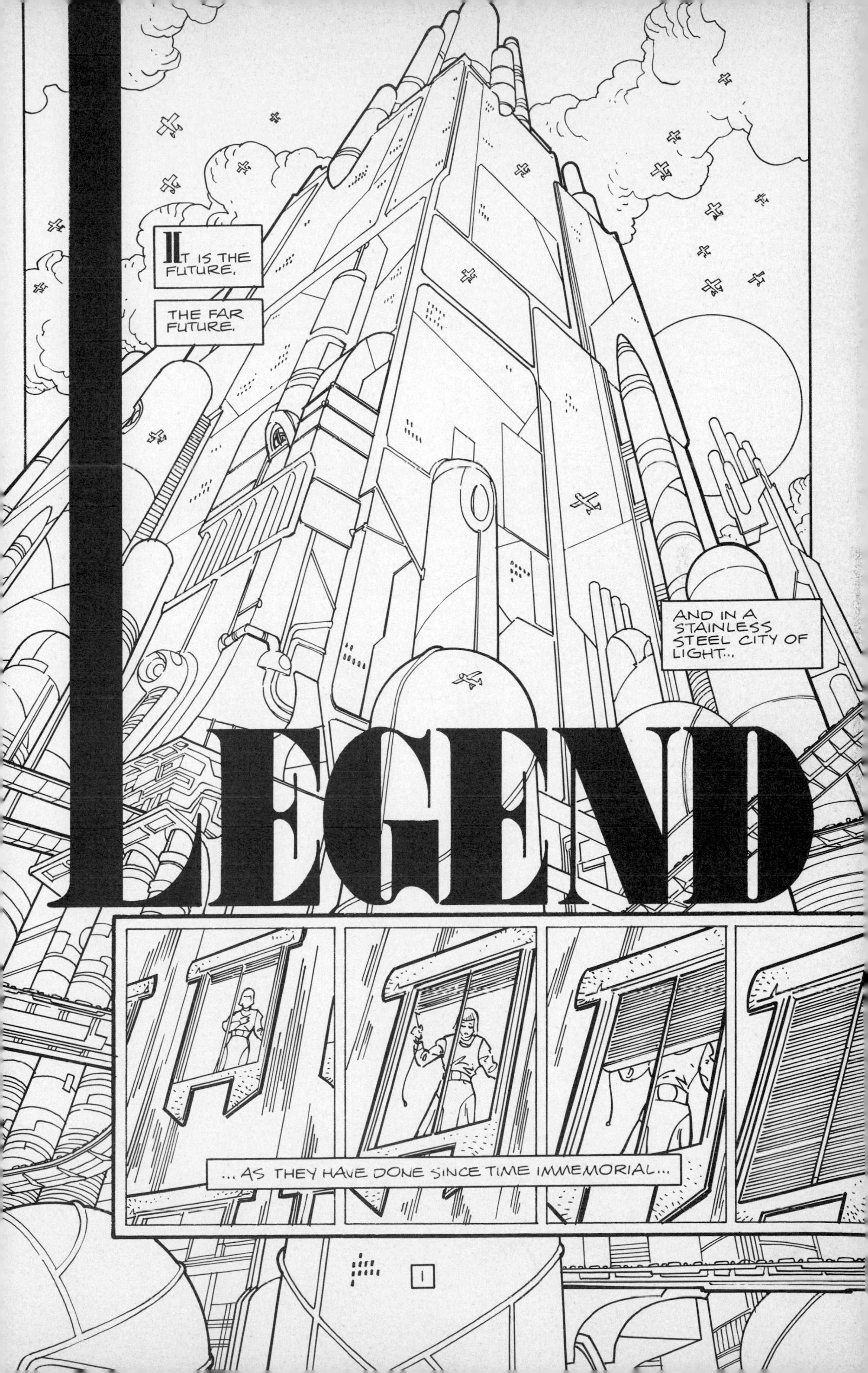
IT IS THE FUTURE.
THE FAR FUTURE.
AND IN A STAINLESS STEEL CITY OF LIGHT...
LEGEND
...AS THEY HAVE DONE SINCE TIME IMMEMORIAL...

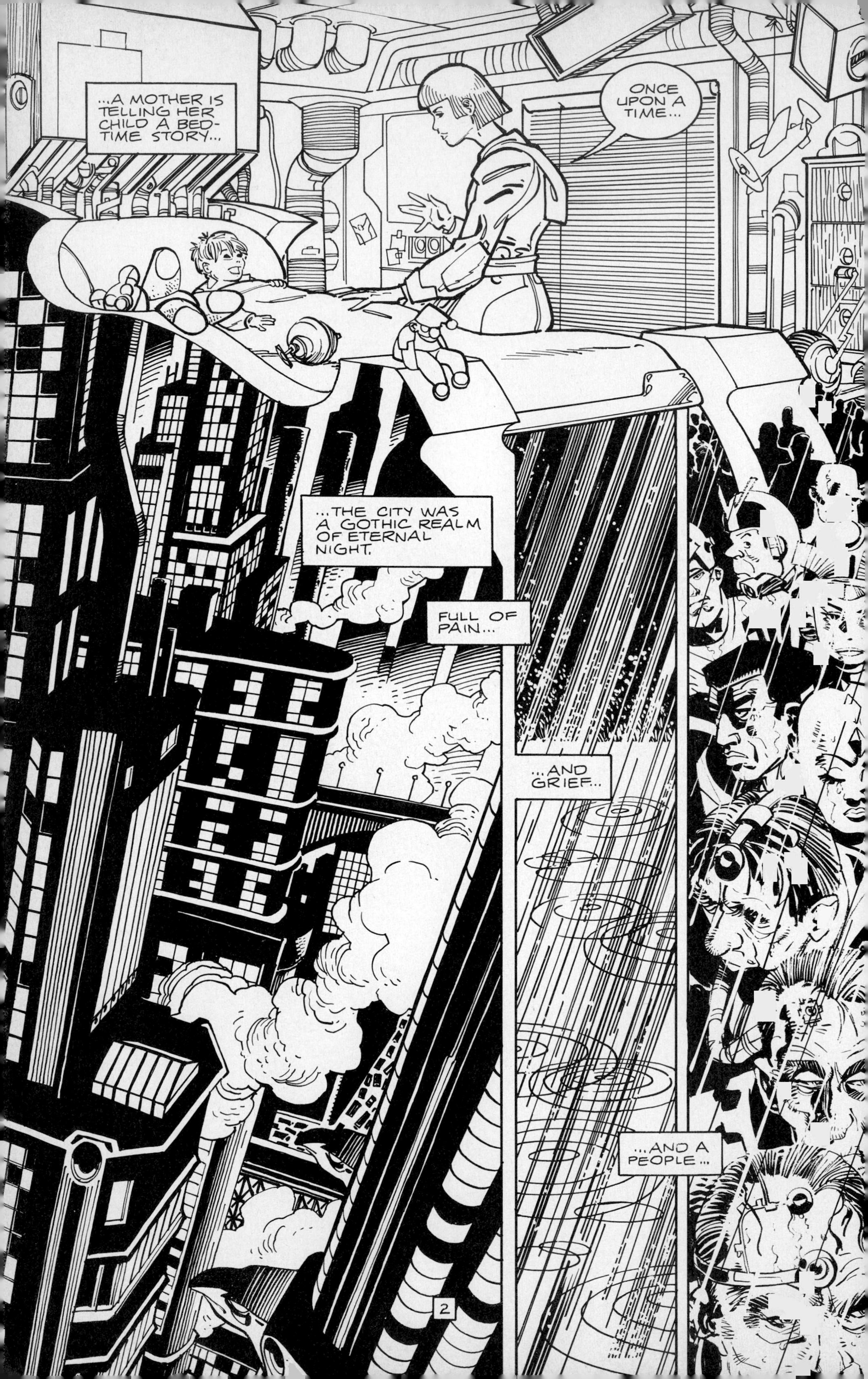
...A MOTHER IS TELLING HER CHILD A BED-TIME STORY...
ONCE UPON A TIME...
...THE CITY WAS A GOTHIC REALM OF ETERNAL NIGHT.
FULL OF PAIN...
...AND GRIEF...
...AND A PEOPLE...

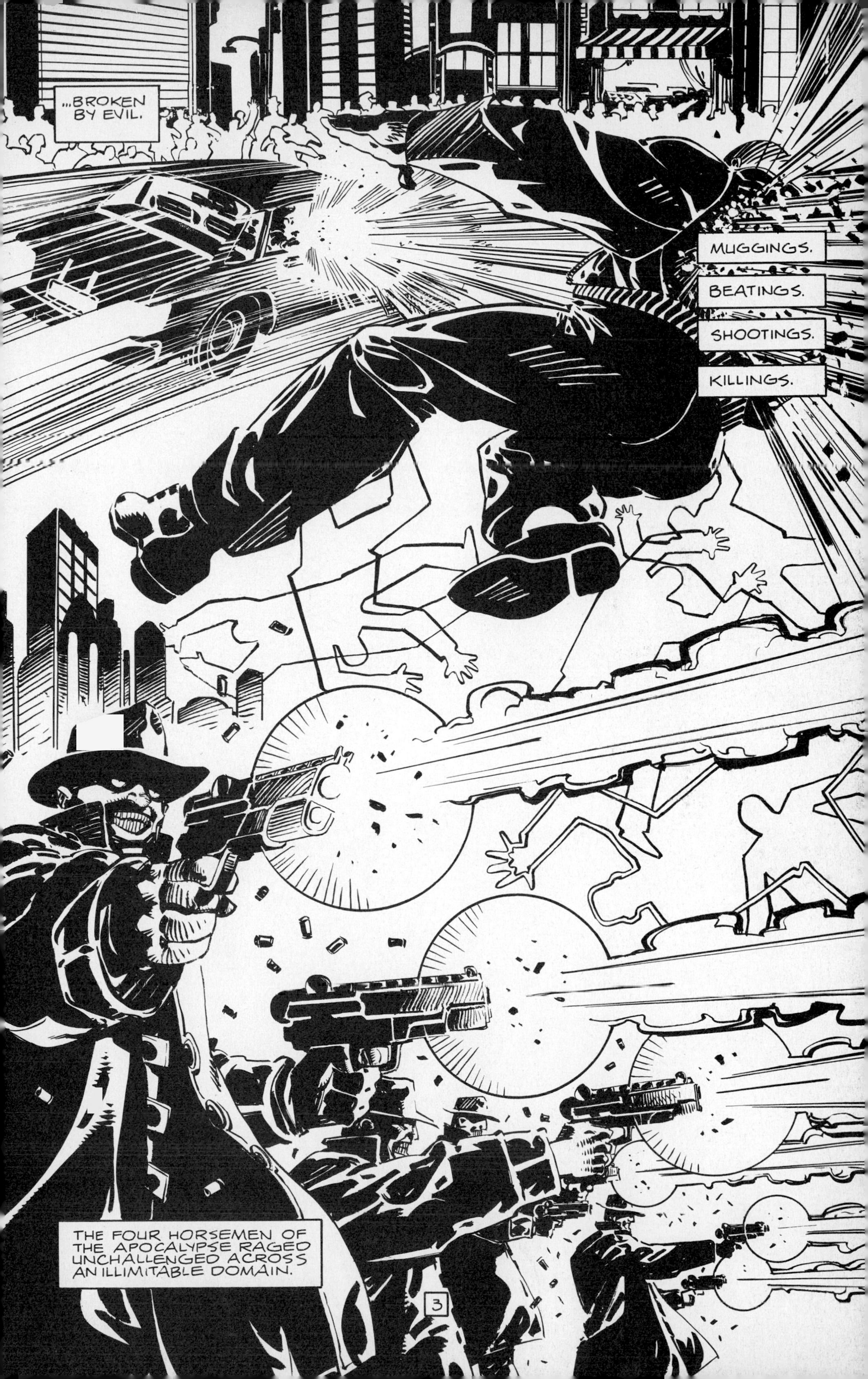
...BROKEN BY EVIL.
MUGGINGS.
BEATINGS.
SHOOTINGS.
KILLINGS.
THE FOUR HORSEMEN OF THE APOCALYPSE RAGED UNCHALLENGED ACROSS AN ILLIMITABLE DOMAIN.
3

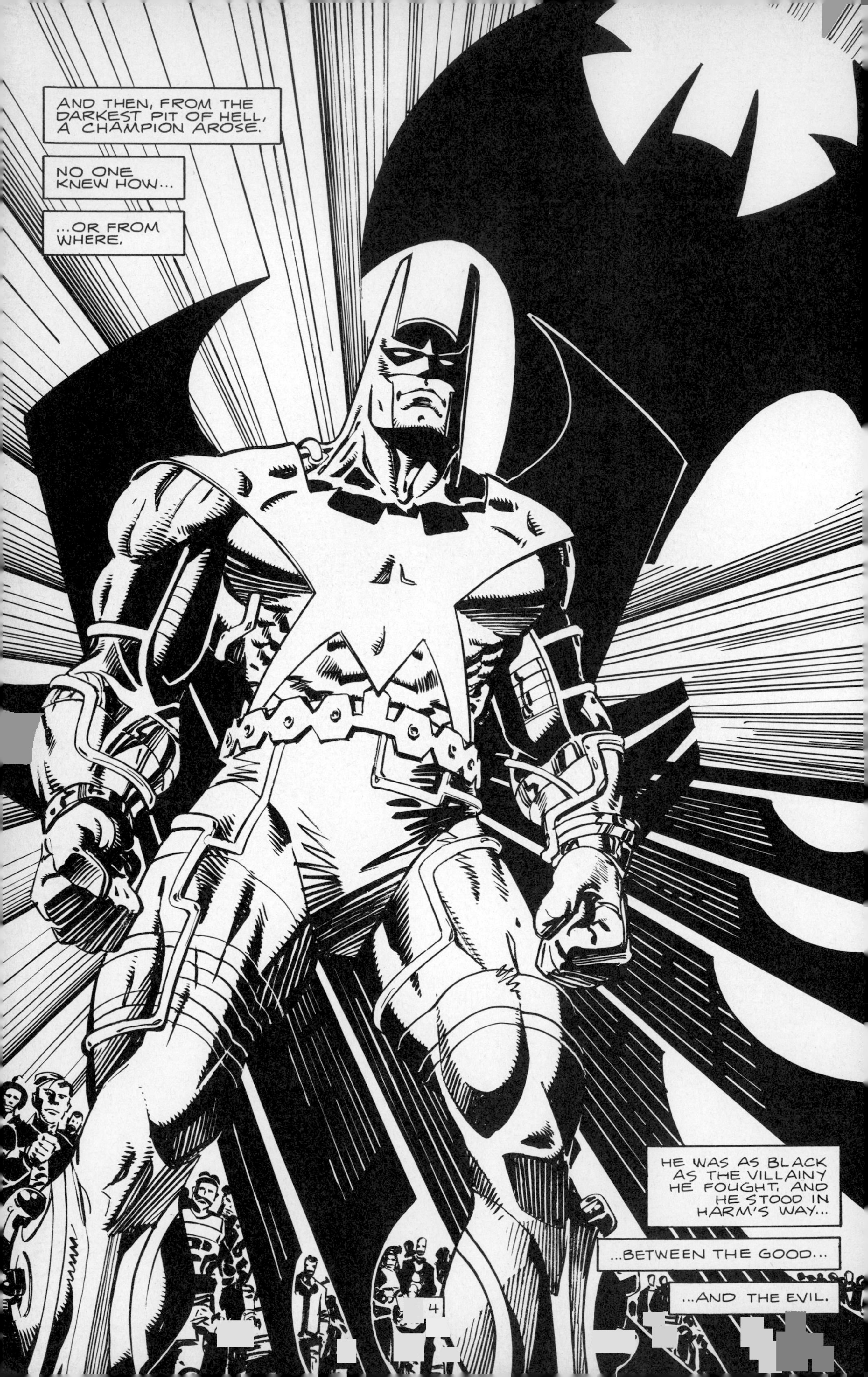
AND THEN, FROM THE DARKEST PIT OF HELL, A CHAMPION AROSE.
NO ONE KNEW HOW...
...OR FROM WHERE.
HE WAS AS BLACK AS THE VILLAINY HE FOUGHT, AND HE STOOD IN HARM'S WAY...
...BETWEEN THE GOOD...
...AND THE EVIL.

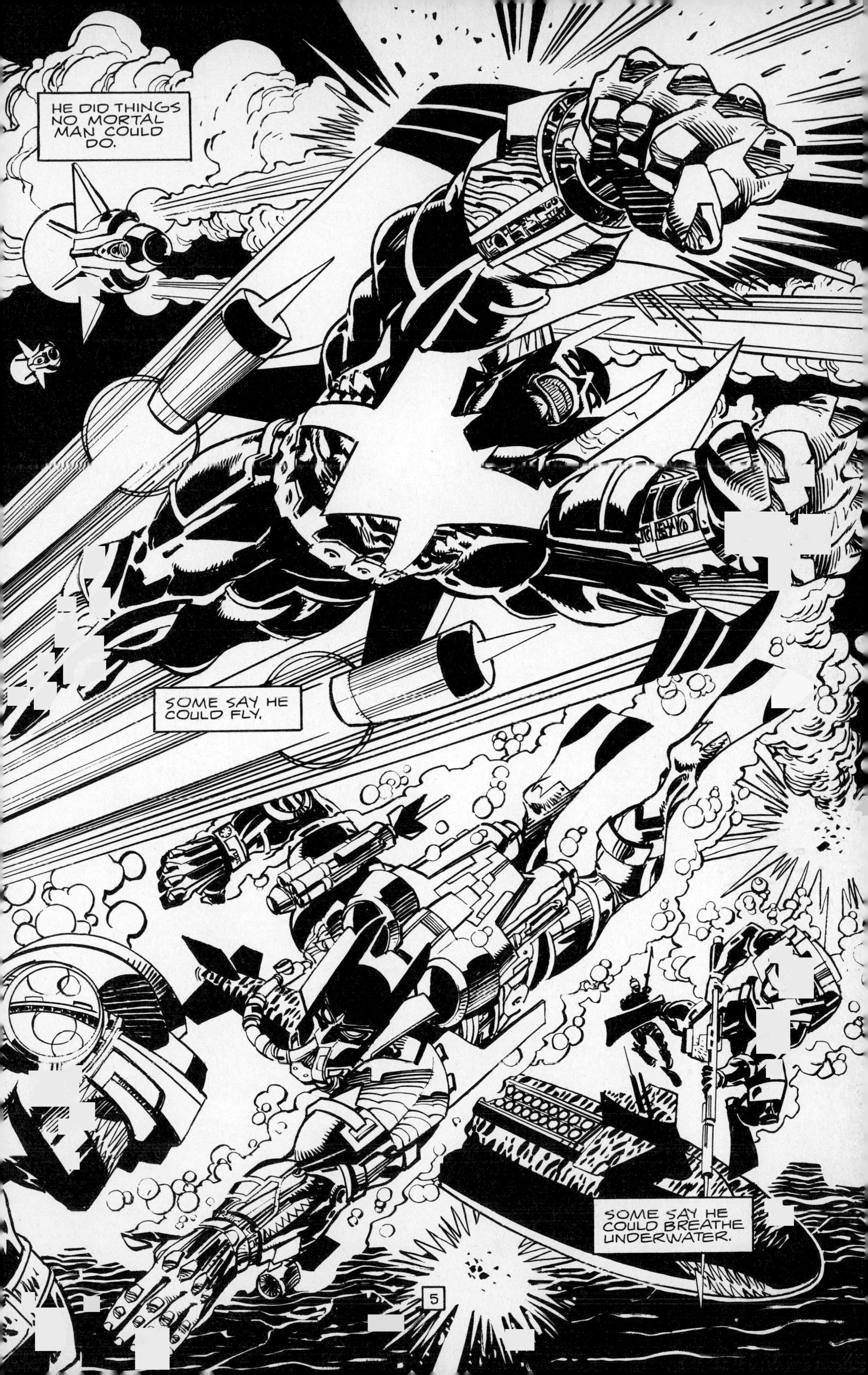
HE DID THINGS NO MORTAL MAN COULD DO.
SOME SAY HE COULD FLY.
SOME SAY HE COULD BREATHE UNDERWATER.

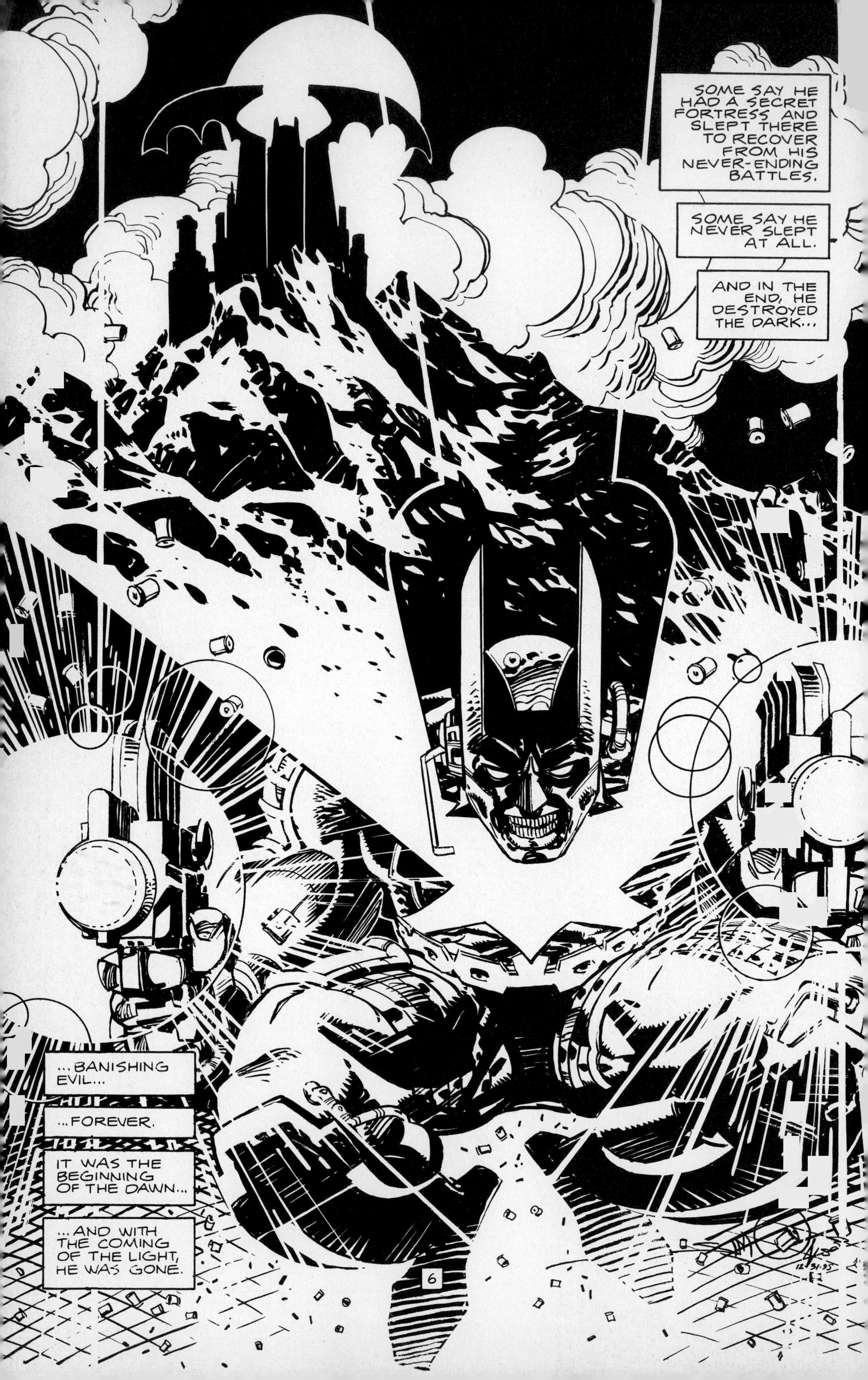
SOME SAY HE HAD A SECRET FORTRESS AND SLEPT THERE TO RECOVER FROM HIS NEVER-ENDING BATTLES.
SOME SAY HE NEVER SLEPT AT ALL.
AND IN THE END, HE DESTROYED THE DARK...
...BANISHING EVIL...
...FOREVER.
IT WAS THE BEGINNING OF THE DAWN...
...AND WITH THE COMING OF THE LIGHT, HE WAS GONE.

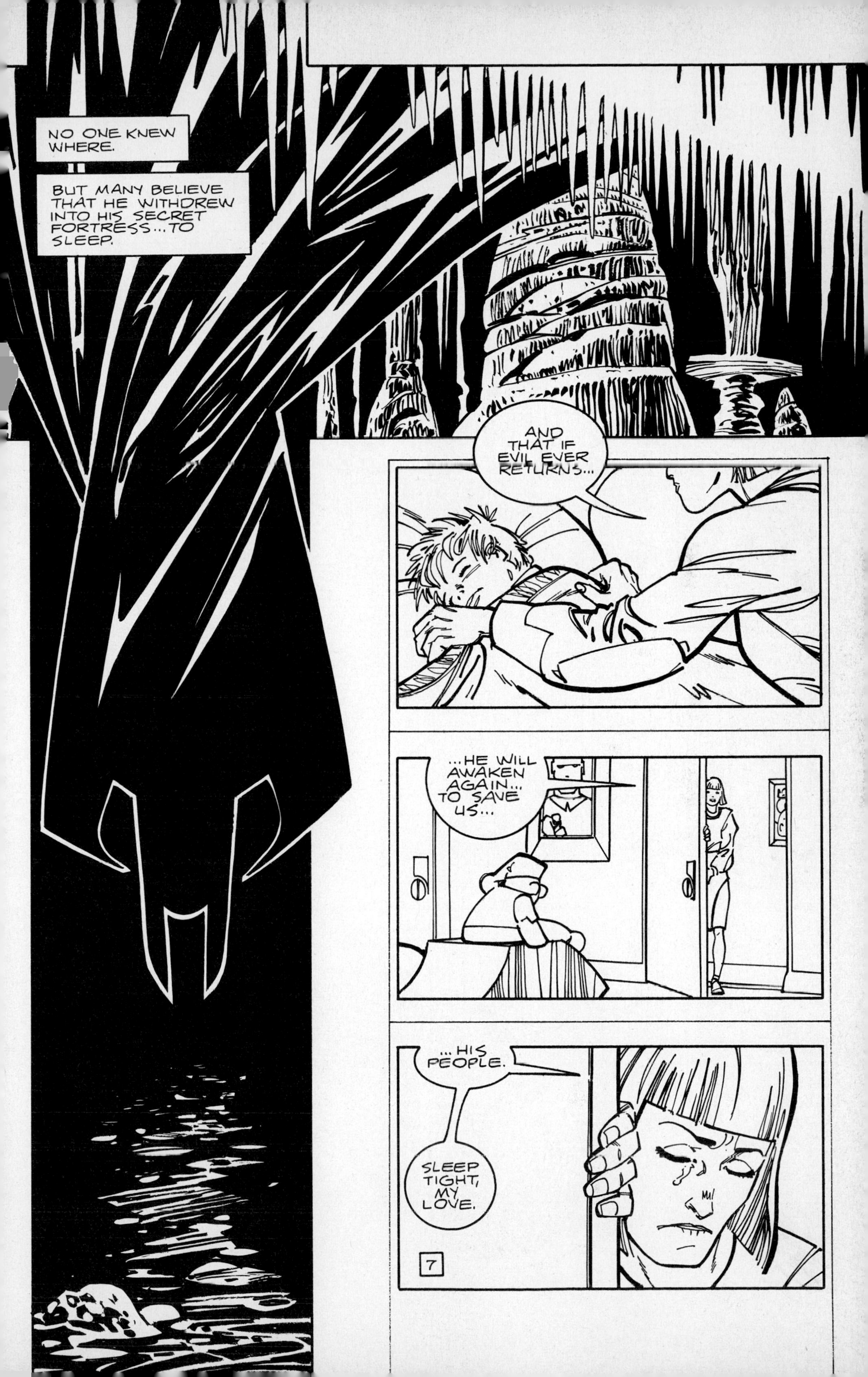
NO ONE KNEW WHERE.
BUT MANY BELIEVE THAT HE WITHDREW INTO HIS SECRET FORTRESS... TO SLEEP.
AND THAT IF EVIL EVER RETURNS...
...HE WILL AWAKEN AGAIN... TO SAVE US...
...HIS PEOPLE.
SLEEP TIGHT, MY LOVE.
7

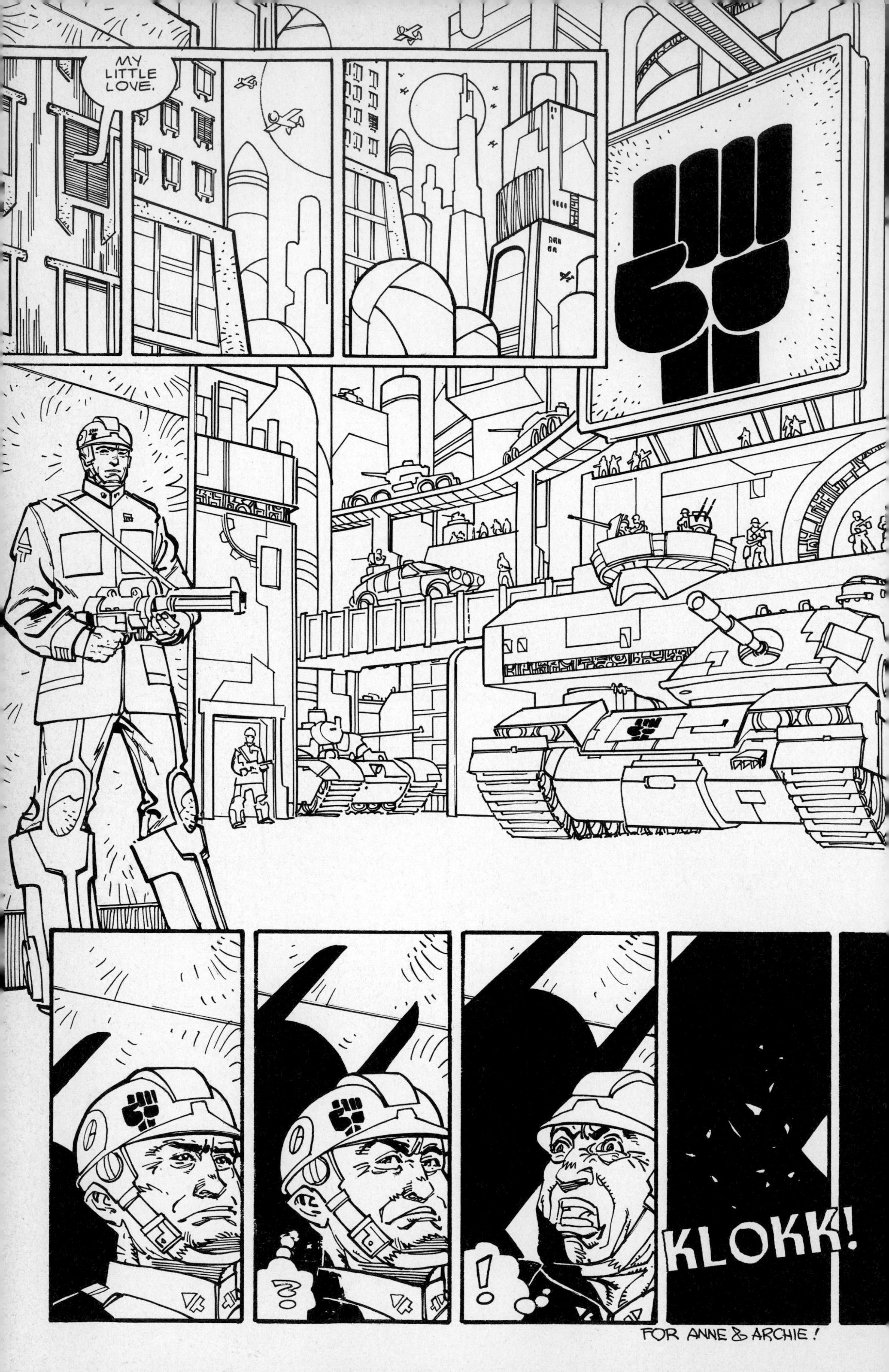

MY LITTLE LOVE.
?
!
KLOKK!

FOR ANNE & ARCHIE!

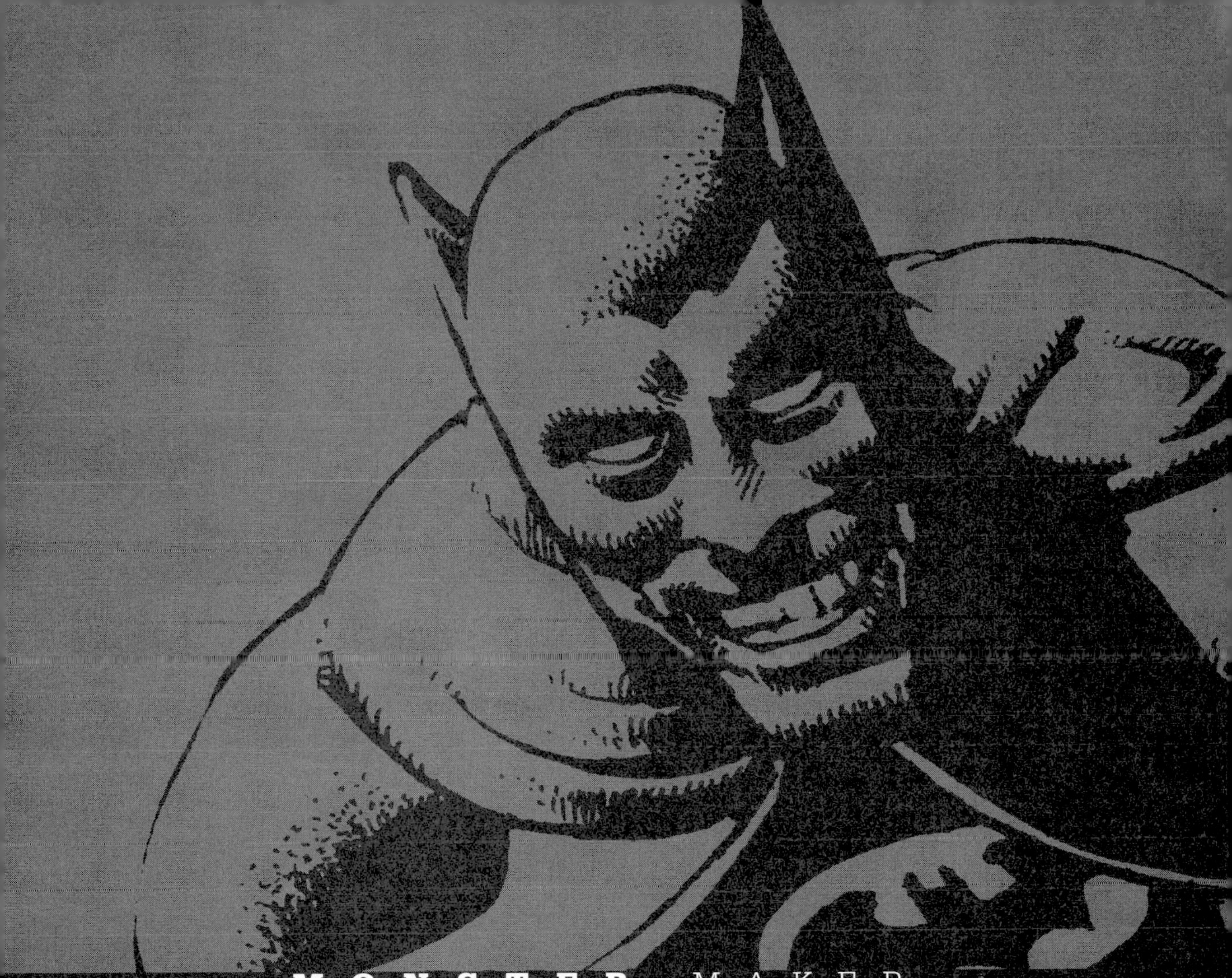

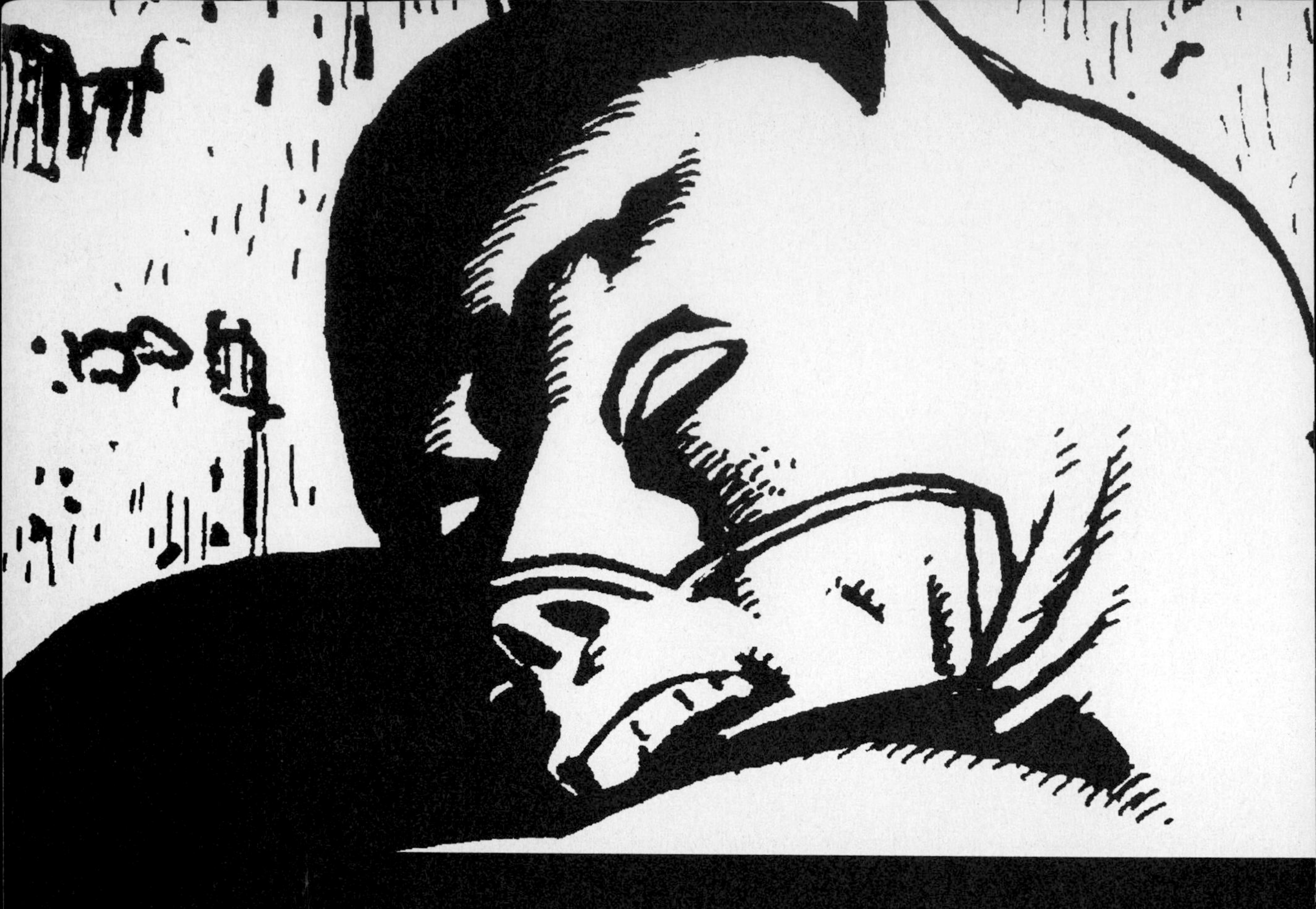

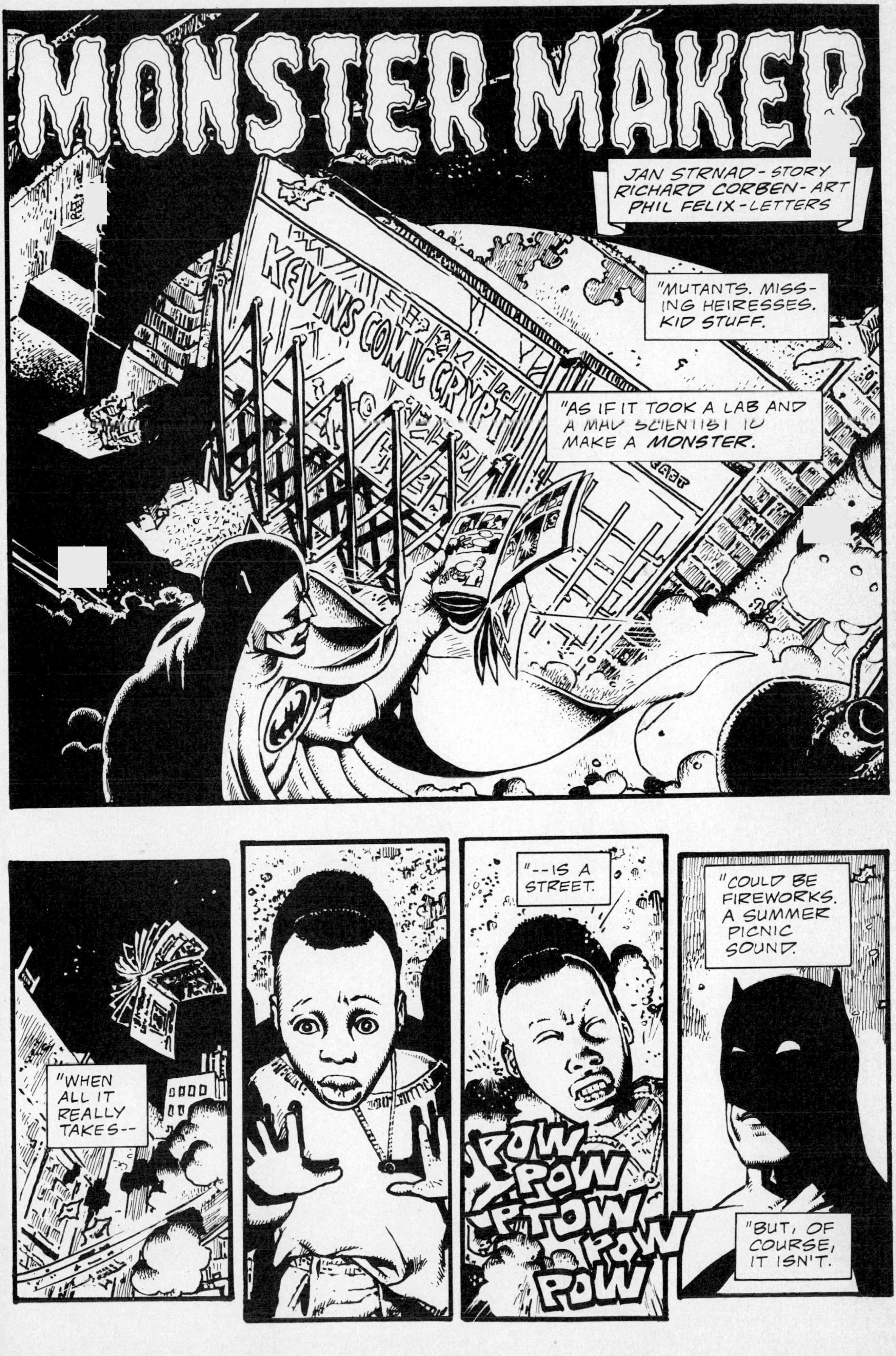
MONSTER MAKER
JAN STRNAD - STORY
RICHARD CORBEN - ART
PHIL FELIX - LETTERS
KEVINS COMIC CRYPT
"MUTANTS. MISSING HEIRESSES. KID STUFF.
"AS IF IT TOOK A LAB AND A MAD SCIENTIST TO MAKE A MONSTER.
"WHEN ALL IT REALLY TAKES--
"--IS A STREET.
POW POW PTOW POW POW
"COULD BE FIREWORKS. A SUMMER PICNIC SOUND.
"BUT, OF COURSE, IT ISN'T.

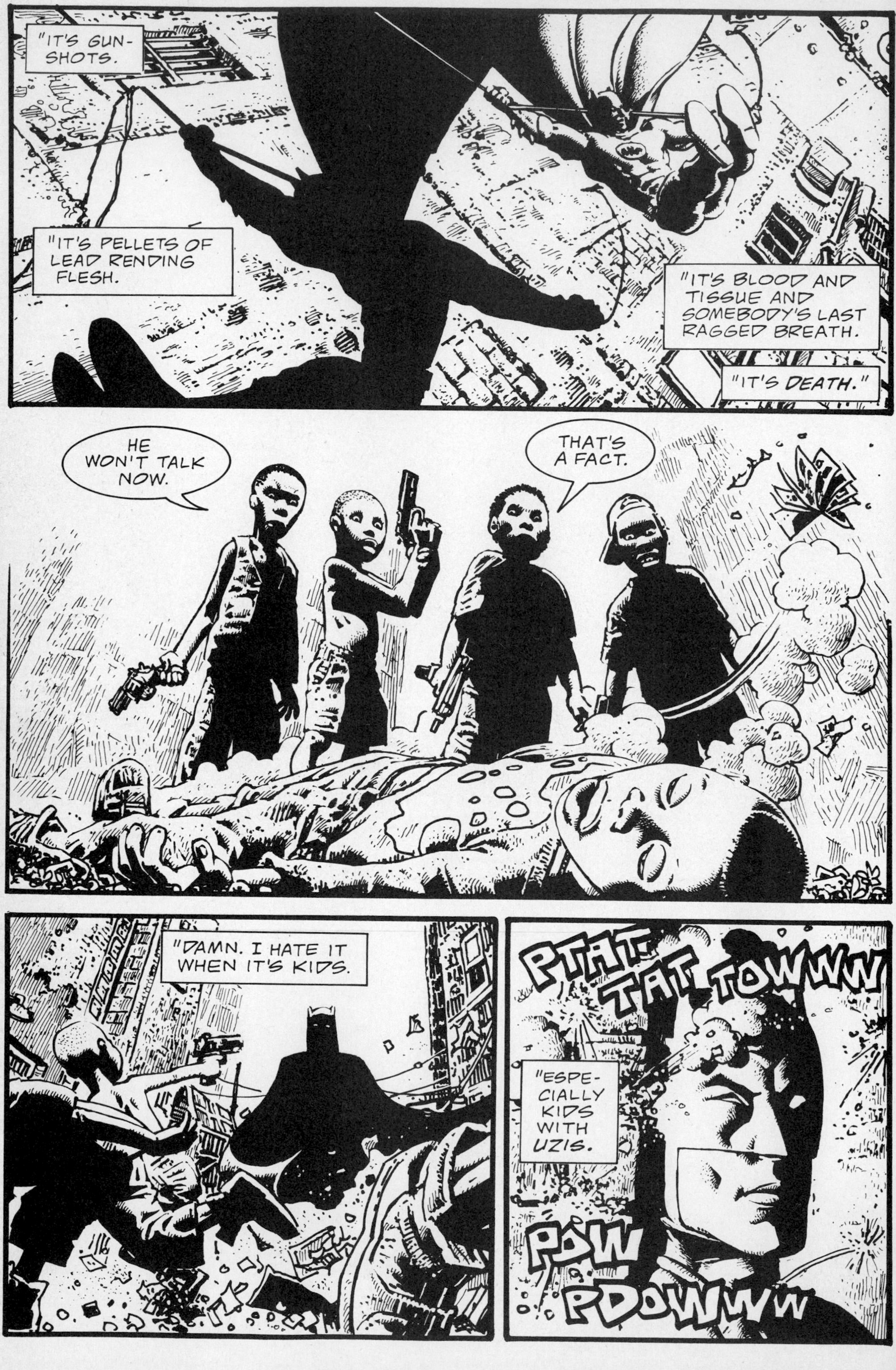
"IT'S GUN-SHOTS.
"IT'S PELLETS OF LEAD RENDING FLESH.
"IT'S BLOOD AND TISSUE AND SOMEBODY'S LAST RAGGED BREATH.
"IT'S *DEATH.*"
HE WON'T TALK NOW.
THAT'S A FACT.
"DAMN. I HATE IT WHEN IT'S KIDS.
PTAT TAT TOWWW
"ESPE-CIALLY KIDS WITH UZIS.
POW
PDOWWWW

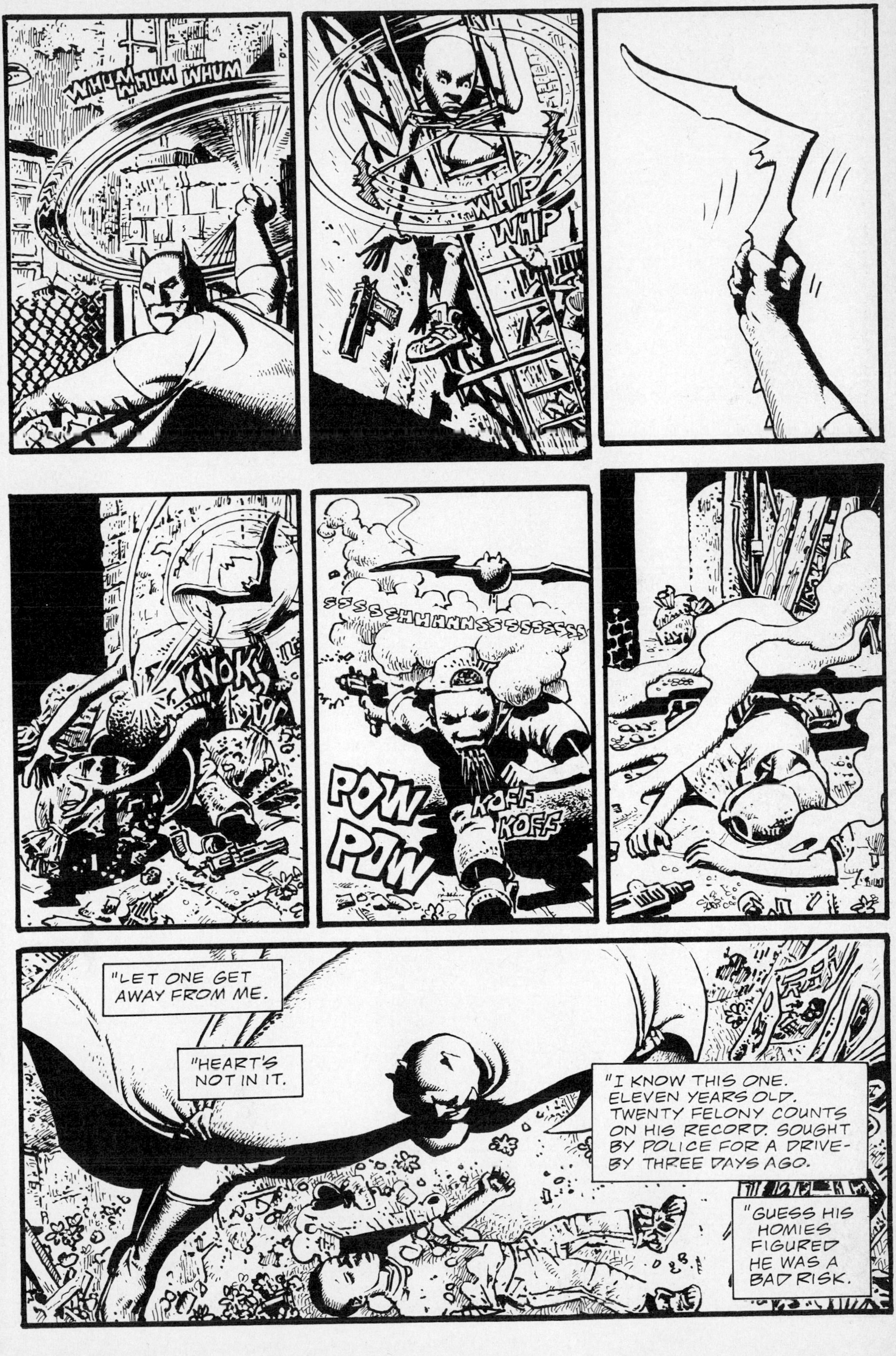
WHUM WHUM WHUM
WHIP
WHIP
KNOK
SSSSSHHHHNNSSSSSSSSS
POW
POW
KOFF
KOFF
"LET ONE GET AWAY FROM ME.
"HEART'S NOT IN IT.
"I KNOW THIS ONE. ELEVEN YEARS OLD. TWENTY FELONY COUNTS ON HIS RECORD. SOUGHT BY POLICE FOR A DRIVE-BY THREE DAYS AGO.
"GUESS HIS HOMIES FIGURED HE WAS A BAD RISK.

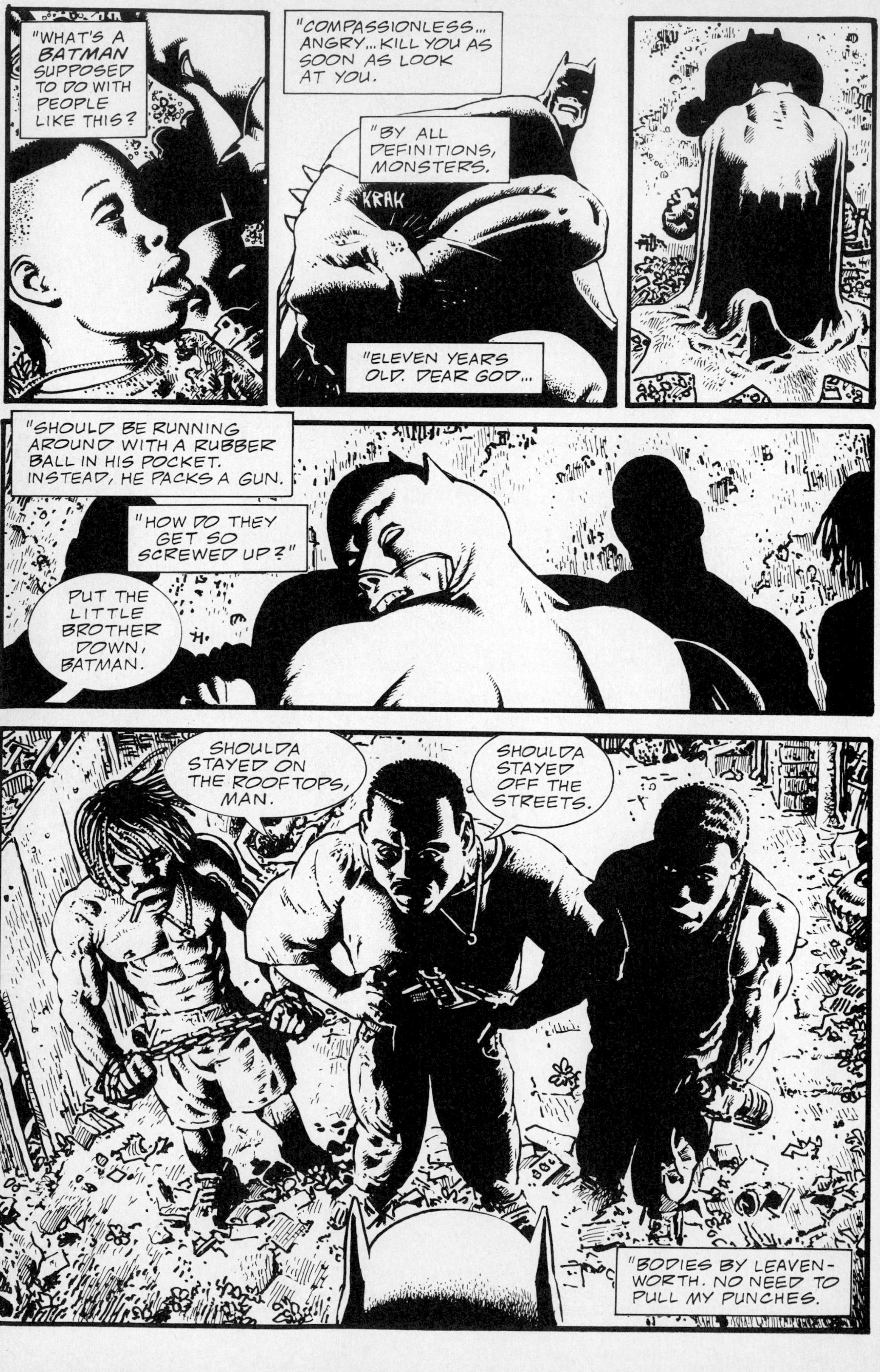
"WHAT'S A BATMAN SUPPOSED TO DO WITH PEOPLE LIKE THIS?
"COMPASSIONLESS... ANGRY... KILL YOU AS SOON AS LOOK AT YOU.
"BY ALL DEFINITIONS, MONSTERS.
KRAK
"ELEVEN YEARS OLD. DEAR GOD...
"SHOULD BE RUNNING AROUND WITH A RUBBER BALL IN HIS POCKET. INSTEAD, HE PACKS A GUN.
"HOW DO THEY GET SO SCREWED UP?"
PUT THE LITTLE BROTHER DOWN, BATMAN.
SHOULDA STAYED ON THE ROOFTOPS, MAN.
SHOULDA STAYED OFF THE STREETS.
"BODIES BY LEAVEN-WORTH. NO NEED TO PULL MY PUNCHES.

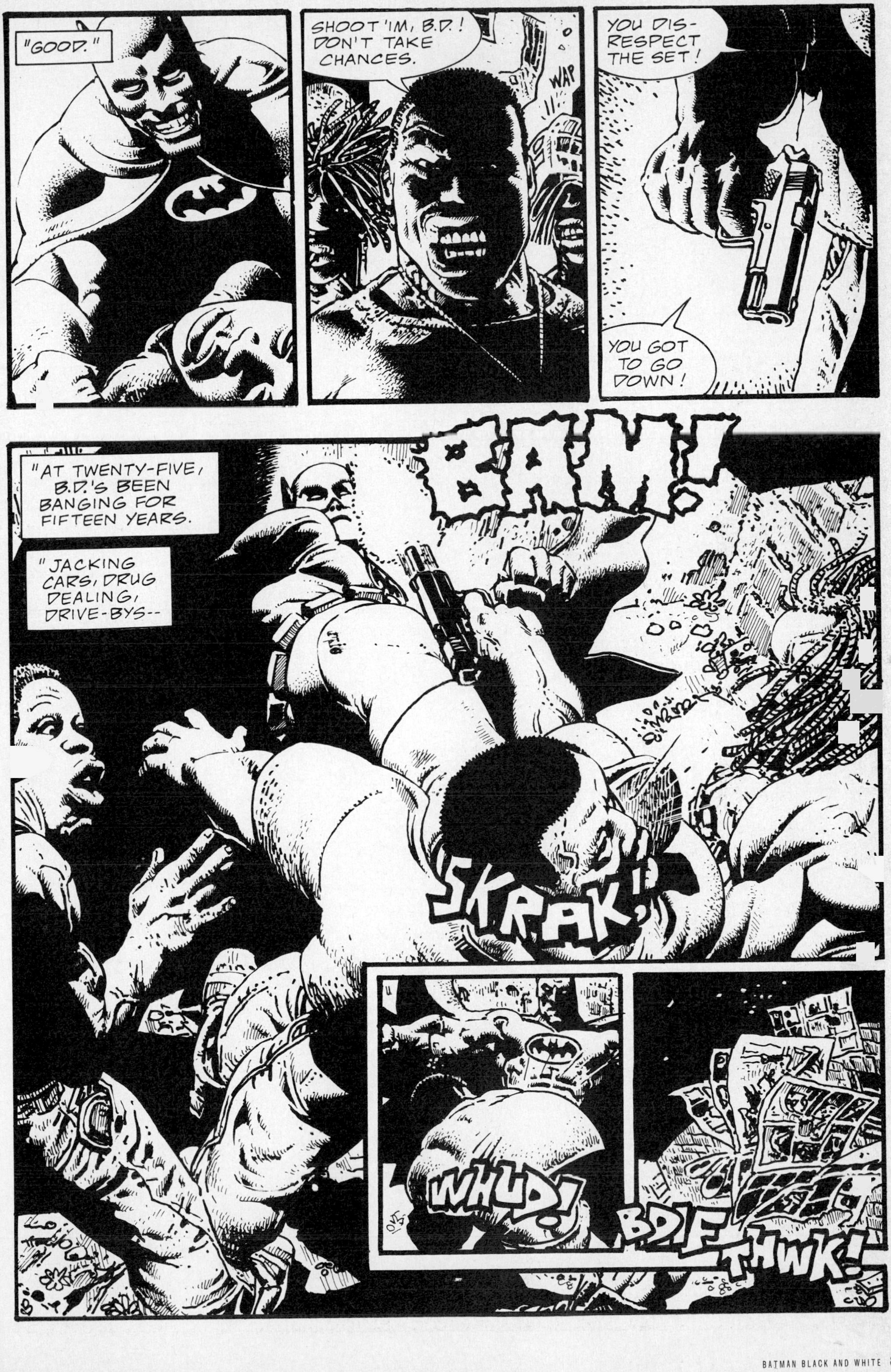

"GOOD."
SHOOT 'IM, B.D.! DON'T TAKE CHANCES.
WAP
YOU DIS-RESPECT THE SET!
YOU GOT TO GO DOWN!
BAM!
"AT TWENTY-FIVE, B.D.'S BEEN BANGING FOR FIFTEEN YEARS.
"JACKING CARS, DRUG DEALING, DRIVE-BYS--
SKRAK!
WHUD!
BDIF
THWK!

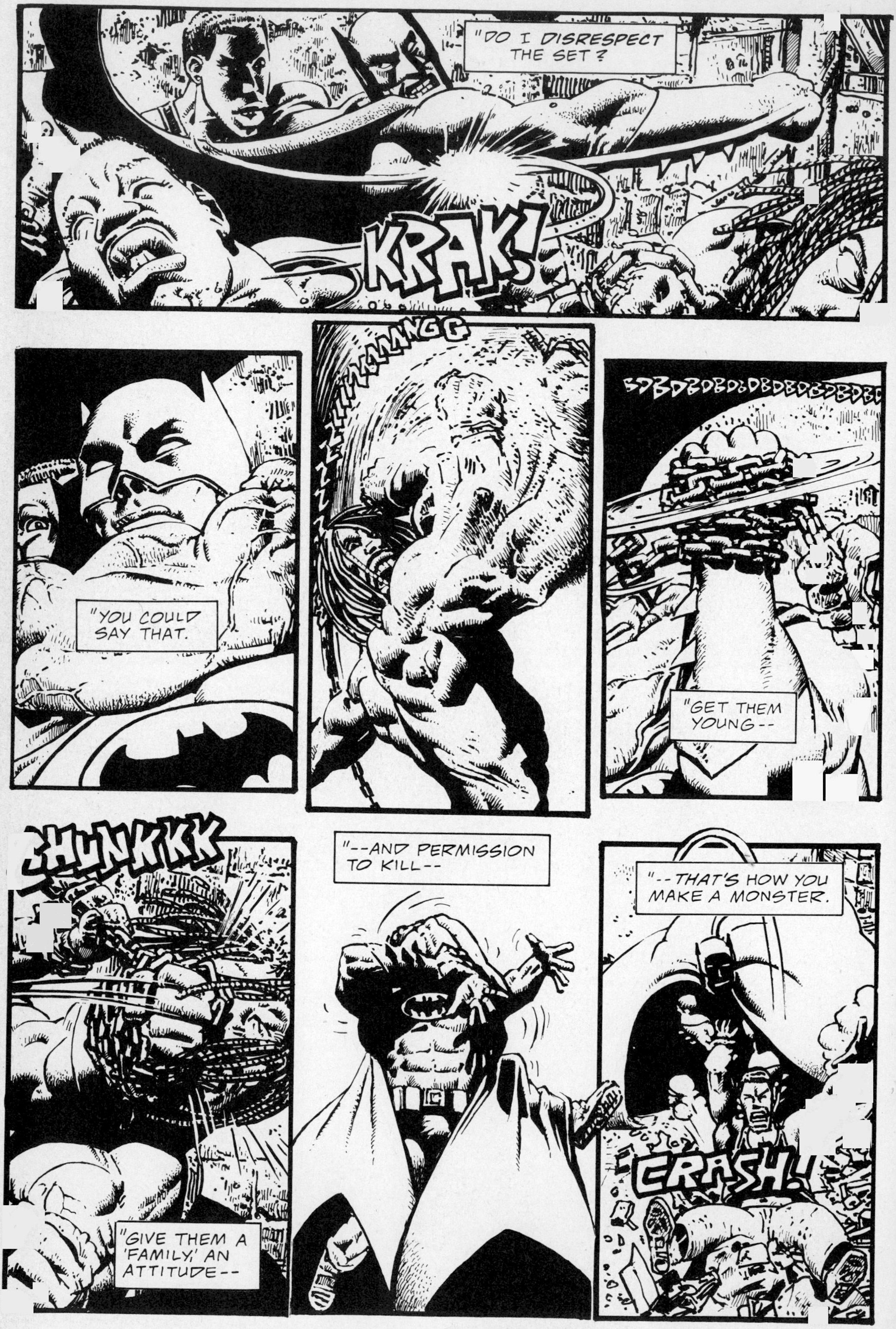
"DO I DISRESPECT THE SET?
KRAK!
"YOU COULD SAY THAT.
"GET THEM YOUNG--
CHUNKKK
"GIVE THEM A 'FAMILY,' AN ATTITUDE--
"--AND PERMISSION TO KILL--
"--THAT'S HOW YOU MAKE A MONSTER.
CRASH!

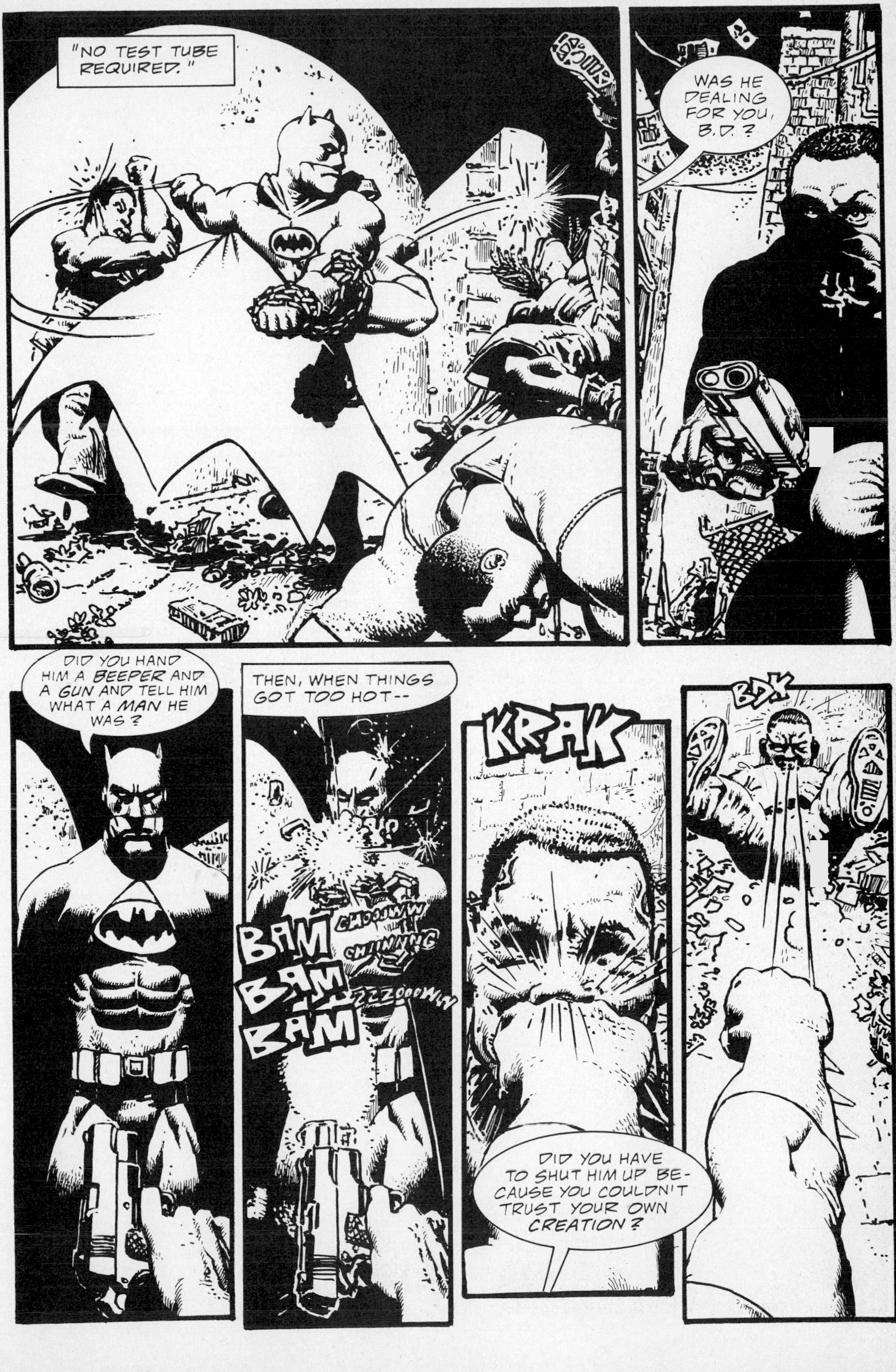
"NO TEST TUBE REQUIRED."
WAS HE DEALING FOR YOU, B.D.?
DID YOU HAND HIM A BEEPER AND A GUN AND TELL HIM WHAT A MAN HE WAS?
THEN, WHEN THINGS GOT TOO HOT--
BAM BAM BAM
KRAK
DID YOU HAVE TO SHUT HIM UP BE-CAUSE YOU COULDN'T TRUST YOUR OWN CREATION?

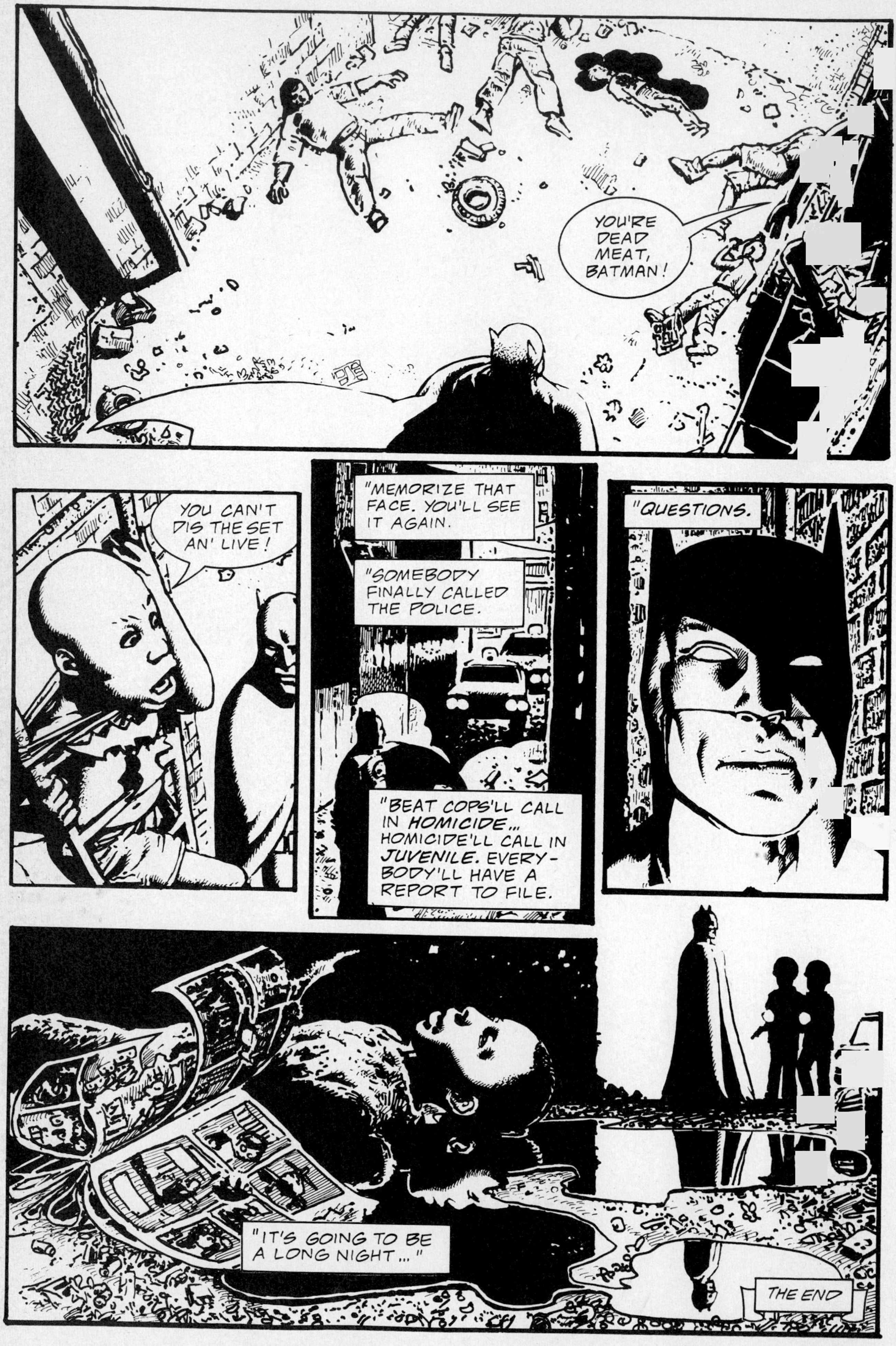
YOU'RE DEAD MEAT, BATMAN!
YOU CAN'T DIS THE SET AN' LIVE!
"MEMORIZE THAT FACE. YOU'LL SEE IT AGAIN.
"SOMEBODY FINALLY CALLED THE POLICE.
"BEAT COPS'LL CALL IN HOMICIDE... HOMICIDE'LL CALL IN JUVENILE. EVERY-BODY'LL HAVE A REPORT TO FILE.
"QUESTIONS.
"IT'S GOING TO BE A LONG NIGHT..."
THE END

DEAD BOYS EYES

KENT **WILLIAMS**

Kent Williams is a bit of an anomaly in the comics business. His fine-art work fetches handsome prices in galleries, and his book and magazine illustrations have won several awards from the Society of Illustrators.

He brings to the comics medium an edgy, impressionistic style that showcases exceptional draftsmanship and raw power. Among Kent's memorable comic work is BLOOD: A TALE, TELL ME, DARK and *Havok & Wolverine: Meltdown*.

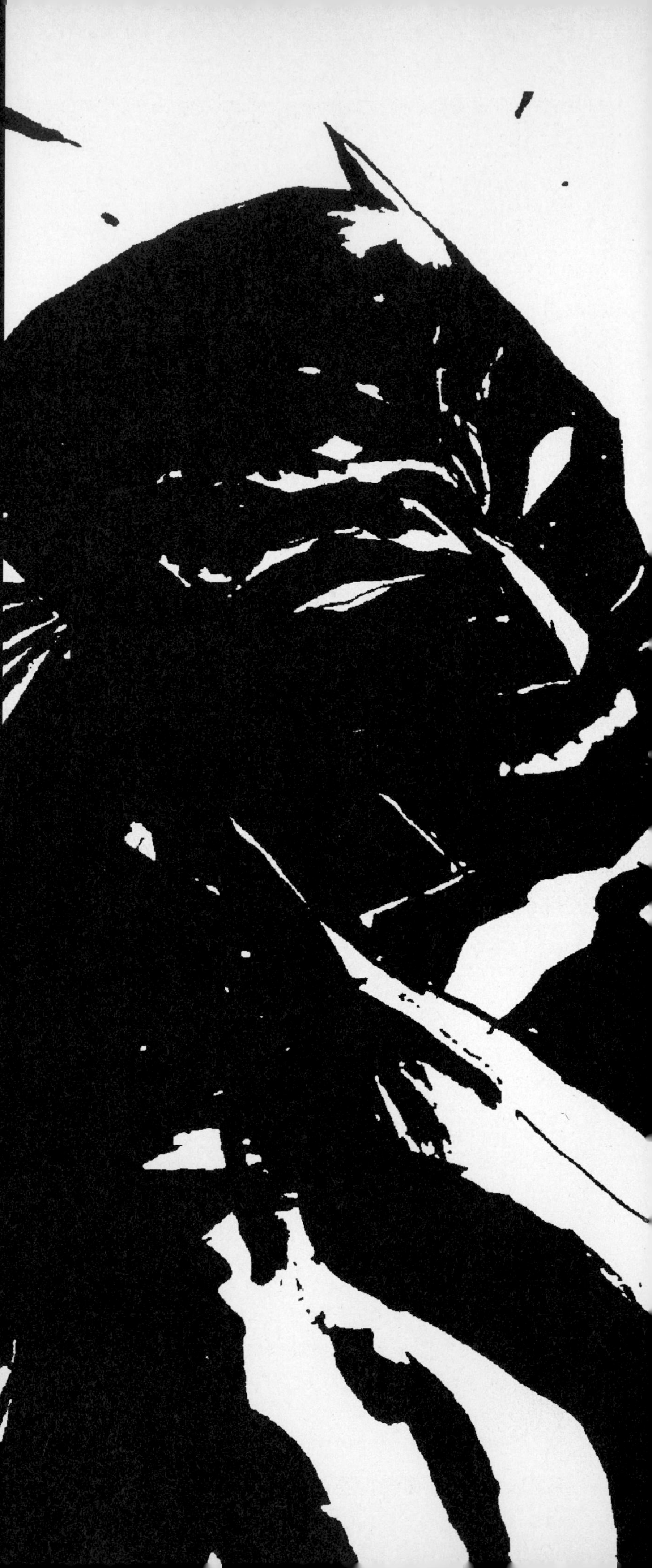

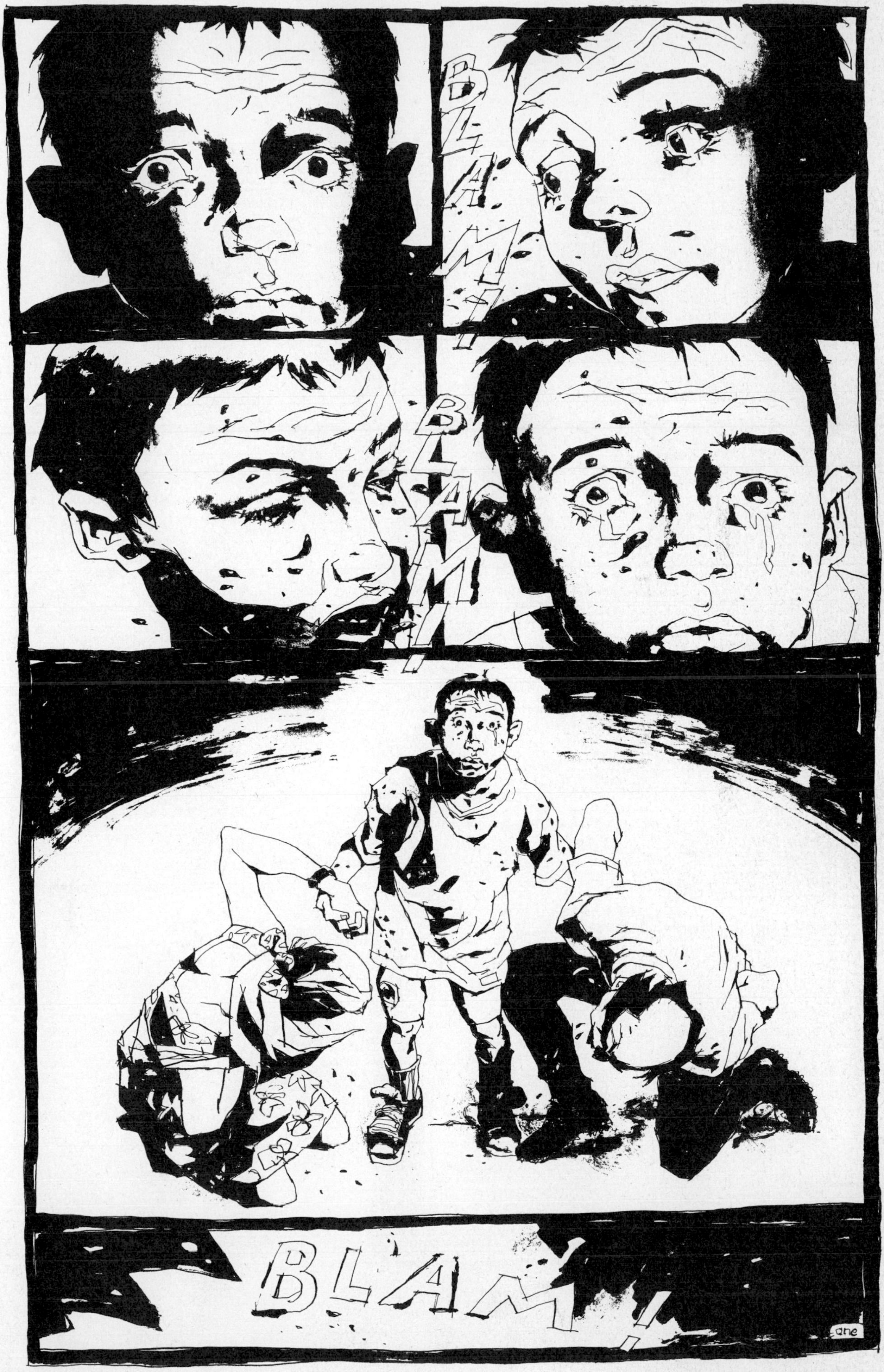
BLAM!
BLAM!
BLAM!
one

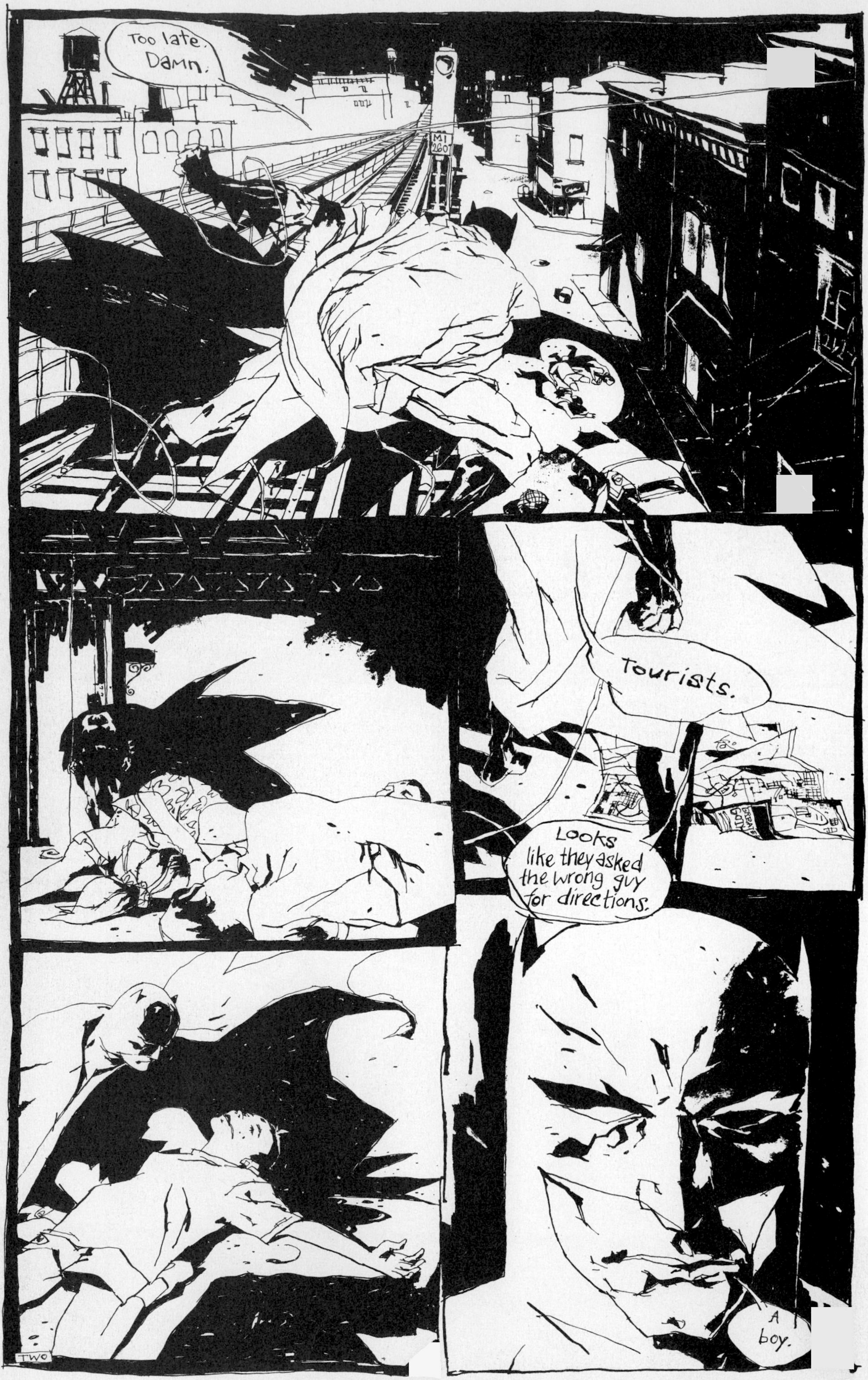
Too late. Damn.
M1 260
Tourists.
Looks like they asked the wrong guy for directions.
TWO
A boy.

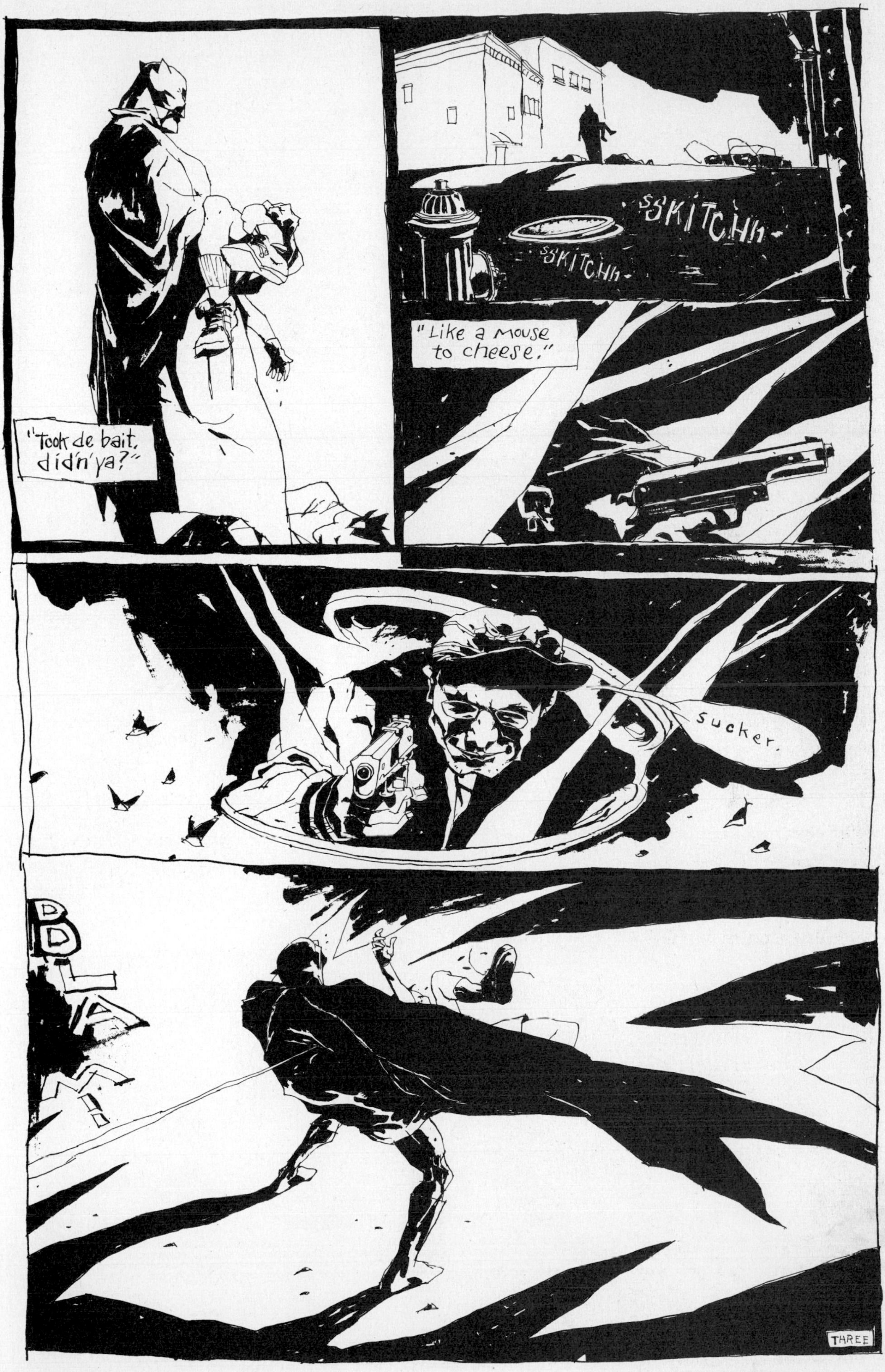
"Took de bait, did'n'ya?"
SSKITCHH
SSKITCHH
"Like a mouse to cheese."
sucker.
THREE

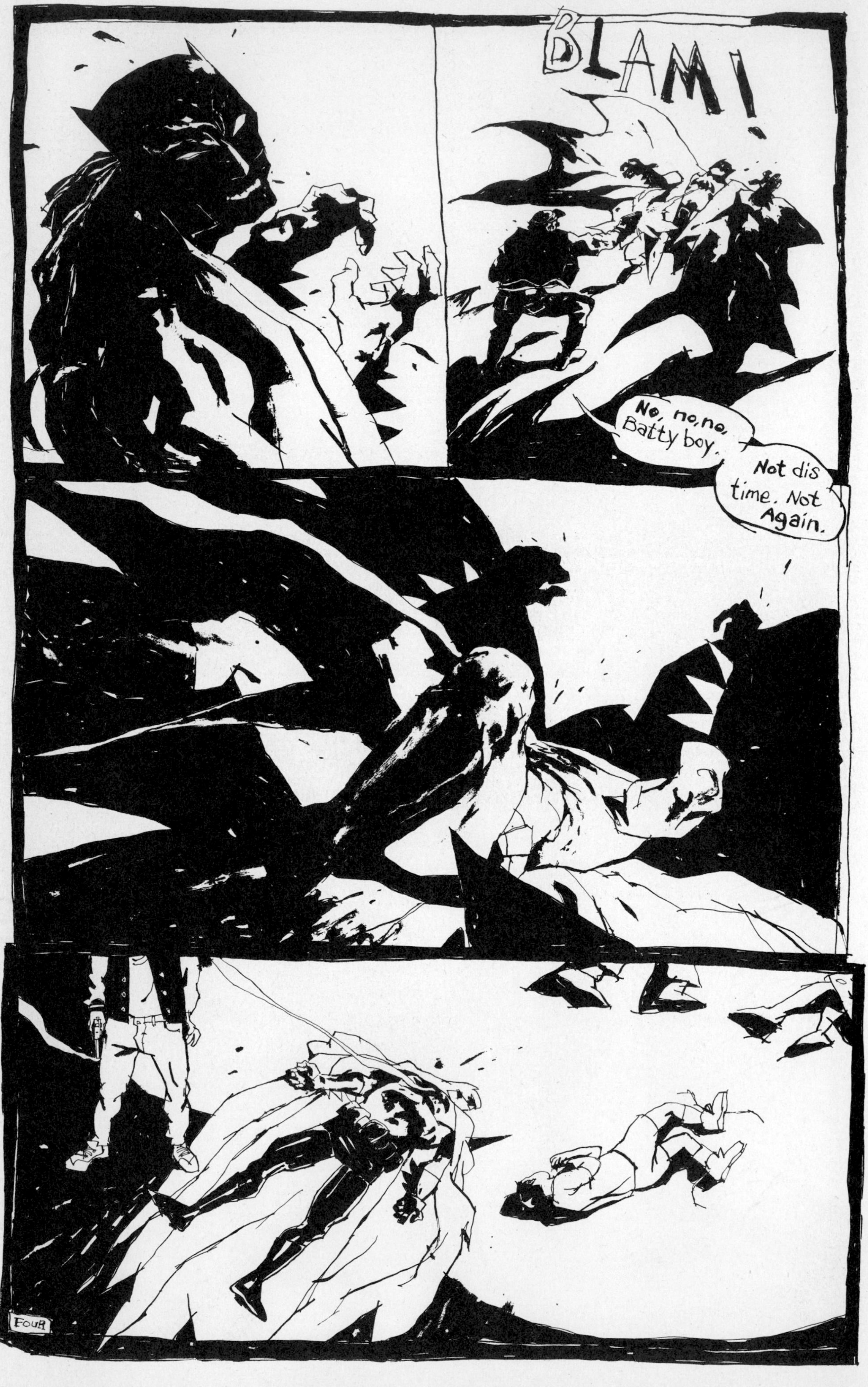
BLAM!
No, no, no, Batty boy.
Not dis time. Not Again.
FOUR

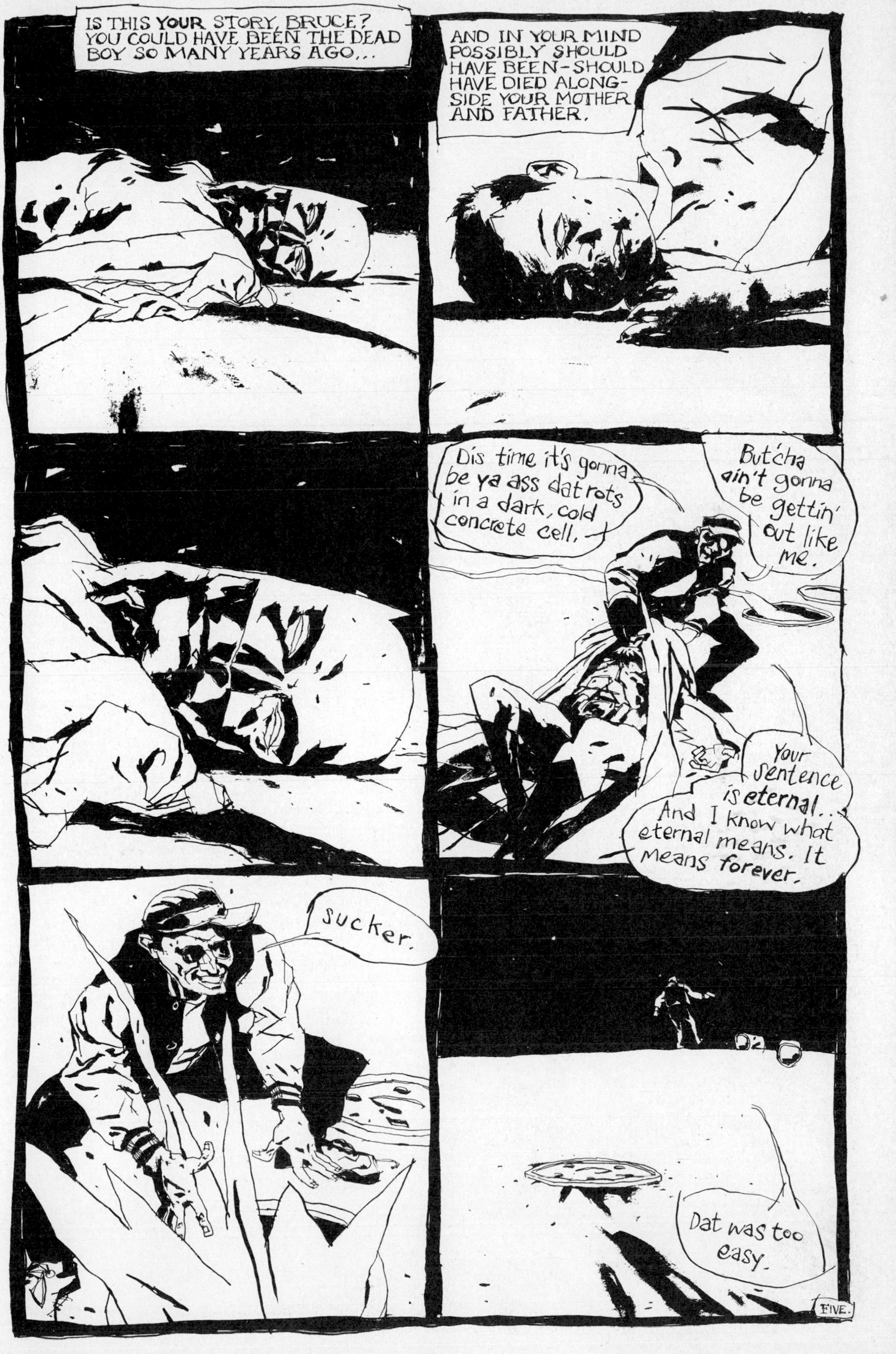
IS THIS YOUR STORY, BRUCE? YOU COULD HAVE BEEN THE DEAD BOY SO MANY YEARS AGO...
AND IN YOUR MIND POSSIBLY SHOULD HAVE BEEN-SHOULD HAVE DIED ALONG-SIDE YOUR MOTHER AND FATHER.
Dis time it's gonna be ya ass dat rots in a dark, cold concrete cell.
But'cha ain't gonna be gettin' out like me.
Your sentence is eternal..
And I know what eternal means. It means forever.
sucker.
Dat was too easy.
FIVE.

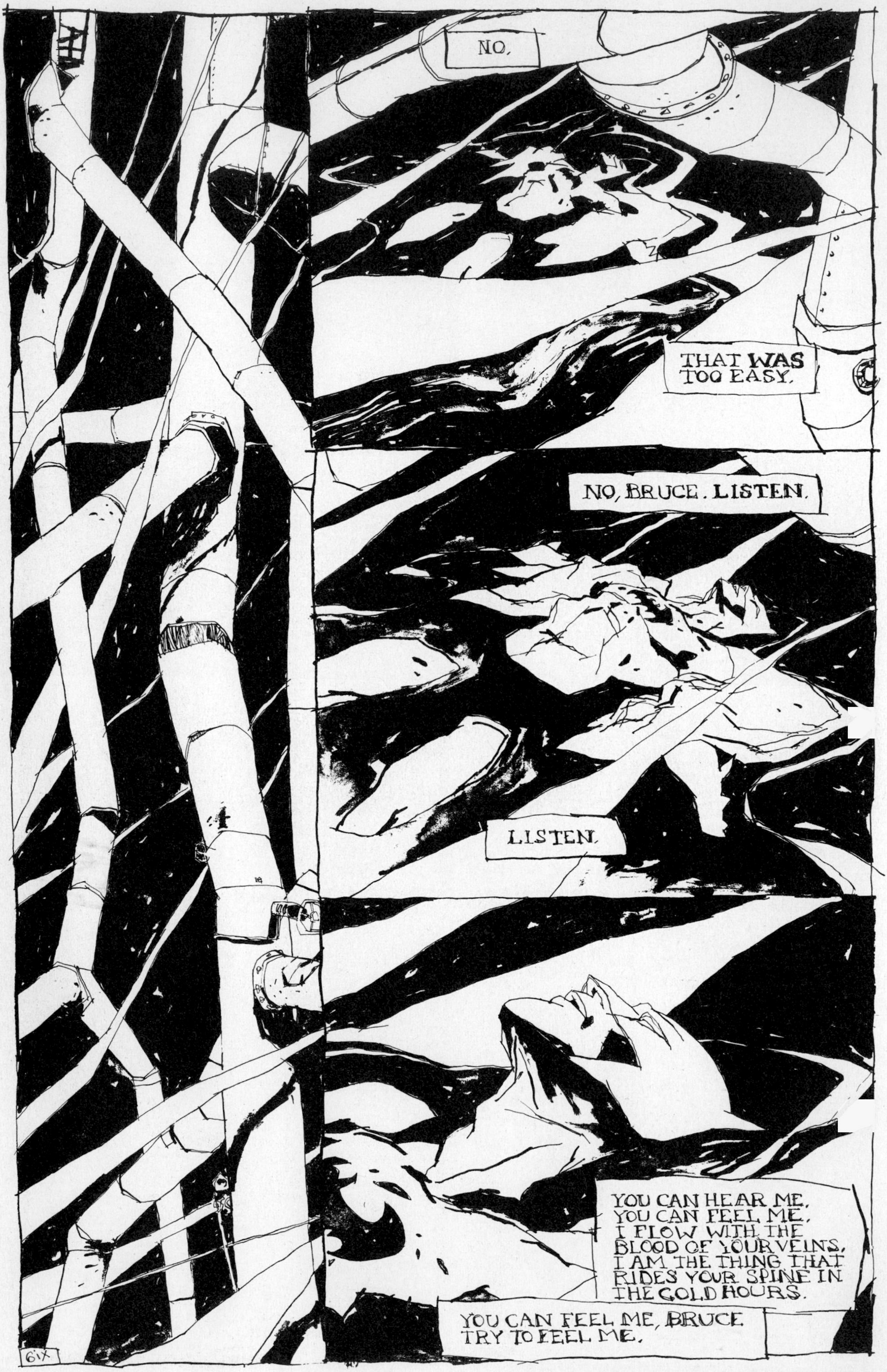
NO.
THAT WAS TOO EASY.
NO, BRUCE. LISTEN.
LISTEN.
YOU CAN HEAR ME. YOU CAN FEEL ME. I FLOW WITH THE BLOOD OF YOUR VEINS. I AM THE THING THAT RIDES YOUR SPINE IN THE COLD HOURS.
YOU CAN FEEL ME, BRUCE. TRY TO FEEL ME.
6IX

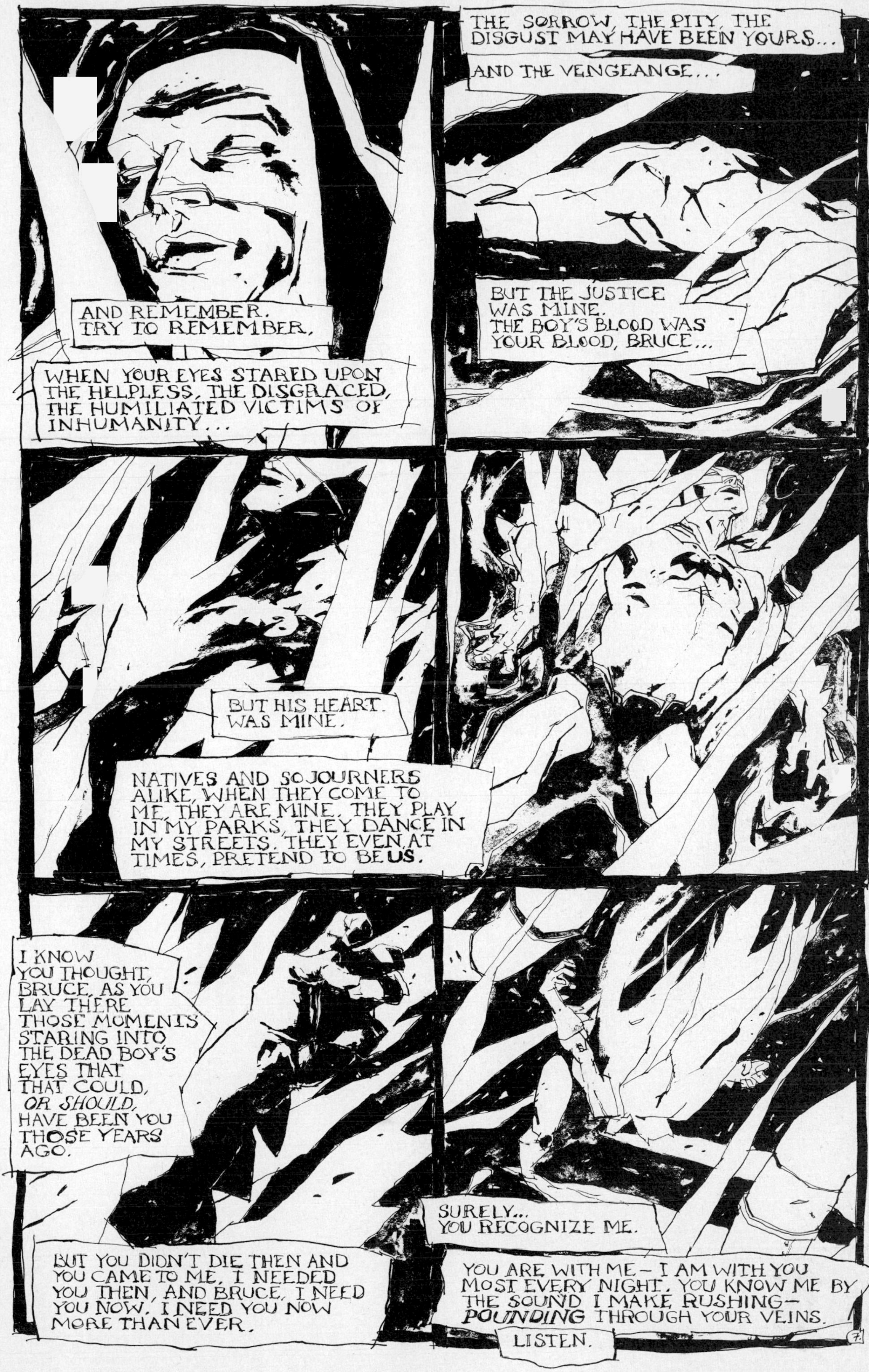
AND REMEMBER.
TRY TO REMEMBER,
WHEN YOUR EYES STARED UPON THE HELPLESS, THE DISGRACED, THE HUMILIATED VICTIMS OF INHUMANITY...
THE SORROW, THE PITY, THE DISGUST MAY HAVE BEEN YOURS...
AND THE VENGEANCE...
BUT THE JUSTICE WAS MINE.
THE BOY'S BLOOD WAS YOUR BLOOD, BRUCE...
BUT HIS HEART WAS MINE.
NATIVES AND SOJOURNERS ALIKE, WHEN THEY COME TO ME, THEY ARE MINE. THEY PLAY IN MY PARKS, THEY DANCE IN MY STREETS. THEY EVEN, AT TIMES, PRETEND TO BE US.
I KNOW YOU THOUGHT, BRUCE, AS YOU LAY THERE THOSE MOMENTS STARING INTO THE DEAD BOY'S EYES THAT THAT COULD, OR SHOULD, HAVE BEEN YOU THOSE YEARS AGO.
BUT YOU DIDN'T DIE THEN AND YOU CAME TO ME. I NEEDED YOU THEN, AND BRUCE, I NEED YOU NOW. I NEED YOU NOW MORE THAN EVER.
SURELY... YOU RECOGNIZE ME.
YOU ARE WITH ME— I AM WITH YOU MOST EVERY NIGHT. YOU KNOW ME BY THE SOUND I MAKE RUSHING— POUNDING THROUGH YOUR VEINS.
LISTEN.
7.

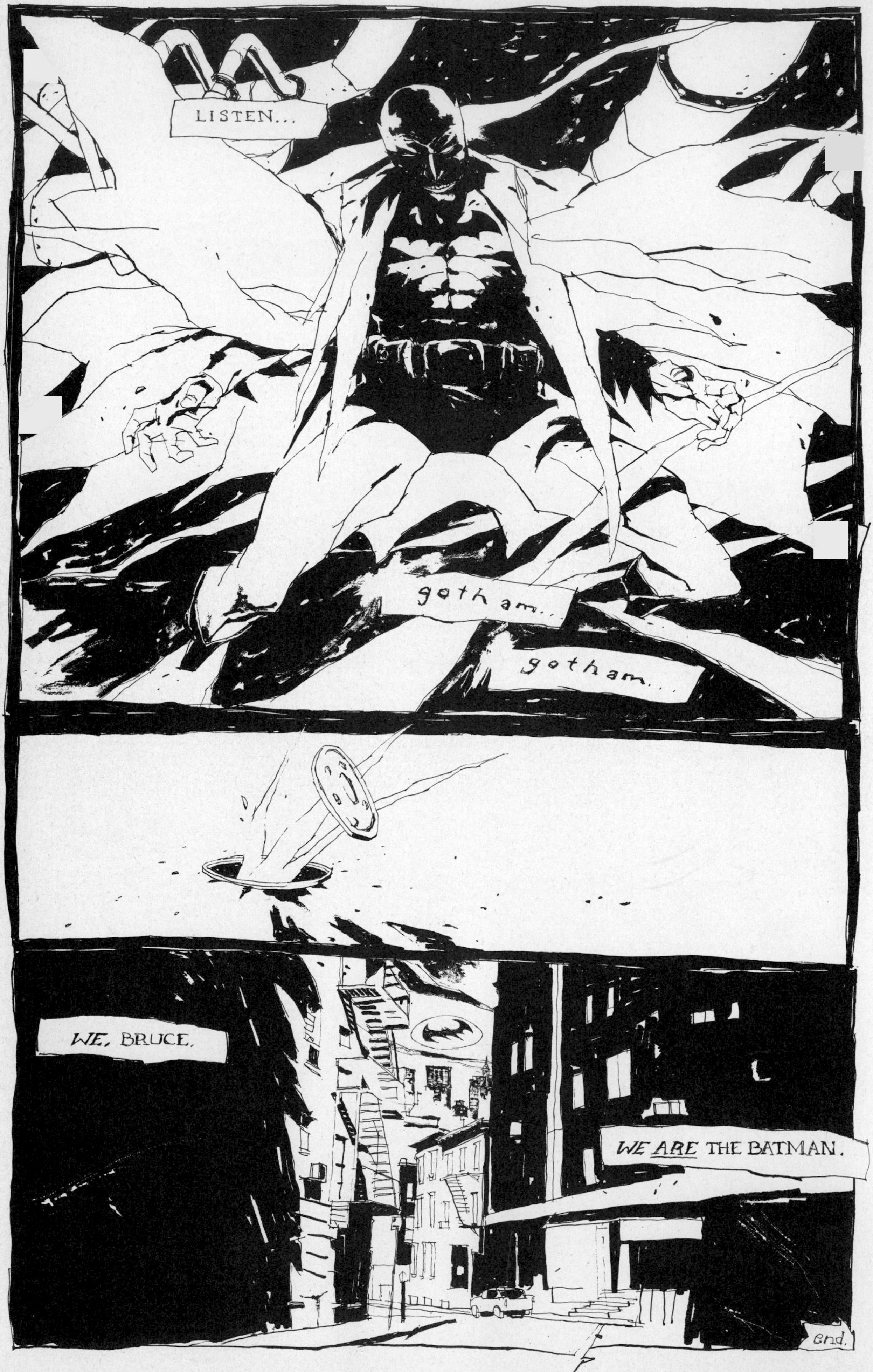
LISTEN...
gotham...
gotham...
WE, BRUCE,
WE ARE THE BATMAN.
end.

THE **DEVIL'S CHILDREN**

JORGE ZAFFINO

Born in Argentina, Jorge Zaffino has been drawing comics since the age of sixteen. His work for South American, European and North American comics is widely hailed for its brutal richness and striking draftsmanship.

Zaffino's work on the 1987 series *Winterworld* is widely considered some of the most impressive comics work of the past decade.

CHUCK DIXON

Chuck Dixon was born in Philadelphia in 1954. From time to time he has held the title "Comics' Most Prolific Writer" without shame.

He currently writes DETECTIVE COMICS, ROBIN, NIGHTWING and GREEN ARROW for DC Comics. Chuck lives in the Brandywine Valley of Pennsylvania with his lovely wife Elma, his lively sons Cullen and Gavin and his pit schnauzer Squire.

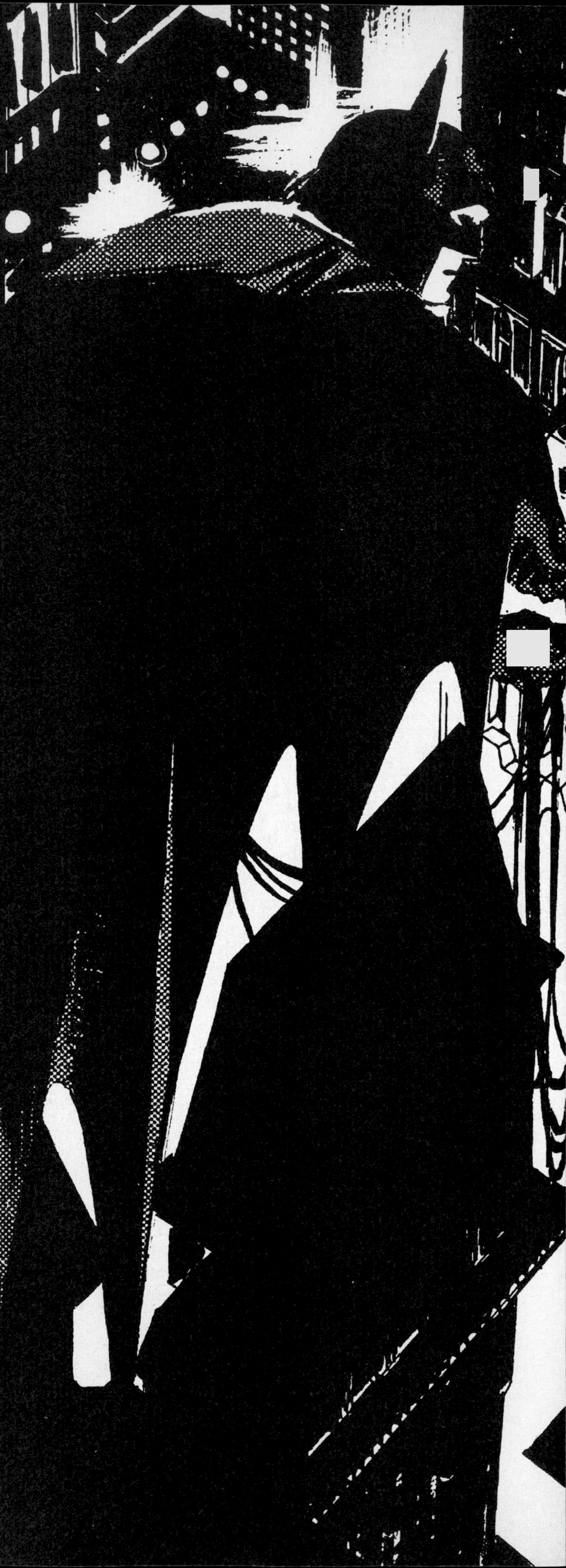

THE DEVIL'S CHILDREN

Story by: Chuck Dixon
Art by: Jorge Zaffino
Lettered by: John Costanza

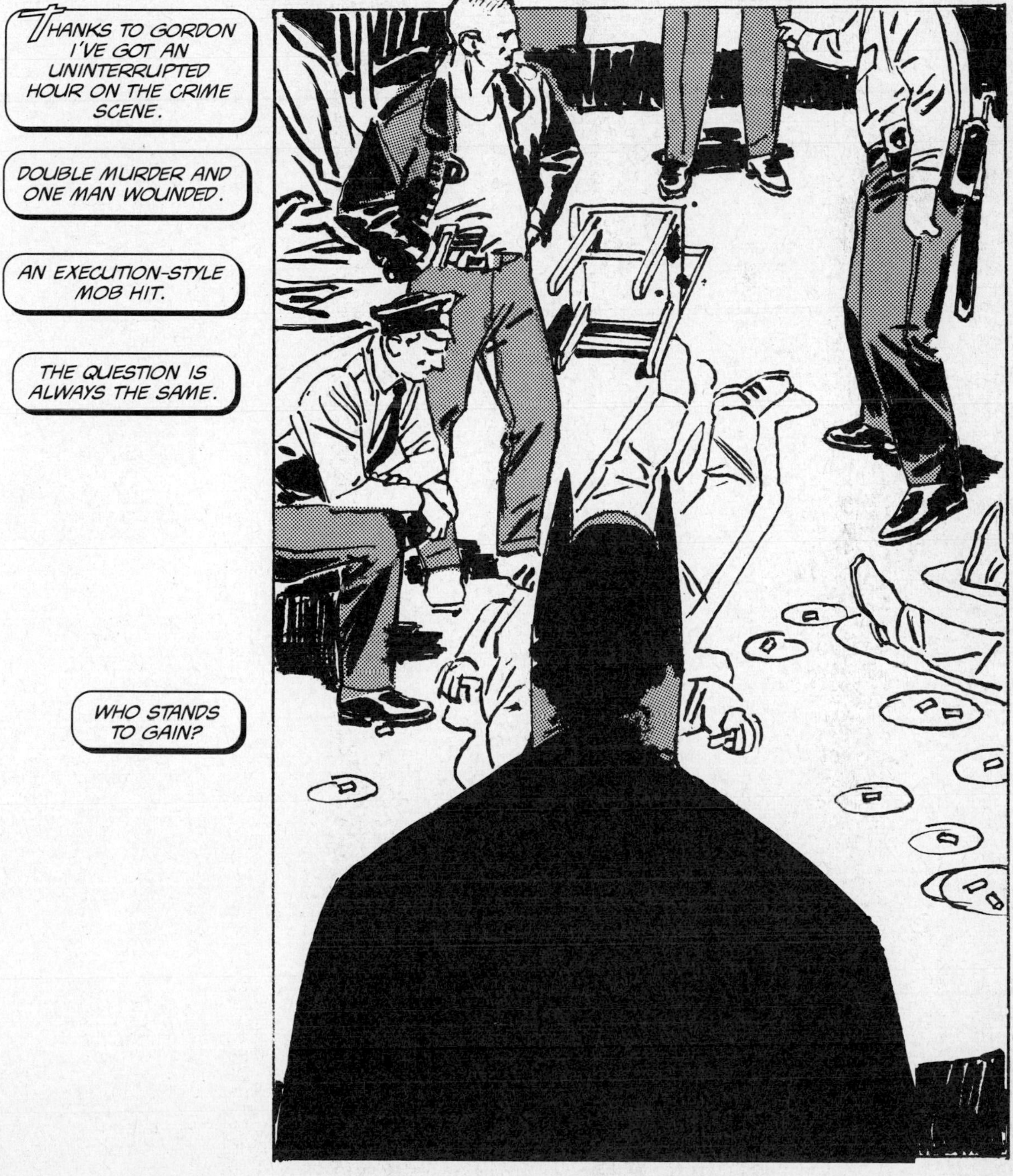
THANKS TO GORDON I'VE GOT AN UNINTERRUPTED HOUR ON THE CRIME SCENE.
DOUBLE MURDER AND ONE MAN WOUNDED.
AN EXECUTION-STYLE MOB HIT.
THE QUESTION IS ALWAYS THE SAME.
WHO STANDS TO GAIN?

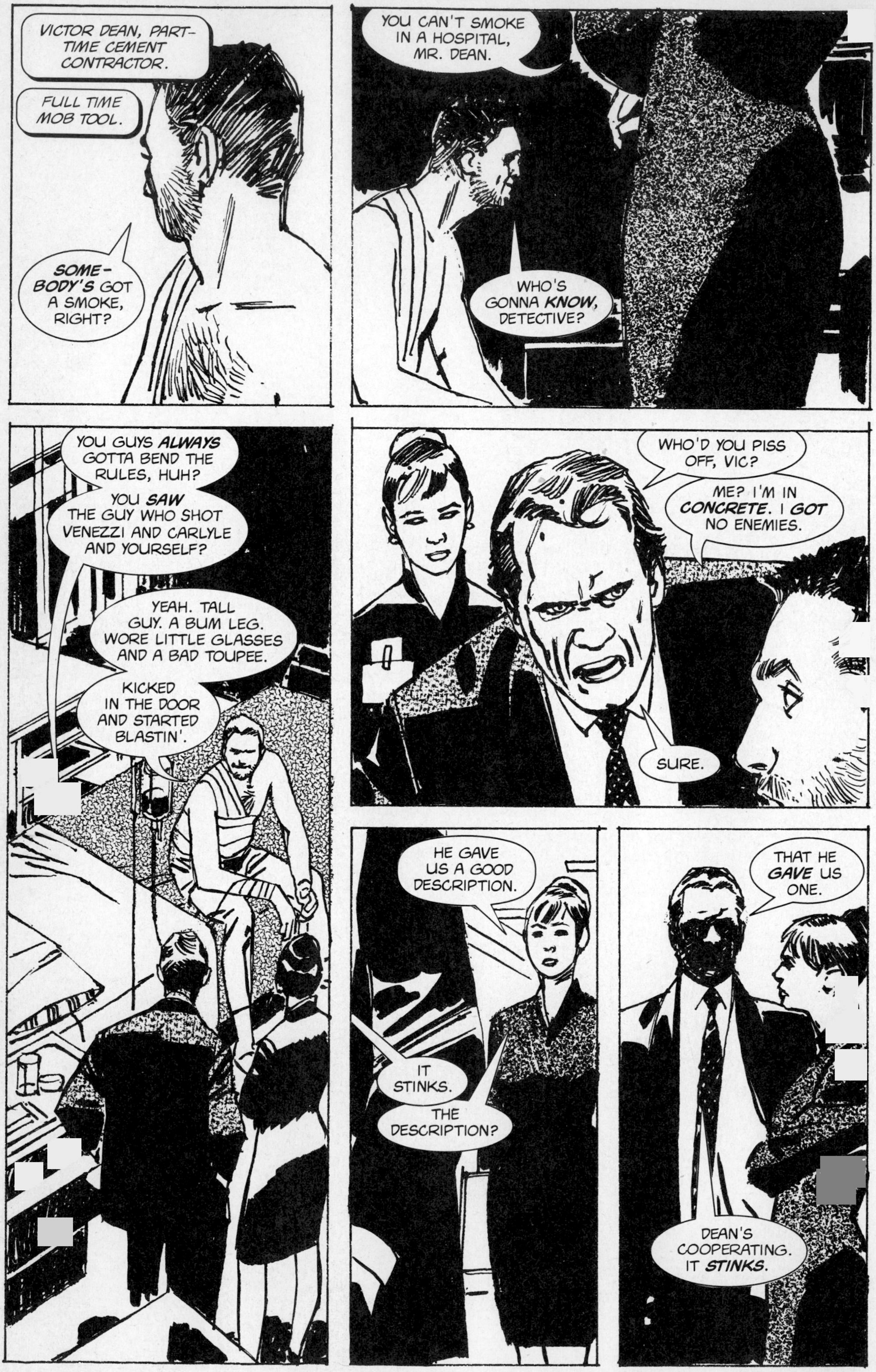
VICTOR DEAN, PART-TIME CEMENT CONTRACTOR.
FULL TIME MOB TOOL.
SOME-BODY'S GOT A SMOKE, RIGHT?
YOU CAN'T SMOKE IN A HOSPITAL, MR. DEAN.
WHO'S GONNA KNOW, DETECTIVE?
YOU GUYS ALWAYS GOTTA BEND THE RULES, HUH?
YOU SAW THE GUY WHO SHOT VENEZZI AND CARLYLE AND YOURSELF?
YEAH. TALL GUY. A BUM LEG. WORE LITTLE GLASSES AND A BAD TOUPEE.
KICKED IN THE DOOR AND STARTED BLASTIN'.
WHO'D YOU PISS OFF, VIC?
ME? I'M IN CONCRETE. I GOT NO ENEMIES.
SURE.
HE GAVE US A GOOD DESCRIPTION.
IT STINKS.
THE DESCRIPTION?
THAT HE GAVE US ONE.
DEAN'S COOPERATING. IT STINKS.

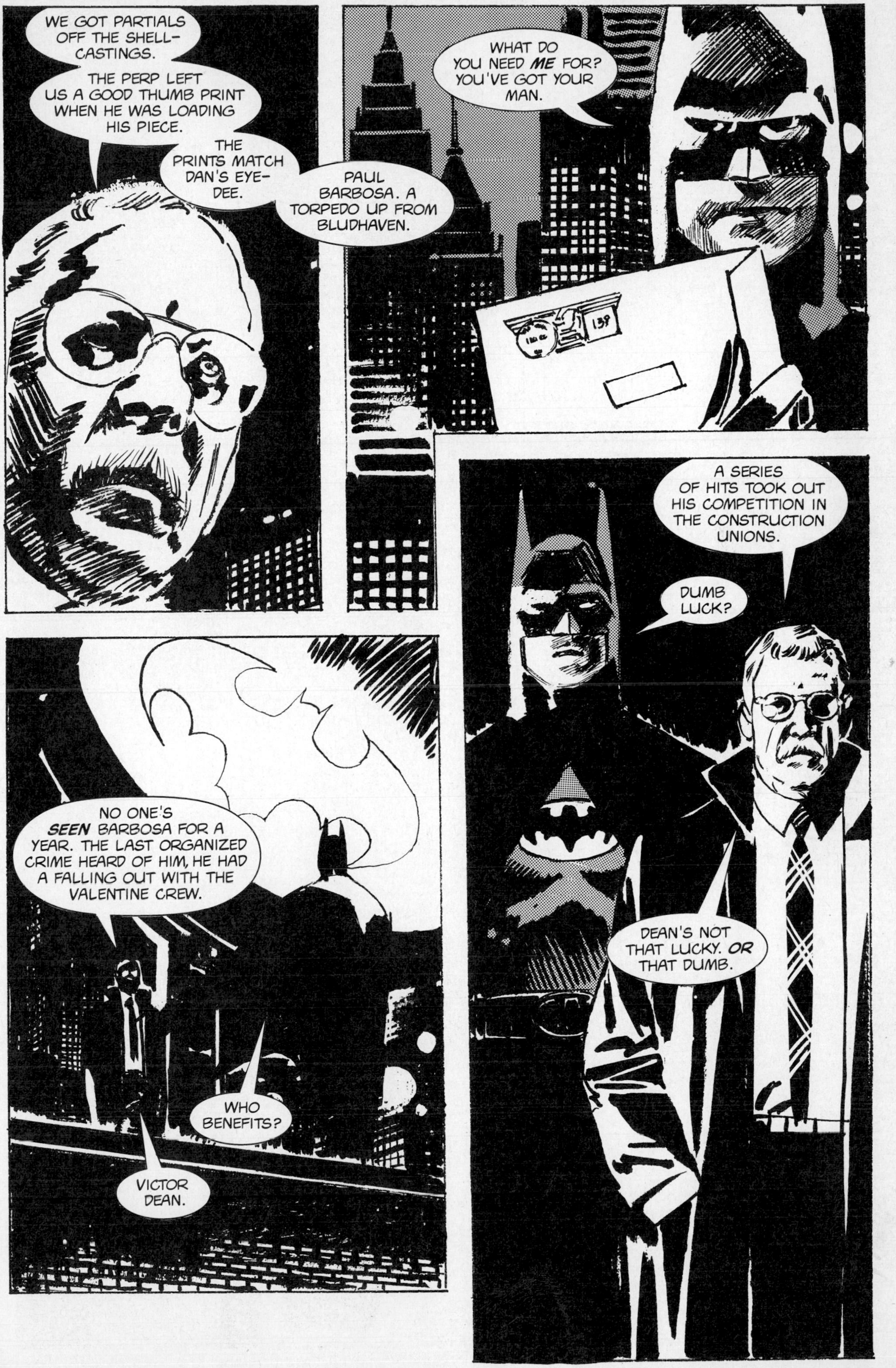
WE GOT PARTIALS OFF THE SHELL-CASTINGS.
THE PERP LEFT US A GOOD THUMB PRINT WHEN HE WAS LOADING HIS PIECE.
THE PRINTS MATCH DAN'S EYE-DEE.
PAUL BARBOSA. A TORPEDO UP FROM BLUDHAVEN.
WHAT DO YOU NEED ME FOR? YOU'VE GOT YOUR MAN.
A SERIES OF HITS TOOK OUT HIS COMPETITION IN THE CONSTRUCTION UNIONS.
DUMB LUCK?
DEAN'S NOT THAT LUCKY. OR THAT DUMB.
NO ONE'S SEEN BARBOSA FOR A YEAR. THE LAST ORGANIZED CRIME HEARD OF HIM, HE HAD A FALLING OUT WITH THE VALENTINE CREW.
WHO BENEFITS?
VICTOR DEAN.

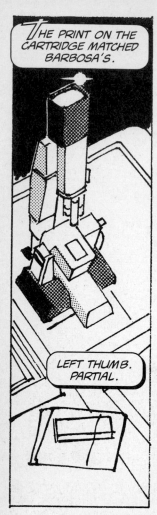

THE PRINT ON THE CARTRIDGE MATCHED BARBOSA'S.

LEFT THUMB. PARTIAL.

BARBOSA WAS RIGHT-HANDED.

HE'D HAVE LOADED HIS GUN WITH THAT HAND.

AND THE PRINT CARRIED A RESIDUE OF SOME KIND OF OIL.

A VEGETABLE OR SEED OIL.

SIX HITS IN SIX WEEKS.

EACH TIME THE HITMAN WAS IDENTIFIED BY PRINTS AND / OR EYEWITNESS.

VICTOR DEAN WAS THE WITNESS IN THREE OF THE HITS.

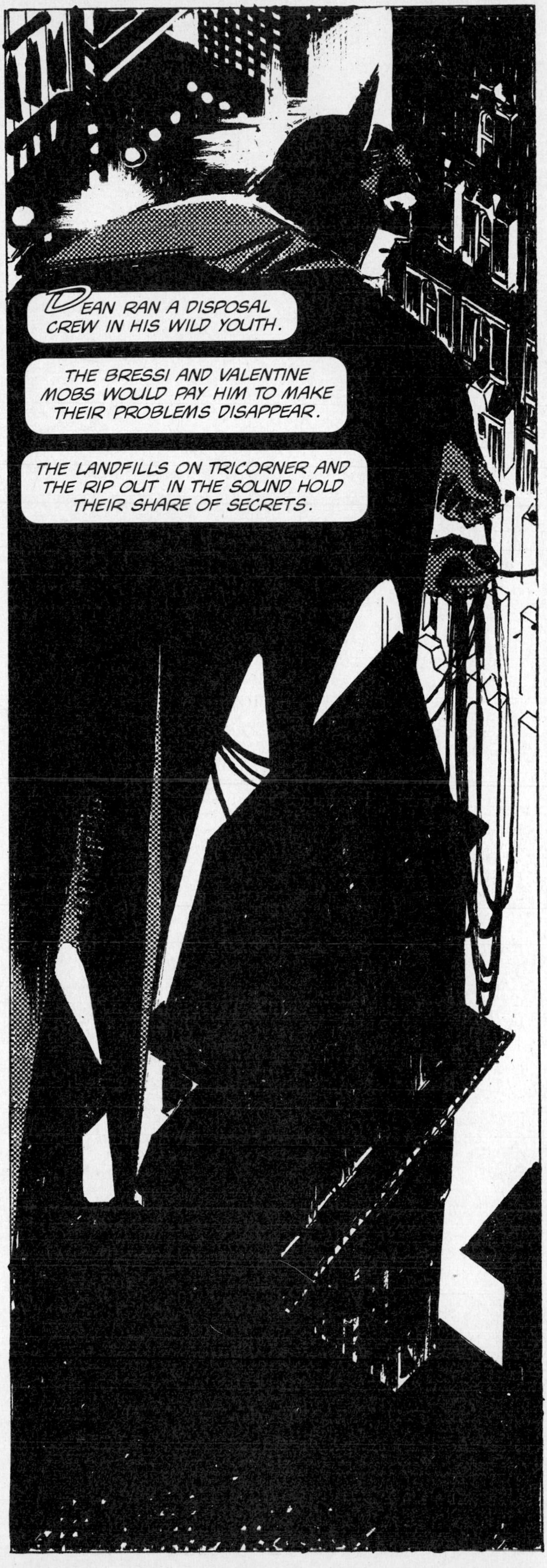
DEAN RAN A DISPOSAL CREW IN HIS WILD YOUTH.
THE BRESSI AND VALENTINE MOBS WOULD PAY HIM TO MAKE THEIR PROBLEMS DISAPPEAR.
THE LANDFILLS ON TRICORNER AND THE RIP OUT IN THE SOUND HOLD THEIR SHARE OF SECRETS.
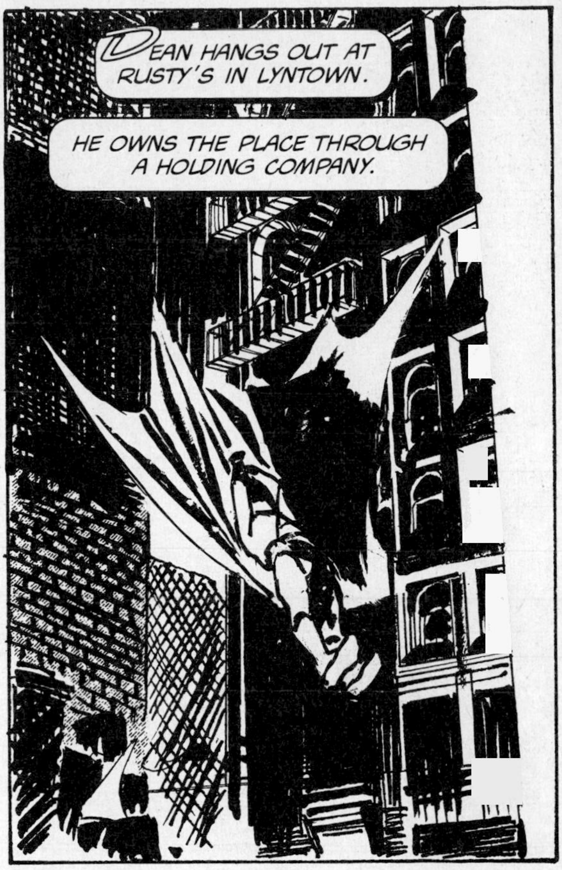
DEAN HANGS OUT AT RUSTY'S IN LYNTOWN.
HE OWNS THE PLACE THROUGH A HOLDING COMPANY.
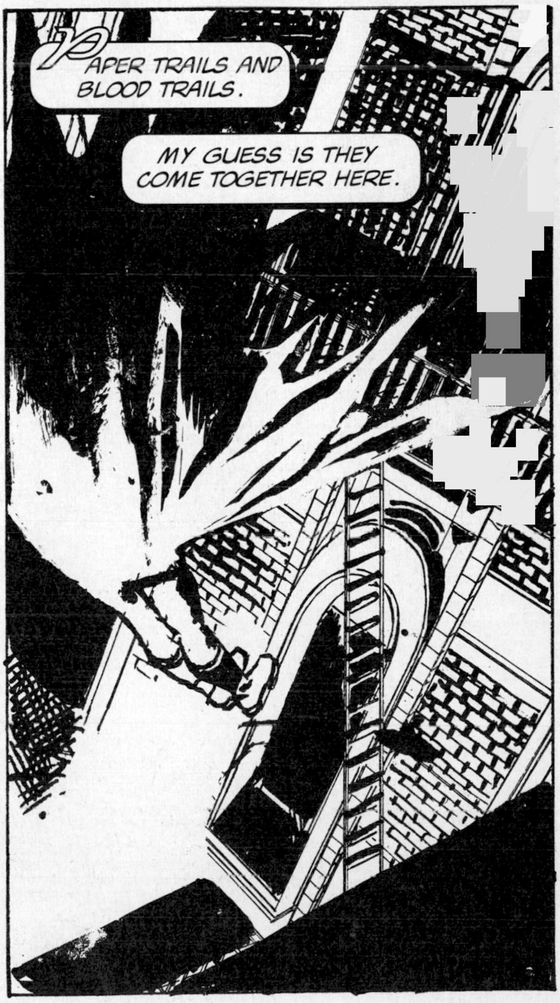
PAPER TRAILS AND BLOOD TRAILS.
MY GUESS IS THEY COME TOGETHER HERE.

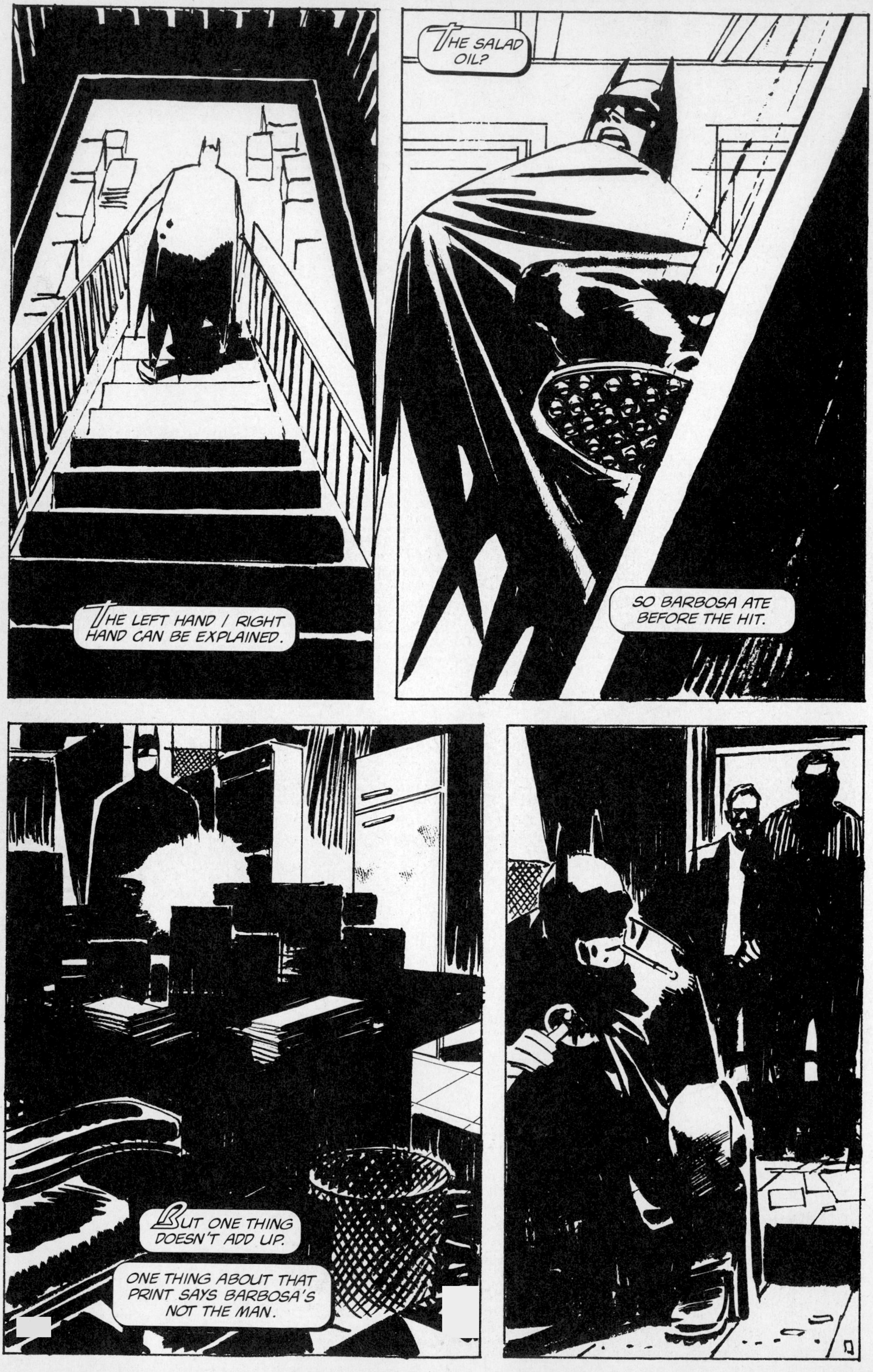
THE LEFT HAND / RIGHT HAND CAN BE EXPLAINED.
THE SALAD OIL?
SO BARBOSA ATE BEFORE THE HIT.
BUT ONE THING DOESN'T ADD UP.
ONE THING ABOUT THAT PRINT SAYS BARBOSA'S NOT THE MAN.

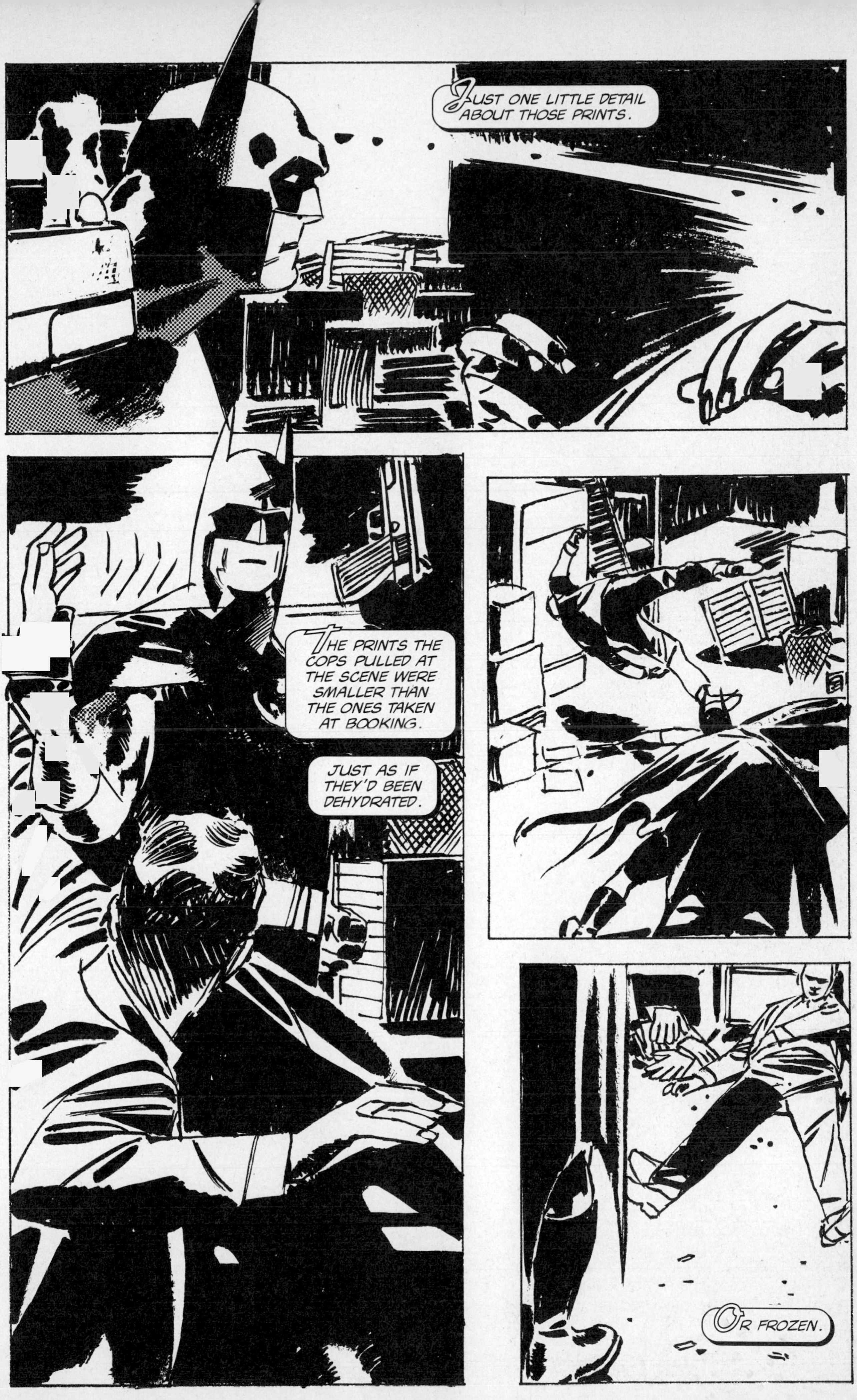
JUST ONE LITTLE DETAIL ABOUT THOSE PRINTS.
THE PRINTS THE COPS PULLED AT THE SCENE WERE SMALLER THAN THE ONES TAKEN AT BOOKING.
JUST AS IF THEY'D BEEN DEHYDRATED.
OR FROZEN.

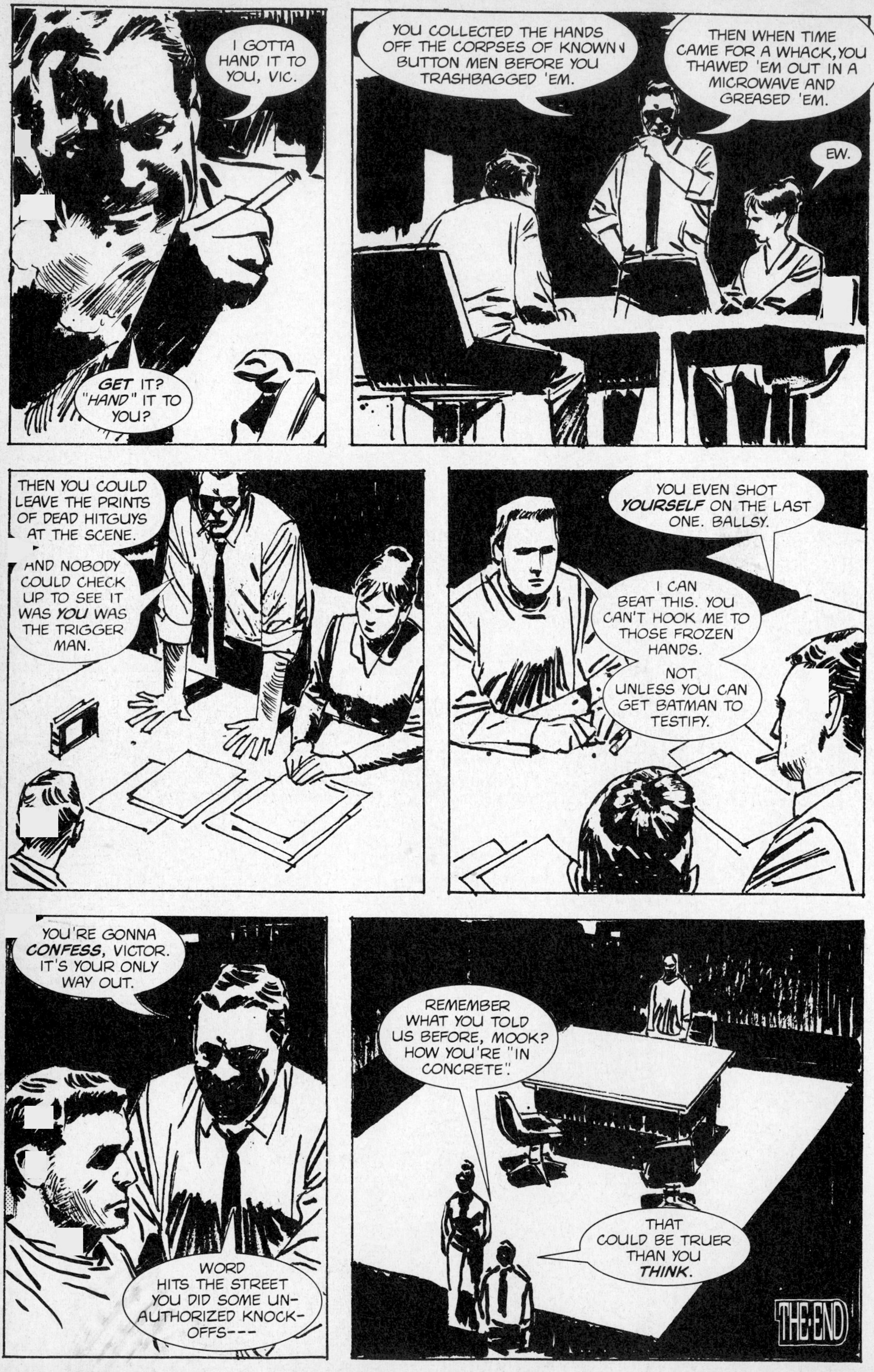
I GOTTA HAND IT TO YOU, VIC.
GET IT? "HAND" IT TO YOU?
YOU COLLECTED THE HANDS OFF THE CORPSES OF KNOWN BUTTON MEN BEFORE YOU TRASHBAGGED 'EM.
THEN WHEN TIME CAME FOR A WHACK, YOU THAWED 'EM OUT IN A MICROWAVE AND GREASED 'EM.
EW.
THEN YOU COULD LEAVE THE PRINTS OF DEAD HITGUYS AT THE SCENE.
AND NOBODY COULD CHECK UP TO SEE IT WAS YOU WAS THE TRIGGER MAN.
YOU EVEN SHOT YOURSELF ON THE LAST ONE. BALLSY.
I CAN BEAT THIS. YOU CAN'T HOOK ME TO THOSE FROZEN HANDS.
NOT UNLESS YOU CAN GET BATMAN TO TESTIFY.
YOU'RE GONNA CONFESS, VICTOR. IT'S YOUR ONLY WAY OUT.
WORD HITS THE STREET YOU DID SOME UN-AUTHORIZED KNOCK-OFFS---
REMEMBER WHAT YOU TOLD US BEFORE, MOOK? HOW YOU'RE "IN CONCRETE".
THAT COULD BE TRUER THAN YOU THINK.
THE END

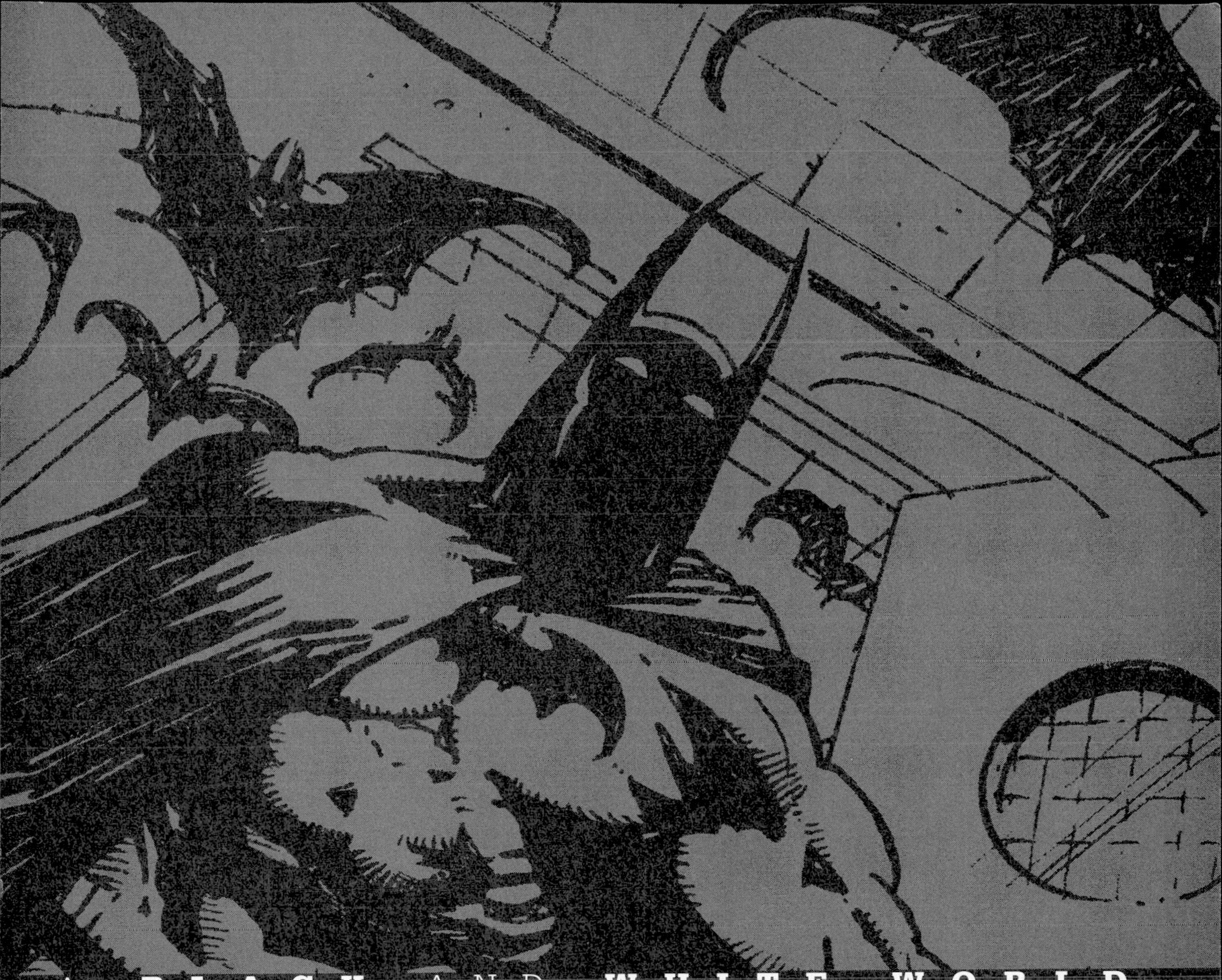

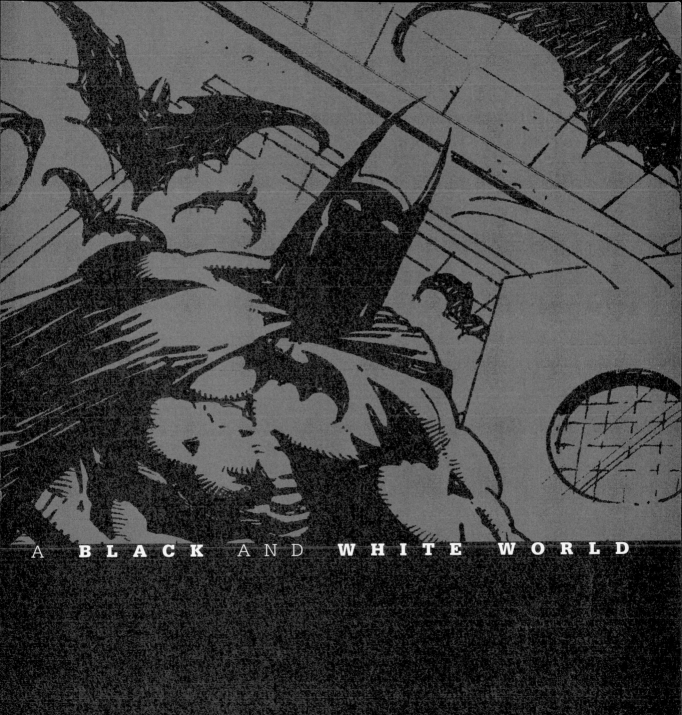

A BLACK AND WHITE WORLD

SIMON **BISLEY**

Simon Bisley exploded onto the comics scene with his work on *Slaine* for England's Fleetway Comics. His major American comics debut was on LOBO: THE LAST CZARNIAN, the first Lobo miniseries, where his frantic, pyrotechnic style completely bowled fans over. He followed that with the fully-painted BATMAN/JUDGE DREDD: JUDGMENT ON GOTHAM crossover, as well as several other Lobo projects before basically dropping out of sight. He resurfaces occasionally to do some project or other. This is one of those.

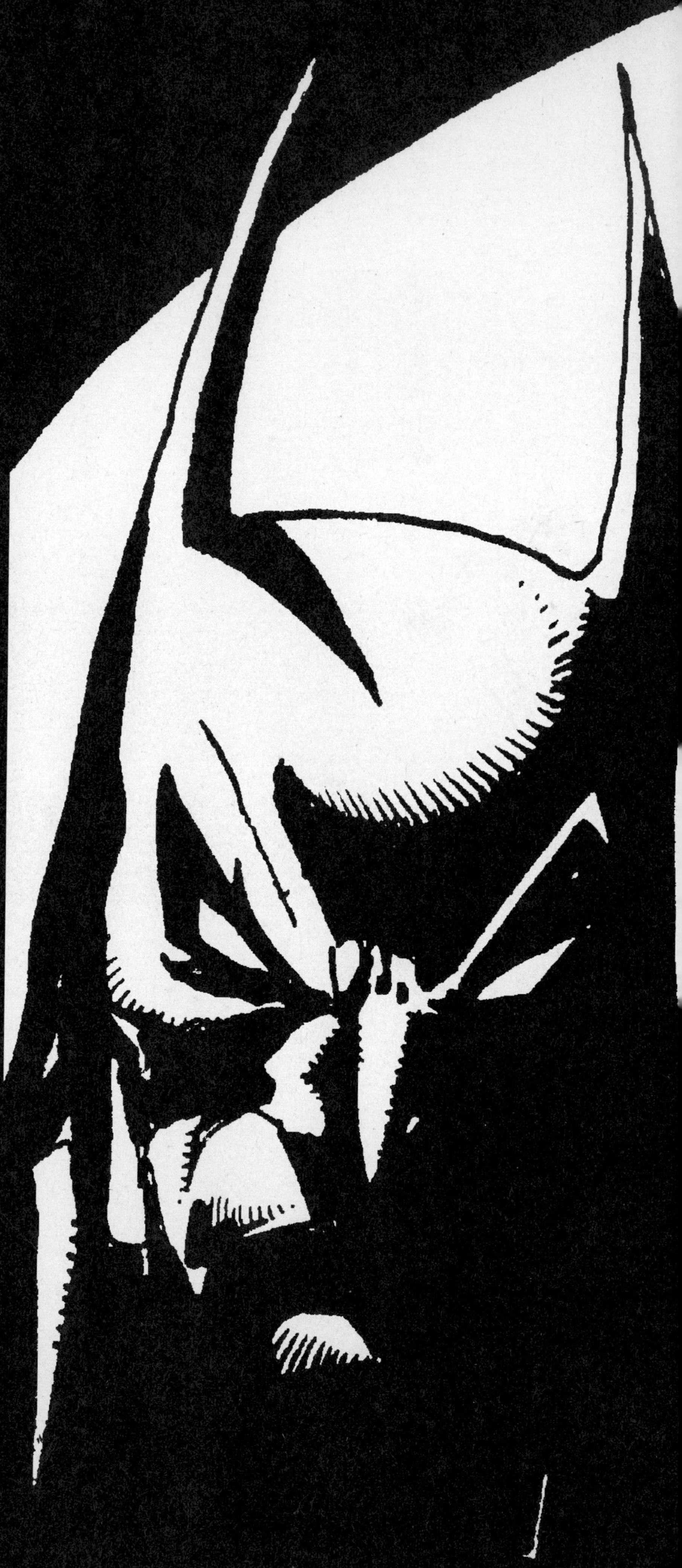

NEIL **GAIMAN**

Neil Gaiman is one of the eleven authors listed as the ten most important post-modern writers in the *Dictionary of Literary Biography*.

He has received awards for many of his comics and books.

His most recent works are *Neverwhere*, a novel, published by Avon Books, and *The Day I Swapped My Dad For Two Goldfish*, a children's book with pictures by Dave McKean.

He is currently working on STARDUST, an illustrated fairy tale drawn by Charles Vess, the *Neverwhere* movie, and, with writer/director Roger Avary, a film of *Beowulf*.

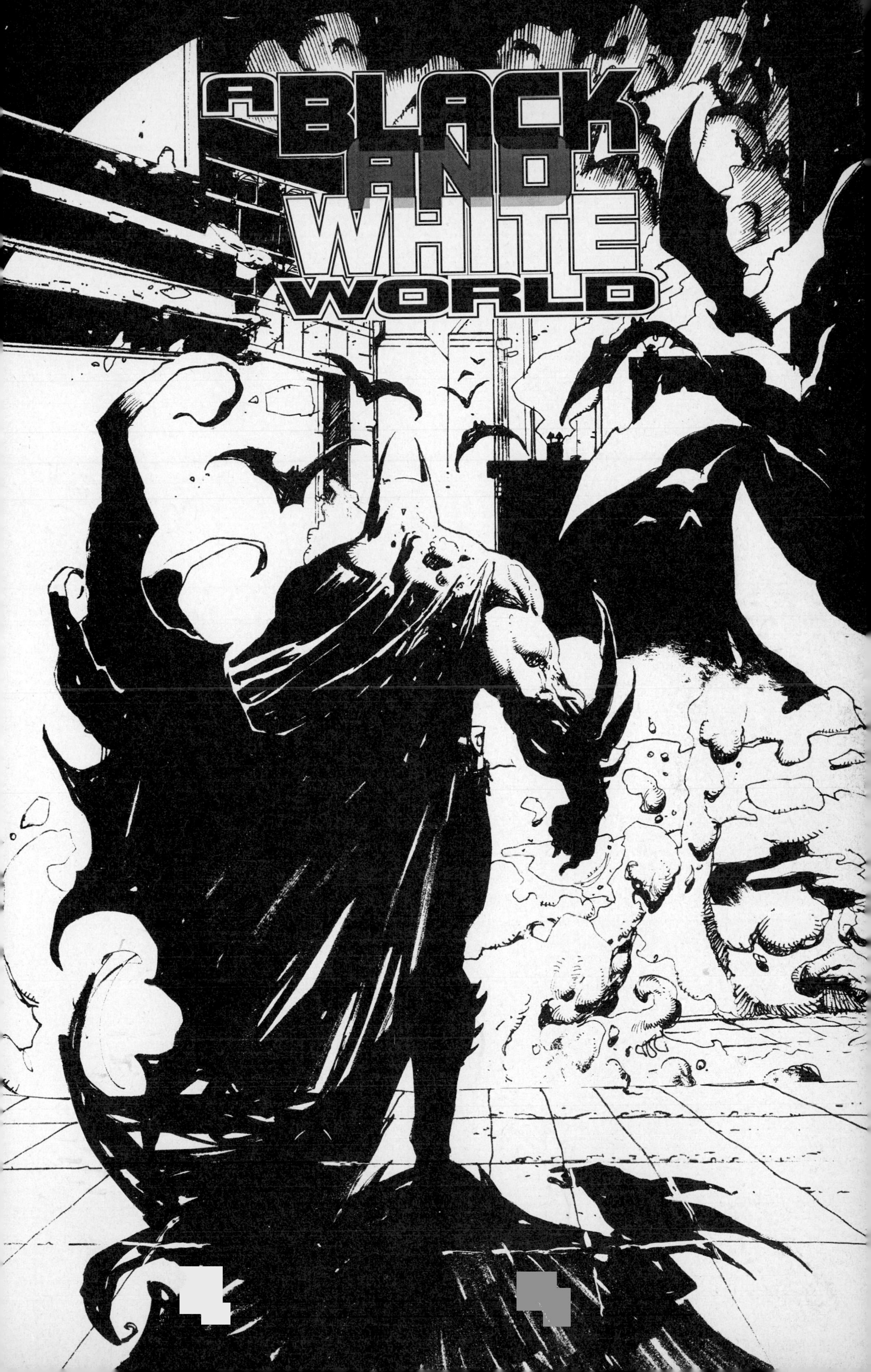
A BLACK AND WHITE WORLD

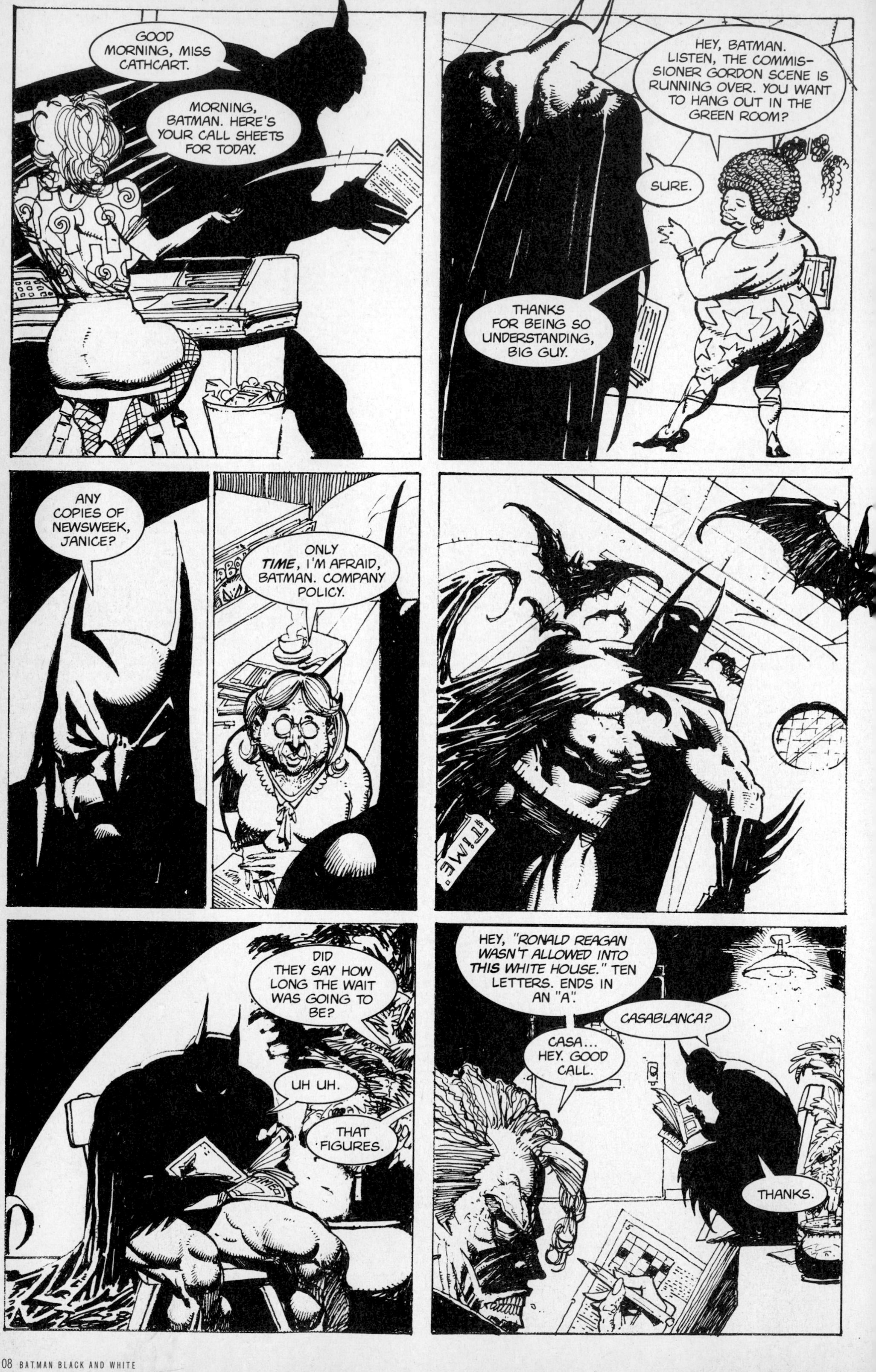
GOOD MORNING, MISS CATHCART.
MORNING, BATMAN. HERE'S YOUR CALL SHEETS FOR TODAY.
HEY, BATMAN. LISTEN, THE COMMIS-SIONER GORDON SCENE IS RUNNING OVER. YOU WANT TO HANG OUT IN THE GREEN ROOM?
SURE.
THANKS FOR BEING SO UNDERSTANDING, BIG GUY.
ANY COPIES OF NEWSWEEK, JANICE?
ONLY *TIME*, I'M AFRAID, BATMAN. COMPANY POLICY.
TIME
DID THEY SAY HOW LONG THE WAIT WAS GOING TO BE?
UH UH.
THAT FIGURES.
HEY, "*RONALD REAGAN WASN'T ALLOWED INTO* **THIS** *WHITE HOUSE*." TEN LETTERS. ENDS IN AN "A".
CASABLANCA?
CASA... HEY. GOOD CALL.
THANKS.

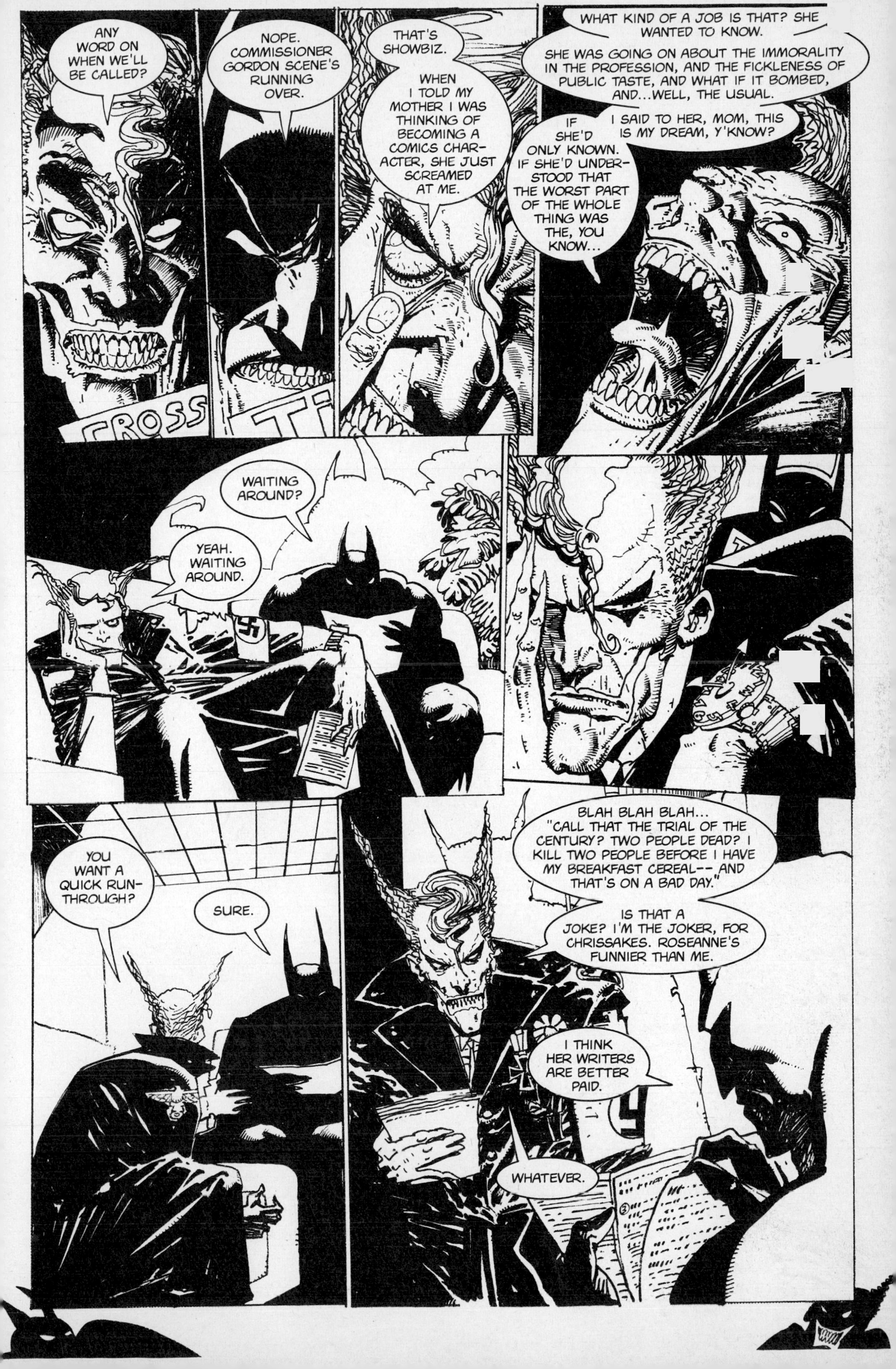
ANY WORD ON WHEN WE'LL BE CALLED?
NOPE. COMMISSIONER GORDON SCENE'S RUNNING OVER.
CROSS
THAT'S SHOWBIZ.
WHEN I TOLD MY MOTHER I WAS THINKING OF BECOMING A COMICS CHARACTER, SHE JUST SCREAMED AT ME.
WHAT KIND OF A JOB IS THAT? SHE WANTED TO KNOW.
SHE WAS GOING ON ABOUT THE IMMORALITY IN THE PROFESSION, AND THE FICKLENESS OF PUBLIC TASTE, AND WHAT IF IT BOMBED, AND...WELL, THE USUAL.
I SAID TO HER, MOM, THIS IS MY DREAM, Y'KNOW?
IF SHE'D ONLY KNOWN. IF SHE'D UNDERSTOOD THAT THE WORST PART OF THE WHOLE THING WAS THE, YOU KNOW...
WAITING AROUND?
YEAH. WAITING AROUND.
YOU WANT A QUICK RUN-THROUGH?
SURE.
BLAH BLAH BLAH... "CALL THAT THE TRIAL OF THE CENTURY? TWO PEOPLE DEAD? I KILL TWO PEOPLE BEFORE I HAVE MY BREAKFAST CEREAL-- AND THAT'S ON A BAD DAY."
IS THAT A JOKE? I'M THE JOKER, FOR CHRISSAKES. ROSEANNE'S FUNNIER THAN ME.
I THINK HER WRITERS ARE BETTER PAID.
WHATEVER.

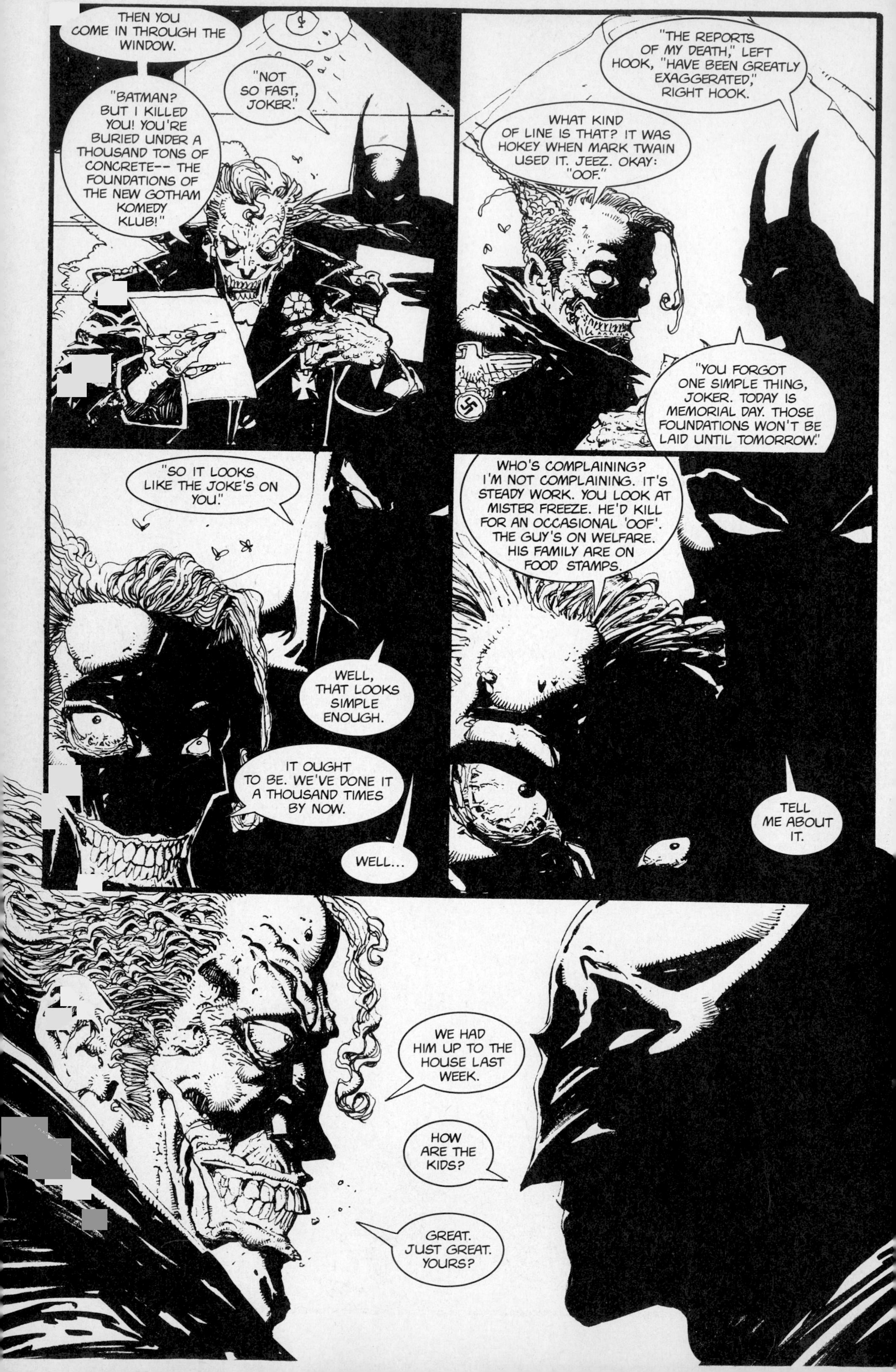
THEN YOU COME IN THROUGH THE WINDOW.
"BATMAN? BUT I KILLED YOU! YOU'RE BURIED UNDER A THOUSAND TONS OF CONCRETE-- THE FOUNDATIONS OF THE NEW GOTHAM KOMEDY KLUB!"
"NOT SO FAST, JOKER."
"THE REPORTS OF MY DEATH," LEFT HOOK, "HAVE BEEN GREATLY EXAGGERATED," RIGHT HOOK.
WHAT KIND OF LINE IS THAT? IT WAS HOKEY WHEN MARK TWAIN USED IT. JEEZ. OKAY: "OOF."
"YOU FORGOT ONE SIMPLE THING, JOKER. TODAY IS MEMORIAL DAY. THOSE FOUNDATIONS WON'T BE LAID UNTIL TOMORROW."
"SO IT LOOKS LIKE THE JOKE'S ON YOU."
WELL, THAT LOOKS SIMPLE ENOUGH.
IT OUGHT TO BE. WE'VE DONE IT A THOUSAND TIMES BY NOW.
WELL...
WHO'S COMPLAINING? I'M NOT COMPLAINING. IT'S STEADY WORK. YOU LOOK AT MISTER FREEZE. HE'D KILL FOR AN OCCASIONAL 'OOF'. THE GUY'S ON WELFARE. HIS FAMILY ARE ON FOOD STAMPS.
TELL ME ABOUT IT.
WE HAD HIM UP TO THE HOUSE LAST WEEK.
HOW ARE THE KIDS?
GREAT. JUST GREAT. YOURS?

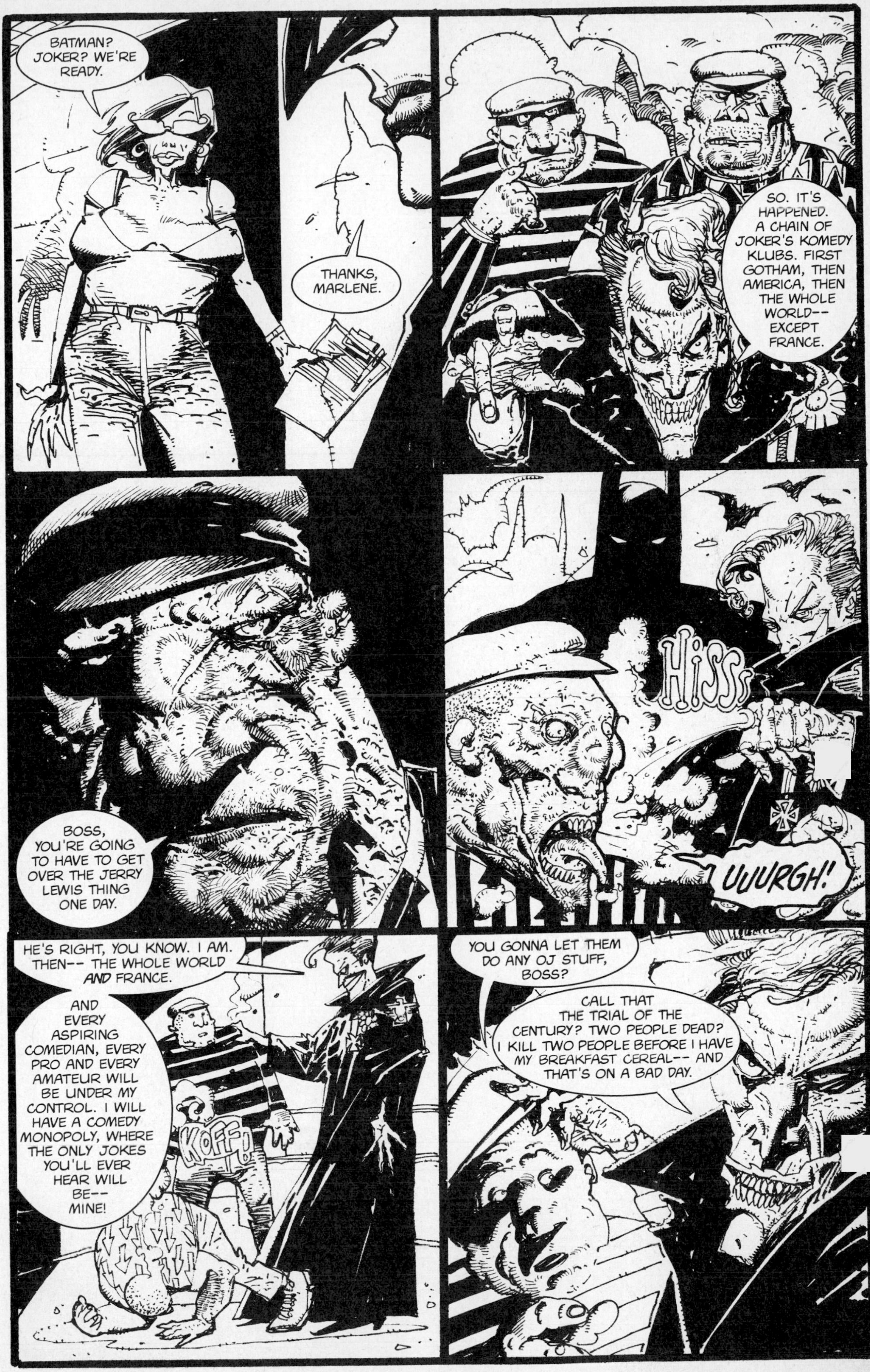
BATMAN? JOKER? WE'RE READY.
THANKS, MARLENE.
SO. IT'S HAPPENED. A CHAIN OF JOKER'S KOMEDY KLUBS. FIRST GOTHAM, THEN AMERICA, THEN THE WHOLE WORLD-- EXCEPT FRANCE.
BOSS, YOU'RE GOING TO HAVE TO GET OVER THE JERRY LEWIS THING ONE DAY.
HISSS
UUURGH!
HE'S RIGHT, YOU KNOW. I AM. THEN-- THE WHOLE WORLD *AND* FRANCE.
AND EVERY ASPIRING COMEDIAN, EVERY PRO AND EVERY AMATEUR WILL BE UNDER MY CONTROL. I WILL HAVE A COMEDY MONOPOLY, WHERE THE ONLY JOKES YOU'LL EVER HEAR WILL BE-- MINE!
KOFF!
YOU GONNA LET THEM DO ANY OJ STUFF, BOSS?
CALL THAT THE TRIAL OF THE CENTURY? TWO PEOPLE DEAD? I KILL TWO PEOPLE BEFORE I HAVE MY BREAKFAST CEREAL-- AND THAT'S ON A BAD DAY.

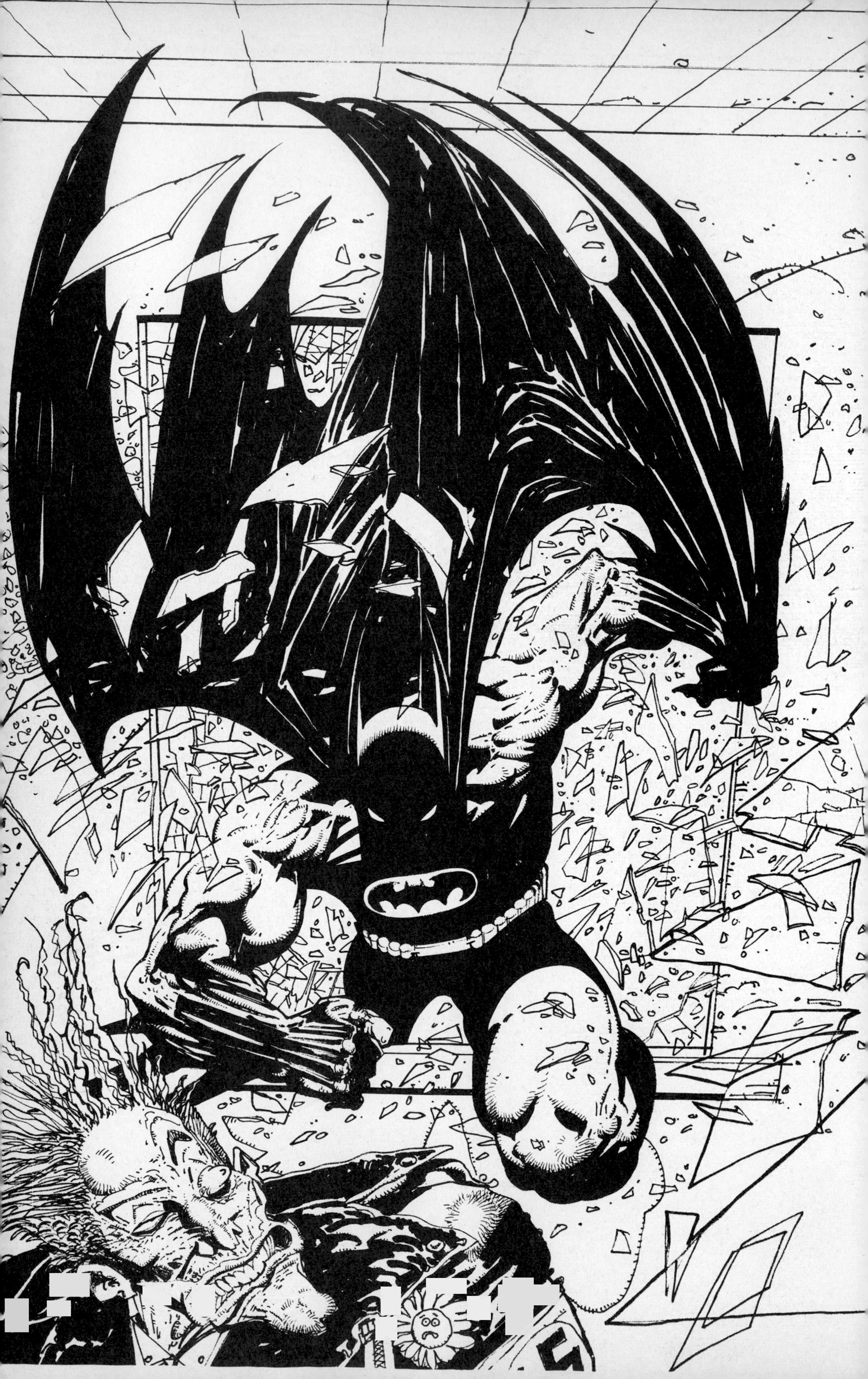

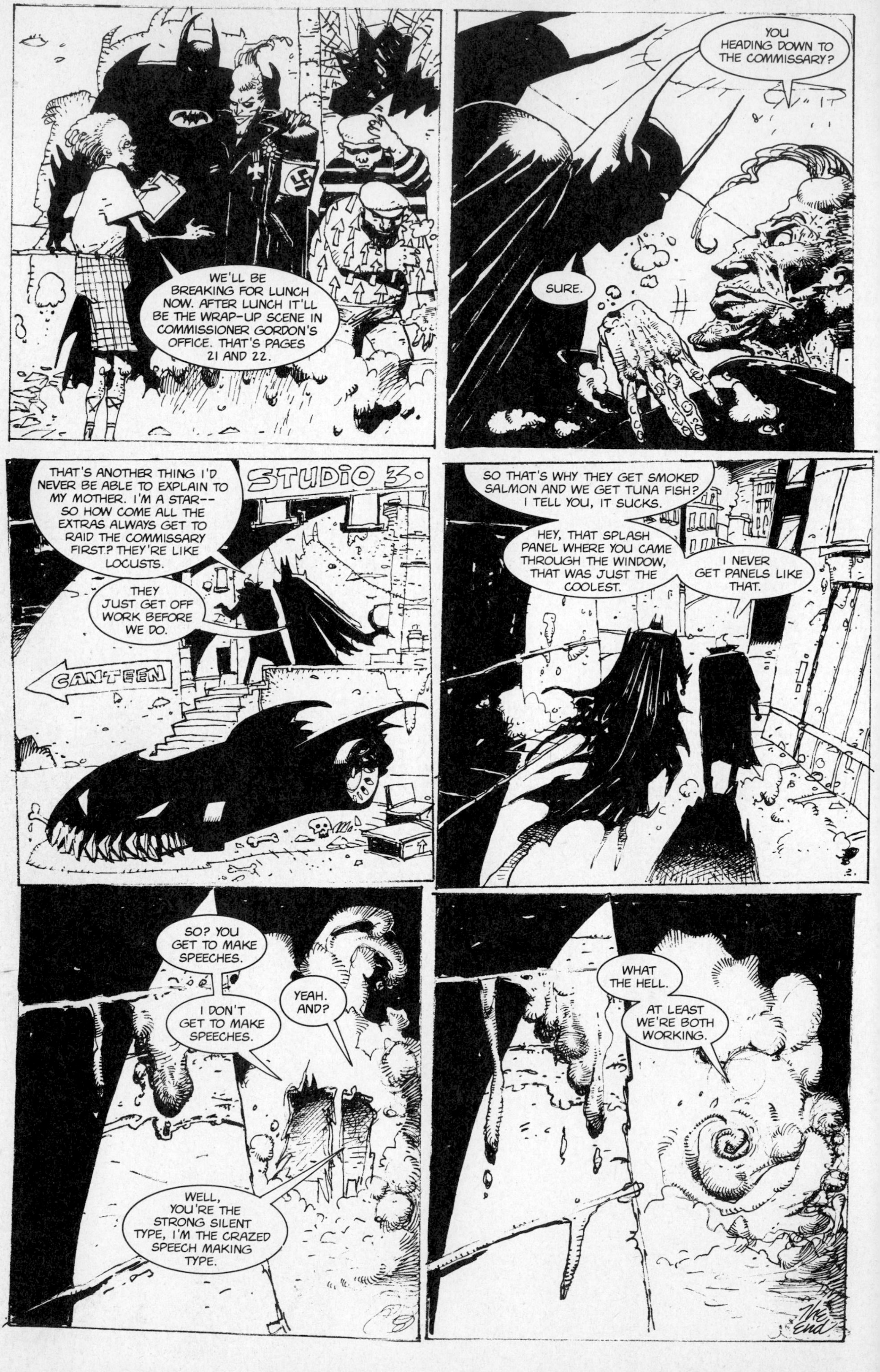
WE'LL BE BREAKING FOR LUNCH NOW. AFTER LUNCH IT'LL BE THE WRAP-UP SCENE IN COMMISSIONER GORDON'S OFFICE. THAT'S PAGES 21 AND 22.
YOU HEADING DOWN TO THE COMMISSARY?
SURE.
STUDIO 3
THAT'S ANOTHER THING I'D NEVER BE ABLE TO EXPLAIN TO MY MOTHER. I'M A STAR-- SO HOW COME ALL THE EXTRAS ALWAYS GET TO RAID THE COMMISSARY FIRST? THEY'RE LIKE LOCUSTS.
THEY JUST GET OFF WORK BEFORE WE DO.
CANTEEN
SO THAT'S WHY THEY GET SMOKED SALMON AND WE GET TUNA FISH? I TELL YOU, IT SUCKS.
HEY, THAT SPLASH PANEL WHERE YOU CAME THROUGH THE WINDOW, THAT WAS JUST THE COOLEST.
I NEVER GET PANELS LIKE THAT.
SO? YOU GET TO MAKE SPEECHES.
I DON'T GET TO MAKE SPEECHES.
YEAH. AND?
WELL, YOU'RE THE STRONG SILENT TYPE, I'M THE CRAZED SPEECH MAKING TYPE.
WHAT THE HELL.
AT LEAST WE'RE BOTH WORKING.
THE END

MICHAEL KALUTA PINUP SKETCH

So, Michael Kaluta leaves a sketch on my desk while I'm out to lunch, and I don't have the slightest idea what it's supposed to be. When I call Mike up an hour later, he says, "Mark, don't worry, trust me." This is usually the kiss of death from a freelancer, but being such a big fan of Mike's work, I tell him to go ahead with the piece. Needless to say, I was not disappointed.

WALT SIMONSON LAYOUT

When an artist is laying out a cover image or story page, it's pretty easy for him to capture a lot of power and dynamics in his thumbnail sketch. After all, thumbnails are simple gestural scribbles that don't need to be weighed down with correct perspective or musculature detail. Unfortunately, it's almost impossible to completely recapture that feeling of power and strength in your final pencil drawing. It's something every artist struggles with— every artist except Walter Simonson. Walt's natural talents have made him the successor to Jack Kirby as comicdom's most dynamic artist.

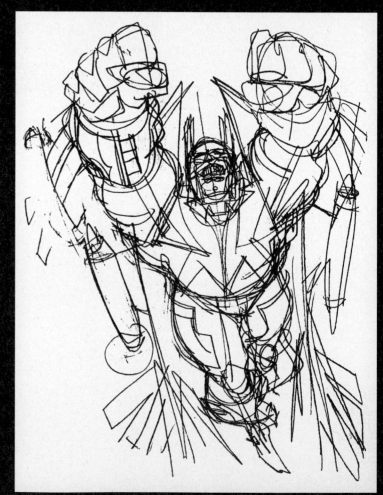

KENT WILLIAMS
PREPRODUCTION DRAWINGS
Every comics artist has a favorite
character they've always wanted to
draw. Some would love to do a
Superman story, others have always
wanted to draw Spider-Man ever
since they were little. The odd thing
is *every* comic-book artist wants to
draw Batman. The tough thing is
when it actually comes time to sit
down and draw comics' most enig-
matic character, it's the moment of
truth. What will *your* version look

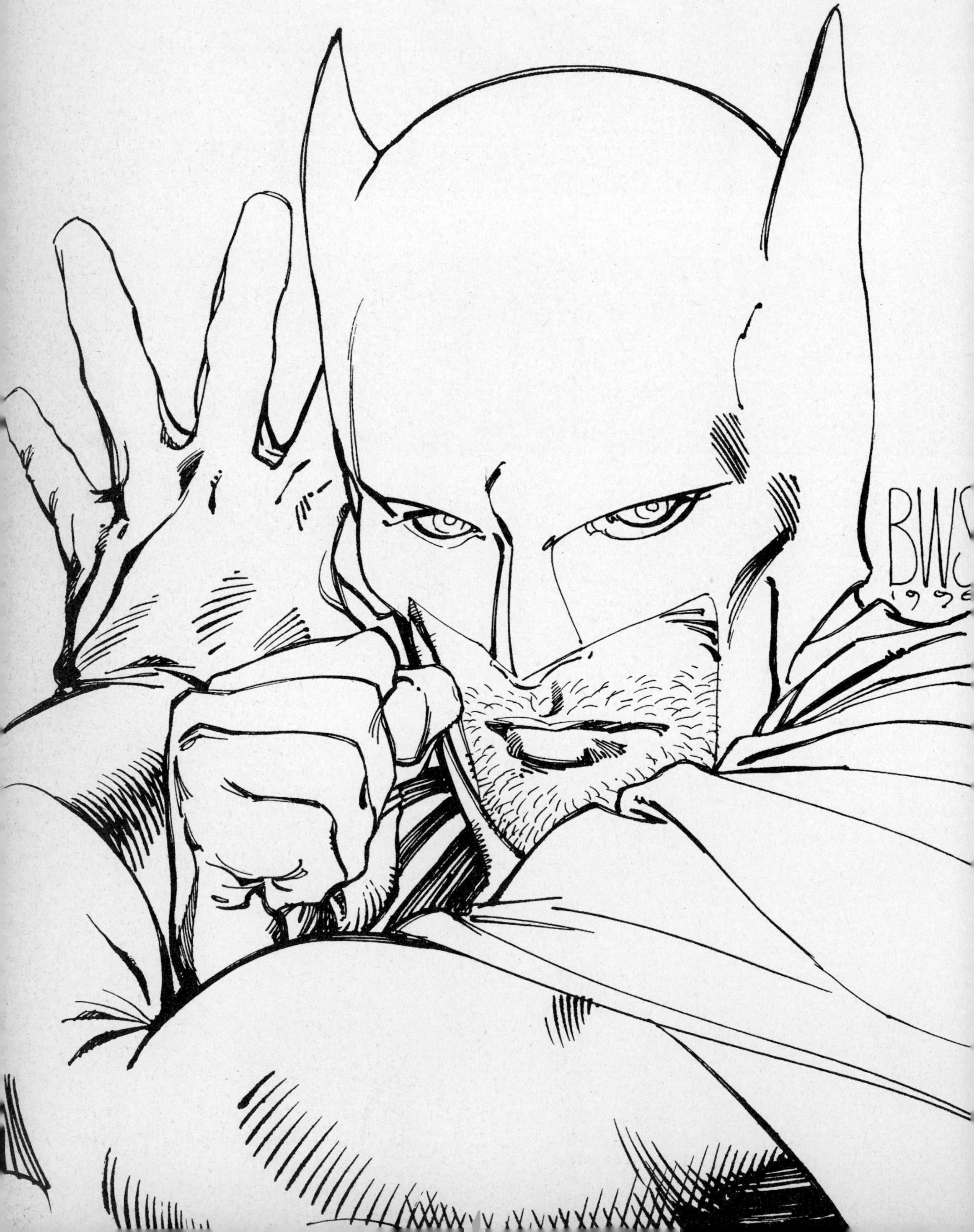

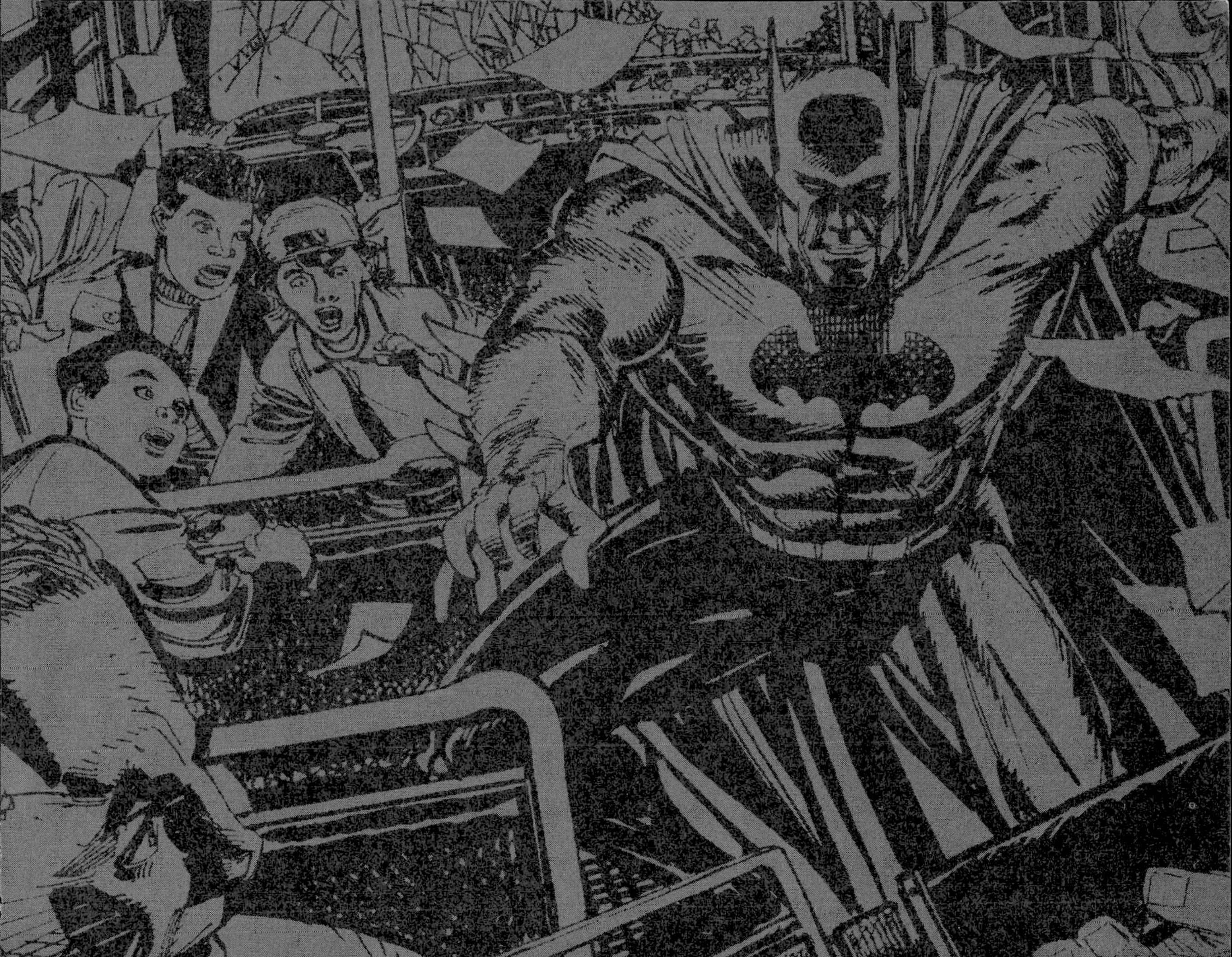

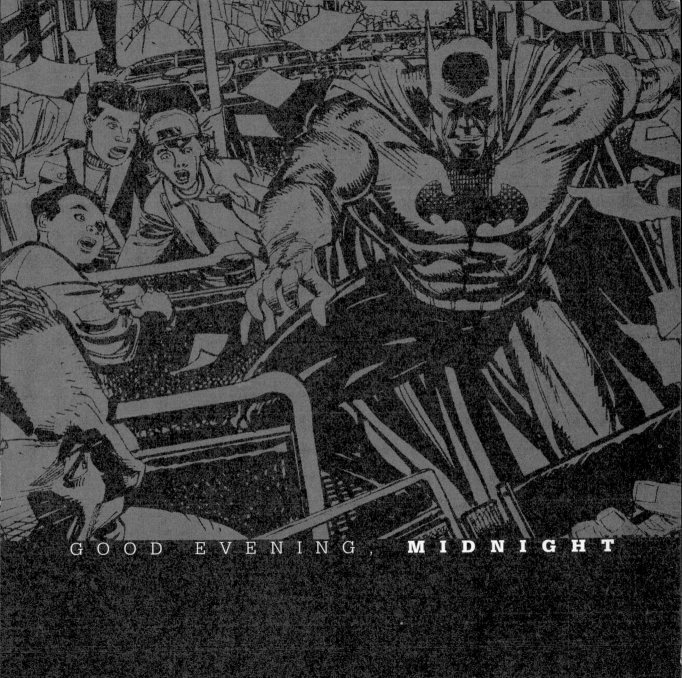

GOOD EVENING, **MIDNIGHT**

KLAUS **JANSON**

It has long been accepted as fact that Klaus Janson is the premier inker in the world of comics. In the past decade, however, he has also gained considerable acclaim as a penciller and colorist as well. First gaining widespread attention on *Daredevil*, Janson later worked on the groundbreaking BATMAN: THE DARK KNIGHT RETURNS and followed that with BATMAN: GOTHIC.

Janson believes he has a greater affinity for Batman than any other character and, consequently, has always done his best work on the Dark Knight.

Astonishingly, *Good Evening, Midnight* is Janson's very first writing for comics.

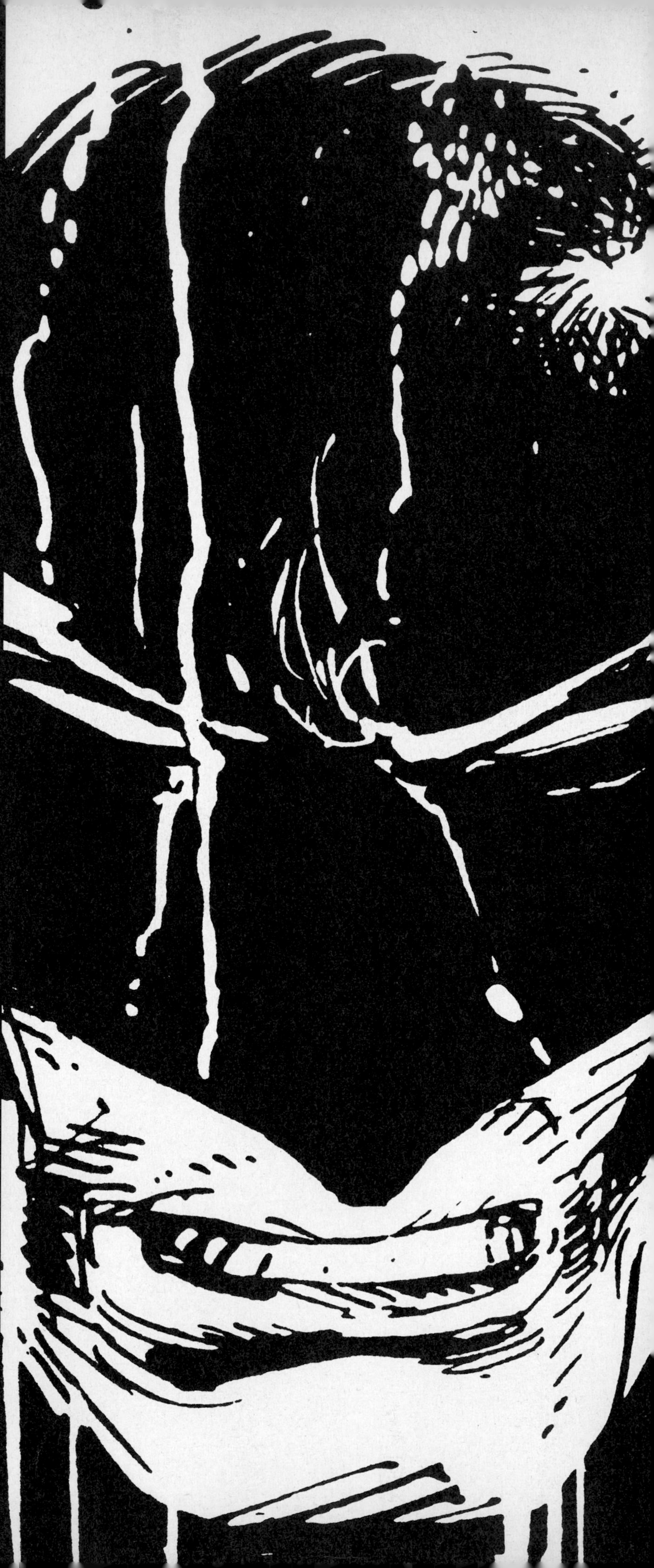

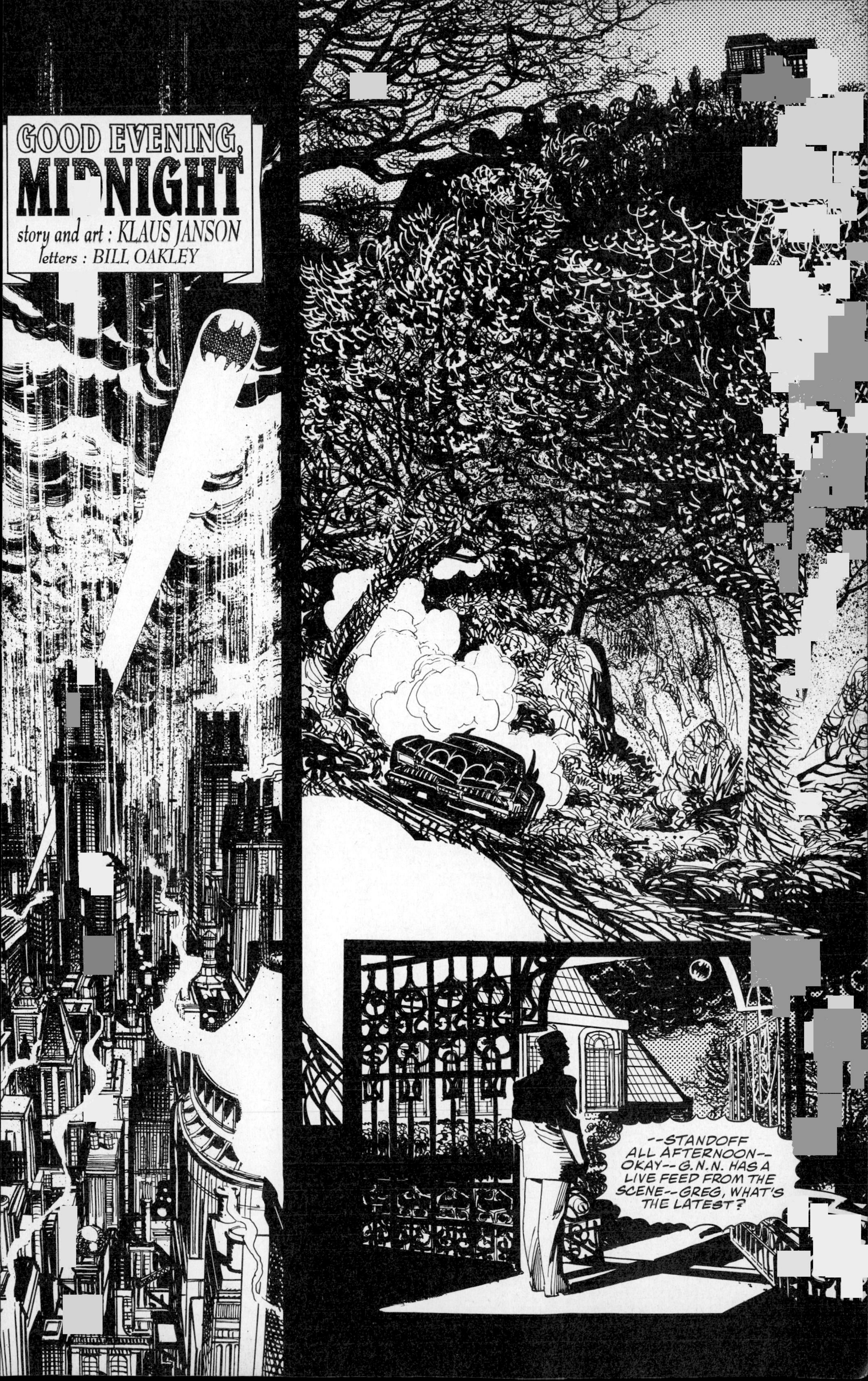
GOOD EVENING, MIDNIGHT
story and art : KLAUS JANSON
letters : BILL OAKLEY
--STANDOFF ALL AFTERNOON-- OKAY-- G.N.N. HAS A LIVE FEED FROM THE SCENE--GREG, WHAT'S THE LATEST?

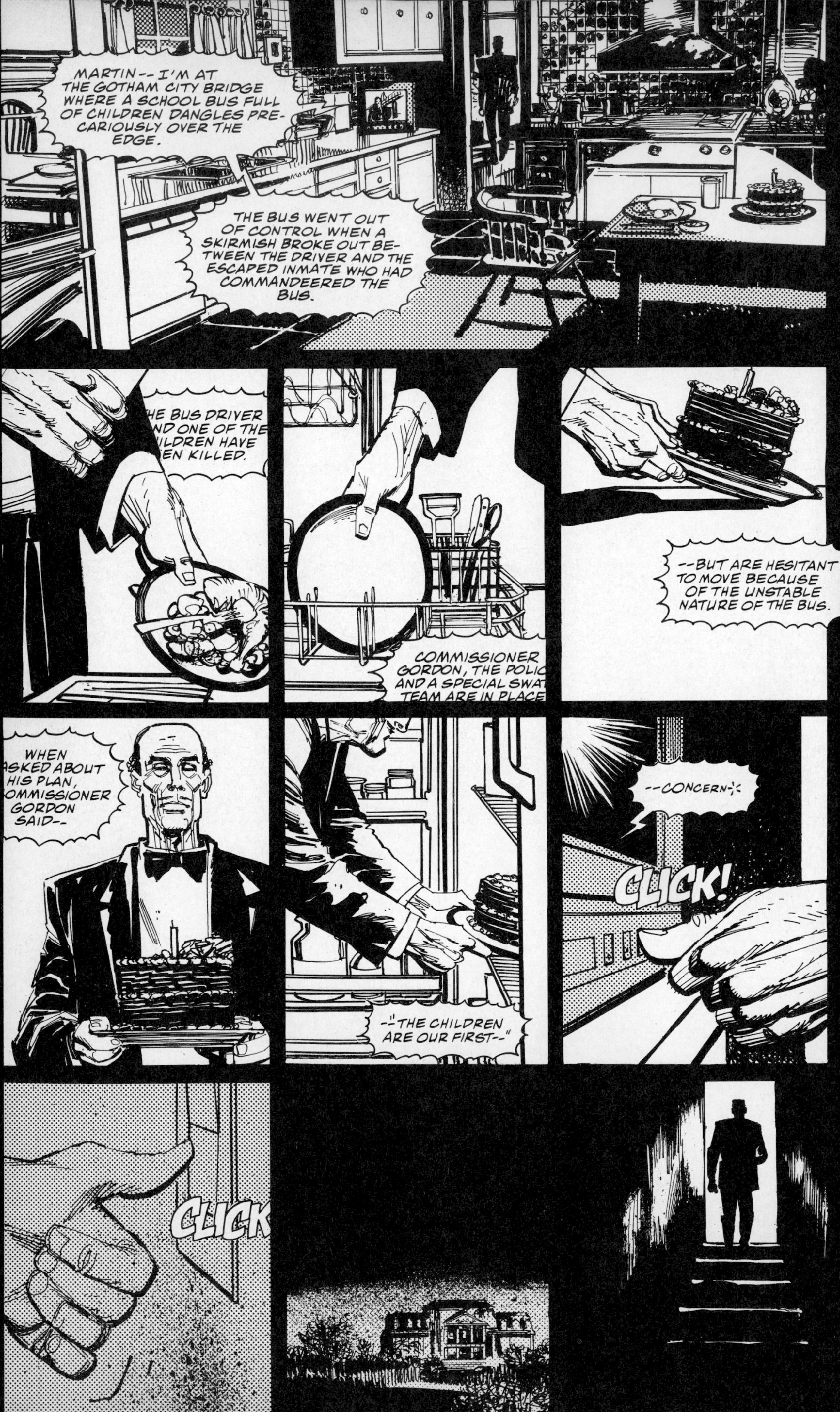
MARTIN-- I'M AT THE GOTHAM CITY BRIDGE WHERE A SCHOOL BUS FULL OF CHILDREN DANGLES PRECARIOUSLY OVER THE EDGE.
THE BUS WENT OUT OF CONTROL WHEN A SKIRMISH BROKE OUT BETWEEN THE DRIVER AND THE ESCAPED INMATE WHO HAD COMMANDEERED THE BUS.
HE BUS DRIVER ND ONE OF THE ILDREN HAVE EN KILLED.
COMMISSIONER GORDON, THE POLIC AND A SPECIAL SWAT TEAM ARE IN PLACE
--BUT ARE HESITANT TO MOVE BECAUSE OF THE UNSTABLE NATURE OF THE BUS.
WHEN ASKED ABOUT HIS PLAN, OMMISSIONER GORDON SAID--
--"THE CHILDREN ARE OUR FIRST--"
--CONCERN--
CLICK!
CLICK

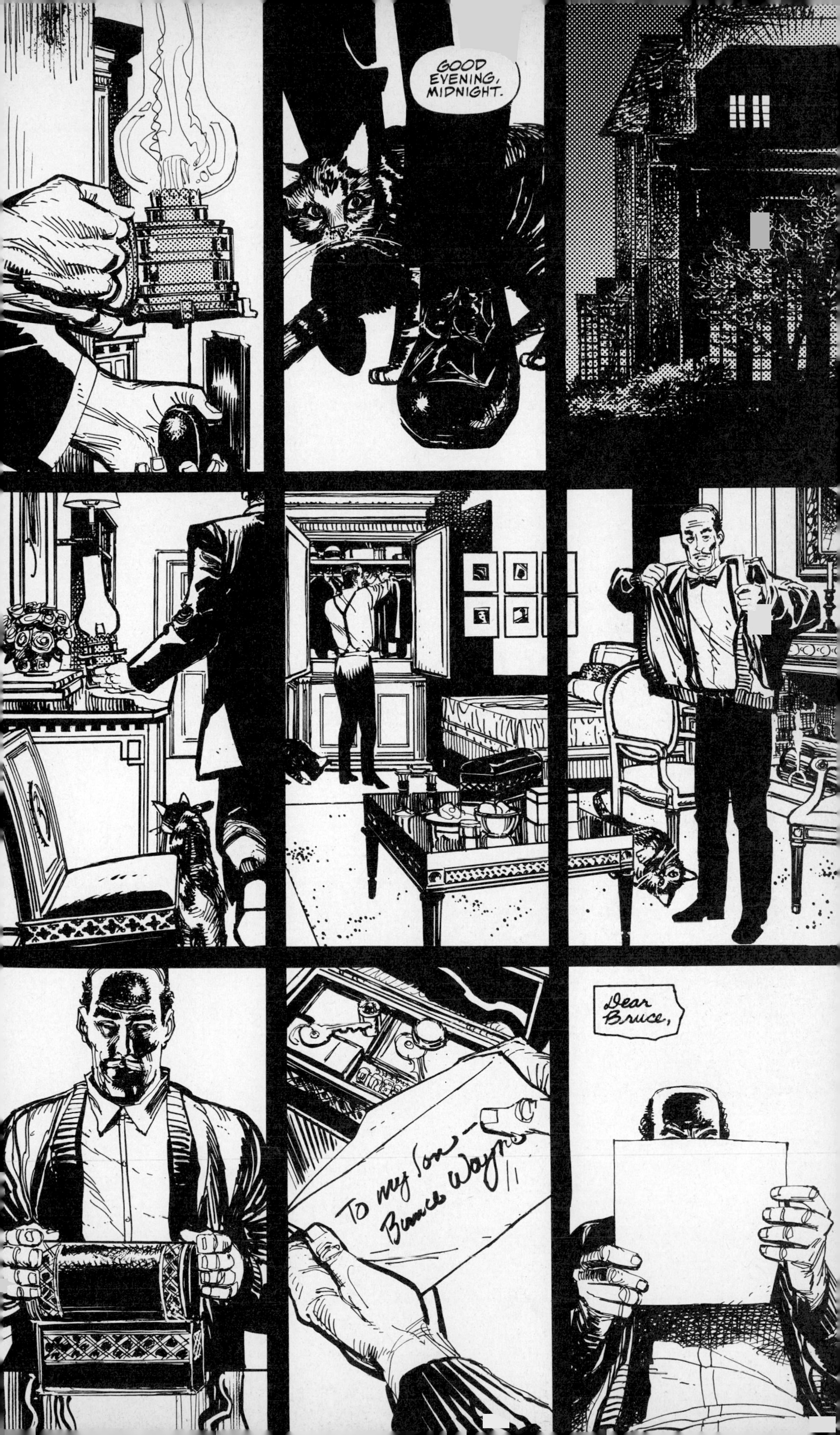
GOOD EVENING, MIDNIGHT.
To my son — Bruce Wayne
Dear Bruce,

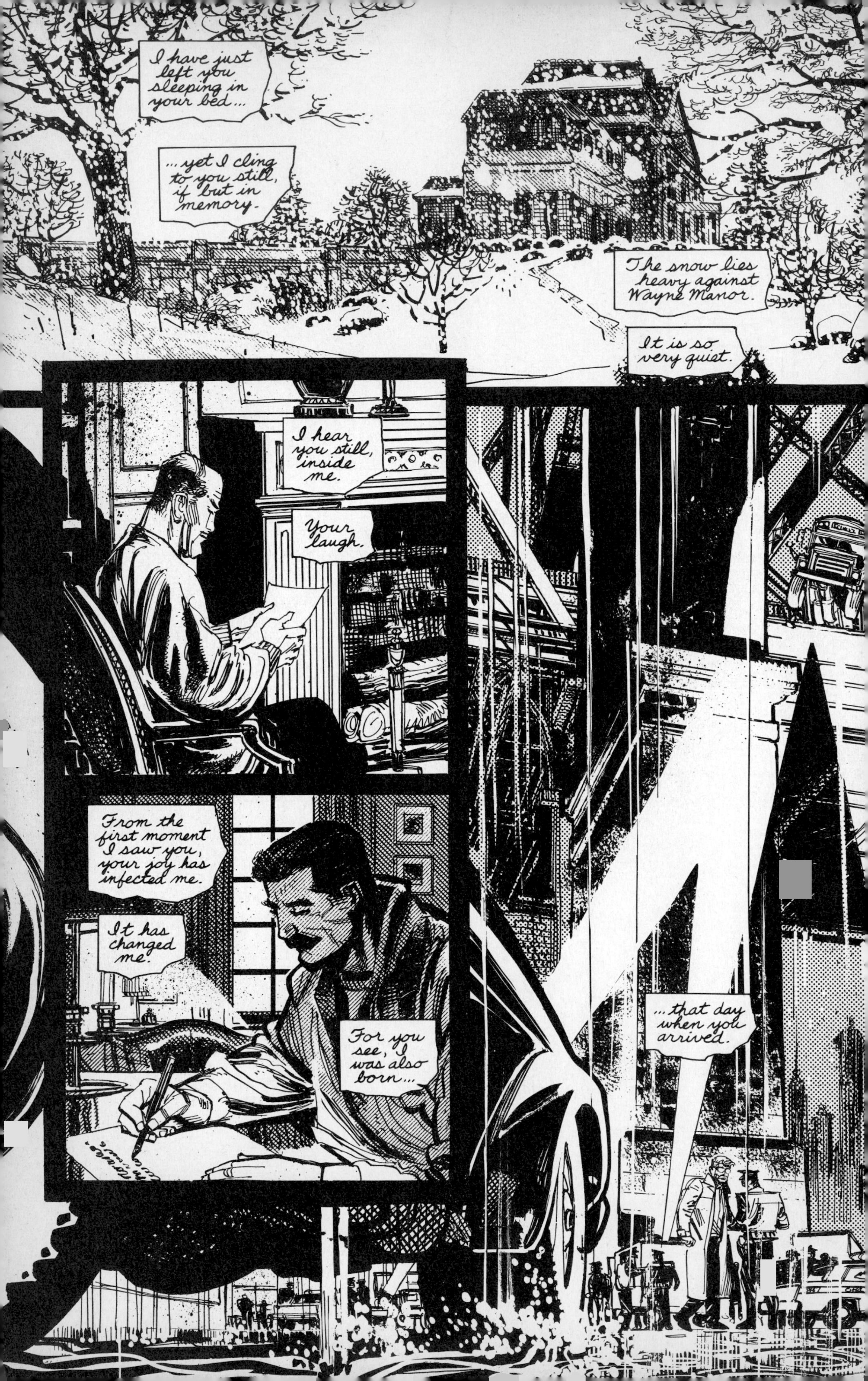
I have just left you sleeping in your bed...
...yet I cling to you still, if but in memory.
The snow lies heavy against Wayne Manor.
It is so very quiet.
I hear you still, inside me.
Your laugh.
From the first moment I saw you, your joy has infected me.
It has changed me.
For you see, I was also born...
...that day when you arrived.

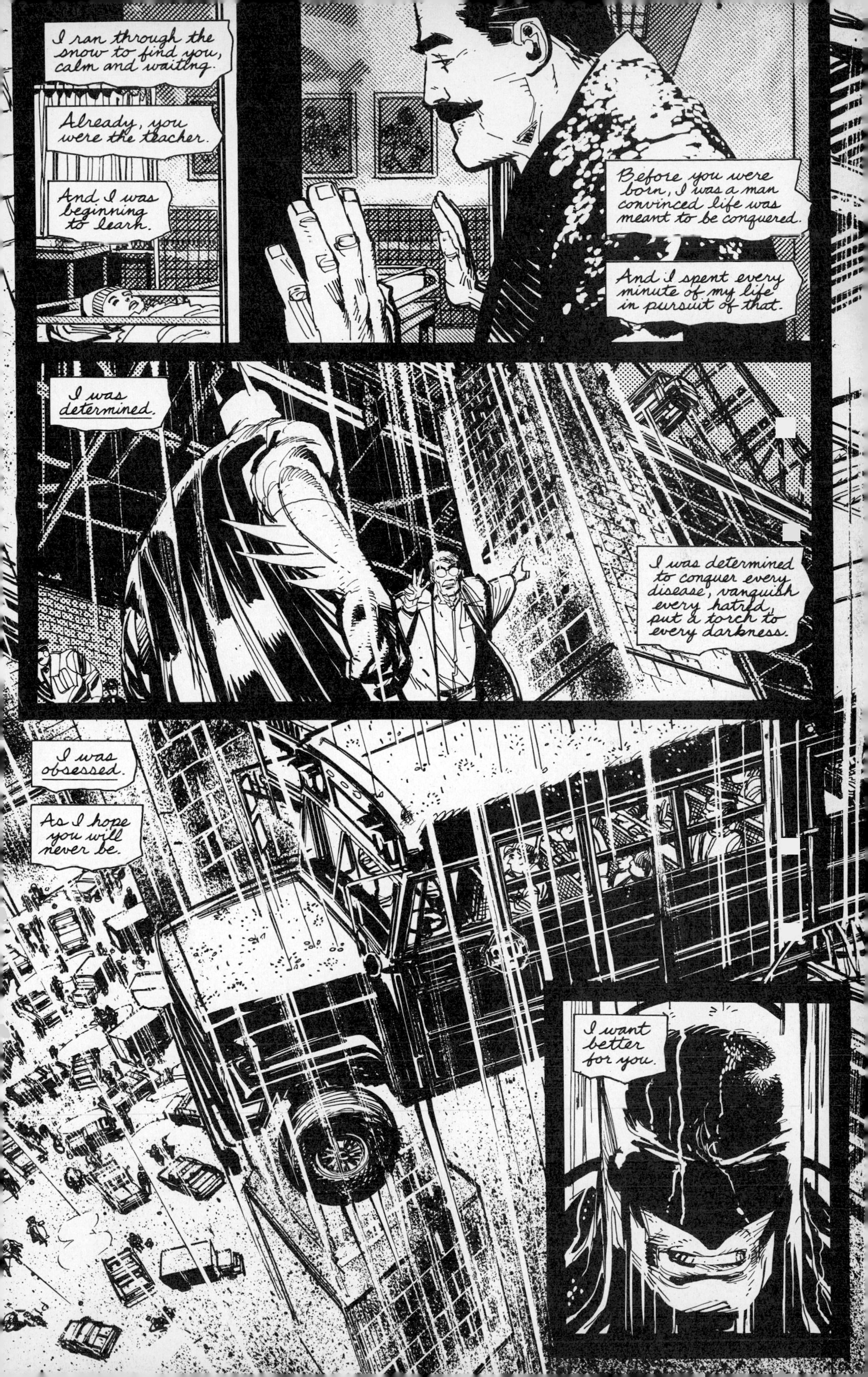

I ran through the snow to find you, calm and waiting.
Already, you were the teacher.
And I was beginning to learn.
Before you were born, I was a man convinced life was meant to be conquered.
And I spent every minute of my life in pursuit of that.
I was determined.
I was determined to conquer every disease, vanquish every hatred, put a torch to every darkness.
I was obsessed.
As I hope you will never be.
I want better for you.

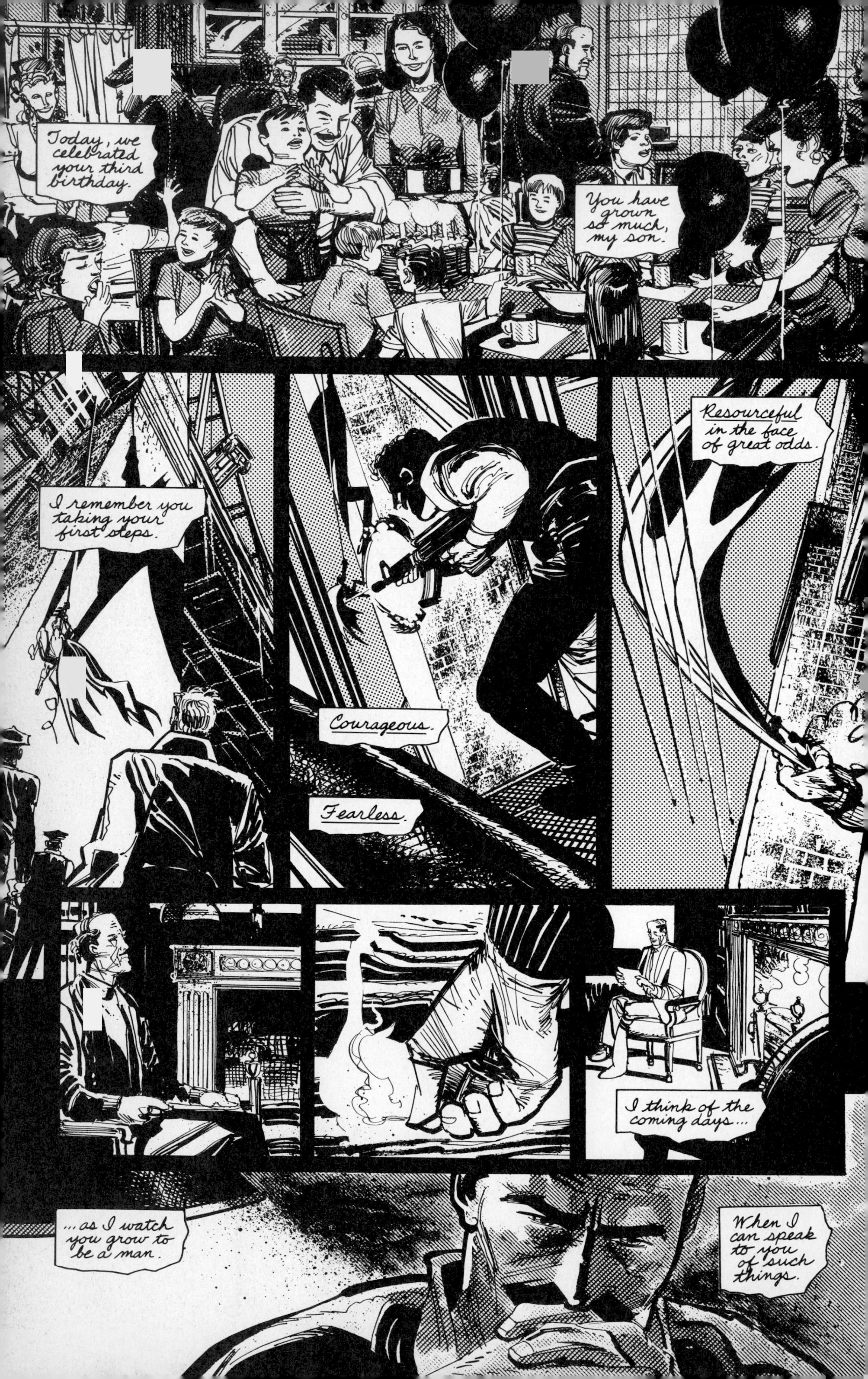

Today, we celebrated your third birthday.
You have grown so much, my son.
I remember you taking your first steps.
Courageous.
Fearless.
Resourceful in the face of great odds.
I think of the coming days...
...as I watch you grow to be a man.
When I can speak to you of such things.

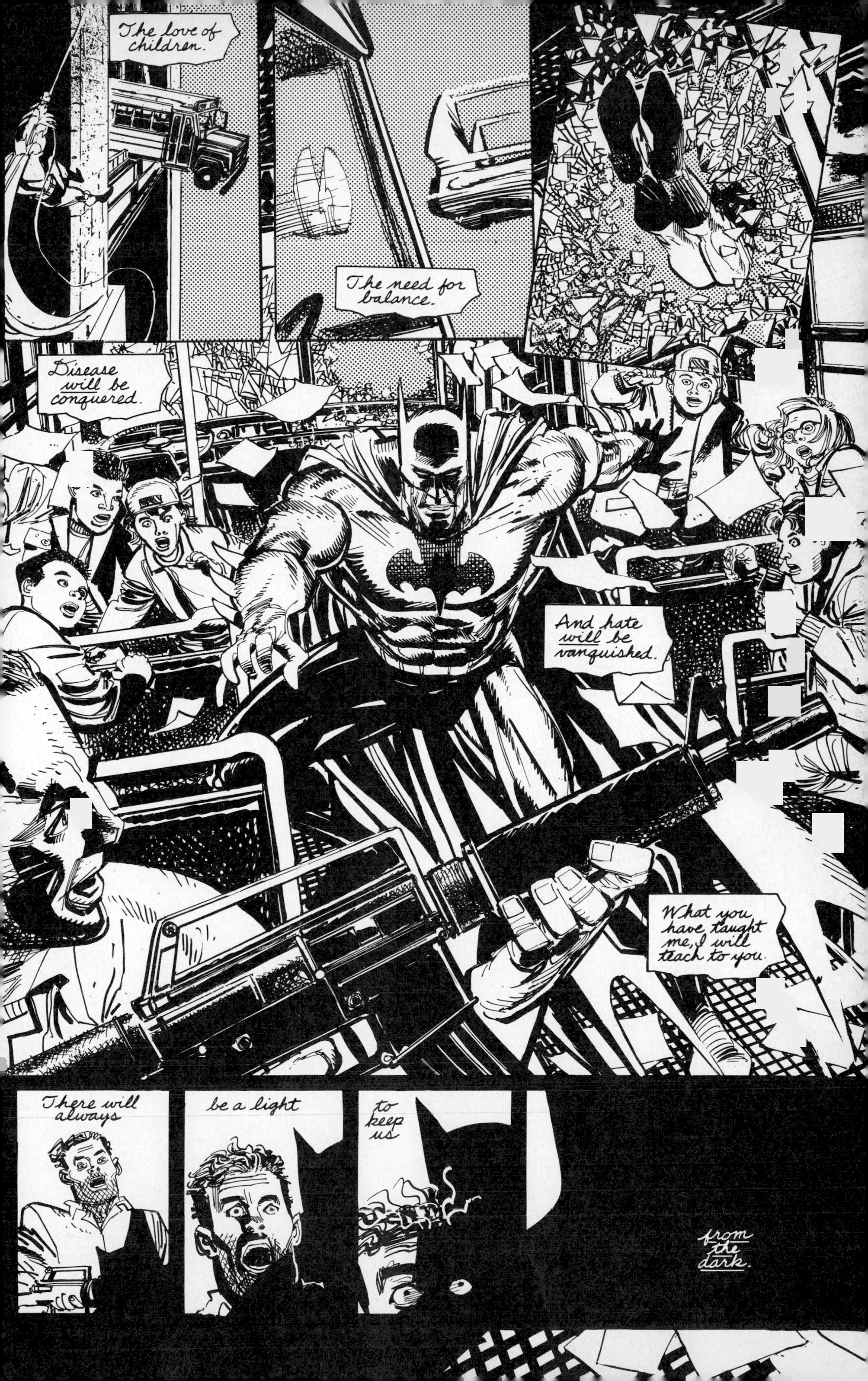
The love of children.
The need for balance.
Disease will be conquered.
And hate will be vanquished.
What you have taught me, I will teach to you.
There will always
be a light
to keep us
from the dark.

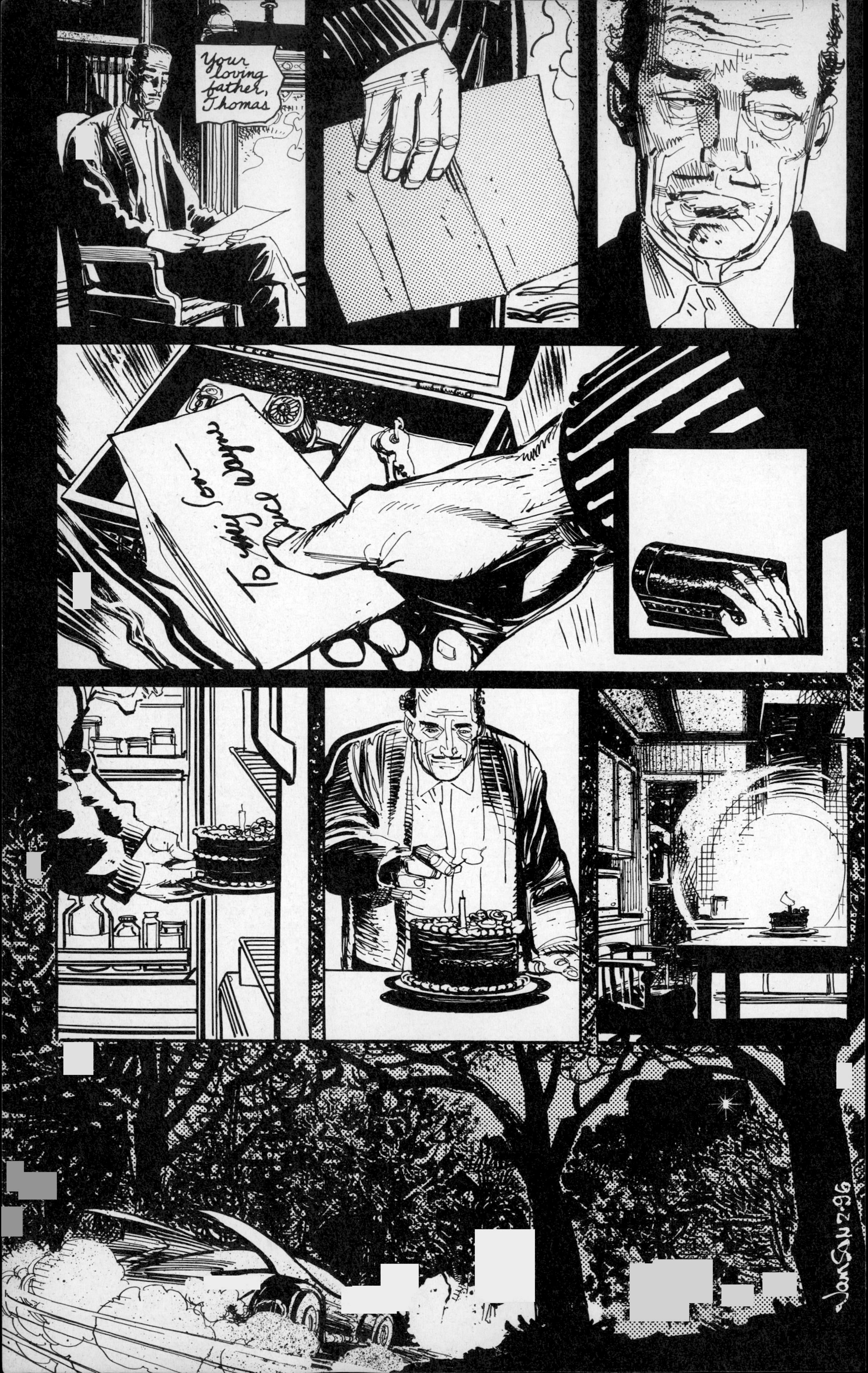
Your loving father, Thomas
To my son—
Bruce Wayne

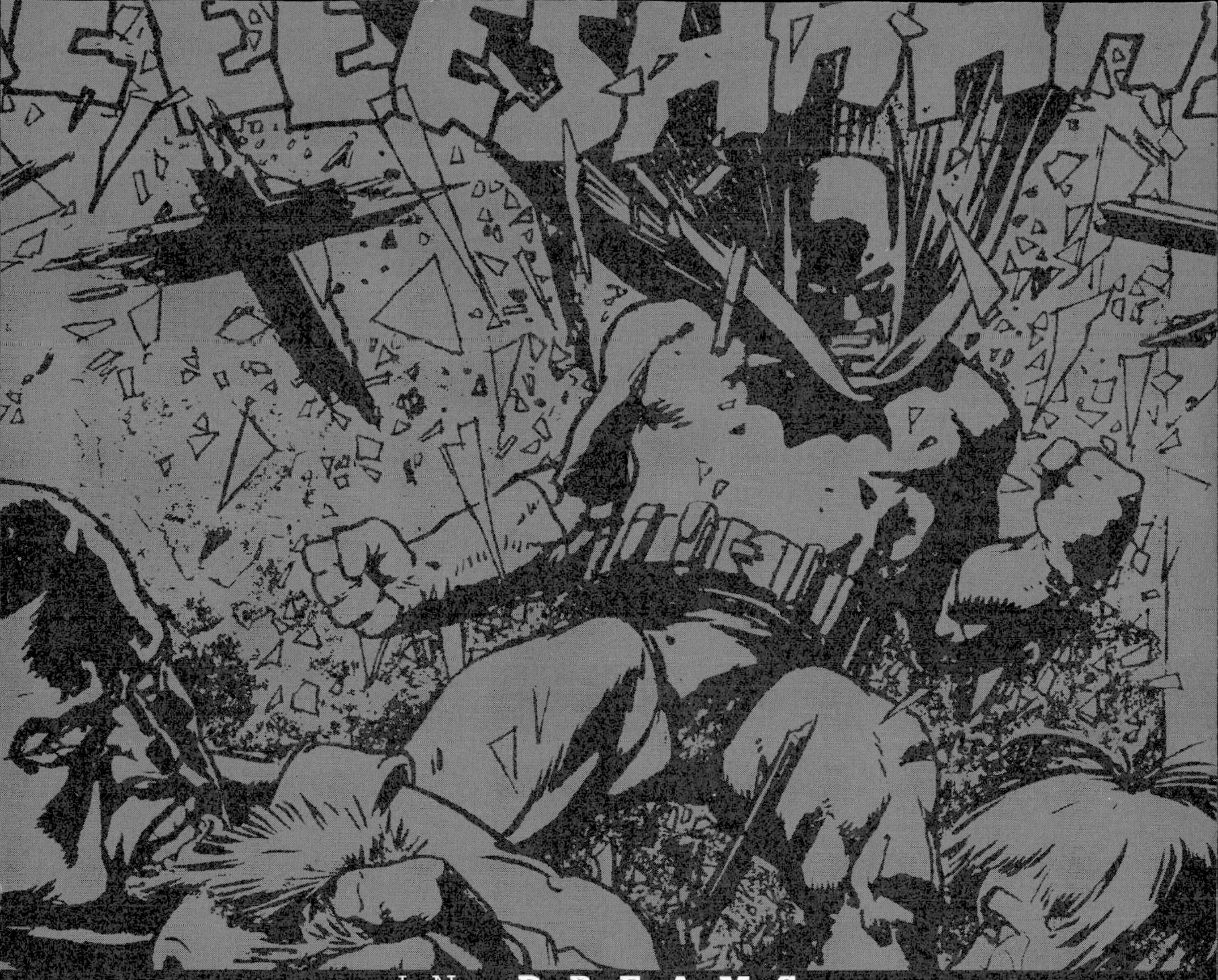

IN DREAMS

LIBERATORE

Italian artist Tanino Liberatore blew the comics world apart in the mid-1980's with his explosive creation *Ranxerox*, serialized in America in *Heavy Metal* magazine. Co-created with writer Stefano Tamburini, *Ranxerox* was an ultra-punk look at the absurdity of exaggerated super-heroic comic-book violence. Response from readers and fellow professionals was astounding, leading to some of *Heavy Metal's* biggest-selling issues. Liberatore takes a radical stylistic departure here with a much more sedate approach to storytelling for *In Dreams*.

ANDREW**HELFER**

In Dreams is not the first time Andrew Helfer has reinterpreted a classic character. His highly original take on THE SHADOW in the late 1980's was as controversial as it was groundbreaking.

He has also written television shows, children's books and film novelizations.

As an editor, Helfer has worked on practically every character in the DC Universe. He is currently Group Editor of DC's Paradox Press, which publishes the popular BIG BOOK series.

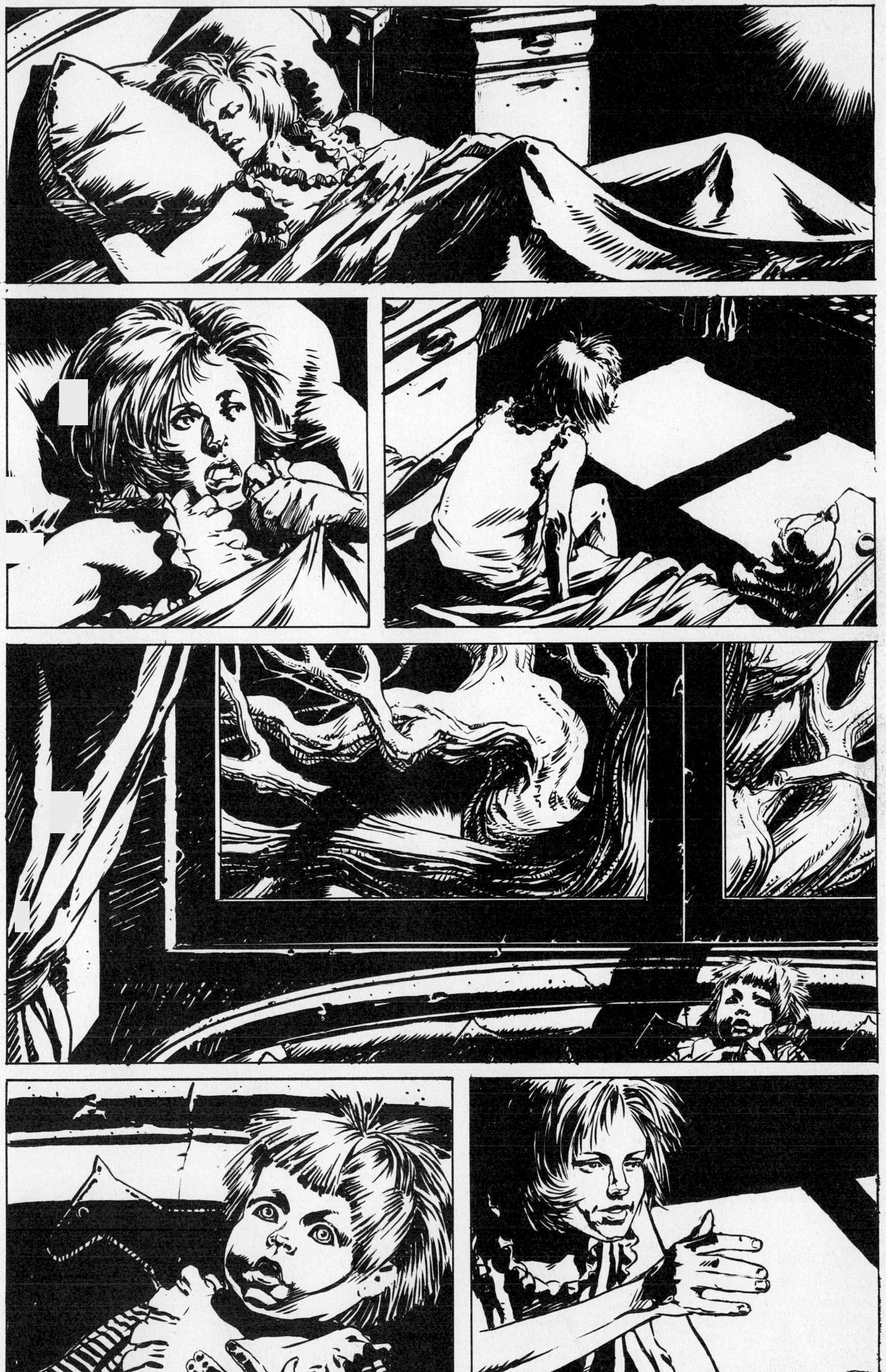

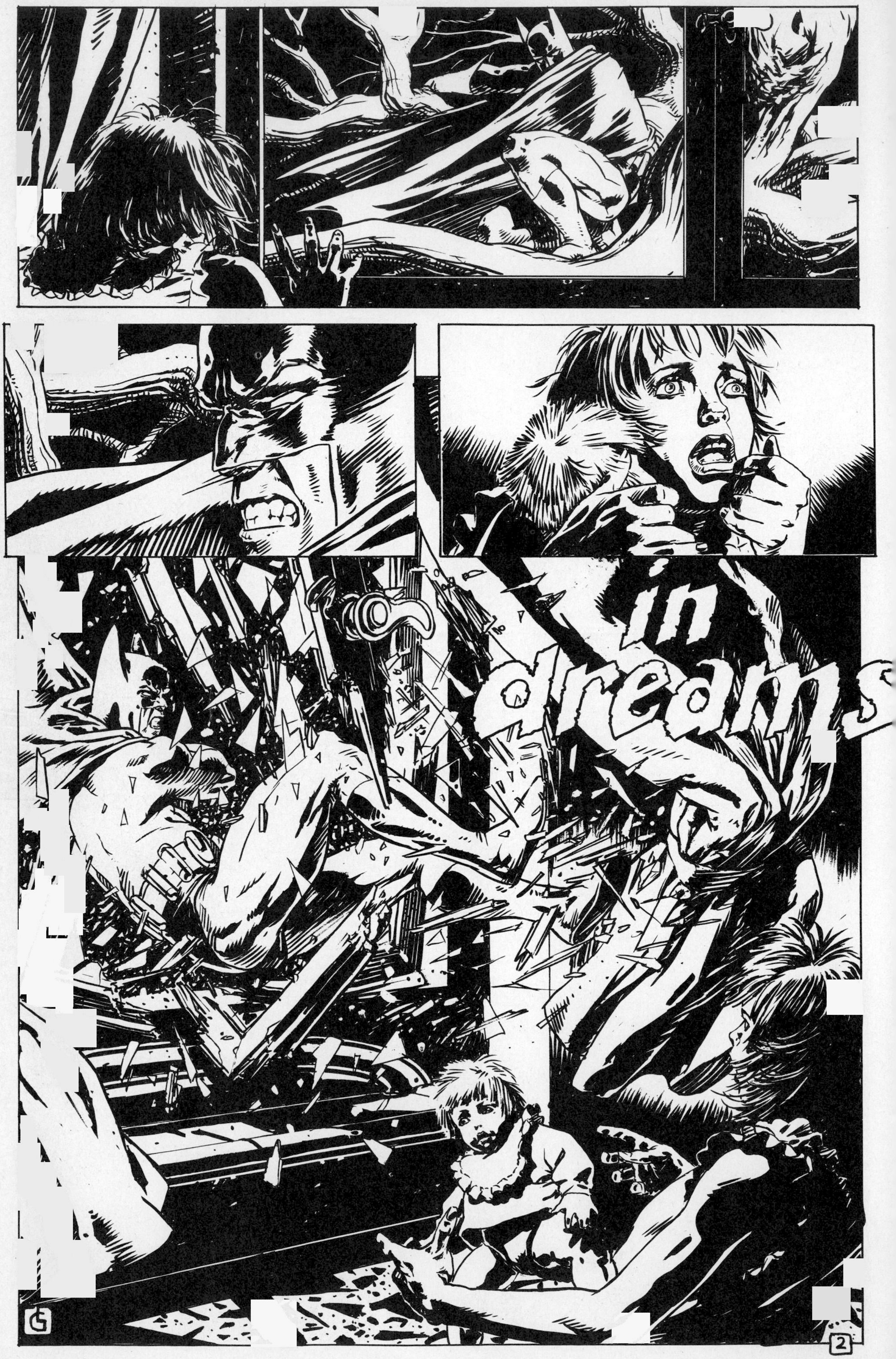
in dreams
2

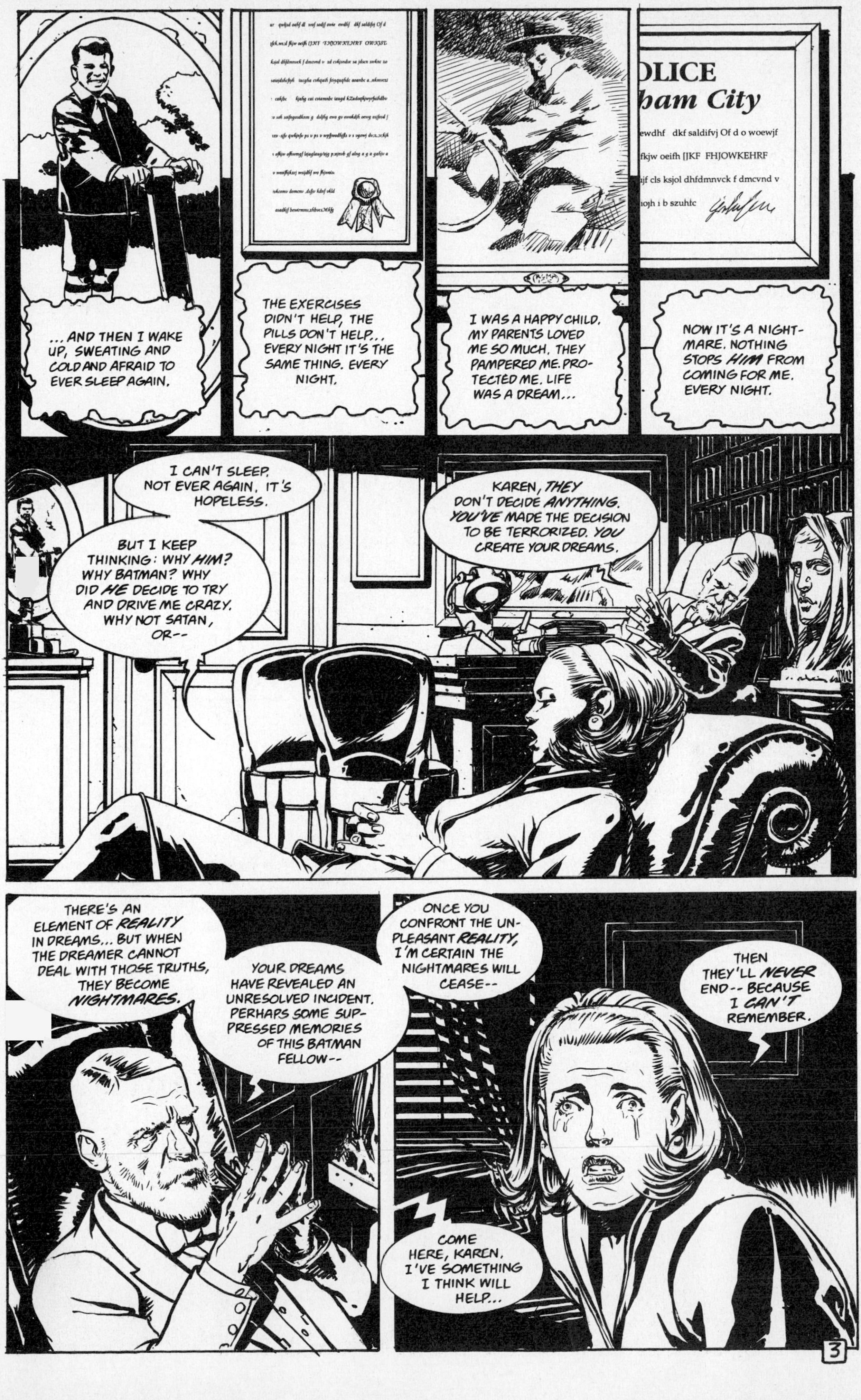
...AND THEN I WAKE UP, SWEATING AND COLD AND AFRAID TO EVER SLEEP AGAIN.
THE EXERCISES DIDN'T HELP, THE PILLS DON'T HELP... EVERY NIGHT IT'S THE SAME THING. EVERY NIGHT.
I WAS A HAPPY CHILD. MY PARENTS LOVED ME SO MUCH. THEY PAMPERED ME. PROTECTED ME. LIFE WAS A DREAM...
NOW IT'S A NIGHTMARE. NOTHING STOPS HIM FROM COMING FOR ME. EVERY NIGHT.
I CAN'T SLEEP. NOT EVER AGAIN. IT'S HOPELESS.
BUT I KEEP THINKING: WHY HIM? WHY BATMAN? WHY DID HE DECIDE TO TRY AND DRIVE ME CRAZY. WHY NOT SATAN, OR--
KAREN, THEY DON'T DECIDE ANYTHING. YOU'VE MADE THE DECISION TO BE TERRORIZED. YOU CREATE YOUR DREAMS.
THERE'S AN ELEMENT OF REALITY IN DREAMS... BUT WHEN THE DREAMER CANNOT DEAL WITH THOSE TRUTHS, THEY BECOME NIGHTMARES.
YOUR DREAMS HAVE REVEALED AN UNRESOLVED INCIDENT. PERHAPS SOME SUPPRESSED MEMORIES OF THIS BATMAN FELLOW--
ONCE YOU CONFRONT THE UNPLEASANT REALITY, I'M CERTAIN THE NIGHTMARES WILL CEASE--
THEN THEY'LL NEVER END-- BECAUSE I CAN'T REMEMBER.
COME HERE, KAREN. I'VE SOMETHING I THINK WILL HELP...
3

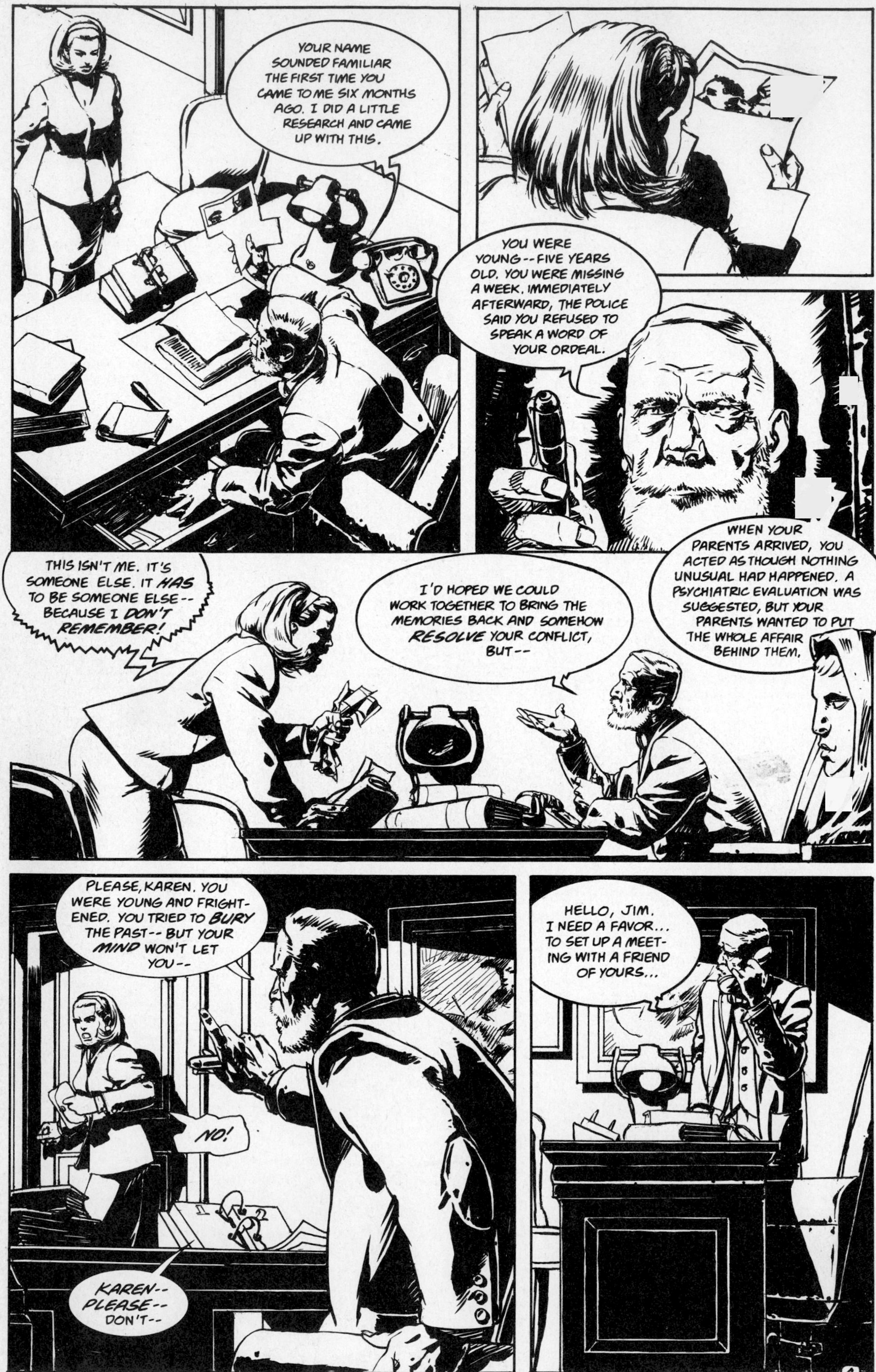
YOUR NAME SOUNDED FAMILIAR THE FIRST TIME YOU CAME TO ME SIX MONTHS AGO. I DID A LITTLE RESEARCH AND CAME UP WITH THIS.
YOU WERE YOUNG--FIVE YEARS OLD. YOU WERE MISSING A WEEK. IMMEDIATELY AFTERWARD, THE POLICE SAID YOU REFUSED TO SPEAK A WORD OF YOUR ORDEAL.
WHEN YOUR PARENTS ARRIVED, YOU ACTED AS THOUGH NOTHING UNUSUAL HAD HAPPENED. A PSYCHIATRIC EVALUATION WAS SUGGESTED, BUT YOUR PARENTS WANTED TO PUT THE WHOLE AFFAIR BEHIND THEM.
THIS ISN'T ME. IT'S SOMEONE ELSE. IT HAS TO BE SOMEONE ELSE--BECAUSE I DON'T REMEMBER!
I'D HOPED WE COULD WORK TOGETHER TO BRING THE MEMORIES BACK AND SOMEHOW RESOLVE YOUR CONFLICT, BUT--
PLEASE, KAREN. YOU WERE YOUNG AND FRIGHT-ENED. YOU TRIED TO BURY THE PAST--BUT YOUR MIND WON'T LET YOU--
NO!
KAREN--PLEASE--DON'T--
HELLO, JIM. I NEED A FAVOR... TO SET UP A MEET-ING WITH A FRIEND OF YOURS...
4

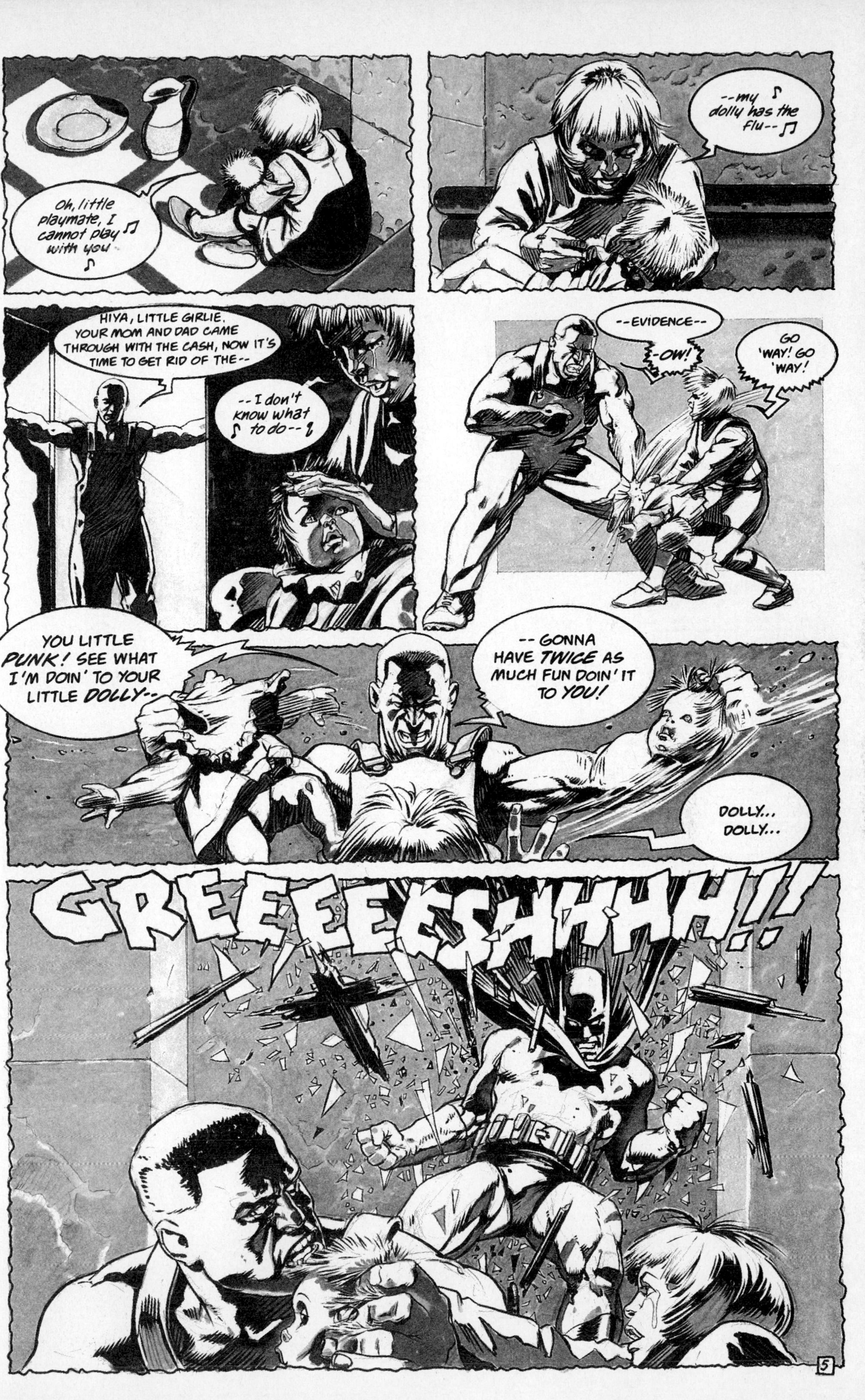
Oh, little playmate, I cannot play with you
--my dolly has the flu--
HIYA, LITTLE GIRLIE. YOUR MOM AND DAD CAME THROUGH WITH THE CASH, NOW IT'S TIME TO GET RID OF THE--
--I don't know what to do--
--EVIDENCE--
-OW!
GO 'WAY! GO 'WAY!
YOU LITTLE PUNK! SEE WHAT I'M DOIN' TO YOUR LITTLE DOLLY--
--GONNA HAVE TWICE AS MUCH FUN DOIN' IT TO YOU!
DOLLY... DOLLY...
GREEEEESHHHH!!
5

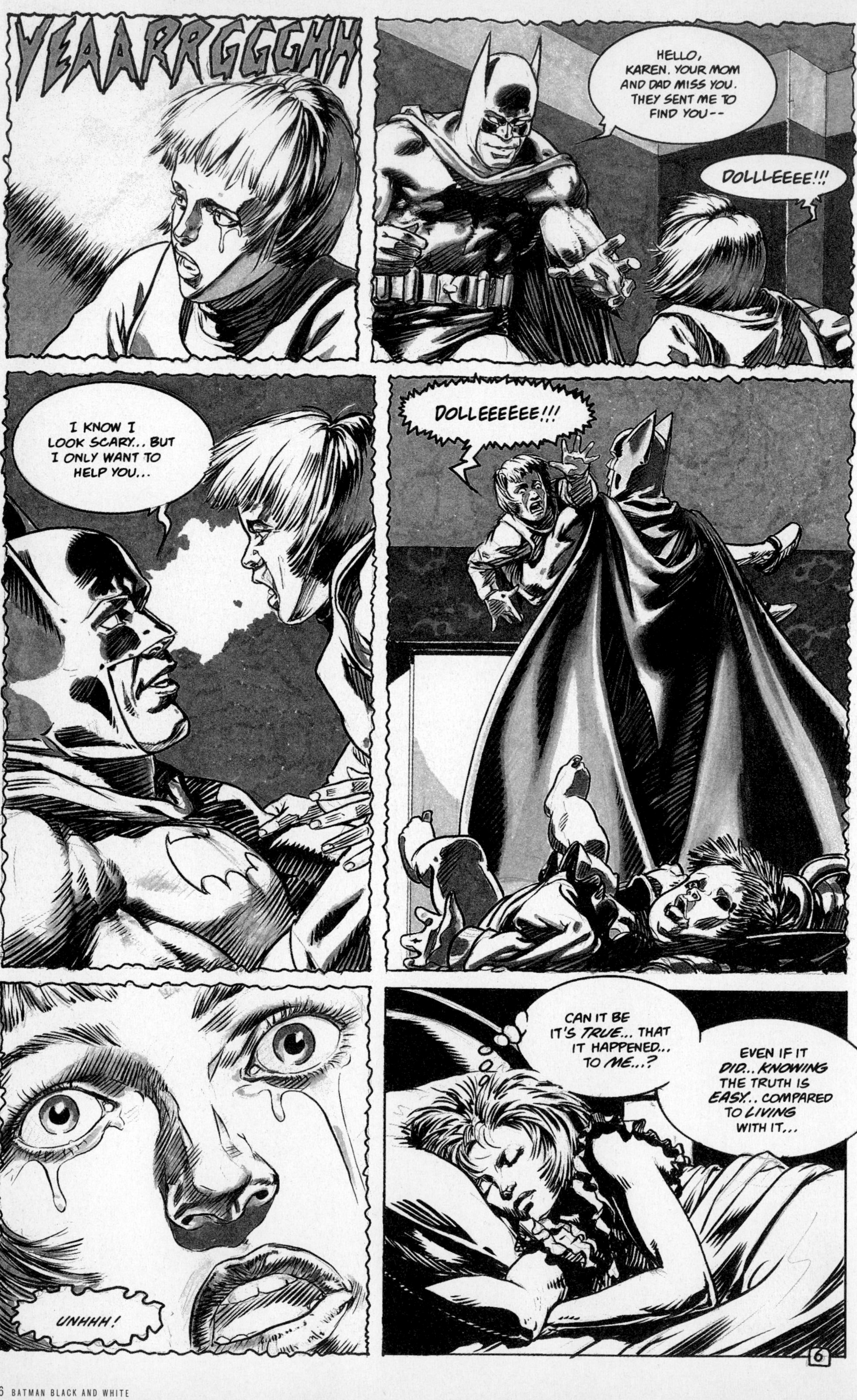
YEAARRGGGHH
HELLO, KAREN. YOUR MOM AND DAD MISS YOU. THEY SENT ME TO FIND YOU--
DOLLLEEEE!!!
I KNOW I LOOK SCARY... BUT I ONLY WANT TO HELP YOU...
DOLLEEEEEEE!!!
UNHHH!
CAN IT BE IT'S TRUE... THAT IT HAPPENED... TO ME...?
EVEN IF IT DID... KNOWING THE TRUTH IS EASY... COMPARED TO LIVING WITH IT...
6

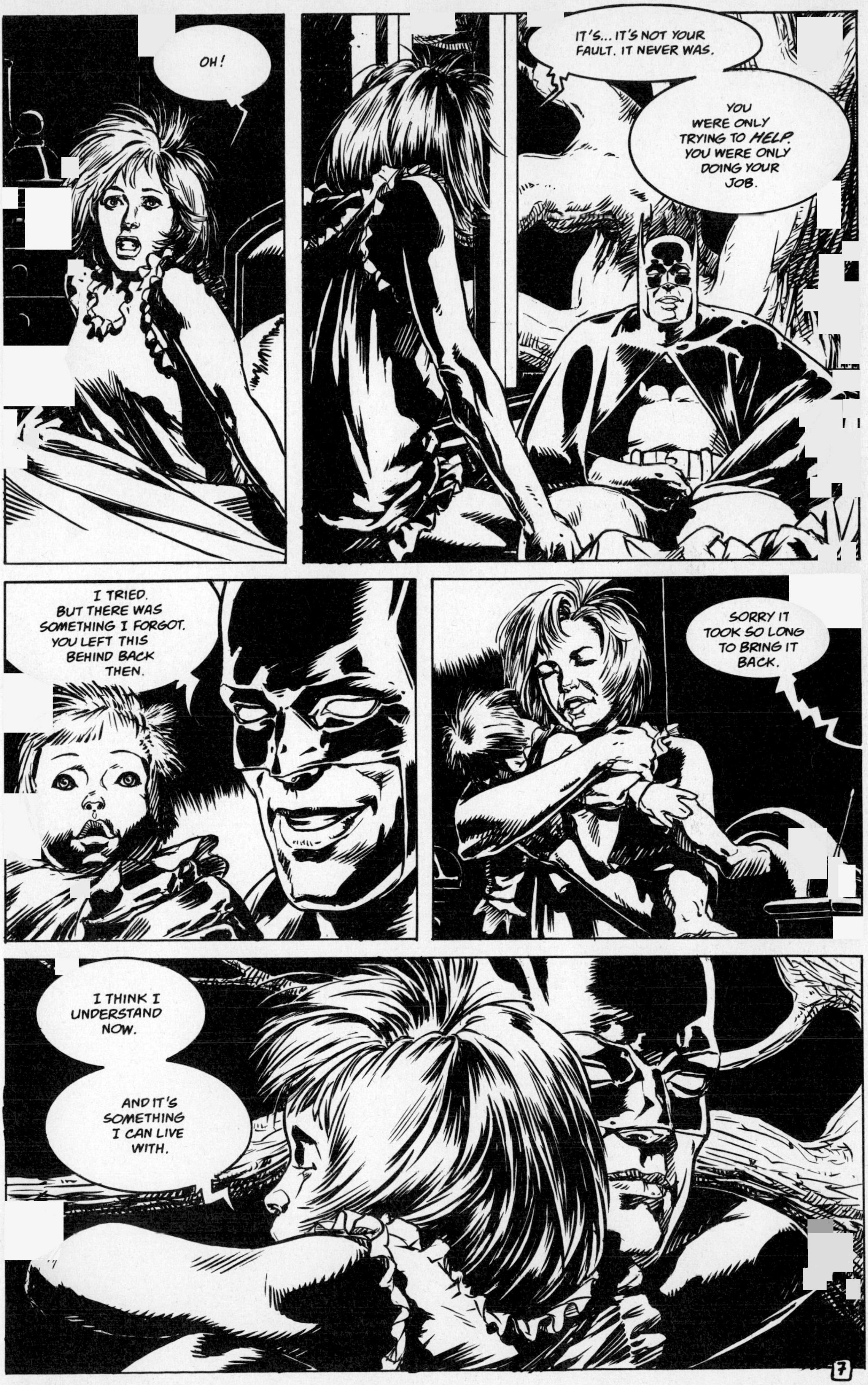
OH!
IT'S... IT'S NOT YOUR FAULT. IT NEVER WAS.
YOU WERE ONLY TRYING TO HELP. YOU WERE ONLY DOING YOUR JOB.
I TRIED. BUT THERE WAS SOMETHING I FORGOT. YOU LEFT THIS BEHIND BACK THEN.
SORRY IT TOOK SO LONG TO BRING IT BACK.
I THINK I UNDERSTAND NOW.
AND IT'S SOMETHING I CAN LIVE WITH.
7

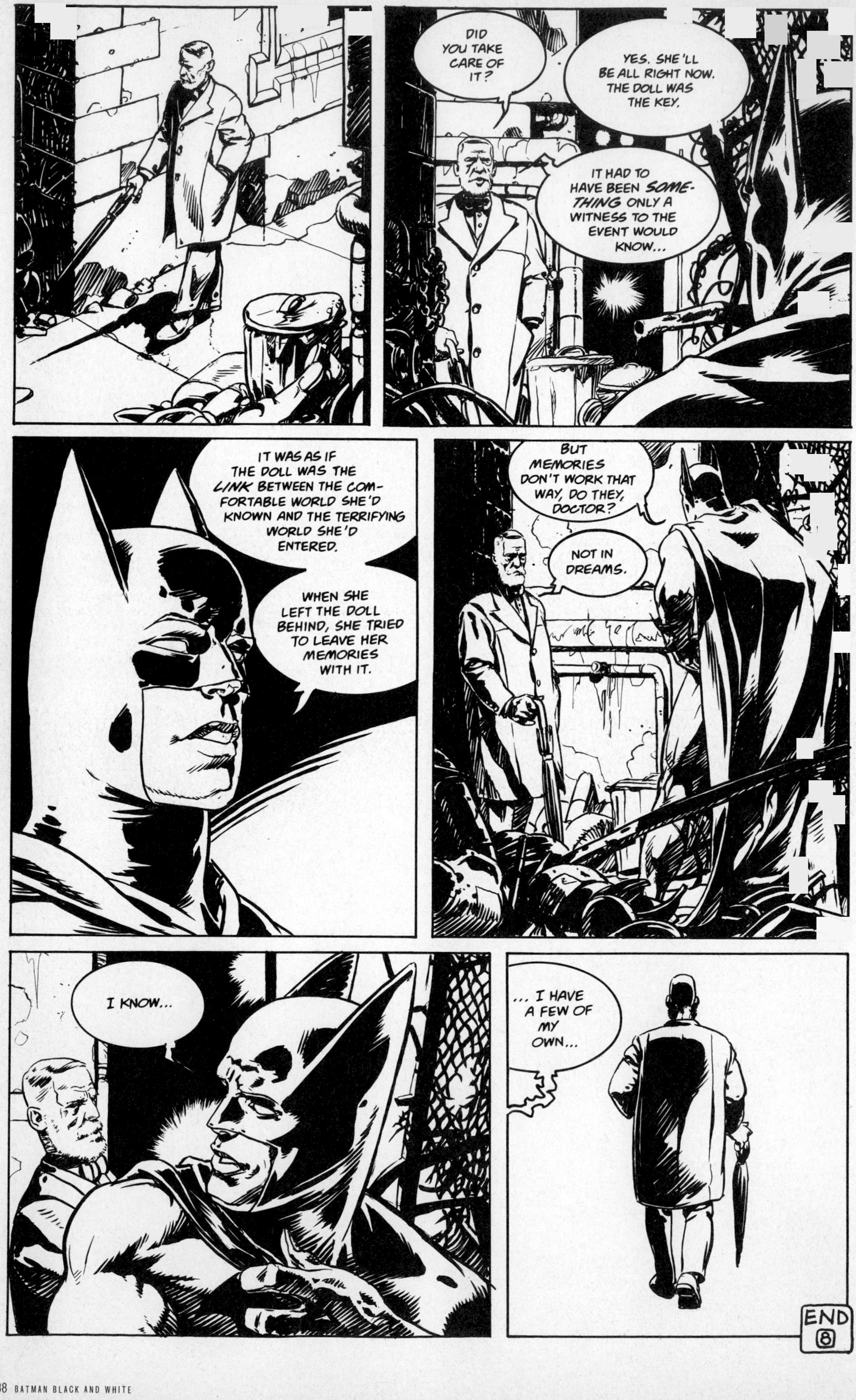

DID YOU TAKE CARE OF IT?
YES. SHE'LL BE ALL RIGHT NOW. THE DOLL WAS THE KEY.
IT HAD TO HAVE BEEN SOME-THING ONLY A WITNESS TO THE EVENT WOULD KNOW...
IT WAS AS IF THE DOLL WAS THE LINK BETWEEN THE COM-FORTABLE WORLD SHE'D KNOWN AND THE TERRIFYING WORLD SHE'D ENTERED.
WHEN SHE LEFT THE DOLL BEHIND, SHE TRIED TO LEAVE HER MEMORIES WITH IT.
BUT MEMORIES DON'T WORK THAT WAY, DO THEY, DOCTOR?
NOT IN DREAMS.
I KNOW...
... I HAVE A FEW OF MY OWN...
END 8

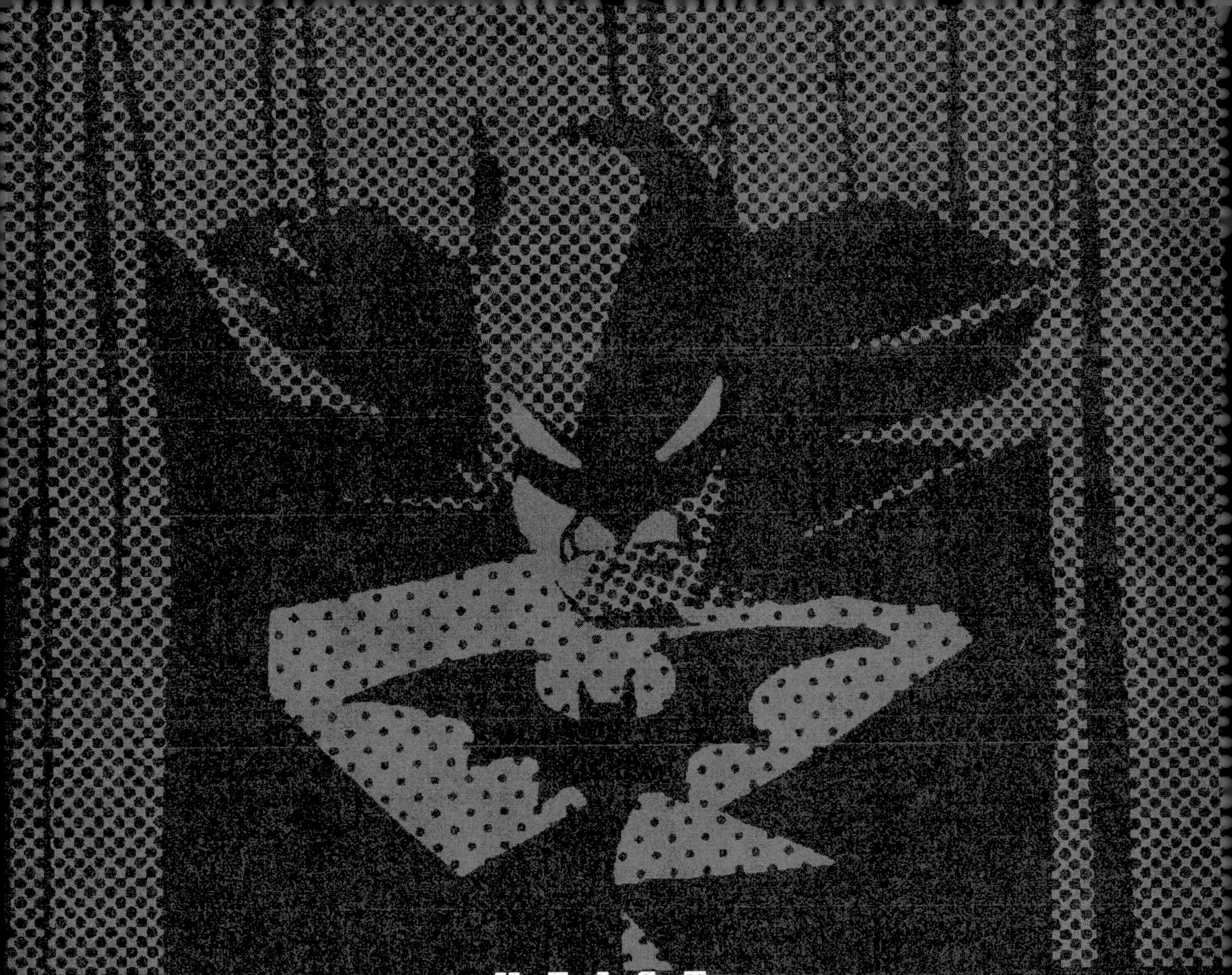

H E I S T

MATT WAGNER

Matt Wagner's work straddles the fence between an eccentric, underground world view and a traditional, highly graphic design and drawing style.

The elaborate worlds of his creator-owned titles *Grendel* and *Mage* have spawned a legion of diehard Matt Wagner fans. Those same fans can get a more mainstream dose of Matt's work in occasional one-shots and miniseries like BATMAN: FACES and BATMAN/GRENDEL as well as Matt's monthly writing chores on SANDMAN MYSTERY THEATRE.

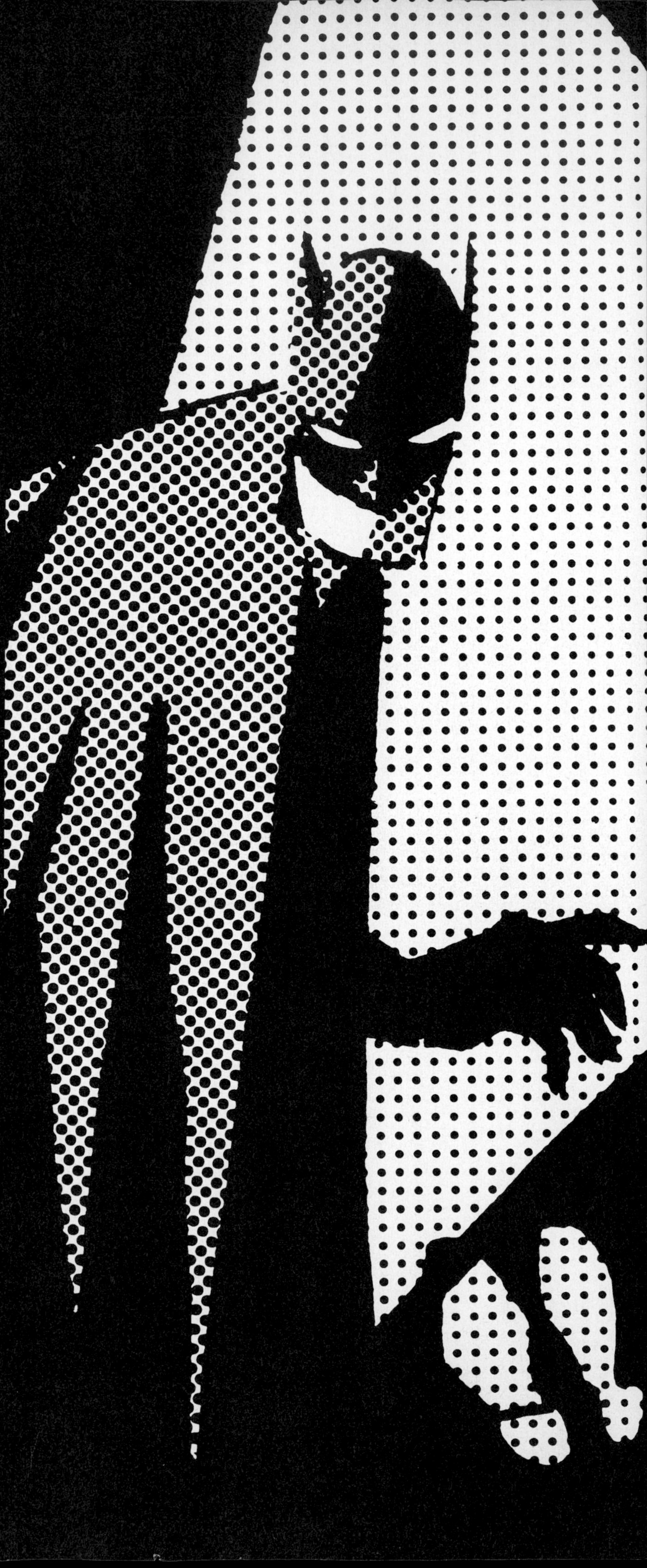

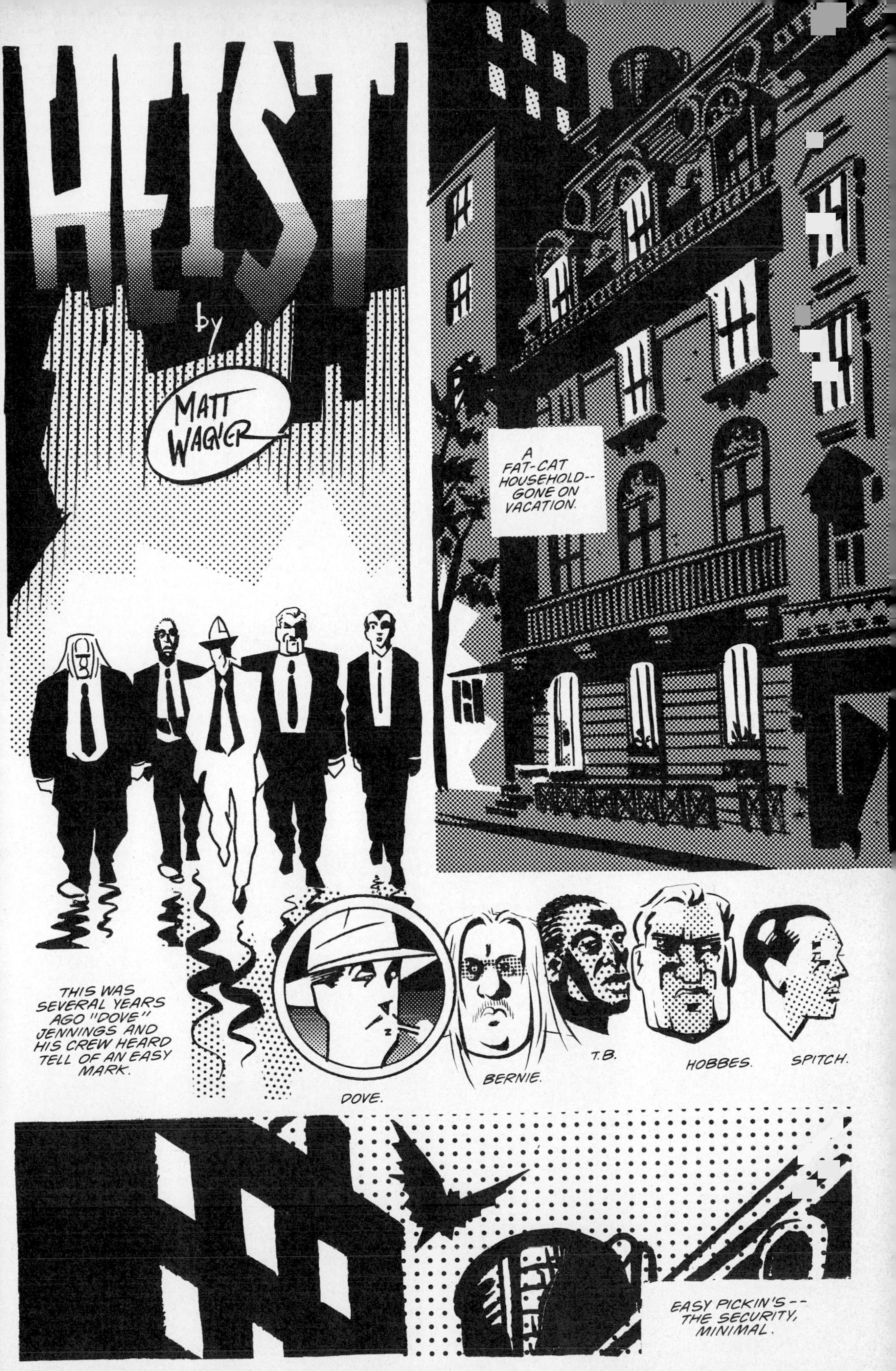
HEIST
by
MATT WAGNER
A FAT-CAT HOUSEHOLD-- GONE ON VACATION.
THIS WAS SEVERAL YEARS AGO "DOVE" JENNINGS AND HIS CREW HEARD TELL OF AN EASY MARK.
DOVE.
BERNIE.
T.B.
HOBBES.
SPITCH.
EASY PICKIN'S -- THE SECURITY, MINIMAL.

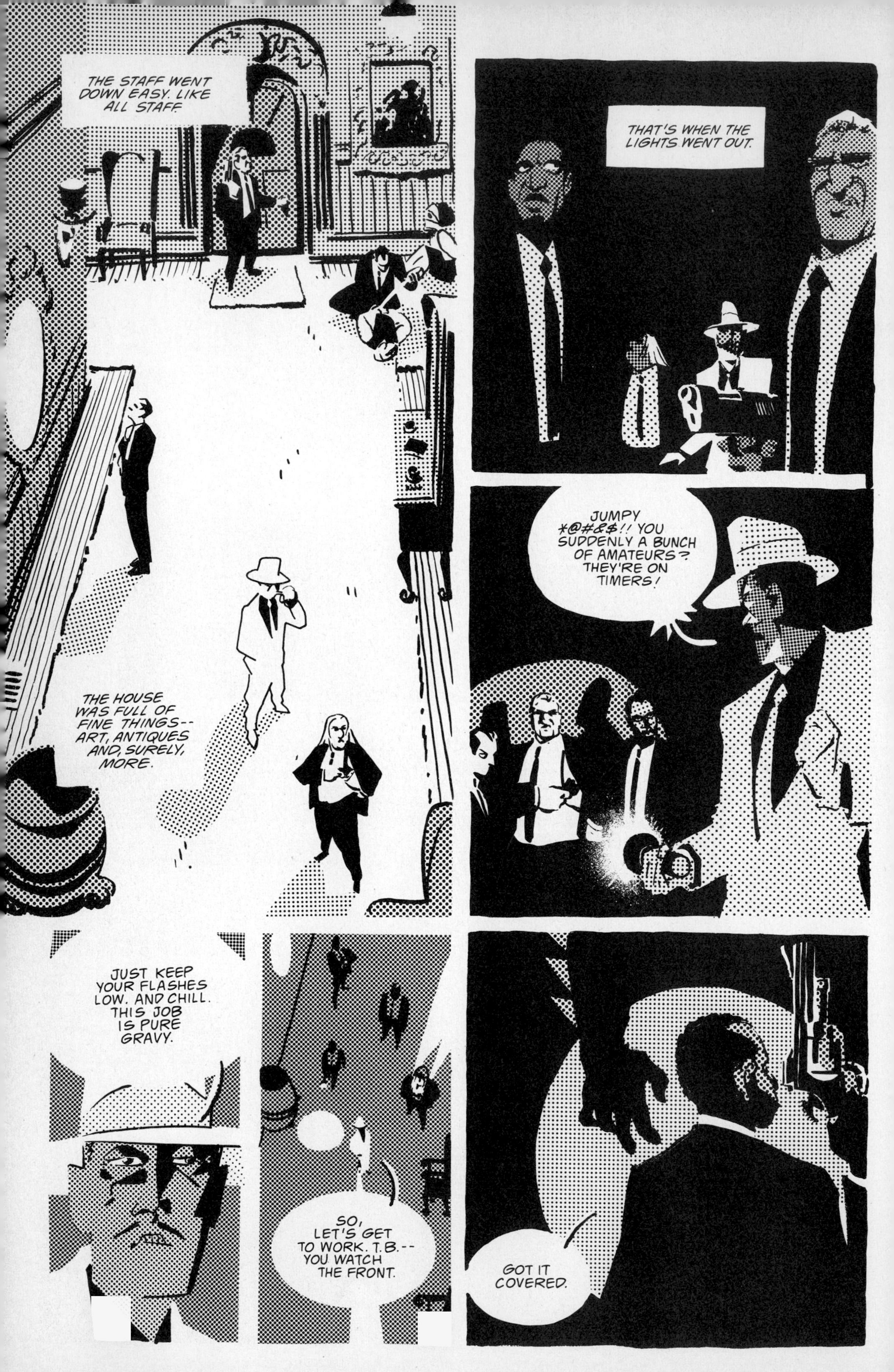

THE STAFF WENT DOWN EASY. LIKE ALL STAFF.
THE HOUSE WAS FULL OF FINE THINGS-- ART, ANTIQUES AND, SURELY, MORE.
THAT'S WHEN THE LIGHTS WENT OUT.
JUMPY *@#&$!! YOU SUDDENLY A BUNCH OF AMATEURS? THEY'RE ON TIMERS!
JUST KEEP YOUR FLASHES LOW. AND CHILL. THIS JOB IS PURE GRAVY.
SO, LET'S GET TO WORK. T.B.-- YOU WATCH THE FRONT.
GOT IT COVERED.

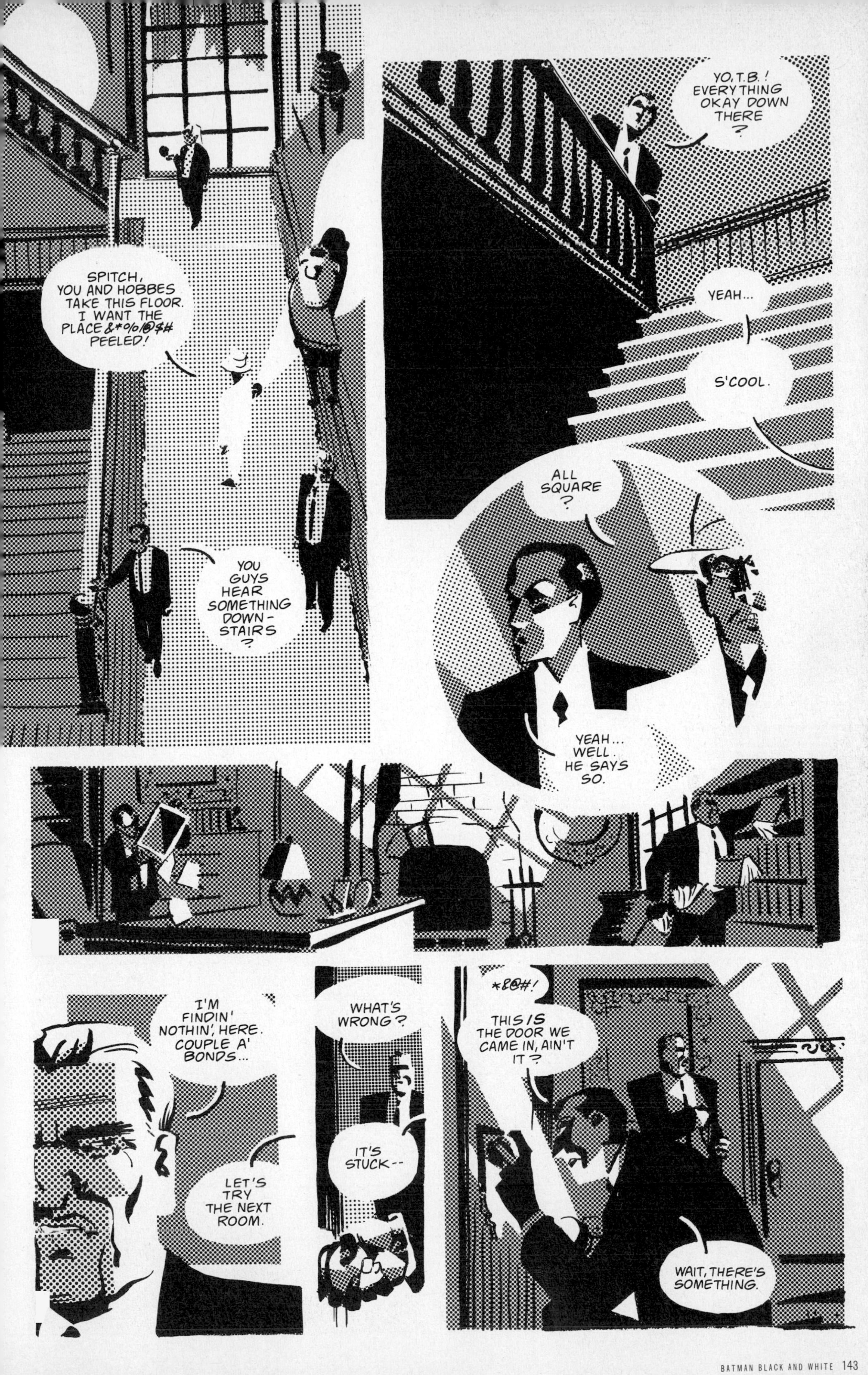
SPITCH, YOU AND HOBBES TAKE THIS FLOOR. I WANT THE PLACE &*%!@$# PEELED!
YOU GUYS HEAR SOMETHING DOWN-STAIRS ?
YO, T.B.! EVERYTHING OKAY DOWN THERE ?
YEAH...
S'COOL.
ALL SQUARE ?
YEAH... WELL. HE SAYS SO.
I'M FINDIN' NOTHIN', HERE. COUPLE A' BONDS...
LET'S TRY THE NEXT ROOM.
WHAT'S WRONG ?
IT'S STUCK--
*&@#!
THIS IS THE DOOR WE CAME IN, AIN'T IT ?
WAIT, THERE'S SOMETHING.

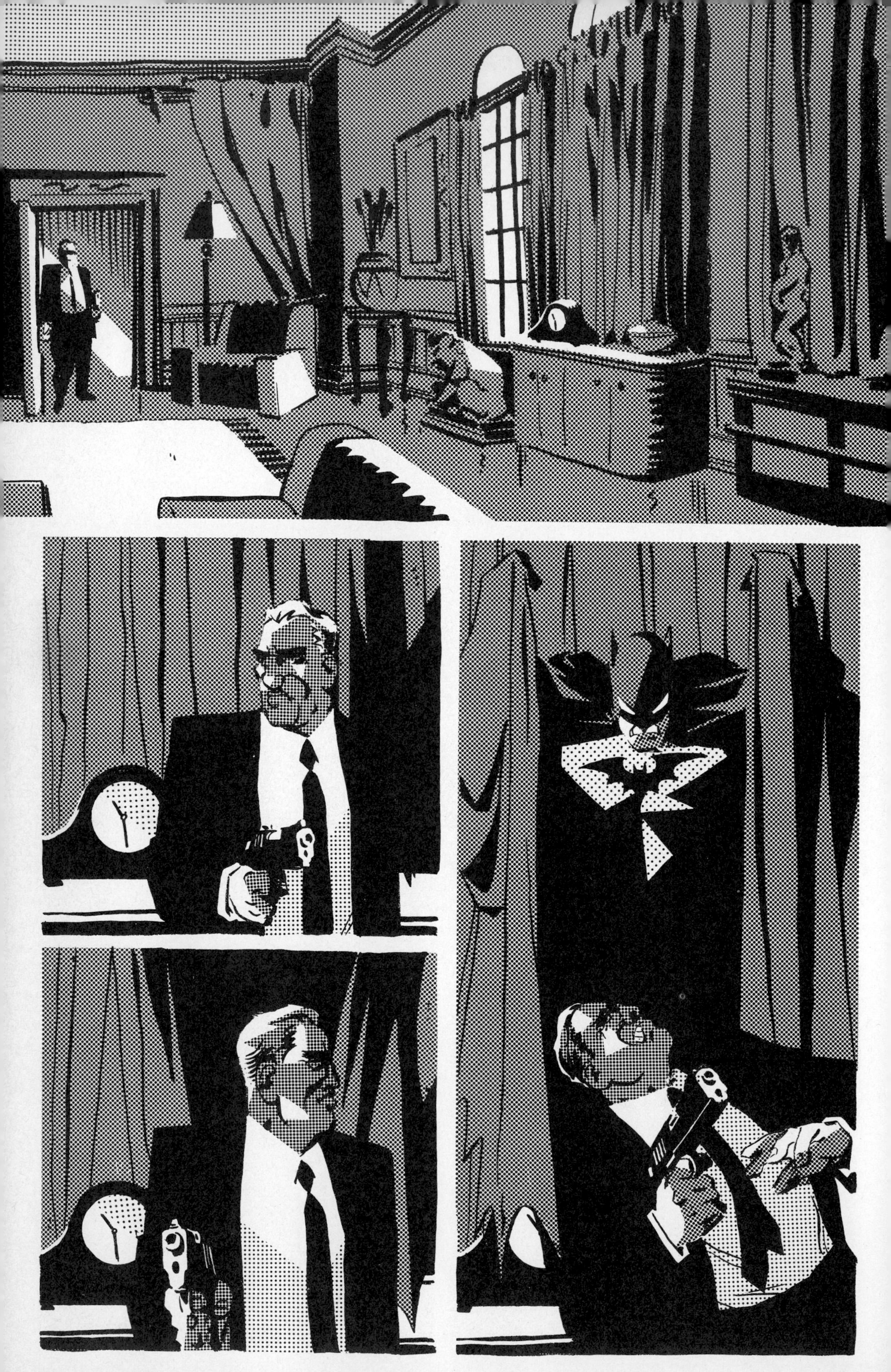

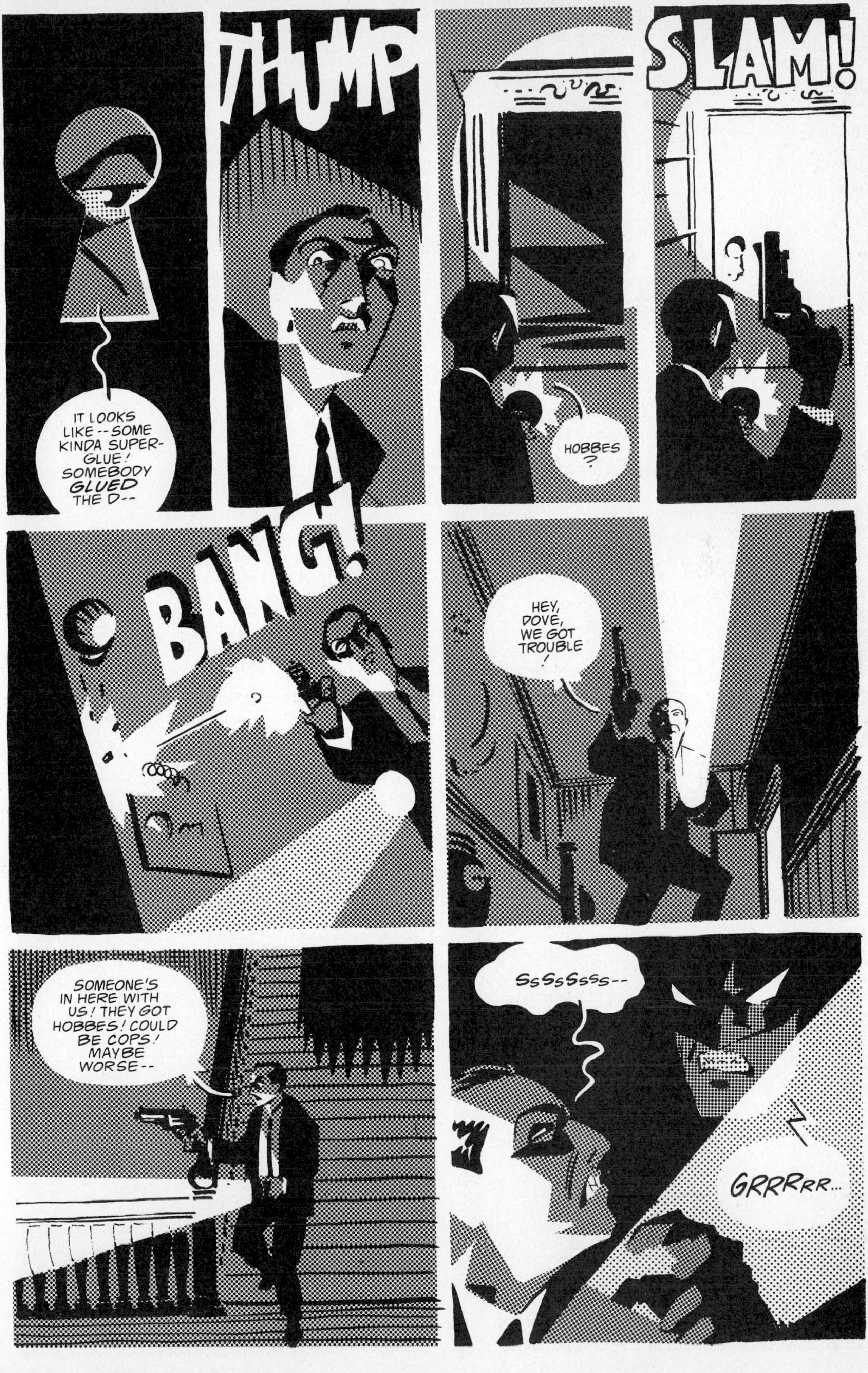
IT LOOKS LIKE -- SOME KINDA SUPER-GLUE! SOMEBODY GLUED THE D--
THUMP
HOBBES?
SLAM!
BANG!
HEY, DOVE, WE GOT TROUBLE!
SOMEONE'S IN HERE WITH US! THEY GOT HOBBES! COULD BE COPS! MAYBE WORSE--
SsSsSsss--
GRRRrr...

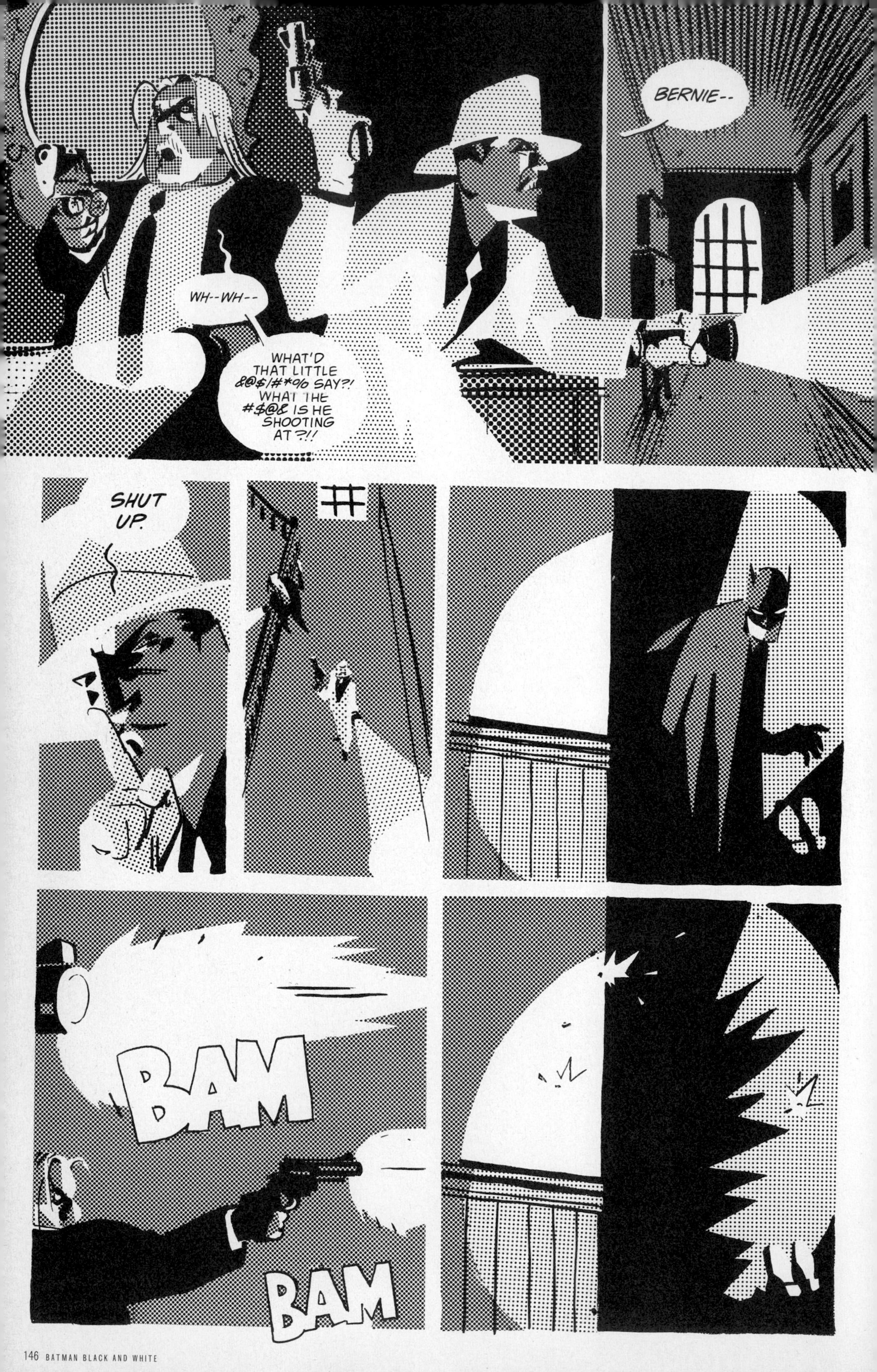
BERNIE--
WH--WH--
WHAT'D THAT LITTLE &@$/#*% SAY?! WHAT THE #$@£ IS HE SHOOTING AT?!!
SHUT UP.
BAM
BAM

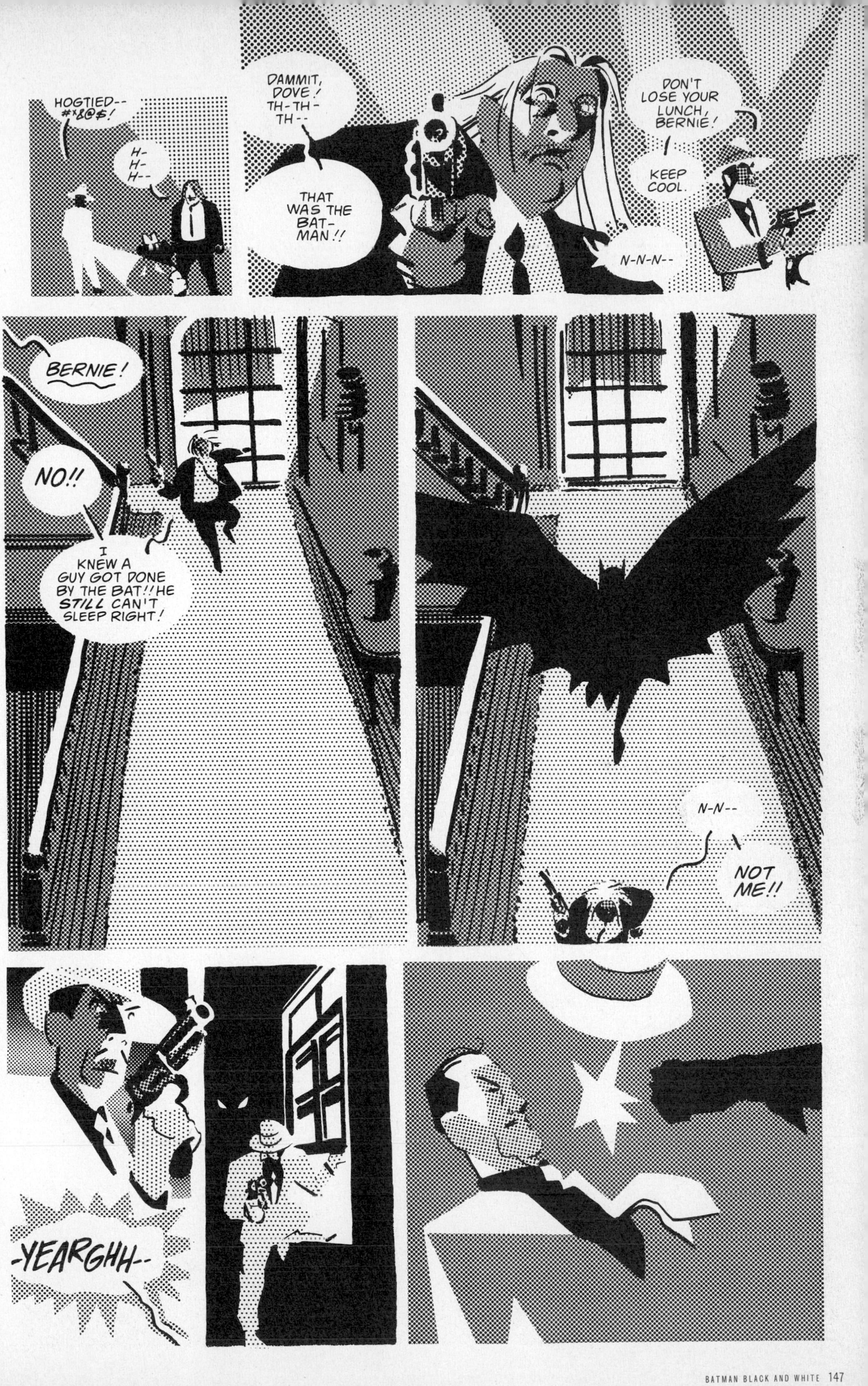
HOGTIED-- #*&@$!
H- H- H--
DAMMIT, DOVE! TH-TH-TH--
THAT WAS THE BAT-MAN!!
DON'T LOSE YOUR LUNCH, BERNIE!
KEEP COOL.
N-N-N--
BERNIE!
NO!!
I KNEW A GUY GOT DONE BY THE BAT!! HE STILL CAN'T SLEEP RIGHT!
N-N--
NOT ME!!
-YEARGHH--

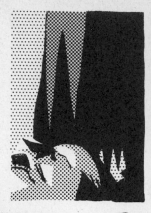

LATER, ACTING ON AN ANONYMOUS TIP--

THE COPS SHOWED UP TO FIND THE DOVE JENNINGS CREW, RED-HANDED AND GIFT-WRAPPED.

THE CALLER HADN'T LEFT HIS NAME, BUT HE DID LEAVE HIS MARK.

HEAR TELL, DOVE STILL CAN'T WIPE

⬙ END ⬙

BENT **TWIGS**

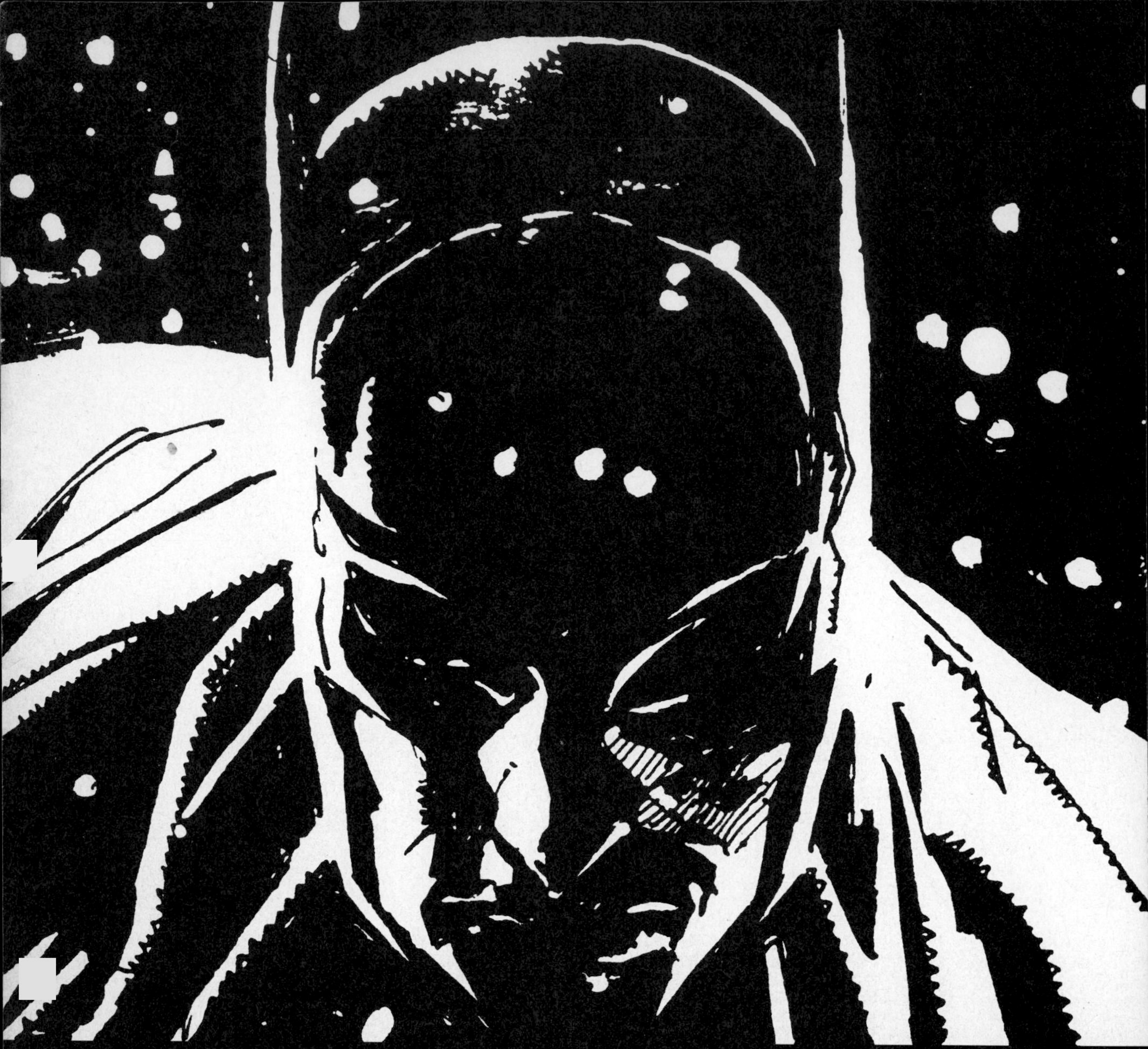

BILL SIENKIEWICZ

Bill Sienkiewicz is a master of incendiary comic art. His astounding drawing ability, design and color sense have assured him a place in comic-book history. Bill has won almost every major award in the comics world including the Eagle, Inkpot, Kirby and Yellow Kid as well as several Merit Awards from the Society of Illustrators.

Among Bill's award-winning credits are *Elektra: Assassin, Stray Toasters* and *Voodoo Child: The Illustrated Legend of Jimi Hendrix.*

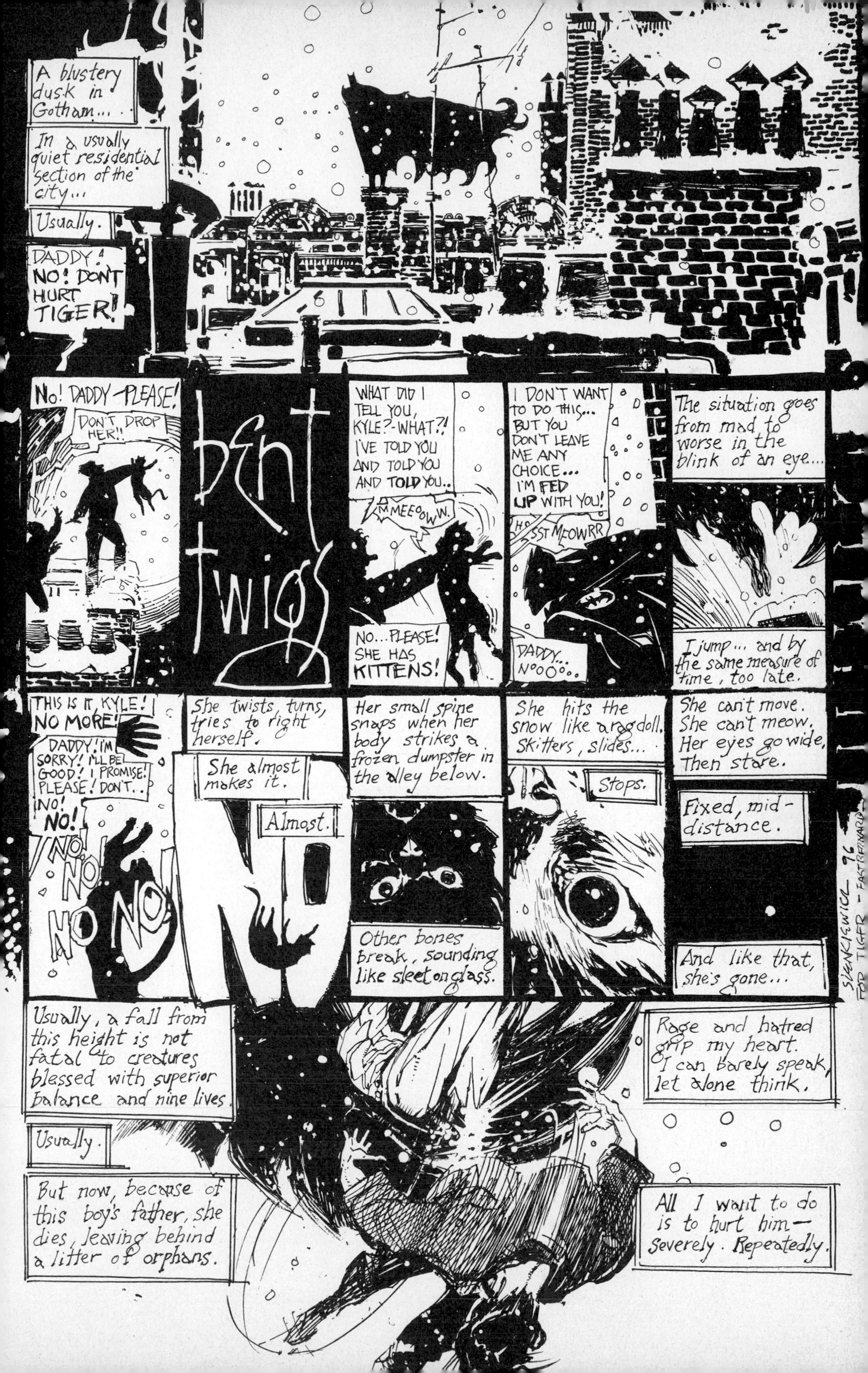

A blustery dusk in Gotham...
In a usually quiet residential section of the city...
Usually.
DADDY! NO! DON'T HURT TIGER!
No! DADDY-PLEASE!
DON'T DROP HER!!
bent twigs
WHAT DID I TELL YOU, KYLE?-WHAT?! I'VE TOLD YOU AND TOLD YOU AND TOLD YOU..
MMEEOOWW.
NO...PLEASE! SHE HAS KITTENS!
I DON'T WANT TO DO THIS... BUT YOU DON'T LEAVE ME ANY CHOICE... I'M FED UP WITH YOU!
SST MEOWRR
DADDY... NOOO...
The situation goes from mad to worse in the blink of an eye...
I jump... and by the same measure of time, too late.
THIS IS IT, KYLE! NO MORE!
DADDY! I'M SORRY! I'LL BE GOOD! I PROMISE! PLEASE! DON'T... NO!
NO!
NO! NO! NO! NO!
She twists, turns, tries to right herself.
She almost makes it.
Almost.
Her small spine snaps when her body strikes a frozen dumpster in the alley below.
Other bones break, sounding like sleet on glass.
She hits the snow like a ragdoll. Skitters, slides...
Stops.
She can't move. She can't meow. Her eyes go wide, then stare.
Fixed, mid-distance.
And like that, she's gone...
SIENKIEWICZ 96
FOR TIGER - FAST BERNARD
Usually, a fall from this height is not fatal to creatures blessed with superior balance and nine lives.
Usually.
But now, because of this boy's father, she dies, leaving behind a litter of orphans.
Rage and hatred grip my heart. I can barely speak, let alone think.
All I want to do is to hurt him—severely. Repeatedly.

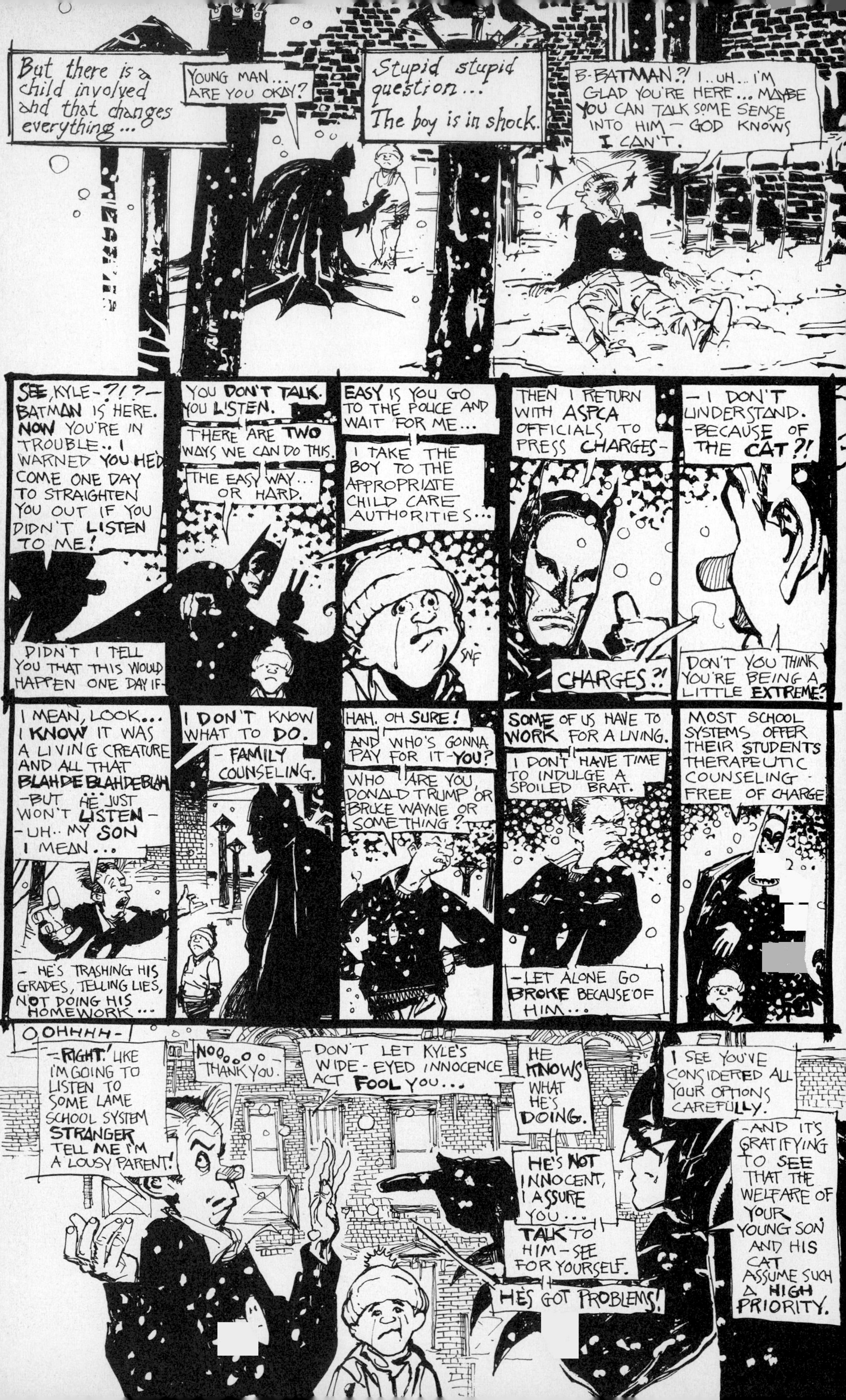
But there is a child involved and that changes everything...
YOUNG MAN... ARE YOU OKAY?
Stupid stupid question...
The boy is in shock.
B-BATMAN?! I...UH... I'M GLAD YOU'RE HERE... MAYBE YOU CAN TALK SOME SENSE INTO HIM — GOD KNOWS I CAN'T.
SEE, KYLE-?!?— BATMAN IS HERE. NOW YOU'RE IN TROUBLE.. I WARNED YOU HE'D COME ONE DAY TO STRAIGHTEN YOU OUT IF YOU DIDN'T LISTEN TO ME!
DIDN'T I TELL YOU THAT THIS WOULD HAPPEN ONE DAY IF-
YOU DON'T TALK. YOU LISTEN.
THERE ARE TWO WAYS WE CAN DO THIS.
THE EASY WAY... OR HARD.
EASY IS YOU GO TO THE POLICE AND WAIT FOR ME...
I TAKE THE BOY TO THE APPROPRIATE CHILD CARE AUTHORITIES...
THEN I RETURN WITH ASPCA OFFICIALS TO PRESS CHARGES-
CHARGES?!
-I DON'T UNDERSTAND. -BECAUSE OF THE CAT?!
DON'T YOU THINK YOU'RE BEING A LITTLE EXTREME?
I MEAN, LOOK... I KNOW IT WAS A LIVING CREATURE AND ALL THAT BLAHDEBLAHDEBLAH. -BUT HE JUST WON'T LISTEN- -UH.. MY SON I MEAN...
- HE'S TRASHING HIS GRADES, TELLING LIES, NOT DOING HIS HOMEWORK...
I DON'T KNOW WHAT TO DO.
- FAMILY COUNSELING.
HAH. OH SURE!
AND WHO'S GONNA PAY FOR IT-YOU?
WHO ARE YOU, DONALD TRUMP OR BRUCE WAYNE OR SOMETHING?
SOME OF US HAVE TO WORK FOR A LIVING.
I DON'T HAVE TIME TO INDULGE A SPOILED BRAT.
-LET ALONE GO BROKE BECAUSE OF HIM...
MOST SCHOOL SYSTEMS OFFER THEIR STUDENTS THERAPEUTIC COUNSELING - FREE OF CHARGE
OOHHHH-
-RIGHT! LIKE I'M GOING TO LISTEN TO SOME LAME SCHOOL SYSTEM STRANGER TELL ME I'M A LOUSY PARENT!
NOooooo THANK YOU.
DON'T LET KYLE'S WIDE-EYED INNOCENCE ACT FOOL YOU...
HE KNOWS WHAT HE'S DOING.
HE'S NOT INNOCENT, I ASSURE YOU...
TALK TO HIM - SEE FOR YOURSELF.
HE'S GOT PROBLEMS!
I SEE YOU'VE CONSIDERED ALL YOUR OPTIONS CAREFULLY.
-AND IT'S GRATIFYING TO SEE THAT THE WELFARE OF YOUR YOUNG SON AND HIS CAT ASSUME SUCH A HIGH PRIORITY.

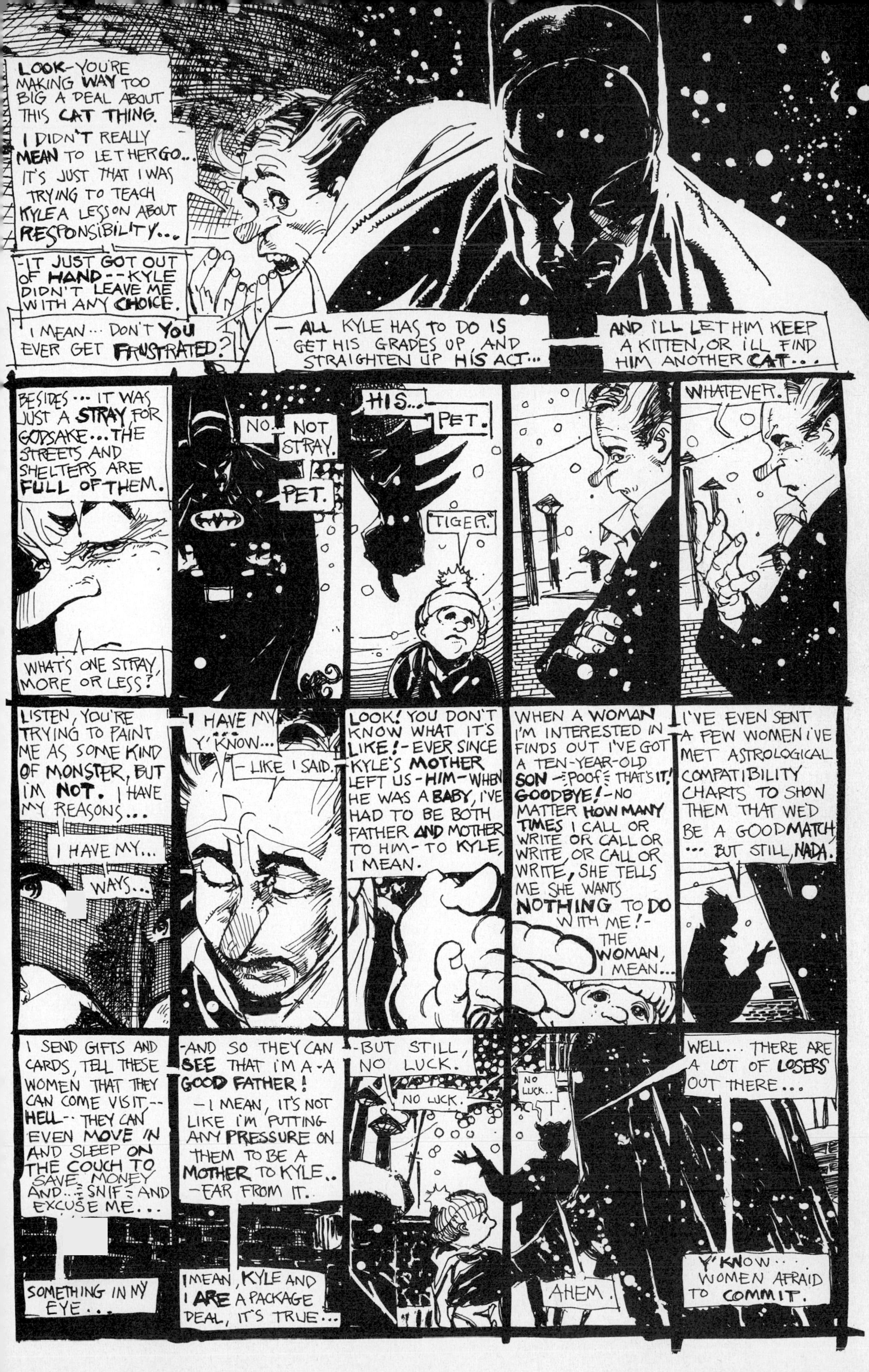
LOOK- YOU'RE MAKING WAY TOO BIG A DEAL ABOUT THIS CAT THING.
I DIDN'T REALLY MEAN TO LET HER GO... IT'S JUST THAT I WAS TRYING TO TEACH KYLE A LESSON ABOUT RESPONSIBILITY...
-IT JUST GOT OUT OF HAND--KYLE DIDN'T LEAVE ME WITH ANY CHOICE.
I MEAN... DON'T YOU EVER GET FRUSTRATED?
-ALL KYLE HAS TO DO IS GET HIS GRADES UP, AND STRAIGHTEN UP HIS ACT...
AND I'LL LET HIM KEEP A KITTEN, OR I'LL FIND HIM ANOTHER CAT...
BESIDES... IT WAS JUST A STRAY FOR GODSAKE... THE STREETS AND SHELTERS ARE FULL OF THEM.
WHAT'S ONE STRAY, MORE OR LESS?
NO... NOT STRAY.
PET.
HIS...
PET.
"TIGER."
WHATEVER.
LISTEN, YOU'RE TRYING TO PAINT ME AS SOME KIND OF MONSTER, BUT I'M NOT. I HAVE MY REASONS...
I HAVE MY...
WAYS...
I HAVE MY... Y'KNOW...
-LIKE I SAID.
LOOK! YOU DON'T KNOW WHAT IT'S LIKE! -EVER SINCE KYLE'S MOTHER LEFT US-HIM-WHEN HE WAS A BABY, I'VE HAD TO BE BOTH FATHER AND MOTHER TO HIM-TO KYLE, I MEAN.
WHEN A WOMAN I'M INTERESTED IN FINDS OUT I'VE GOT A TEN-YEAR-OLD SON -POOF- THAT'S IT! GOODBYE! -NO MATTER HOW MANY TIMES I CALL OR WRITE OR CALL OR WRITE, OR CALL OR WRITE, SHE TELLS ME SHE WANTS NOTHING TO DO WITH ME! -THE WOMAN, I MEAN...
I'VE EVEN SENT A FEW WOMEN I'VE MET ASTROLOGICAL COMPATIBILITY CHARTS TO SHOW THEM THAT WE'D BE A GOOD MATCH, ... BUT STILL, NADA.
I SEND GIFTS AND CARDS, TELL THESE WOMEN THAT THEY CAN COME VISIT--HELL--THEY CAN EVEN MOVE IN AND SLEEP ON THE COUCH TO SAVE MONEY AND... SNIF- AND EXCUSE ME...
SOMETHING IN MY EYE...
-AND SO THEY CAN SEE THAT I'M A-A GOOD FATHER!
-I MEAN, IT'S NOT LIKE I'M PUTTING ANY PRESSURE ON THEM TO BE A MOTHER TO KYLE.. -FAR FROM IT.
I MEAN, KYLE AND I ARE A PACKAGE DEAL, IT'S TRUE...
-BUT STILL, NO LUCK.
NO LUCK.
NO LUCK..
AHEM.
WELL... THERE ARE A LOT OF LOSERS OUT THERE...
Y'KNOW... WOMEN AFRAID TO COMMIT.

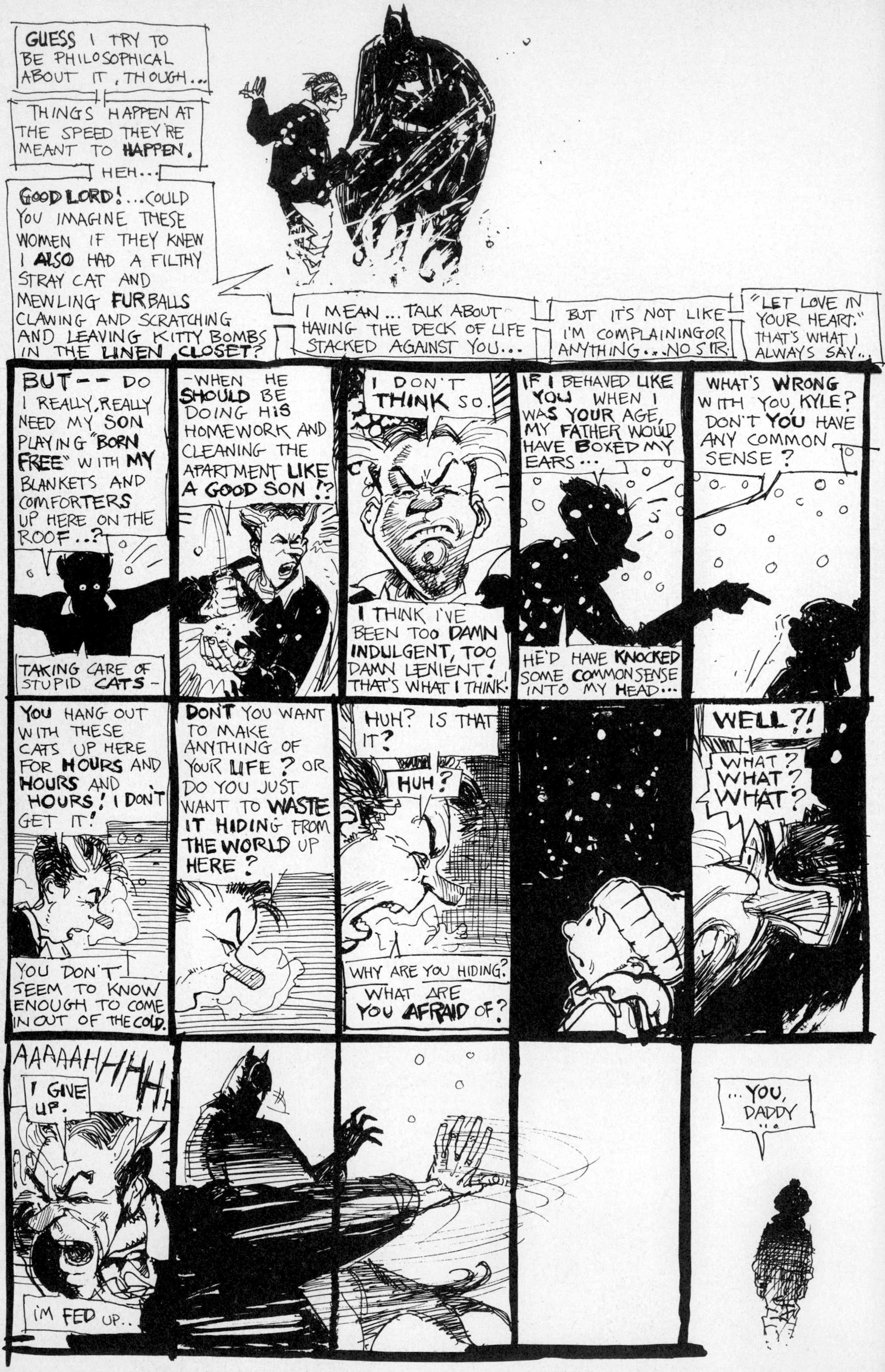
GUESS I TRY TO BE PHILOSOPHICAL ABOUT IT, THOUGH...
THINGS HAPPEN AT THE SPEED THEY'RE MEANT TO HAPPEN.
HEH...
GOOD LORD!...COULD YOU IMAGINE THESE WOMEN IF THEY KNEW I ALSO HAD A FILTHY STRAY CAT AND MEWLING FURBALLS CLAWING AND SCRATCHING AND LEAVING KITTY BOMBS IN THE LINEN CLOSET?
I MEAN... TALK ABOUT HAVING THE DECK OF LIFE STACKED AGAINST YOU...
BUT IT'S NOT LIKE I'M COMPLAINING OR ANYTHING...NO SIR.
"LET LOVE IN YOUR HEART." THAT'S WHAT I ALWAYS SAY..
BUT -- DO I REALLY, REALLY NEED MY SON PLAYING "BORN FREE" WITH MY BLANKETS AND COMFORTERS UP HERE ON THE ROOF..?
TAKING CARE OF STUPID CATS -
-WHEN HE SHOULD BE DOING HIS HOMEWORK AND CLEANING THE APARTMENT LIKE A GOOD SON!?
I DON'T THINK SO.
I THINK I'VE BEEN TOO DAMN INDULGENT, TOO DAMN LENIENT! THAT'S WHAT I THINK!
IF I BEHAVED LIKE YOU WHEN I WAS YOUR AGE, MY FATHER WOULD HAVE BOXED MY EARS...
HE'D HAVE KNOCKED SOME COMMONSENSE INTO MY HEAD...
WHAT'S WRONG WITH YOU, KYLE? DON'T YOU HAVE ANY COMMON SENSE?
YOU HANG OUT WITH THESE CATS UP HERE FOR HOURS AND HOURS AND HOURS! I DON'T GET IT!
YOU DON'T SEEM TO KNOW ENOUGH TO COME IN OUT OF THE COLD.
DON'T YOU WANT TO MAKE ANYTHING OF YOUR LIFE? OR DO YOU JUST WANT TO WASTE IT HIDING FROM THE WORLD UP HERE?
HUH? IS THAT IT?
HUH?
WHY ARE YOU HIDING? WHAT ARE YOU AFRAID OF?
WELL?!
WHAT? WHAT? WHAT?
AAAAAHHHH.
I GIVE UP.
I'M FED UP..
...YOU, DADDY...

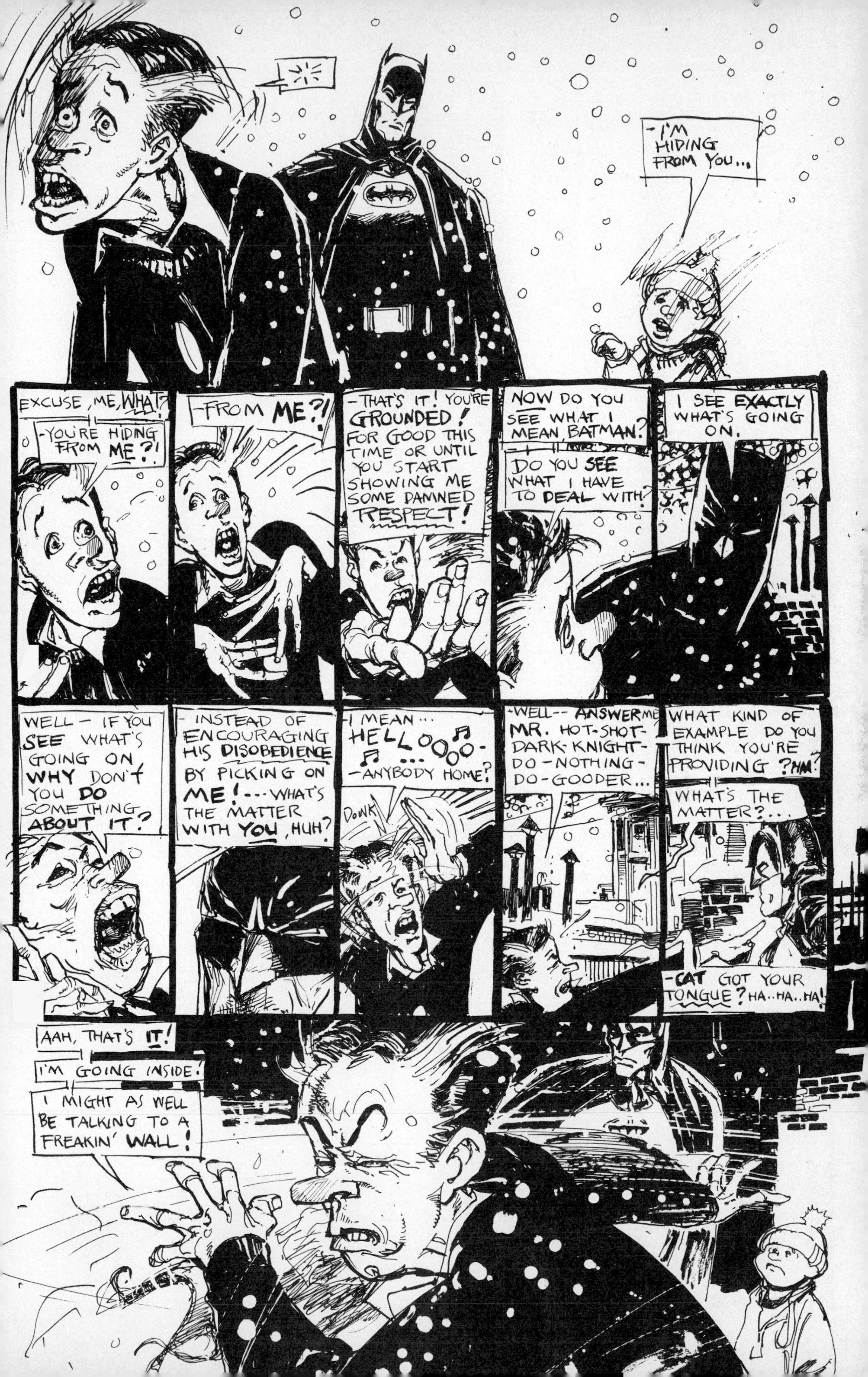
-I'M HIDING FROM YOU...
EXCUSE, ME, WHAT?
-YOU'RE HIDING FROM ME?!
-FROM ME?!
-THAT'S IT! YOU'RE GROUNDED! FOR GOOD THIS TIME OR UNTIL YOU START SHOWING ME SOME DAMNED RESPECT!
NOW DO YOU SEE WHAT I MEAN, BATMAN?
DO YOU SEE WHAT I HAVE TO DEAL WITH?
I SEE EXACTLY WHAT'S GOING ON.
WELL - IF YOU SEE WHAT'S GOING ON, WHY DON'T YOU DO SOMETHING ABOUT IT?
- INSTEAD OF ENCOURAGING HIS DISOBEDIENCE BY PICKING ON ME! --- WHAT'S THE MATTER WITH YOU, HUH?
-I MEAN... HELLOOOO- ... -ANYBODY HOME?
DONK
-WELL -- ANSWER ME MR. HOT-SHOT-DARK-KNIGHT-DO-NOTHING-DO-GOODER...
WHAT KIND OF EXAMPLE DO YOU THINK YOU'RE PROVIDING? HM?
WHAT'S THE MATTER?...
-CAT GOT YOUR TONGUE? HA..HA..HA!
AAH, THAT'S IT!
I'M GOING INSIDE.
I MIGHT AS WELL BE TALKING TO A FREAKIN' WALL!

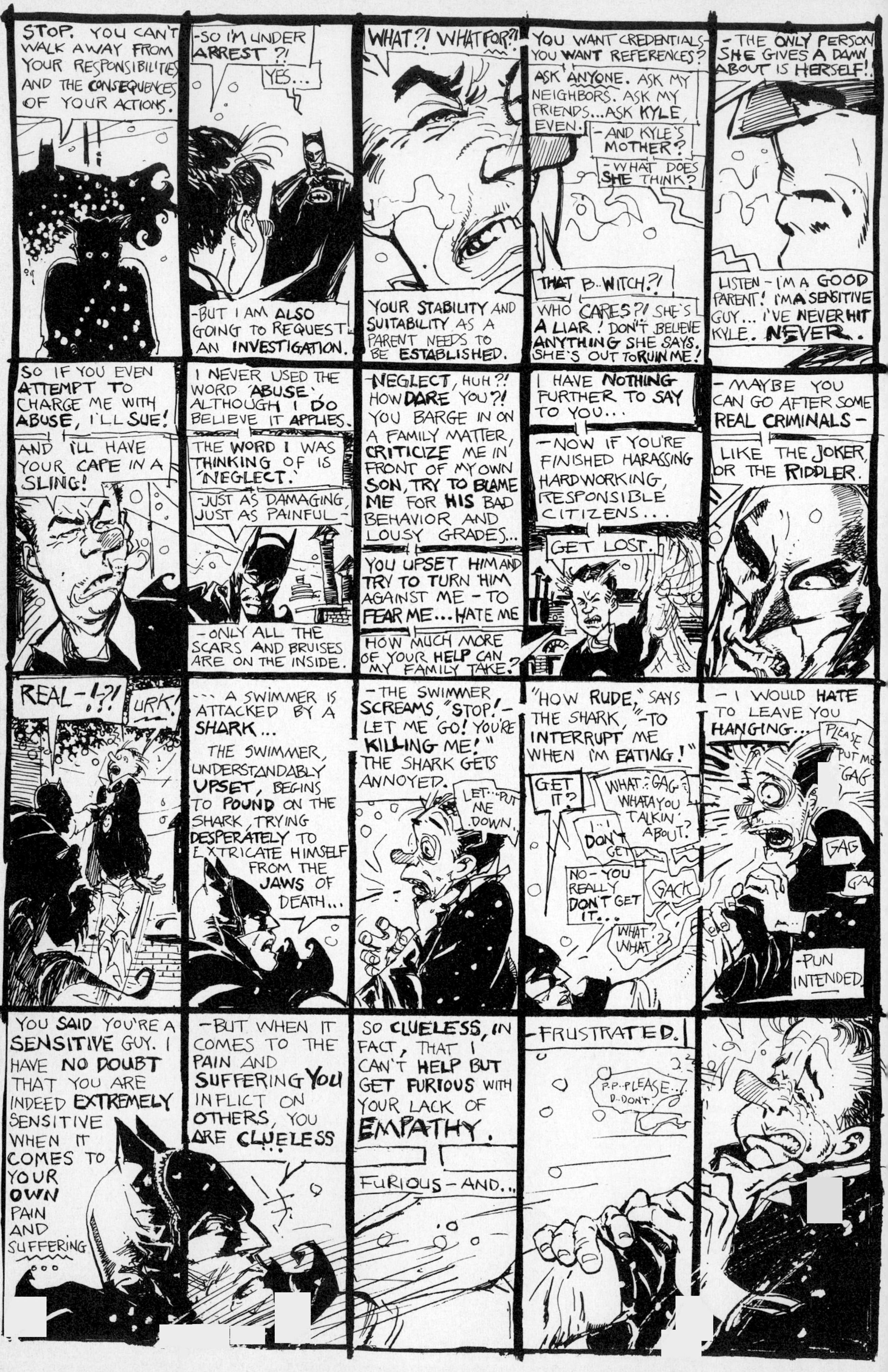
STOP. YOU CAN'T WALK AWAY FROM YOUR RESPONSIBILITIES AND THE CONSEQUENCES OF YOUR ACTIONS.
-SO I'M UNDER ARREST ?!
YES...
-BUT I AM ALSO GOING TO REQUEST AN INVESTIGATION.
WHAT?! WHAT FOR?!
YOUR STABILITY AND SUITABILITY AS A PARENT NEEDS TO BE ESTABLISHED.
YOU WANT CREDENTIALS-YOU WANT REFERENCES?
ASK ANYONE. ASK MY NEIGHBORS. ASK MY FRIENDS...ASK KYLE, EVEN.
-AND KYLE'S MOTHER?
-WHAT DOES SHE THINK?
THAT B..WITCH?!
WHO CARES?! SHE'S A LIAR! DON'T BELIEVE ANYTHING SHE SAYS. SHE'S OUT TO RUIN ME!
-THE ONLY PERSON SHE GIVES A DAMN ABOUT IS HERSELF!
LISTEN-I'M A GOOD PARENT! I'M A SENSITIVE GUY... I'VE NEVER HIT KYLE. NEVER.
SO IF YOU EVEN ATTEMPT TO CHARGE ME WITH ABUSE, I'LL SUE!
AND I'LL HAVE YOUR CAPE IN A SLING!
I NEVER USED THE WORD 'ABUSE' ALTHOUGH I DO BELIEVE IT APPLIES.
THE WORD I WAS THINKING OF IS 'NEGLECT.'
-JUST AS DAMAGING, JUST AS PAINFUL-
-ONLY ALL THE SCARS AND BRUISES ARE ON THE INSIDE.
-NEGLECT, HUH?! HOW DARE YOU?! YOU BARGE IN ON A FAMILY MATTER, CRITICIZE ME IN FRONT OF MY OWN SON, TRY TO BLAME ME FOR HIS BAD BEHAVIOR AND LOUSY GRADES...
YOU UPSET HIM AND TRY TO TURN HIM AGAINST ME-TO FEAR ME...HATE ME
HOW MUCH MORE OF YOUR HELP CAN MY FAMILY TAKE?
I HAVE NOTHING FURTHER TO SAY TO YOU...
-NOW IF YOU'RE FINISHED HARASSING HARDWORKING, RESPONSIBLE CITIZENS...
GET LOST.
-MAYBE YOU CAN GO AFTER SOME REAL CRIMINALS-
LIKE THE JOKER, OR THE RIDDLER.
REAL-!?!
URK!
...A SWIMMER IS ATTACKED BY A SHARK...
THE SWIMMER, UNDERSTANDABLY UPSET, BEGINS TO POUND ON THE SHARK, TRYING DESPERATELY TO EXTRICATE HIMSELF FROM THE JAWS OF DEATH...
-THE SWIMMER SCREAMS, "STOP!-LET ME GO! YOU'RE KILLING ME!" THE SHARK GETS ANNOYED.
LET...PUT ME DOWN.
"HOW RUDE," SAYS THE SHARK, "-TO INTERRUPT ME WHEN I'M EATING!"
GET IT?
WHAT...GAG... WHATAYOU TALKIN' ABOUT?
I...I DON'T GET...
NO-YOU REALLY DON'T GET IT...
GACK
WHAT? WHAT?
-I WOULD HATE TO LEAVE YOU HANGING...
PLEASE PUT ME GAG
GAG
GAG
-PUN INTENDED.
YOU SAID YOU'RE A SENSITIVE GUY. I HAVE NO DOUBT THAT YOU ARE INDEED EXTREMELY SENSITIVE WHEN IT COMES TO YOUR OWN PAIN AND SUFFERING...
-BUT WHEN IT COMES TO THE PAIN AND SUFFERING YOU INFLICT ON OTHERS, YOU ARE CLUELESS...
SO CLUELESS, IN FACT, THAT I CAN'T HELP BUT GET FURIOUS WITH YOUR LACK OF EMPATHY.
FURIOUS-AND...
-FRUSTRATED.
P..P..PLEASE... D..DON'T.

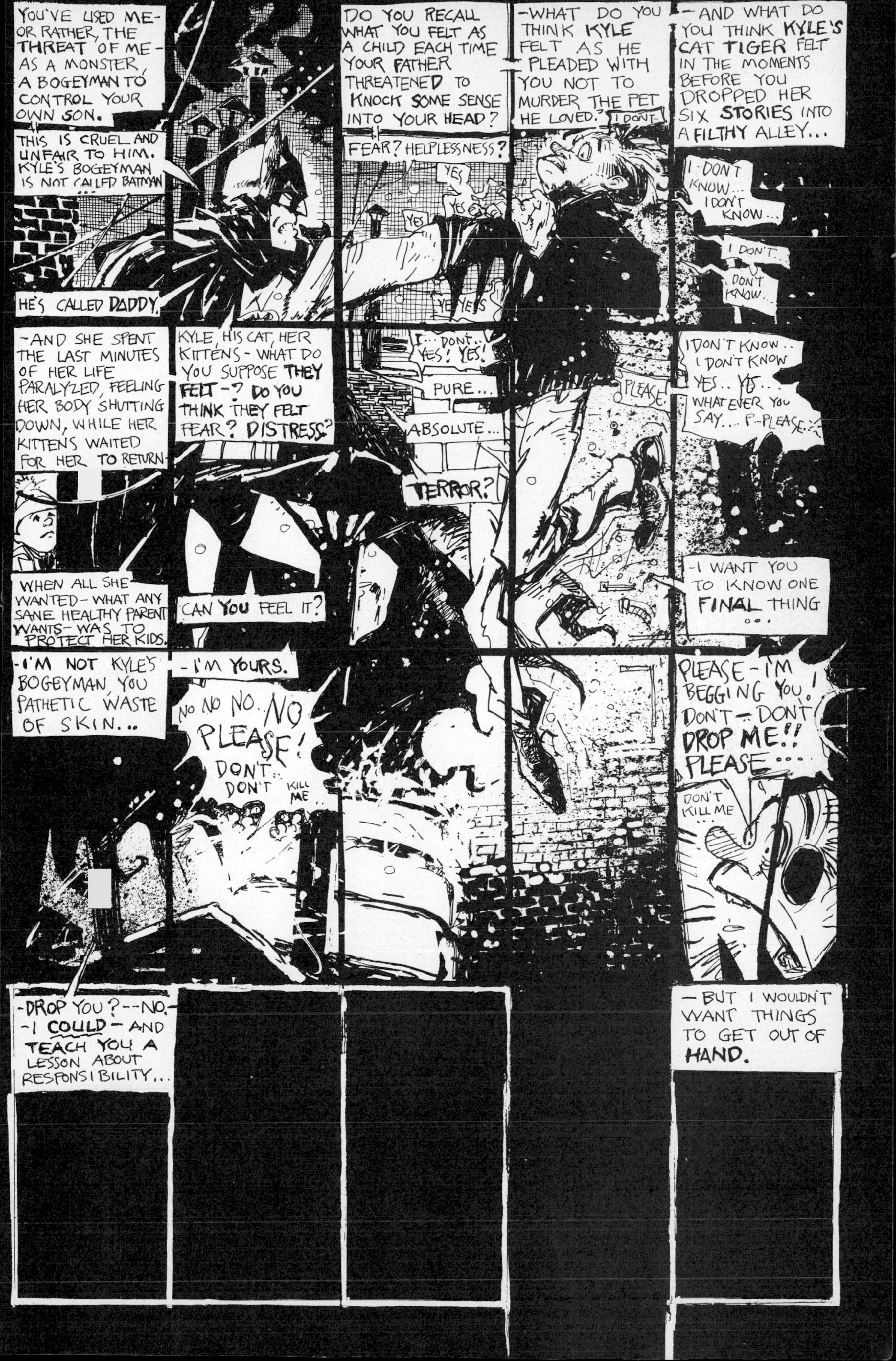

YOU'VE USED ME— OR RATHER, THE THREAT OF ME— AS A MONSTER, A BOGEYMAN TO CONTROL YOUR OWN SON.
THIS IS CRUEL AND UNFAIR TO HIM. KYLE'S BOGEYMAN IS NOT CALLED BATMAN...
HE'S CALLED DADDY.
DO YOU RECALL WHAT YOU FELT AS A CHILD EACH TIME YOUR FATHER THREATENED TO KNOCK SOME SENSE INTO YOUR HEAD?
FEAR? HELPLESSNESS?
YES
YES
YES
YES YES
—WHAT DO YOU THINK KYLE FELT AS HE PLEADED WITH YOU NOT TO MURDER THE PET HE LOVED?
I DON'T..
—AND WHAT DO YOU THINK KYLE'S CAT TIGER FELT IN THE MOMENTS BEFORE YOU DROPPED HER SIX STORIES INTO A FILTHY ALLEY...
I DON'T KNOW... I DON'T KNOW...
I DON'T...
DON'T KNOW...
—AND SHE SPENT THE LAST MINUTES OF HER LIFE PARALYZED, FEELING HER BODY SHUTTING DOWN, WHILE HER KITTENS WAITED FOR HER TO RETURN—
WHEN ALL SHE WANTED— WHAT ANY SANE HEALTHY PARENT WANTS— WAS TO PROTECT HER KIDS.
KYLE, HIS CAT, HER KITTENS— WHAT DO YOU SUPPOSE THEY FELT—? DO YOU THINK THEY FELT FEAR? DISTRESS?
CAN YOU FEEL IT?
I... DON'T.. YES! YES!
PURE...
ABSOLUTE...
TERROR?
PLEASE.
I DON'T KNOW.. I DON'T KNOW YES... YES... WHATEVER YOU SAY... P-PLEASE...
—I WANT YOU TO KNOW ONE FINAL THING...
—I'M NOT KYLE'S BOGEYMAN, YOU PATHETIC WASTE OF SKIN...
—I'M YOURS.
NO NO NO.. NO PLEASE! DON'T.. DON'T KILL ME
PLEASE—I'M BEGGING YOU! DON'T—DON'T DROP ME!! PLEASE...
DON'T KILL ME...
—DROP YOU?—NO. —I COULD— AND TEACH YOU A LESSON ABOUT RESPONSIBILITY...
—BUT I WOULDN'T WANT THINGS TO GET OUT OF HAND.

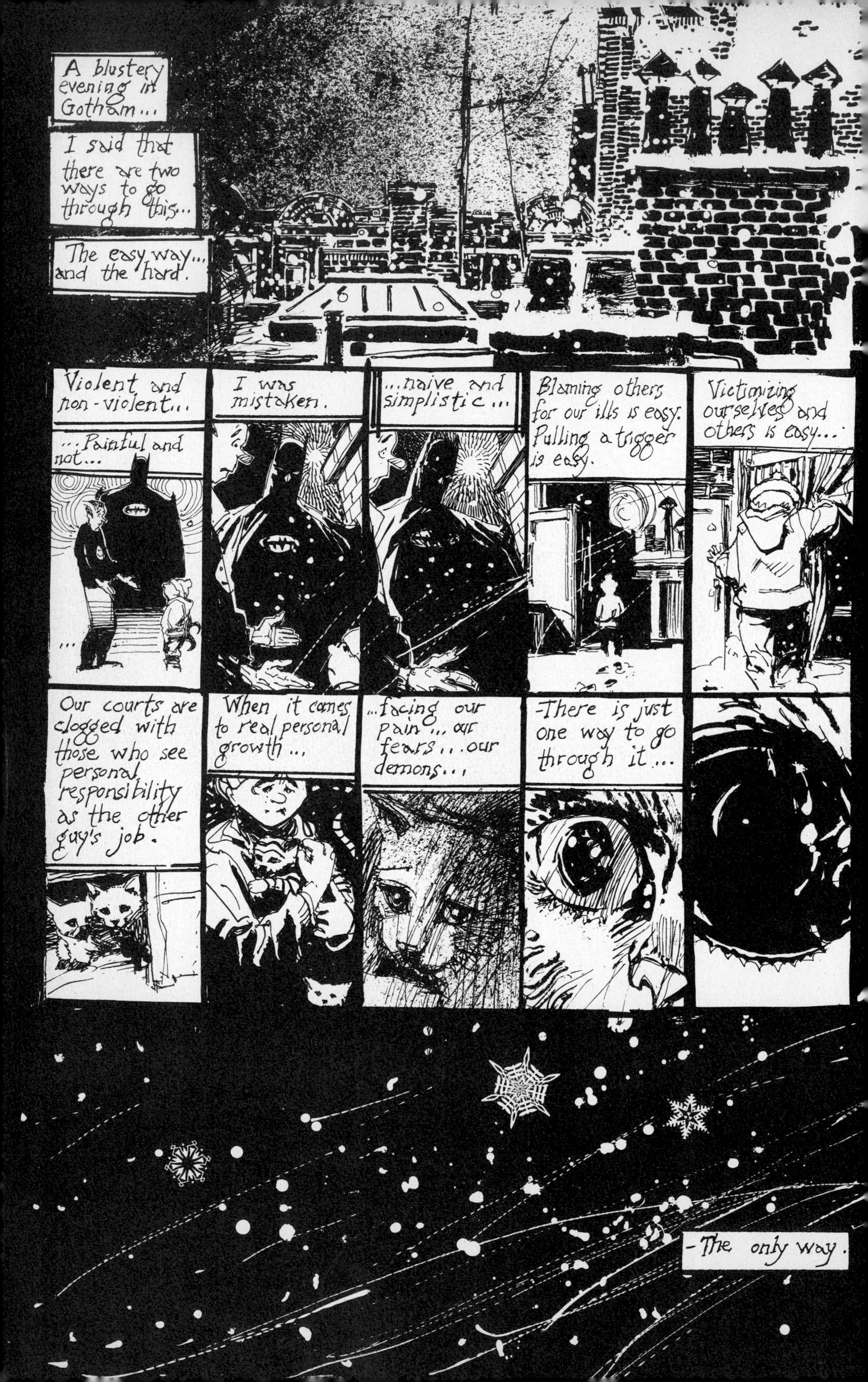

A blustery evening in Gotham...
I said that there are two ways to go through this...
The easy way... and the hard.
Violent and non-violent...
...Painful and not...
...
I was mistaken.
...naive and simplistic...
Blaming others for our ills is easy. Pulling a trigger is easy.
Victimizing ourselves and others is easy...
Our courts are clogged with those who see personal responsibility as the other guy's job.
When it comes to real personal growth...
...facing our pain... our fears... our demons...
-There is just one way to go through it...
-The only way.

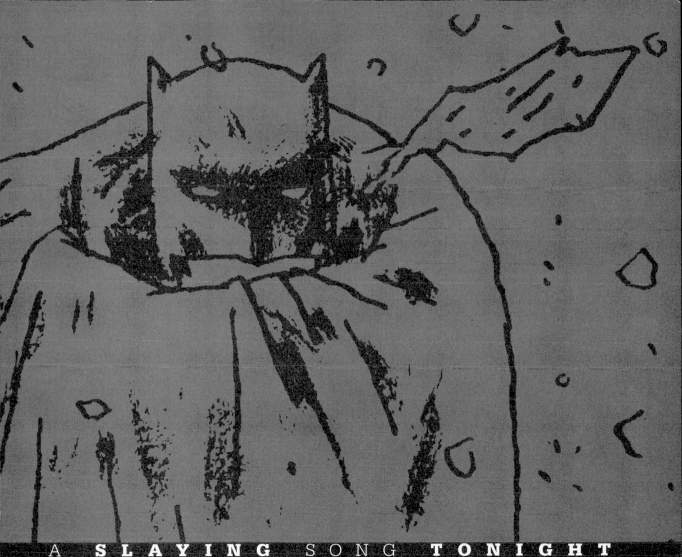

A **SLAYING** SONG **TONIGHT**

world in a very short period of time. Working primarily on limited series and one-shots, he has become one of the most sought-after young artists in the business. Always bold and inventive in its approach, Teddy's work can be seen in issues of *Grendel Tales*, SANDMAN, SANDMAN MYSTERY THEATRE and his own HOUSE OF SECRETS for DC/VERTIGO.

DENNIS **O'NEIL**

For over twenty years, Batman editor and writer Dennis O'Neil has put the "dark" in the Dark Knight and has been the guiding force behind the Batman mythos. He has been praised as a master of the comics form and as the dean of American comics. He prefers to think of himself as, simply, "a working professional storyteller."

Dennis has written most of Marvel's and DC's major characters including Spider-Man, Iron Man, Daredevil, Superman, Wonder Woman, and the Justice League of America. His GREEN LANTERN/GREEN ARROW series in the early '70s is hailed as the first "relevant" comic book, and his late '80s title, THE QUESTION, is credited with being a forerunner of "mature reader" comics.

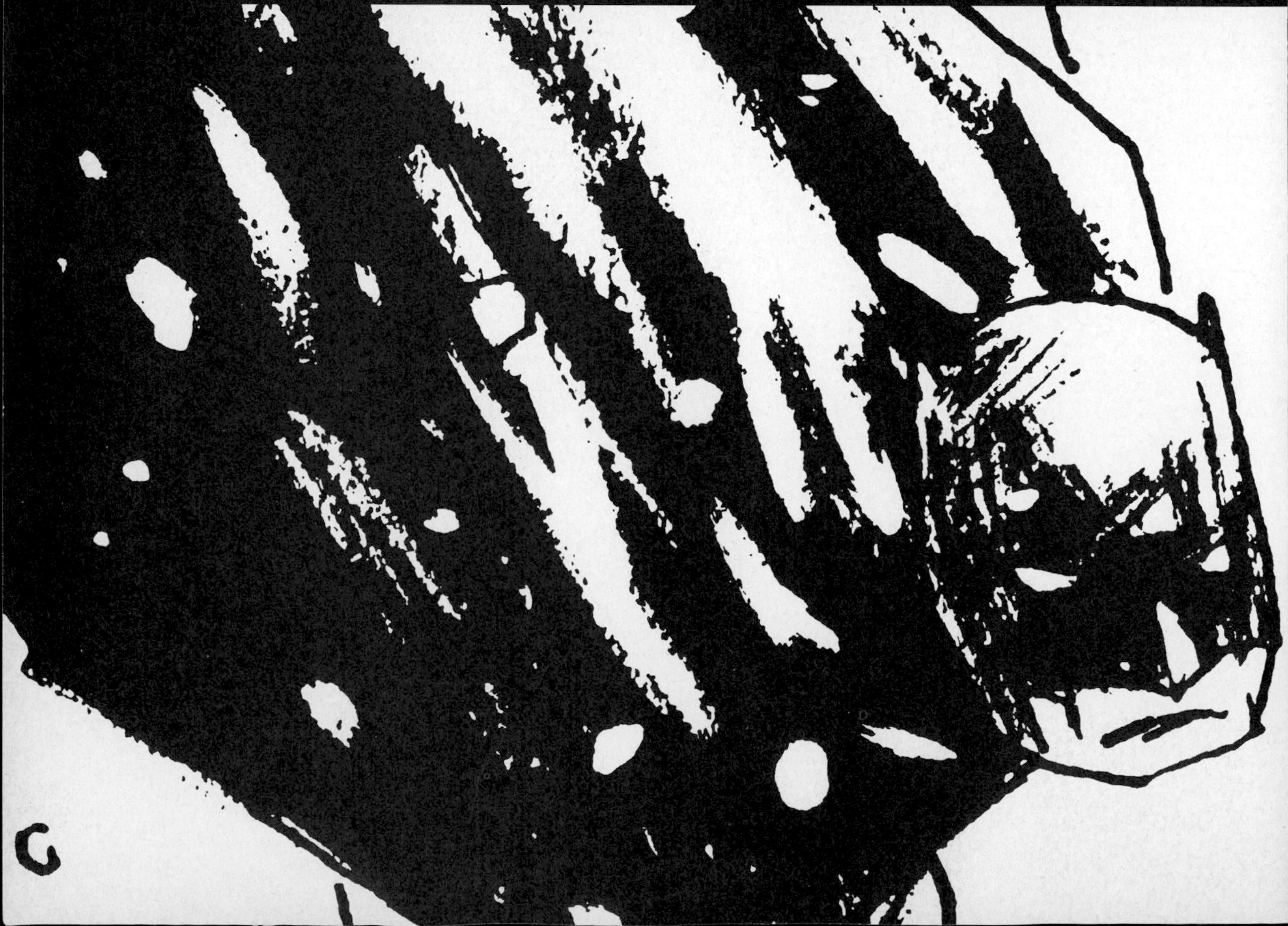

A slaying song tonight

Written by Dennis O'neil   Art by Teddy H. Kristiansen

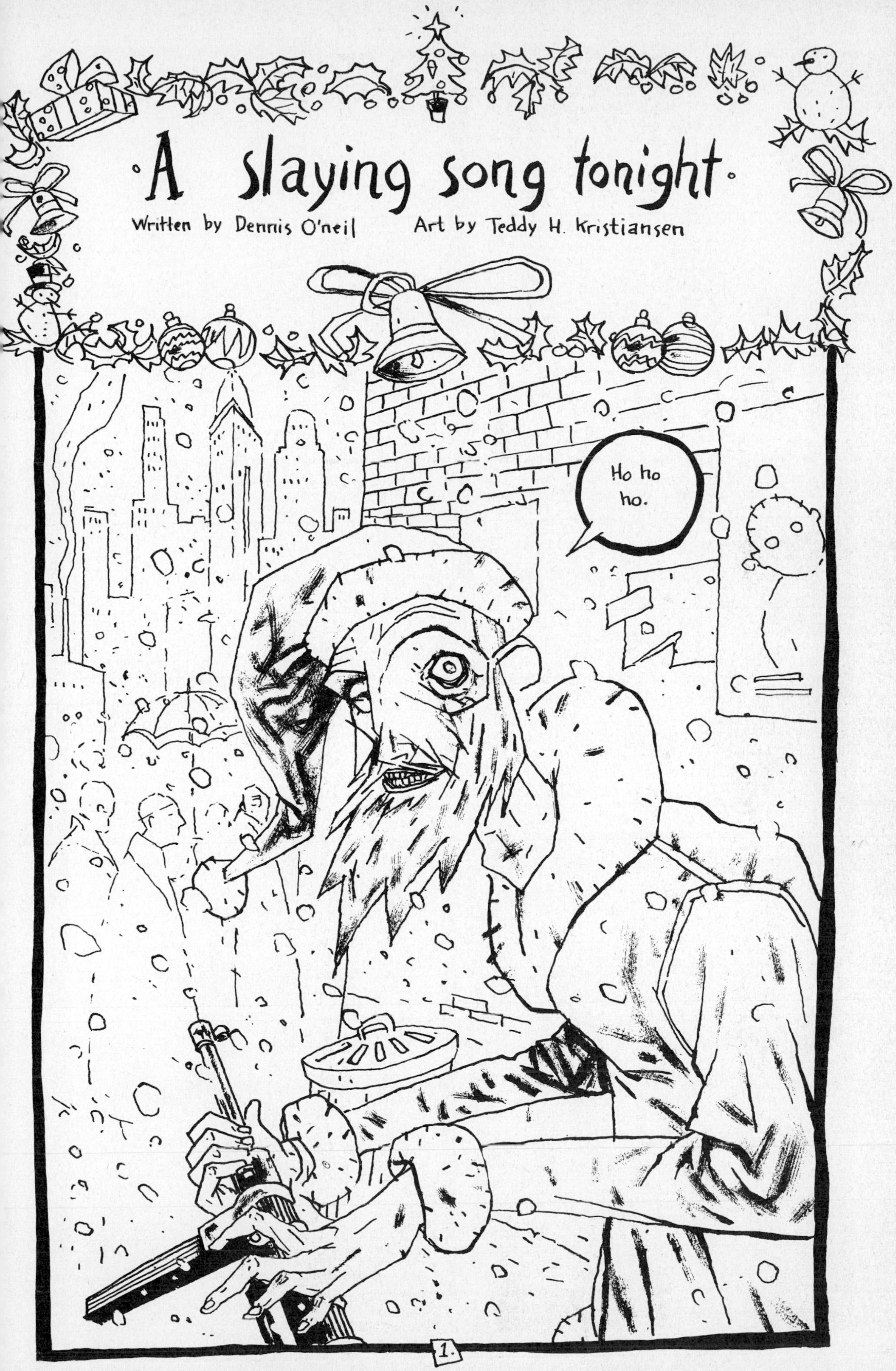

Ho ho ho.

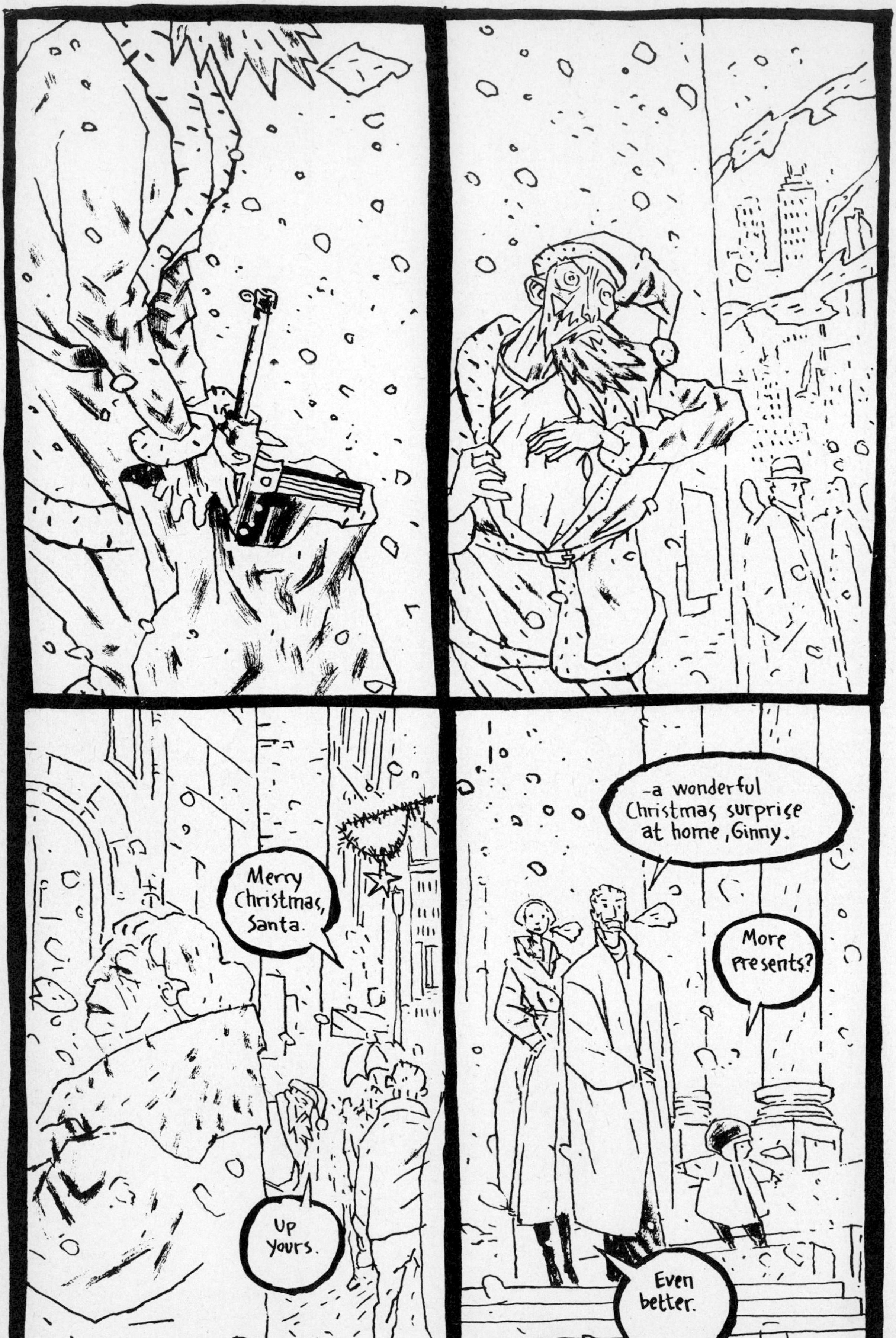
Merry Christmas, Santa.
Up yours.
-a wonderful Christmas surprise at home, Ginny.
More presents?
Even better.
2.

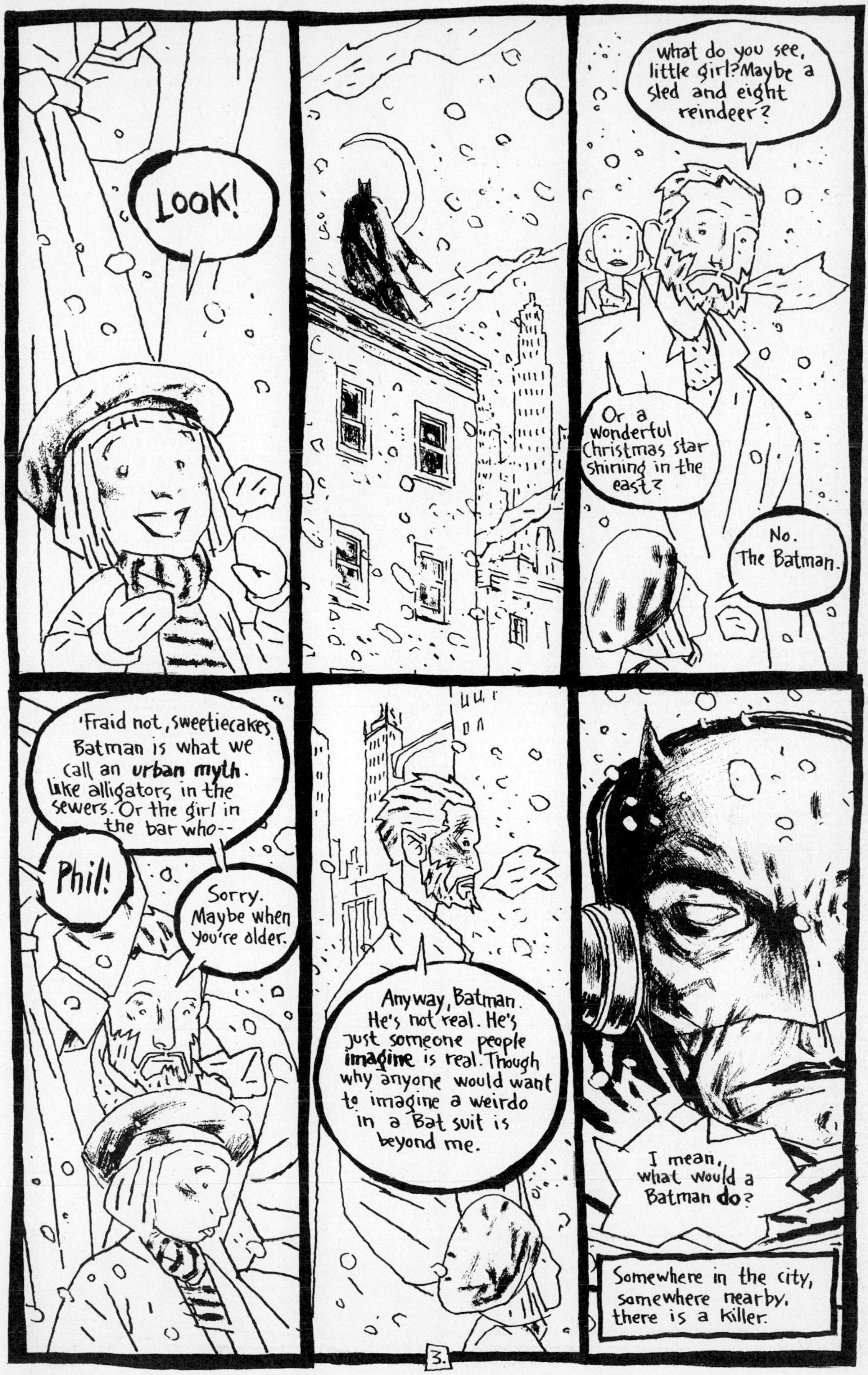
LOOK!
what do you see, little girl? Maybe a sled and eight reindeer?
Or a wonderful Christmas star shining in the east?
No. The Batman.
'Fraid not, sweetiecakes. Batman is what we call an **urban myth**. Like alligators in the sewers. Or the girl in the bar who--
Phil!
Sorry. Maybe when you're older.
Anyway, Batman. He's not real. He's just someone people **imagine** is real. Though why anyone would want to imagine a weirdo in a Bat suit is beyond me.
I mean, what would a Batman **do**?
Somewhere in the city, somewhere nearby, there is a killer.
3.

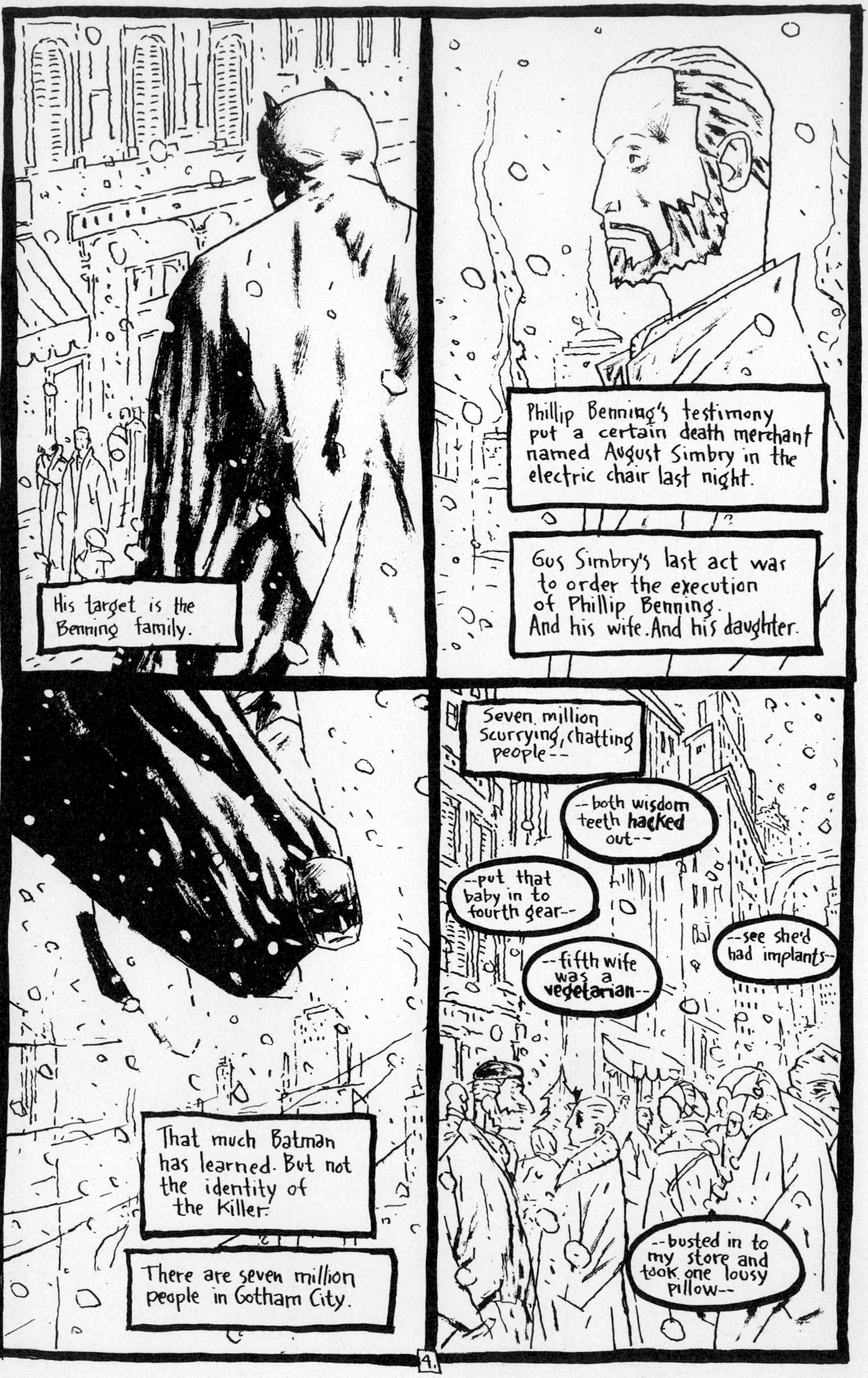
His target is the Benning family.
Phillip Benning's testimony put a certain death merchant named August Simbry in the electric chair last night.
Gus Simbry's last act was to order the execution of Phillip Benning. And his wife. And his daughter.
That much Batman has learned. But not the identity of the killer.
There are seven million people in Gotham City.
Seven million scurrying, chatting people--
--both wisdom teeth hacked out--
--put that baby in to fourth gear--
--fifth wife was a vegetarian--
--see she'd had implants--
--busted in to my store and took one lousy pillow--
4.

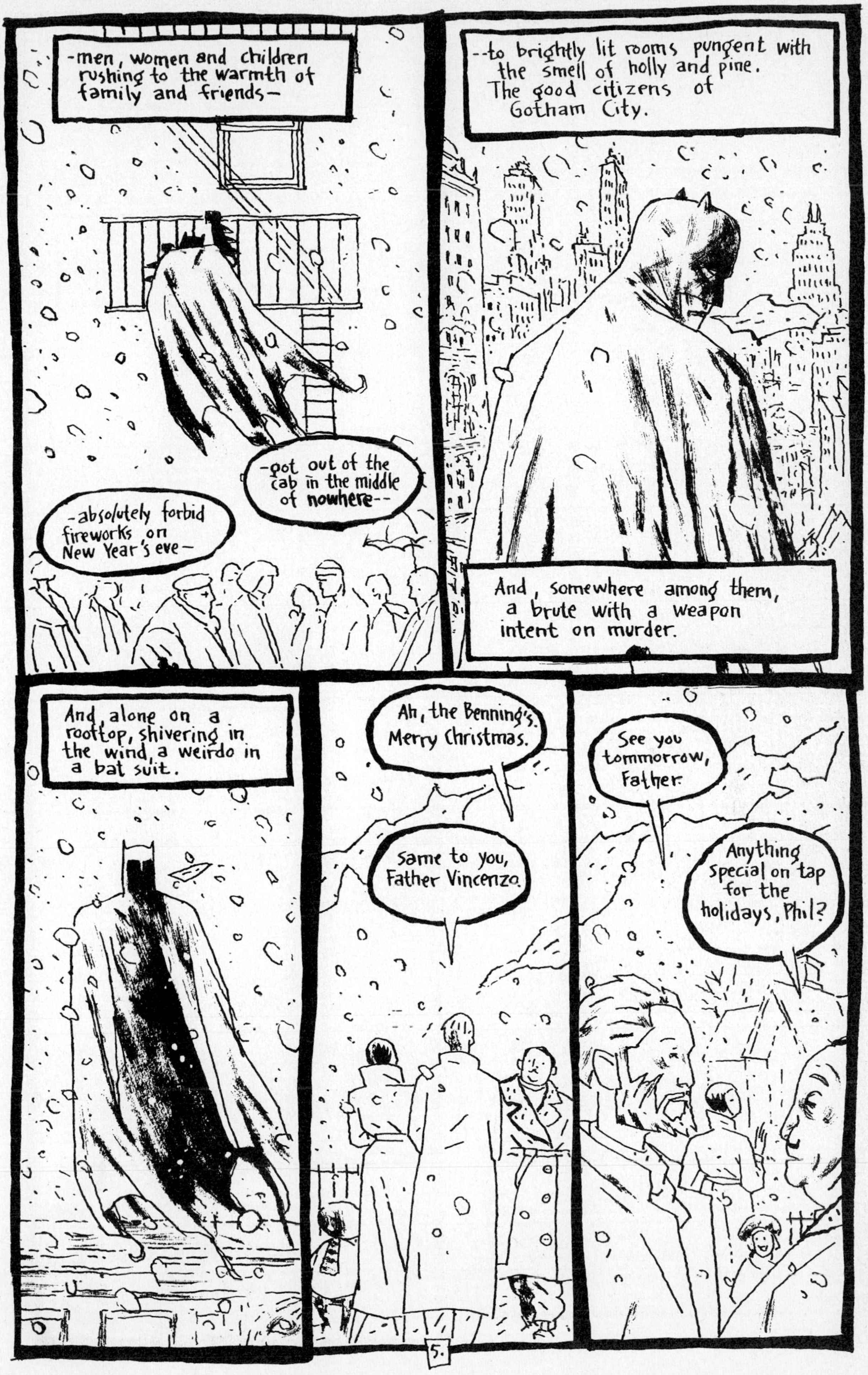
-men, women and children rushing to the warmth of family and friends-
-got out of the cab in the middle of nowhere--
-absolutely forbid fireworks on New Year's eve-
--to brightly lit rooms pungent with the smell of holly and pine. The good citizens of Gotham City.
And, somewhere among them, a brute with a weapon intent on murder.
And, alone on a rooftop, shivering in the wind, a weirdo in a bat suit.
Ah, the Benning's. Merry Christmas.
Same to you, Father Vincenzo.
See you tommorrow, Father.
Anything special on tap for the holidays, Phil?
5.

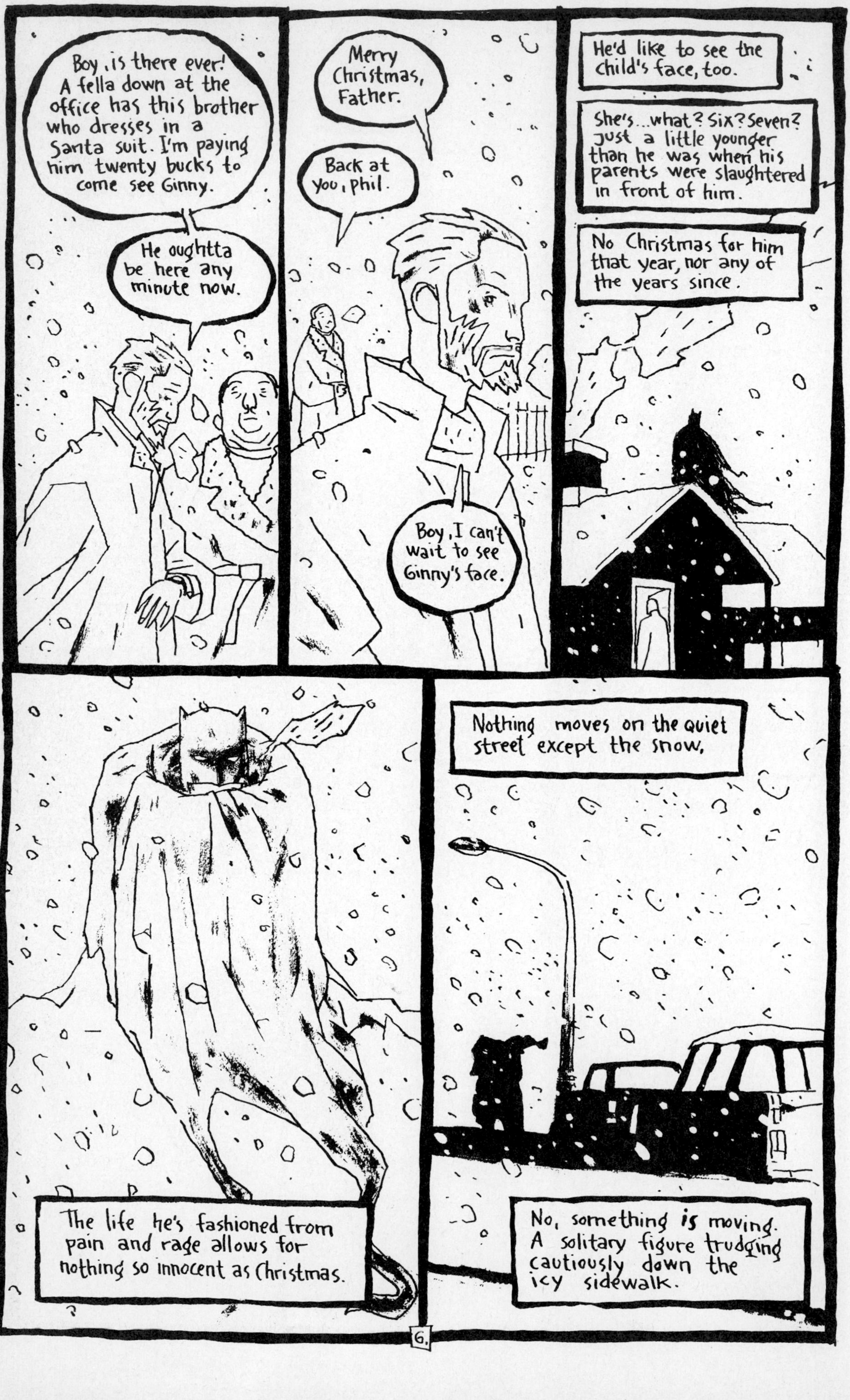
Boy, is there ever! A fella down at the office has this brother who dresses in a Santa suit. I'm paying him twenty bucks to come see Ginny.
He oughtta be here any minute now.
Merry Christmas, Father.
Back at you, Phil.
Boy, I can't wait to see Ginny's face.
He'd like to see the child's face, too.
She's...what? Six? Seven? Just a little younger than he was when his parents were slaughtered in front of him.
No Christmas for him that year, nor any of the years since.
The life he's fashioned from pain and rage allows for nothing so innocent as Christmas.
Nothing moves on the quiet street except the snow.
No, something is moving. A solitary figure trudging cautiously down the icy sidewalk.
6.

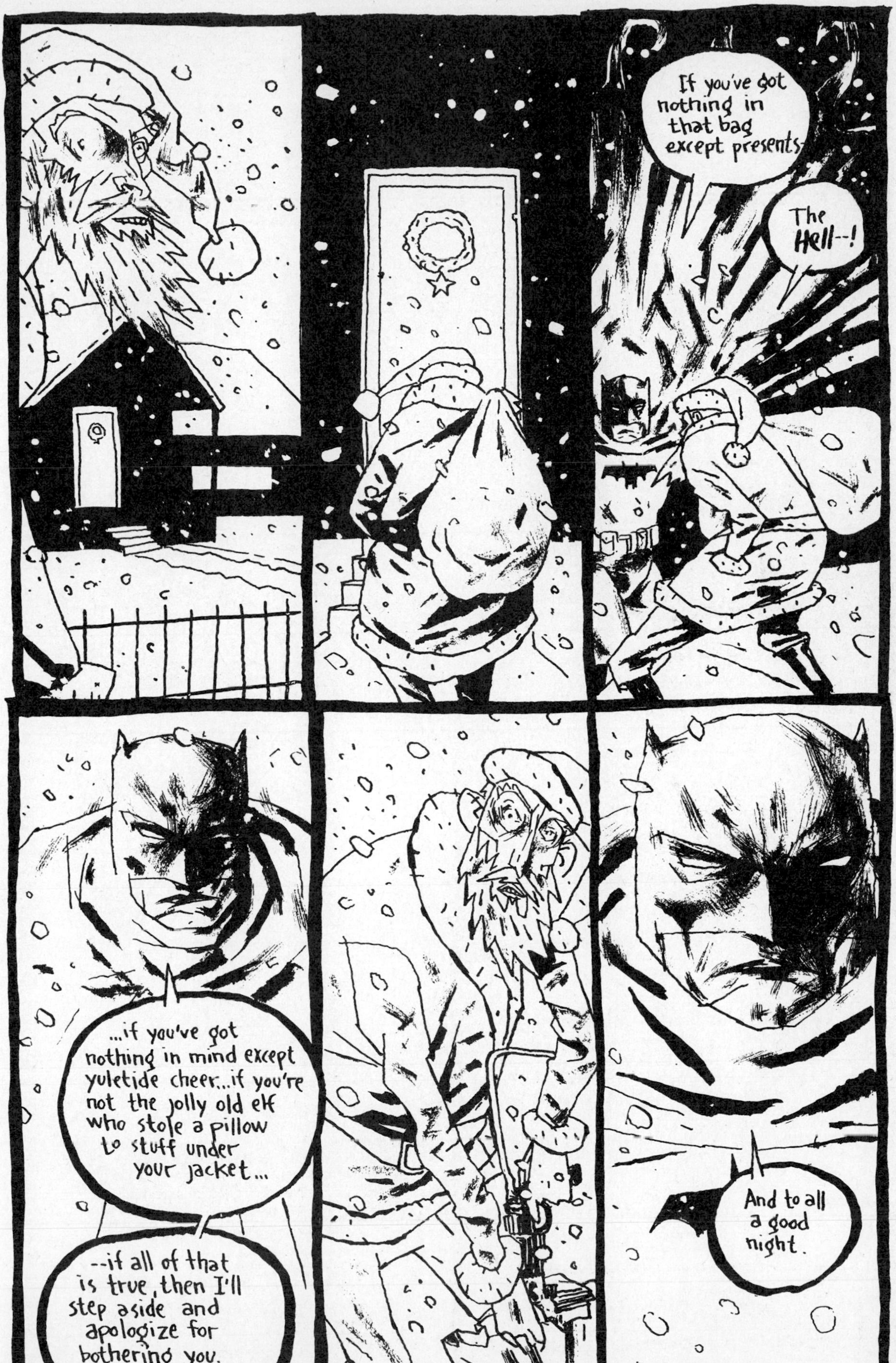
If you've got nothing in that bag except presents--
The Hell--!
...if you've got nothing in mind except yuletide cheer...if you're not the jolly old elf who stole a pillow to stuff under your jacket...
--if all of that is true, then I'll step aside and apologize for bothering you.
And to all a good night.
7.

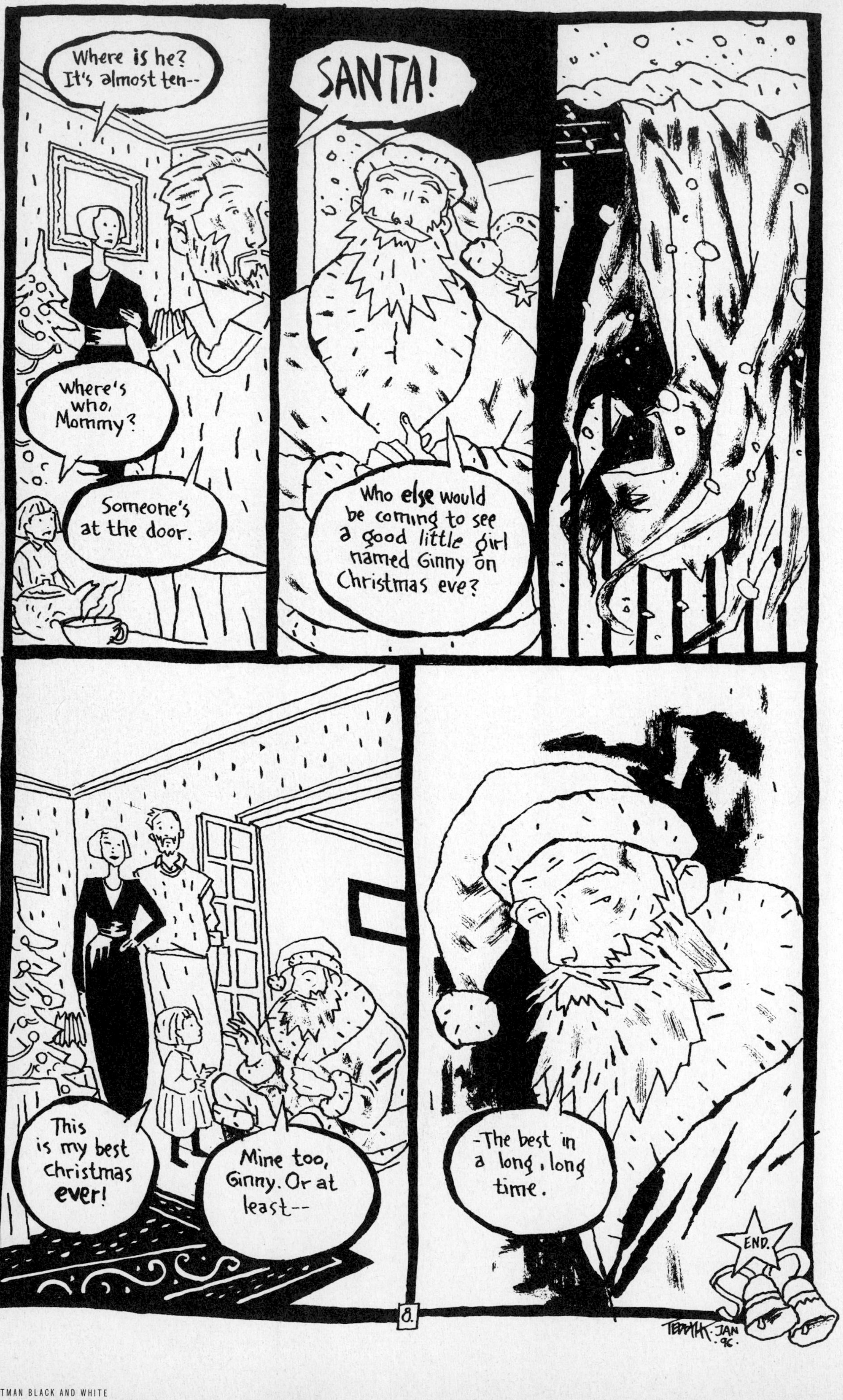
Where is he? It's almost ten--
Where's who, Mommy?
Someone's at the door.
SANTA!
Who else would be coming to see a good little girl named Ginny on Christmas eve?
This is my best christmas ever!
Mine too, Ginny. Or at least--
-The best in a long, long time.
END.
8.
TEBAK. JAN. 96.

BARRY WINDSOR-SMITH

ALTERNATE COVERS

Quite some time after Barry Windsor-Smith agreed to draw the cover for issue #3, he faxed over a sketch. Since it had taken quite a while to actually receive the sketch, I figured Barry had been swamped as usual, and had to wait until there was a hole in his schedule. Well, I OK'd the sketch and then waited. And waited. And waited. Finally the finished piece arrived, only it was completely different from the approach the original sketch showed. Fortunately Scott Peterson and I liked the new piece, but we scratched our heads over what ever happened to the original idea. Months later Barry told me that he agonized over trying to get a grasp of the character and went through half a dozen abortive attempts. Here are a few of his "near misses."

KLAUS JANSON ORIGINAL FINAL PAGE

In the original version of Klaus Janson's story, Alfred eventually burns Thomas Wayne's letter. I thought it was the perfect ending to an exceptional story, but my co-editor Scott Peterson very much disagreed. He felt Alfred would never destroy such a personal item, especially considering it was Thomas Wayne's wish that Bruce would someday read this letter. Scott and I had a major disagreement, he gave me a black eye, and we had Klaus change the panel in question. I still think it's a better story if Alfred burns the note!

Your loving father, Thomas

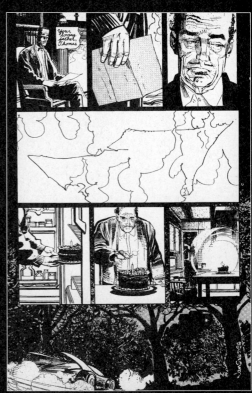

BILL SIENKIEWICZ LAYOUT PAGE

My inevitable question when I got Bill Sienkiewicz's story layouts was: "But Bill, where are you gonna put the art?"

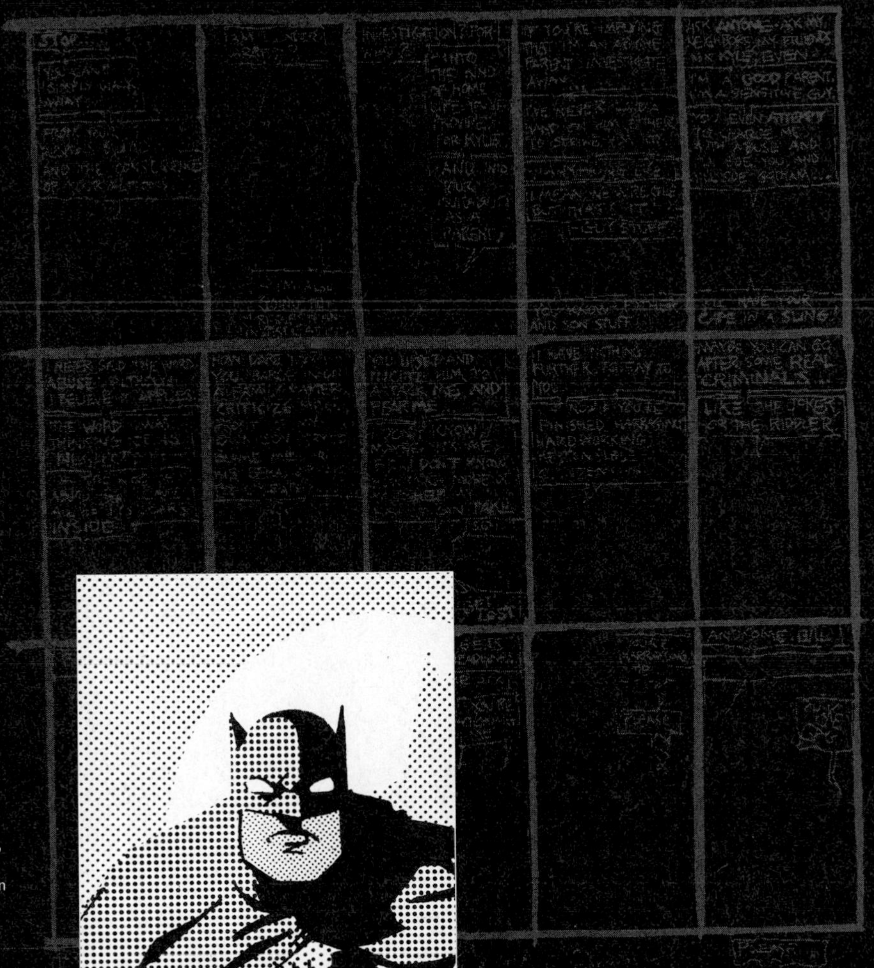

MATT WAGNER POSTER PANEL

"Matt, have you drawn your story yet?"

"Whatta you talking about, Mark? You just called me last week, I haven't even written it yet!"

"Well, you see, we're doing a poster for B&W and I need a panel from your story."

"I wasn't planning on starting the Batman story until after I finish BATMAN/GRENDEL #2."

"How about if you do a separate drawing of Batman that I can use for the poster?"

"OK, but isn't that sorta cheating? I mean, it won't really appear in the actual story."

"Ah, don't worry about it, we'll print it again when we do the big collection."

"OK, you're the boss."

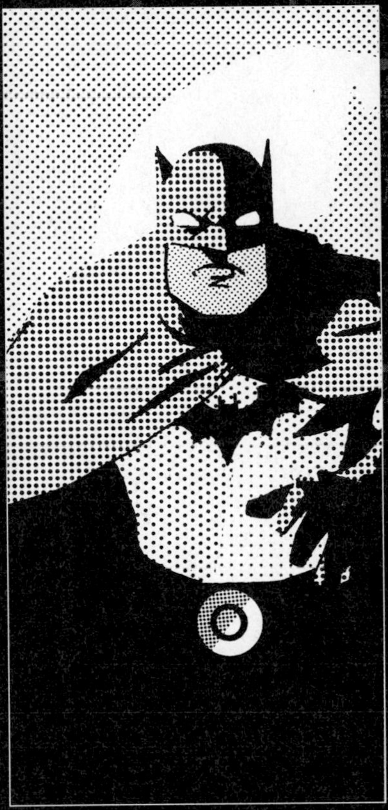

TEDDY KRISTIANSEN BATMAN SKETCH

When you hire the world's greatest comic-book artists (as we did with BATMAN B&W), you've got to use your head. Most of these guys are in such demand, you've got to have a really long deadline or you're not going to get the talent you want. Sometimes you even fib a little to them about when the job is due, keep a cushion of a few weeks between them and the real deadline. As was the case with a few of the creators involved with this series, Teddy Kristiansen bent the hell out of the false deadline and even backed right up to the real one. Being the sweetheart that he is, Teddy called to apologize a million times, assuring me that he actually was working on his story. Towards the end, he even started *faxing* me apologies! Here's a doodle from one of them.

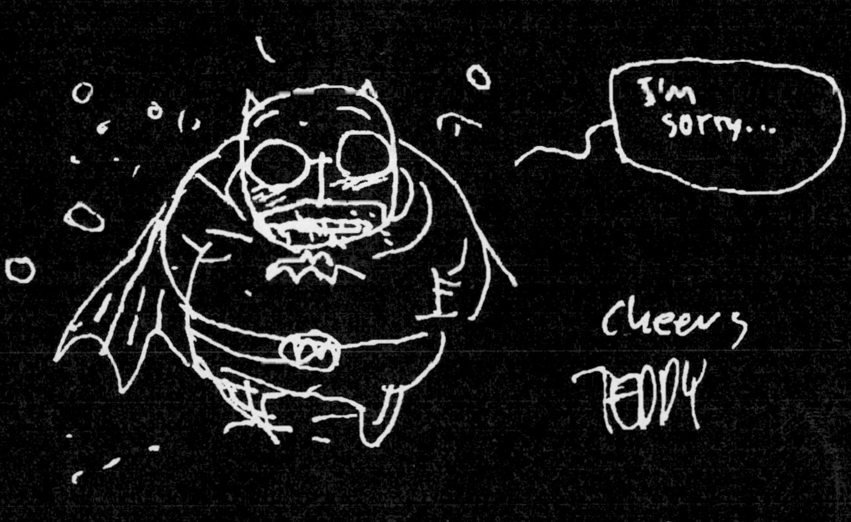
I'm sorry...
Cheers
TEDDY

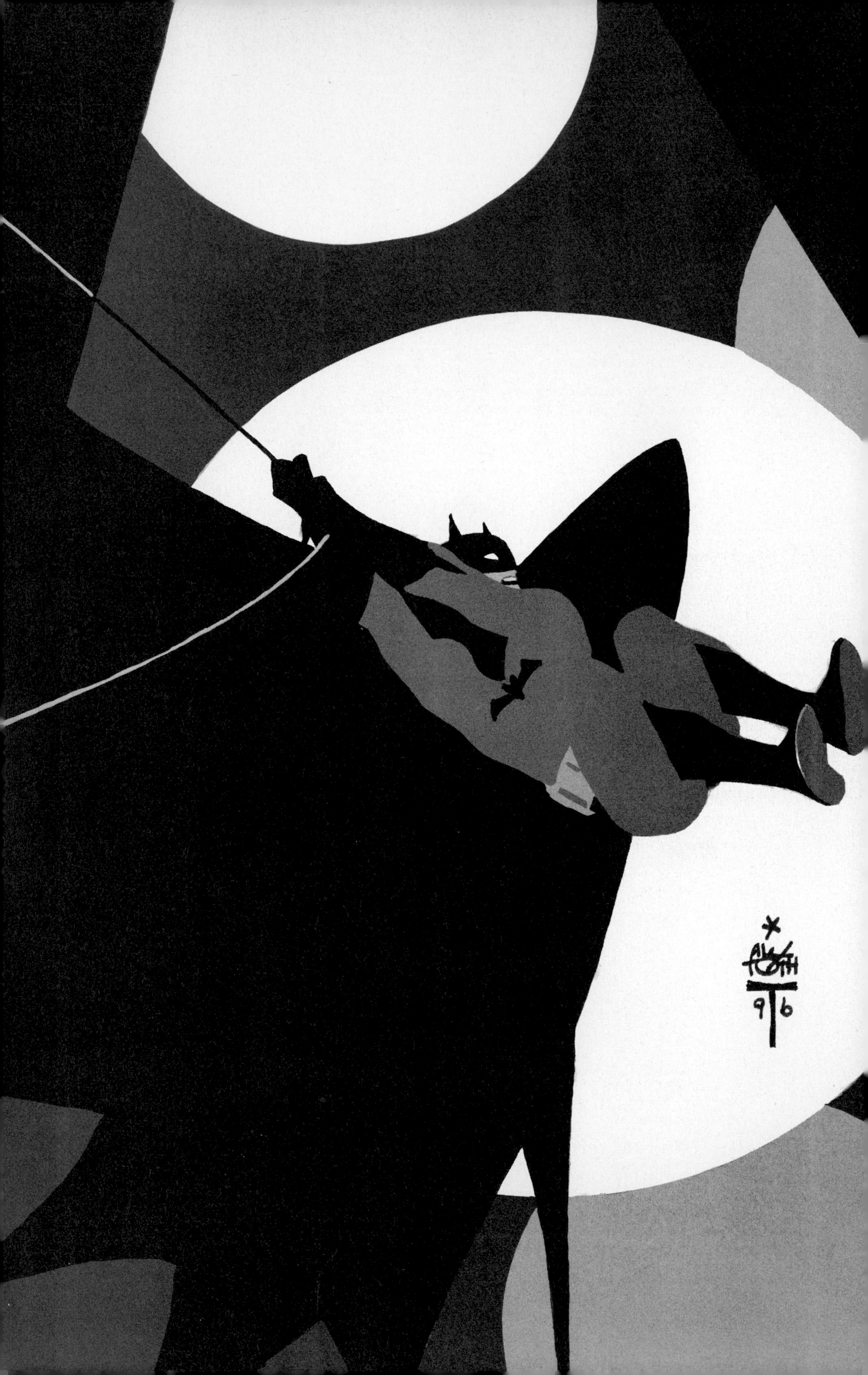

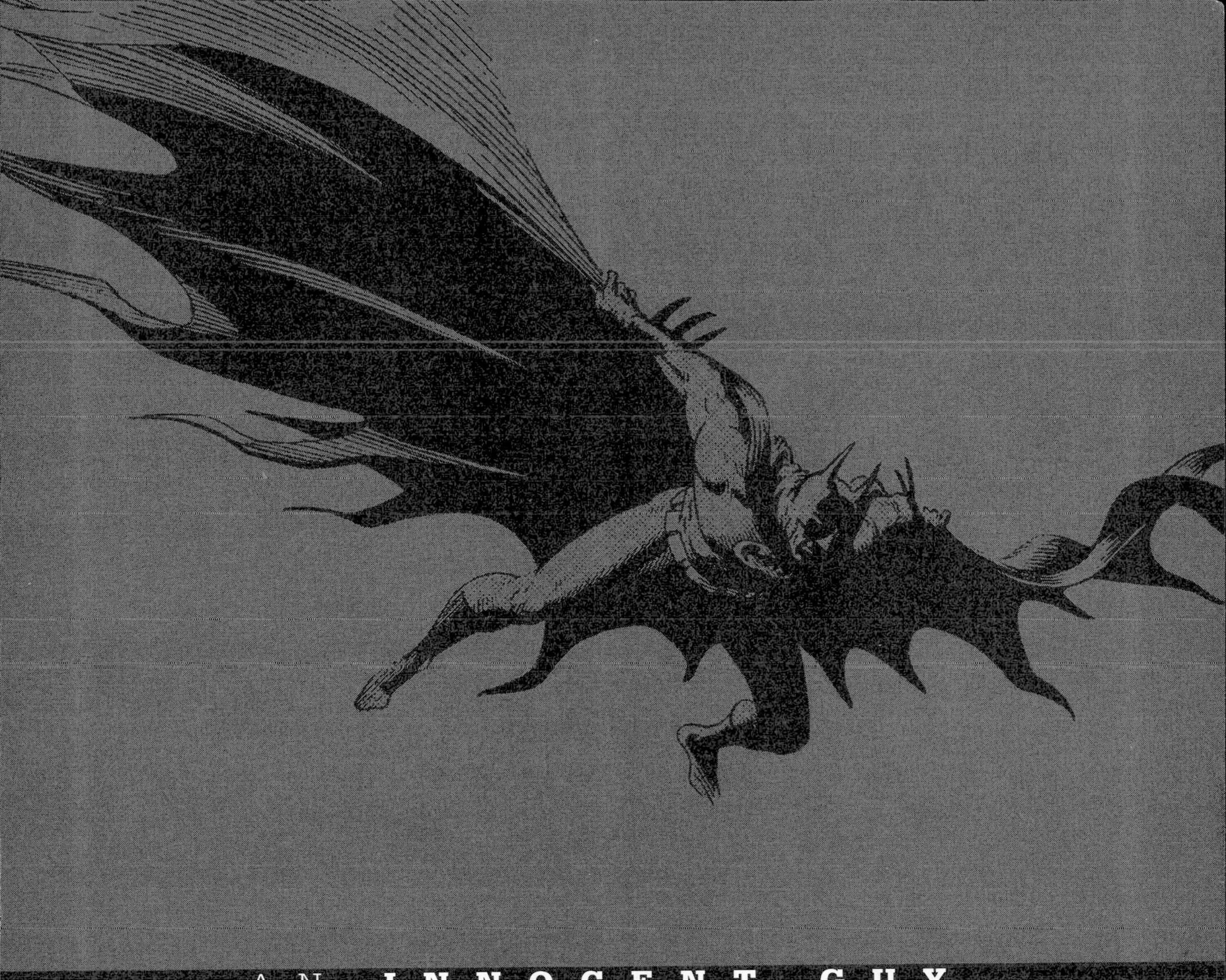

AN INNOCENT GUY

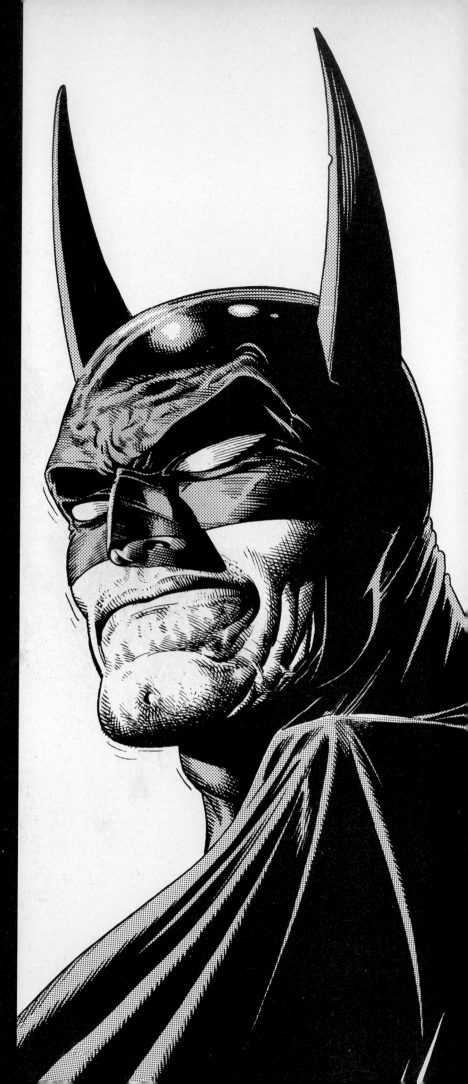

BRIANBOLLAND

From his very first professional
work, it was clear that Brian Bolland
was destined to be one of the all-
time greats. Making his debut back
in the mid-70's with *Powerman*, a
collaboration with Dave Gibbons,
Bolland already showed his
incredible command of anatomy
and perspective, as well as the
razor-sharp linework that has
been his trademark.

Bolland then drew British newspaper strips with Syd Jordan before
moving on to *2000 A.D.*, where he
would produce some of the most
remarkable artwork seen in comics.
Much of his most notable work
there was on *Judge Dredd*, where he
drew the first appearances of both
Judge Death and Judge Anderson.

Brian's first major American work
was the maxiseries CAMELOT 3000,
an epic updating of the classic tale.
He then took two years to draw
BATMAN: THE KILLING JOKE,
often acclaimed as the single
greatest Batman story ever.

Since then, Bolland has chosen
to work primarily on covers,
contributing astonishing artwork to
the fronts of several series, most
notably ANIMAL MAN and
WONDER WOMAN.

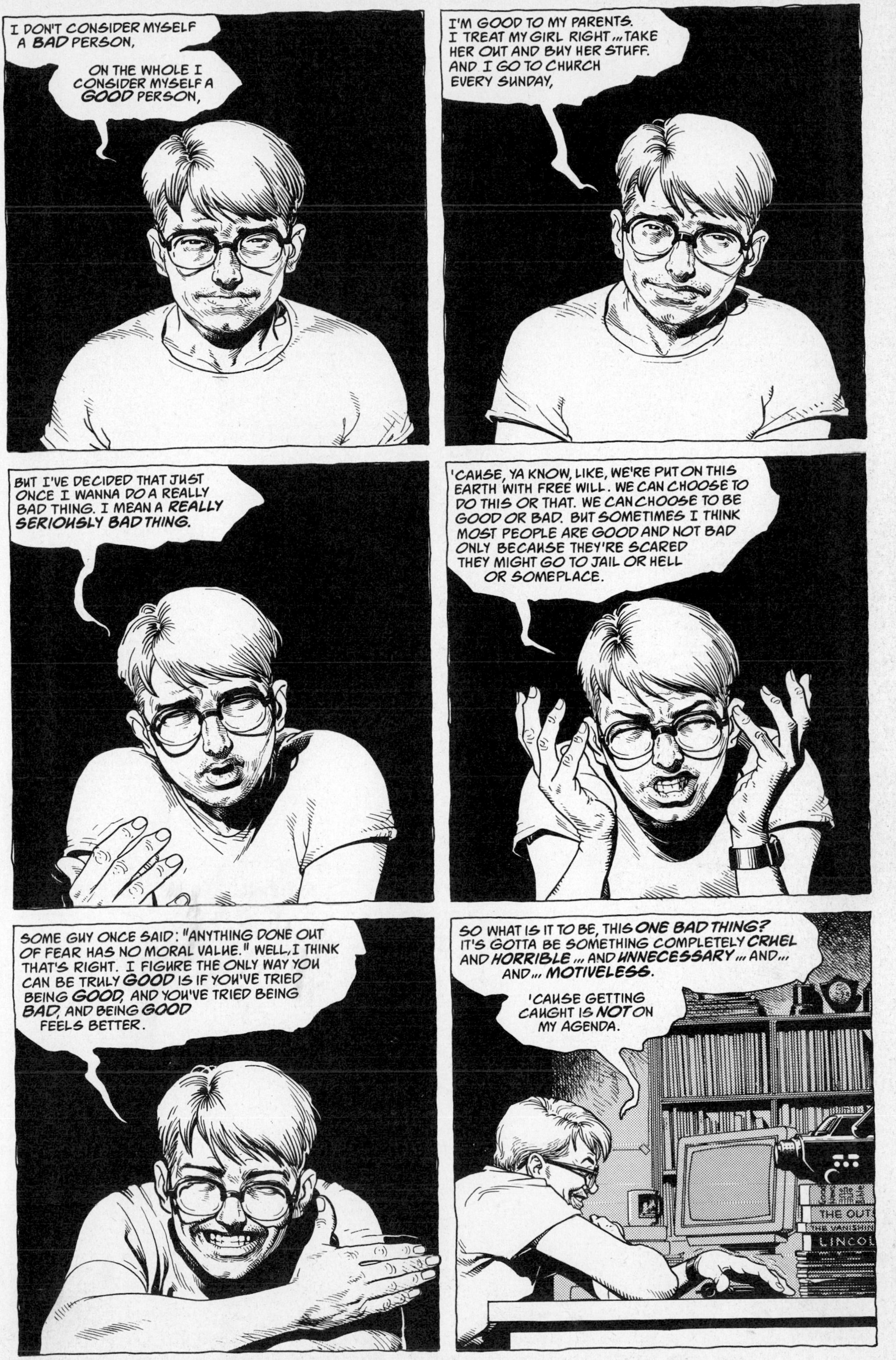
I DON'T CONSIDER MYSELF A BAD PERSON.
ON THE WHOLE I CONSIDER MYSELF A GOOD PERSON.
I'M GOOD TO MY PARENTS. I TREAT MY GIRL RIGHT... TAKE HER OUT AND BUY HER STUFF. AND I GO TO CHURCH EVERY SUNDAY.
BUT I'VE DECIDED THAT JUST ONCE I WANNA DO A REALLY BAD THING. I MEAN A REALLY SERIOUSLY BAD THING.
'CAUSE, YA KNOW, LIKE, WE'RE PUT ON THIS EARTH WITH FREE WILL. WE CAN CHOOSE TO DO THIS OR THAT. WE CAN CHOOSE TO BE GOOD OR BAD. BUT SOMETIMES I THINK MOST PEOPLE ARE GOOD AND NOT BAD ONLY BECAUSE THEY'RE SCARED THEY MIGHT GO TO JAIL OR HELL OR SOMEPLACE.
SOME GUY ONCE SAID: "ANYTHING DONE OUT OF FEAR HAS NO MORAL VALUE." WELL, I THINK THAT'S RIGHT. I FIGURE THE ONLY WAY YOU CAN BE TRULY GOOD IS IF YOU'VE TRIED BEING GOOD, AND YOU'VE TRIED BEING BAD, AND BEING GOOD FEELS BETTER.
SO WHAT IS IT TO BE, THIS ONE BAD THING? IT'S GOTTA BE SOMETHING COMPLETELY CRUEL AND HORRIBLE... AND UNNECESSARY... AND... AND... MOTIVELESS.
'CAUSE GETTING CAUGHT IS NOT ON MY AGENDA.
THE OUTS
THE VANISHIN
LINCOL

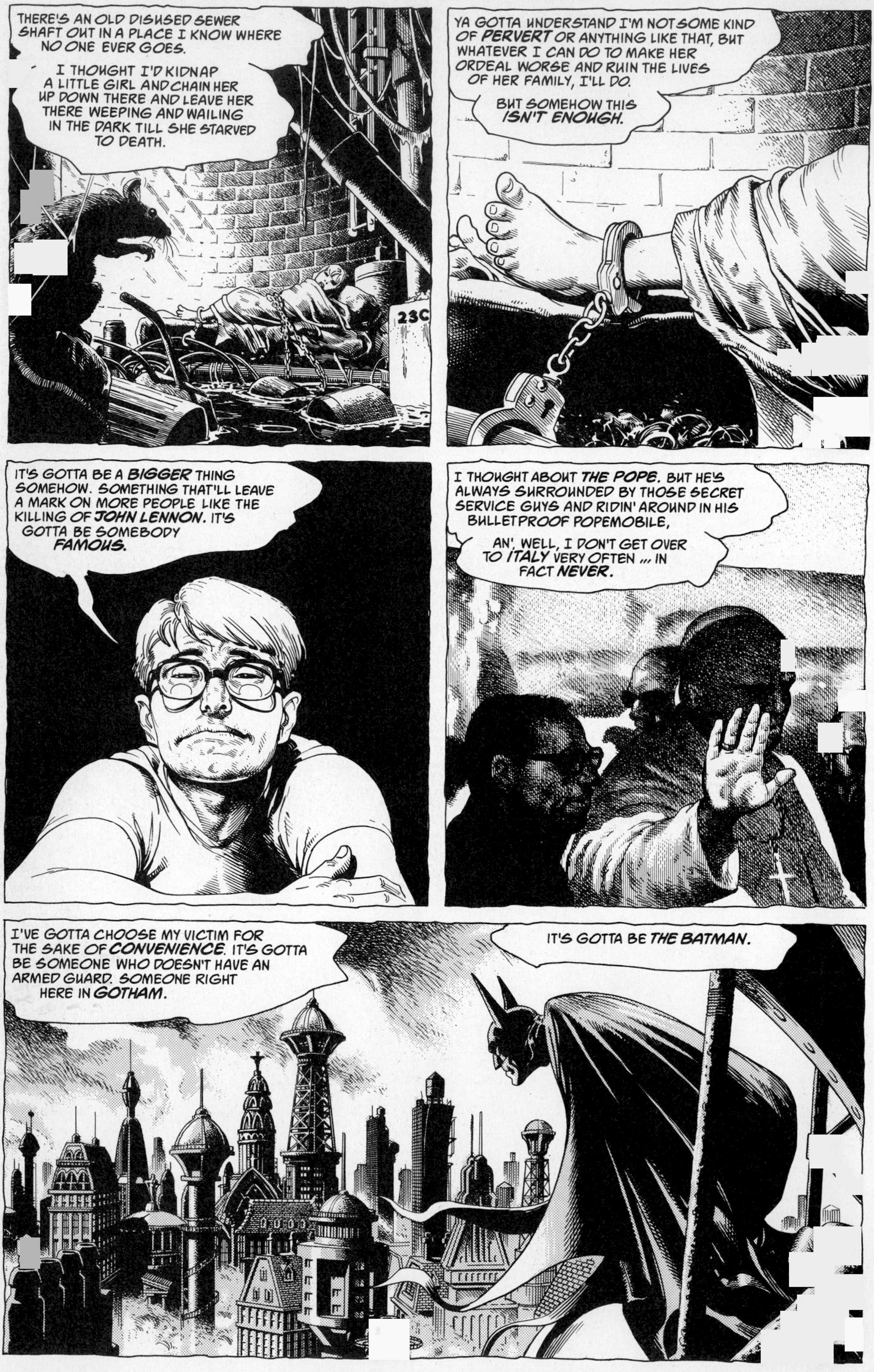
THERE'S AN OLD DISUSED SEWER SHAFT OUT IN A PLACE I KNOW WHERE NO ONE EVER GOES.
I THOUGHT I'D KIDNAP A LITTLE GIRL AND CHAIN HER UP DOWN THERE AND LEAVE HER THERE WEEPING AND WAILING IN THE DARK TILL SHE STARVED TO DEATH.
23C
YA GOTTA UNDERSTAND I'M NOT SOME KIND OF PERVERT OR ANYTHING LIKE THAT, BUT WHATEVER I CAN DO TO MAKE HER ORDEAL WORSE AND RUIN THE LIVES OF HER FAMILY, I'LL DO.
BUT SOMEHOW THIS ISN'T ENOUGH.
IT'S GOTTA BE A BIGGER THING SOMEHOW. SOMETHING THAT'LL LEAVE A MARK ON MORE PEOPLE LIKE THE KILLING OF JOHN LENNON. IT'S GOTTA BE SOMEBODY FAMOUS.
I THOUGHT ABOUT THE POPE. BUT HE'S ALWAYS SURROUNDED BY THOSE SECRET SERVICE GUYS AND RIDIN' AROUND IN HIS BULLETPROOF POPEMOBILE,
AN', WELL, I DON'T GET OVER TO ITALY VERY OFTEN ... IN FACT NEVER.
I'VE GOTTA CHOOSE MY VICTIM FOR THE SAKE OF CONVENIENCE. IT'S GOTTA BE SOMEONE WHO DOESN'T HAVE AN ARMED GUARD. SOMEONE RIGHT HERE IN GOTHAM.
IT'S GOTTA BE THE BATMAN.

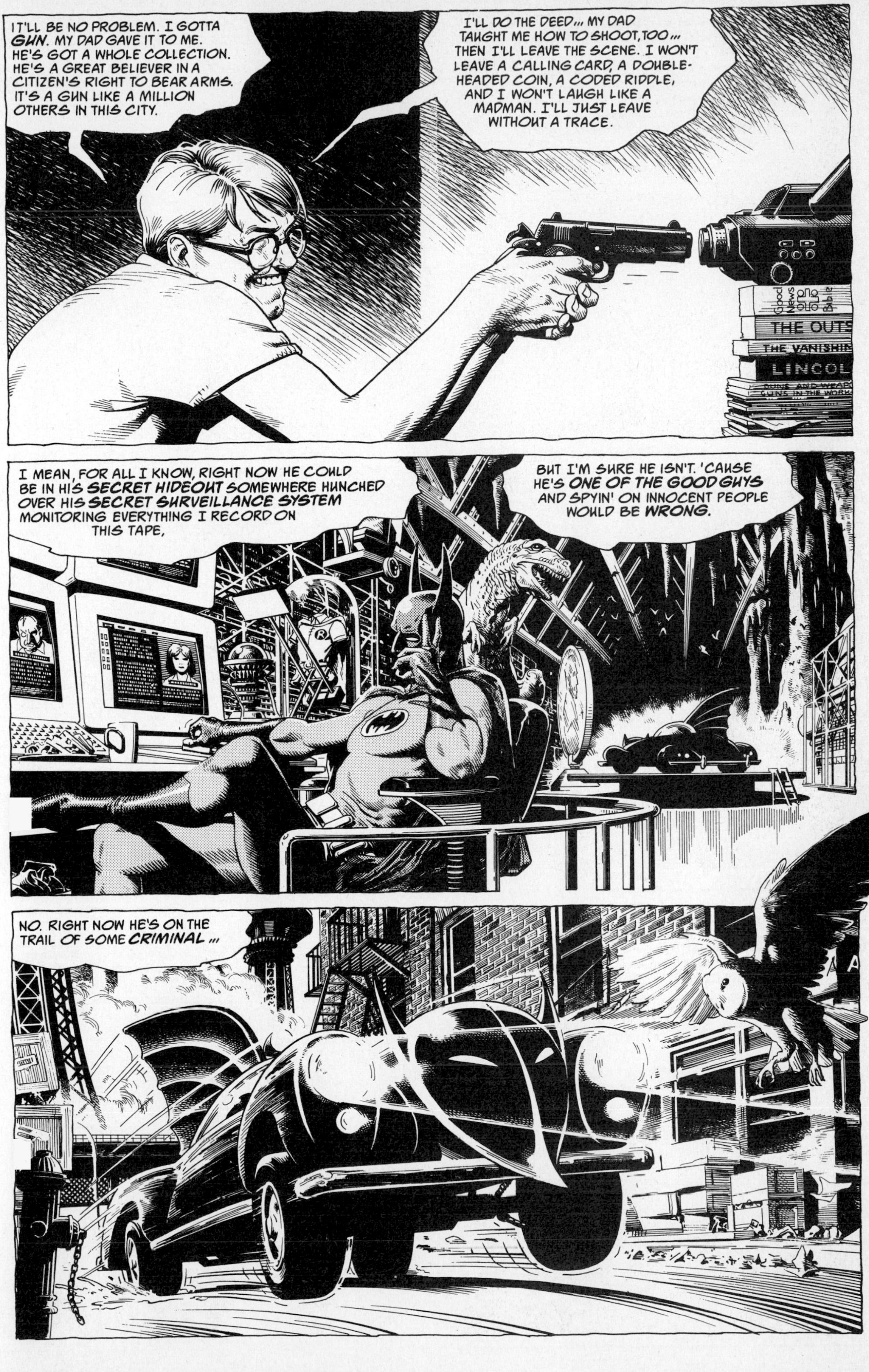
IT'LL BE NO PROBLEM. I GOTTA GUN. MY DAD GAVE IT TO ME. HE'S GOT A WHOLE COLLECTION. HE'S A GREAT BELIEVER IN A CITIZEN'S RIGHT TO BEAR ARMS. IT'S A GUN LIKE A MILLION OTHERS IN THIS CITY.
I'LL DO THE DEED... MY DAD TAUGHT ME HOW TO SHOOT, TOO... THEN I'LL LEAVE THE SCENE. I WON'T LEAVE A CALLING CARD, A DOUBLE-HEADED COIN, A CODED RIDDLE, AND I WON'T LAUGH LIKE A MADMAN. I'LL JUST LEAVE WITHOUT A TRACE.
THE OUTS
THE VANISHIN
LINCOL
I MEAN, FOR ALL I KNOW, RIGHT NOW HE COULD BE IN HIS SECRET HIDEOUT SOMEWHERE HUNCHED OVER HIS SECRET SURVEILLANCE SYSTEM MONITORING EVERYTHING I RECORD ON THIS TAPE,
BUT I'M SURE HE ISN'T. 'CAUSE HE'S ONE OF THE GOOD GUYS AND SPYIN' ON INNOCENT PEOPLE WOULD BE WRONG.
NO. RIGHT NOW HE'S ON THE TRAIL OF SOME CRIMINAL...

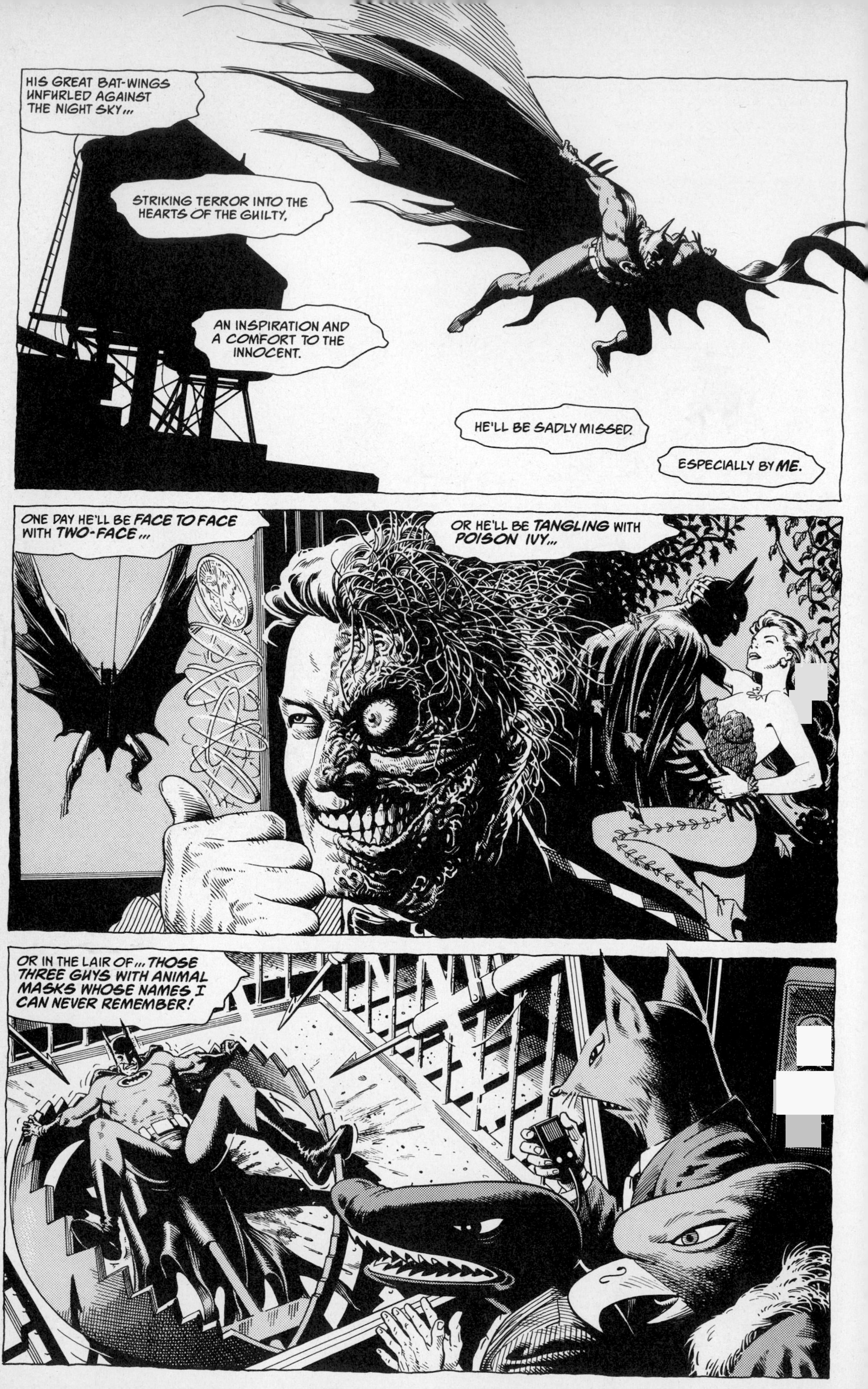
HIS GREAT BAT-WINGS UNFURLED AGAINST THE NIGHT SKY...
STRIKING TERROR INTO THE HEARTS OF THE GUILTY,
AN INSPIRATION AND A COMFORT TO THE INNOCENT.
HE'LL BE SADLY MISSED.
ESPECIALLY BY ME.
ONE DAY HE'LL BE FACE TO FACE WITH TWO-FACE...
OR HE'LL BE TANGLING WITH POISON IVY...
OR IN THE LAIR OF... THOSE THREE GUYS WITH ANIMAL MASKS WHOSE NAMES I CAN NEVER REMEMBER!

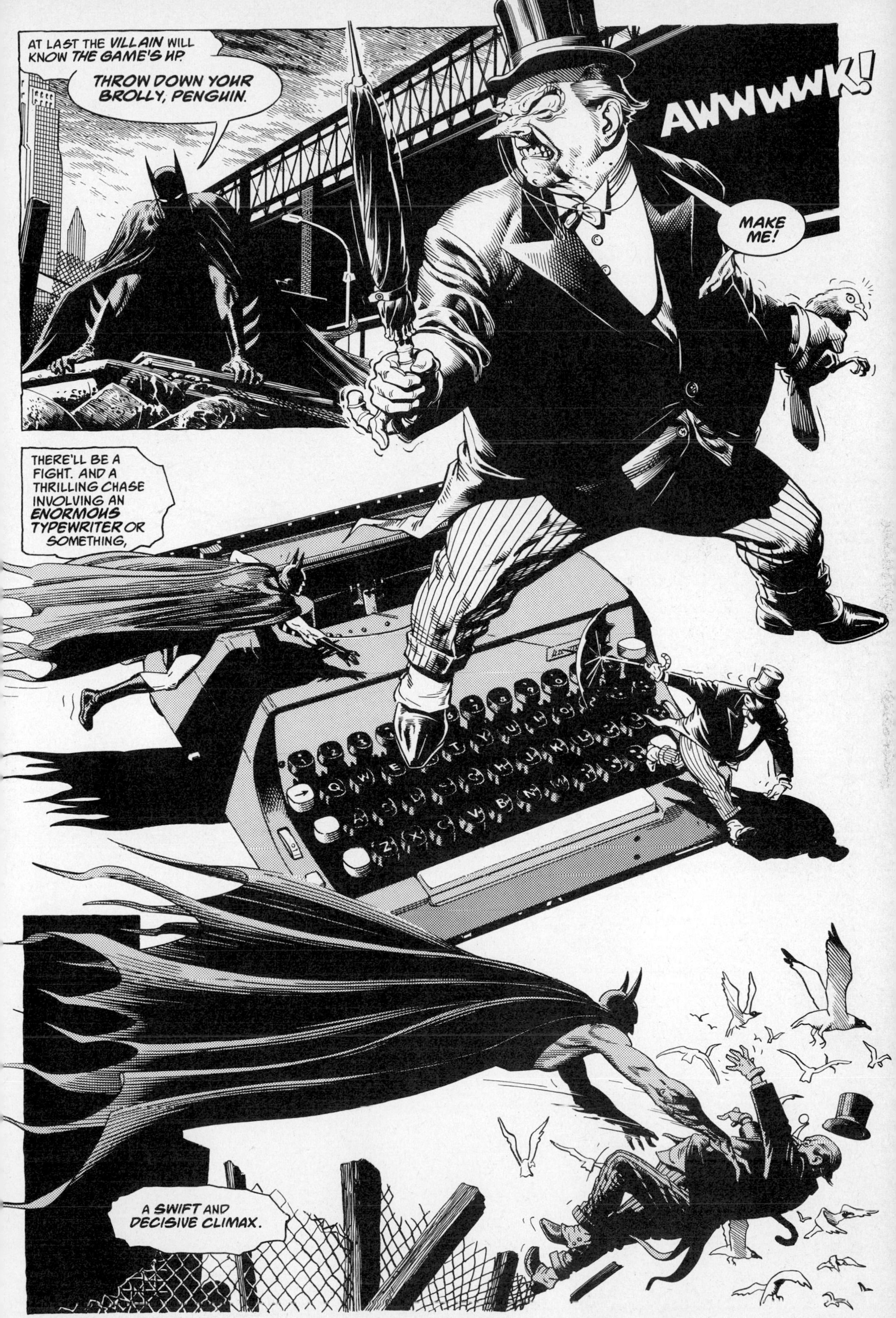
AT LAST THE VILLAIN WILL KNOW THE GAME'S UP.
THROW DOWN YOUR BROLLY, PENGUIN.
AWWWWK!
MAKE ME!
THERE'LL BE A FIGHT. AND A THRILLING CHASE INVOLVING AN ENORMOUS TYPEWRITER OR SOMETHING,
A SWIFT AND DECISIVE CLIMAX.

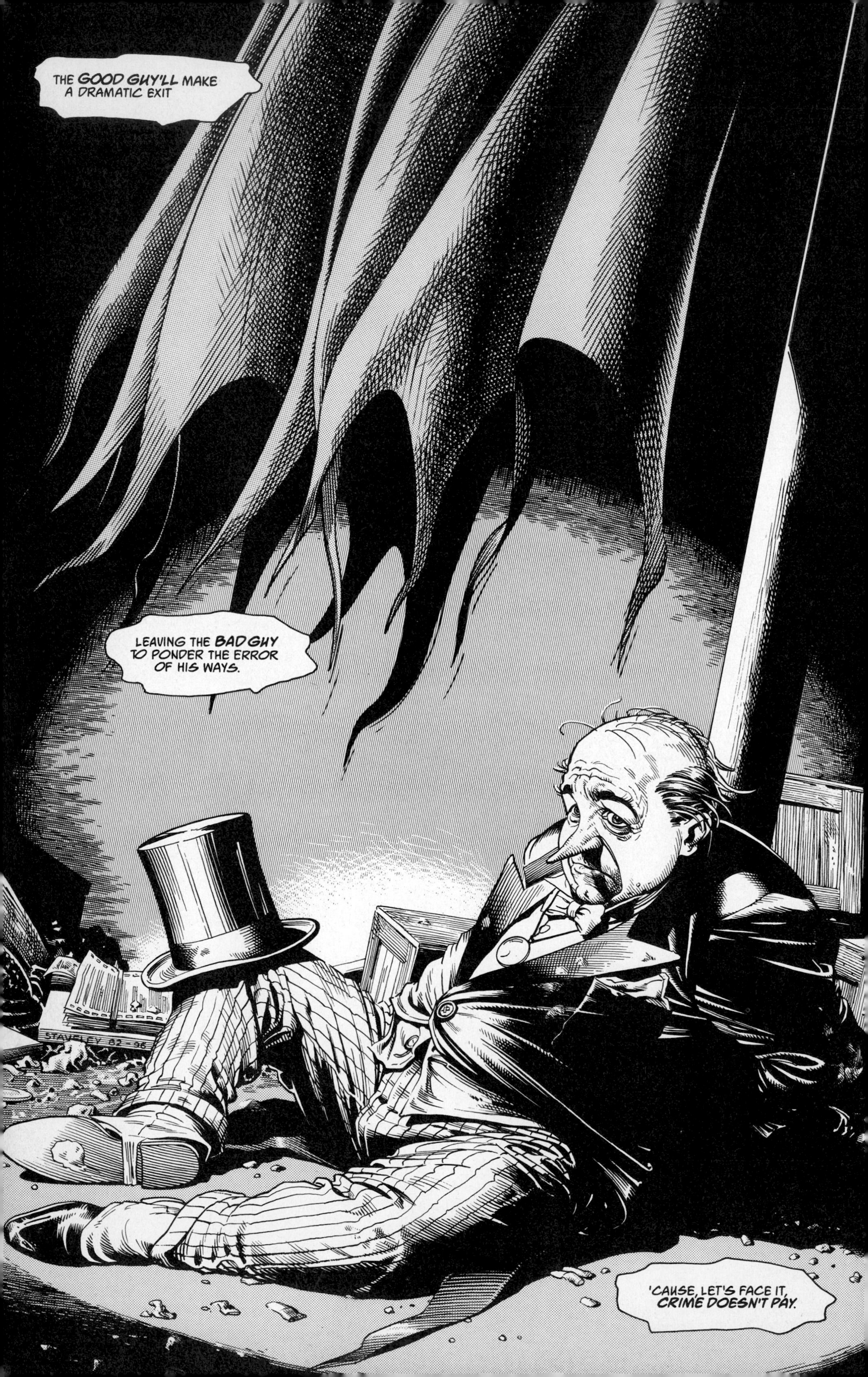
THE GOOD GUY'LL MAKE A DRAMATIC EXIT
LEAVING THE BAD GUY TO PONDER THE ERROR OF HIS WAYS.
'CAUSE, LET'S FACE IT, CRIME DOESN'T PAY.

AND JUST FOR ONE MOMENT THE BATMAN WILL PAUSE. TURN. HIS FACE ILLUMINATED BY A SINGLE LIGHT... A SPLENDID AVENGER OF THE NIGHT.
AND THEN FROM A DARK ALLEY,
OR A WINDOW HIGH UP,
OR A GRASSY KNOLL,
OR SOME OTHER PLACE,
THERE'LL BE A GLINT,
AND THEN
BANG

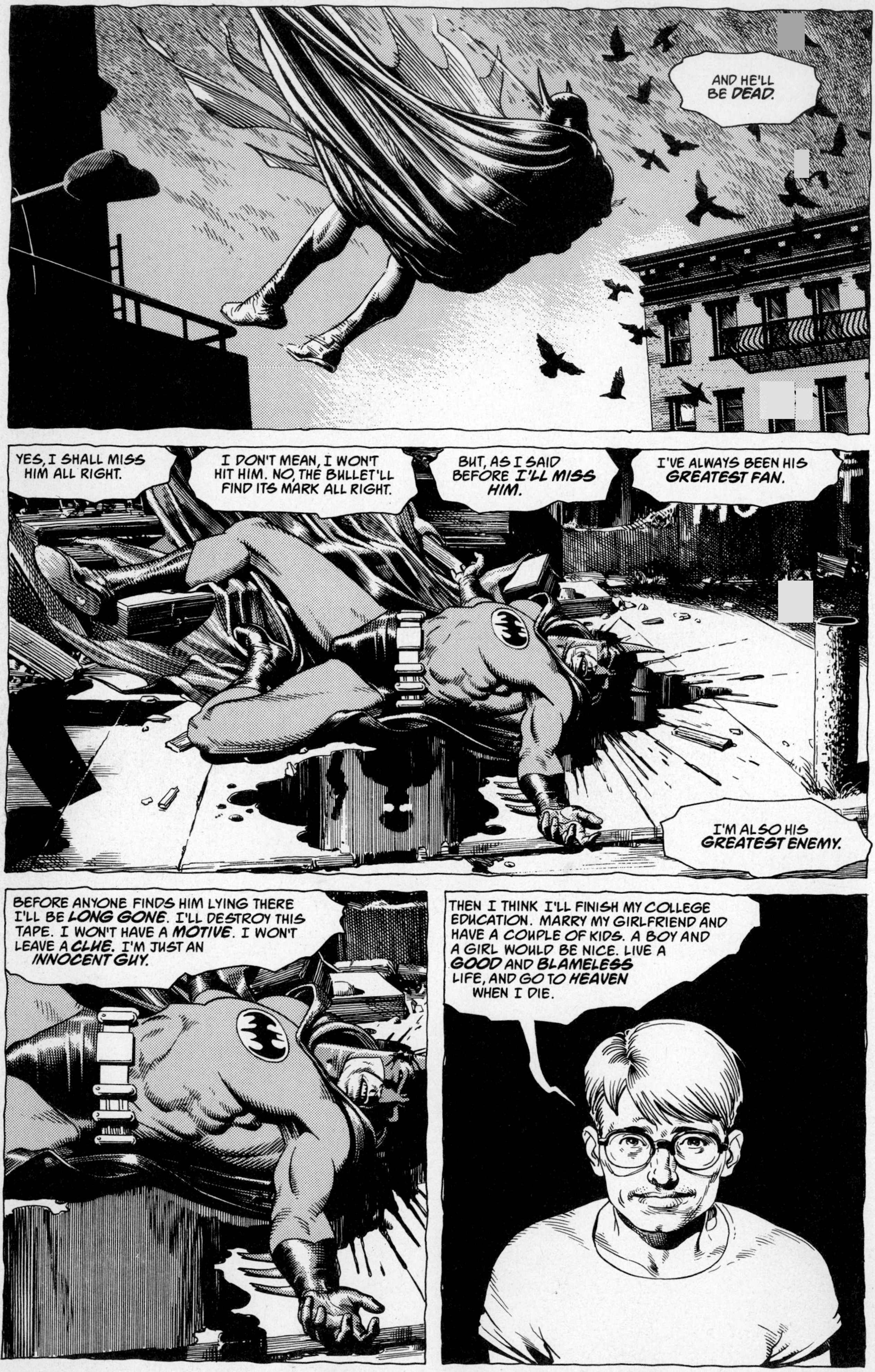
AND HE'LL BE DEAD.
YES, I SHALL MISS HIM ALL RIGHT.
I DON'T MEAN, I WON'T HIT HIM. NO, THE BULLET'LL FIND ITS MARK ALL RIGHT.
BUT, AS I SAID BEFORE I'LL MISS HIM.
I'VE ALWAYS BEEN HIS GREATEST FAN.
I'M ALSO HIS GREATEST ENEMY.
BEFORE ANYONE FINDS HIM LYING THERE I'LL BE LONG GONE. I'LL DESTROY THIS TAPE. I WON'T HAVE A MOTIVE. I WON'T LEAVE A CLUE. I'M JUST AN INNOCENT GUY.
THEN I THINK I'LL FINISH MY COLLEGE EDUCATION. MARRY MY GIRLFRIEND AND HAVE A COUPLE OF KIDS. A BOY AND A GIRL WOULD BE NICE. LIVE A GOOD AND BLAMELESS LIFE, AND GO TO HEAVEN WHEN I DIE.

MONSTERS IN THE CLOSET

KEVIN NOWLAN

Kevin Nowlan is considered the Renaissance man of the comics world. He is easily one of the great pencillers, inkers, colorists and letterers working in the business today. His talents have made him a near-god among his peers, who are simply in awe of his artwork.

JAN STRNAD

Best known to the comics world for his collaborations with comics legend Richard Corben, writer Jan Strnad now spends much of his time writing for television.

Jan has written for an incredible array of comics publishers, including mainstream, independent and underground companies.

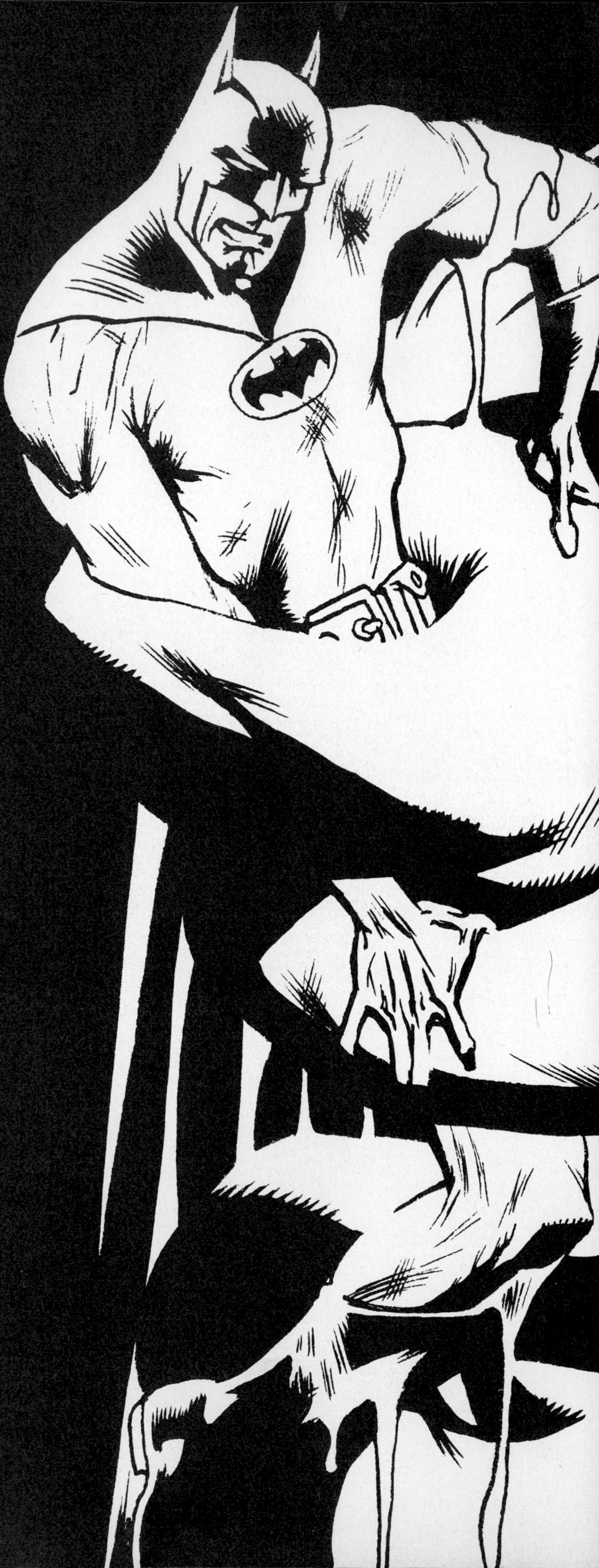

 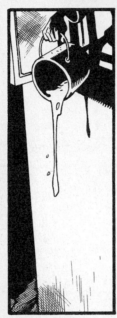  

BE CAREFUL, MARTHA.

HURRY, THESE BIG CITY STREETS AREN'T *SAFE* AFTER DARK.

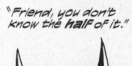

*"Friend, you don't know the **half** of it."*

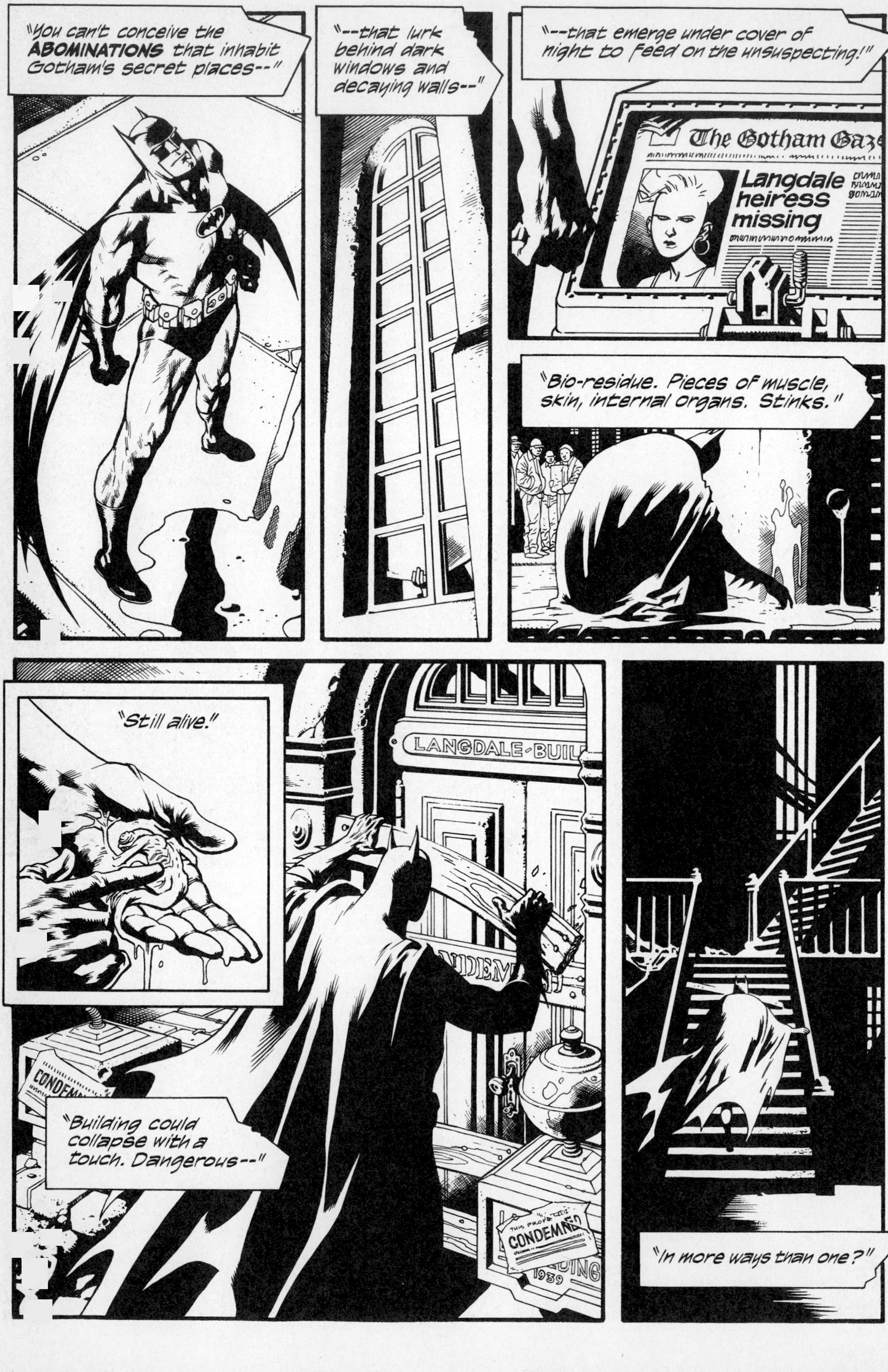
"You can't conceive the ABOMINATIONS that inhabit Gotham's secret places--"
"--that lurk behind dark windows and decaying walls--"
"--that emerge under cover of night to feed on the unsuspecting!"
The Gotham Gaze
Langdale heiress missing
"Bio-residue. Pieces of muscle, skin, internal organs. Stinks."
"Still alive."
LANGDALE-BUIL
CONDEMNED
"Building could collapse with a touch. Dangerous--"
THIS PROPERTY CONDEMNED
1939
"In more ways than one?"

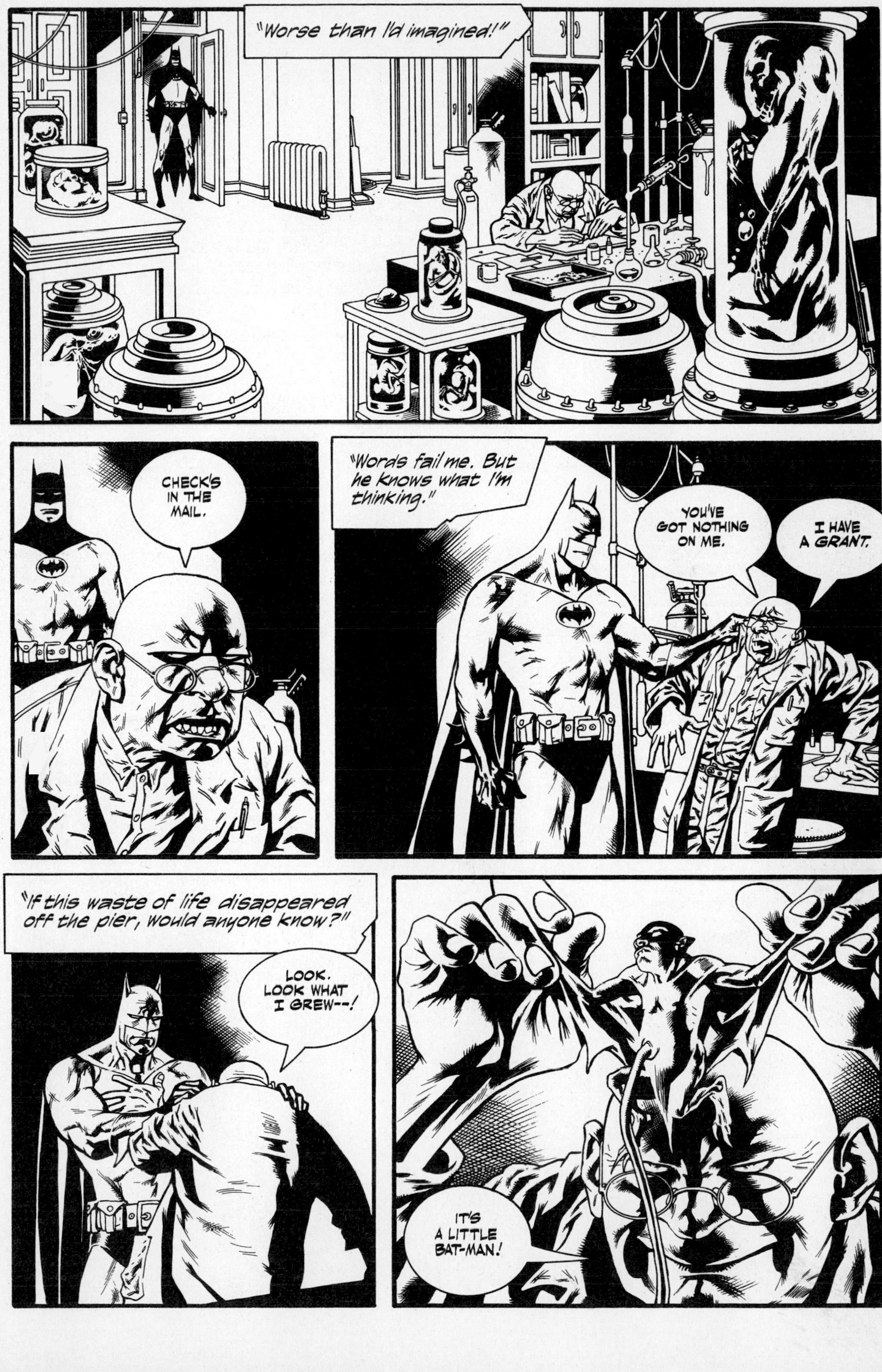
"Worse than I'd imagined!"
CHECK'S IN THE MAIL.
"Words fail me. But he knows what I'm thinking."
YOU'VE GOT NOTHING ON ME.
I HAVE A GRANT.
"If this waste of life disappeared off the pier, would anyone know?"
LOOK. LOOK WHAT I GREW--!
IT'S A LITTLE BAT-MAN!

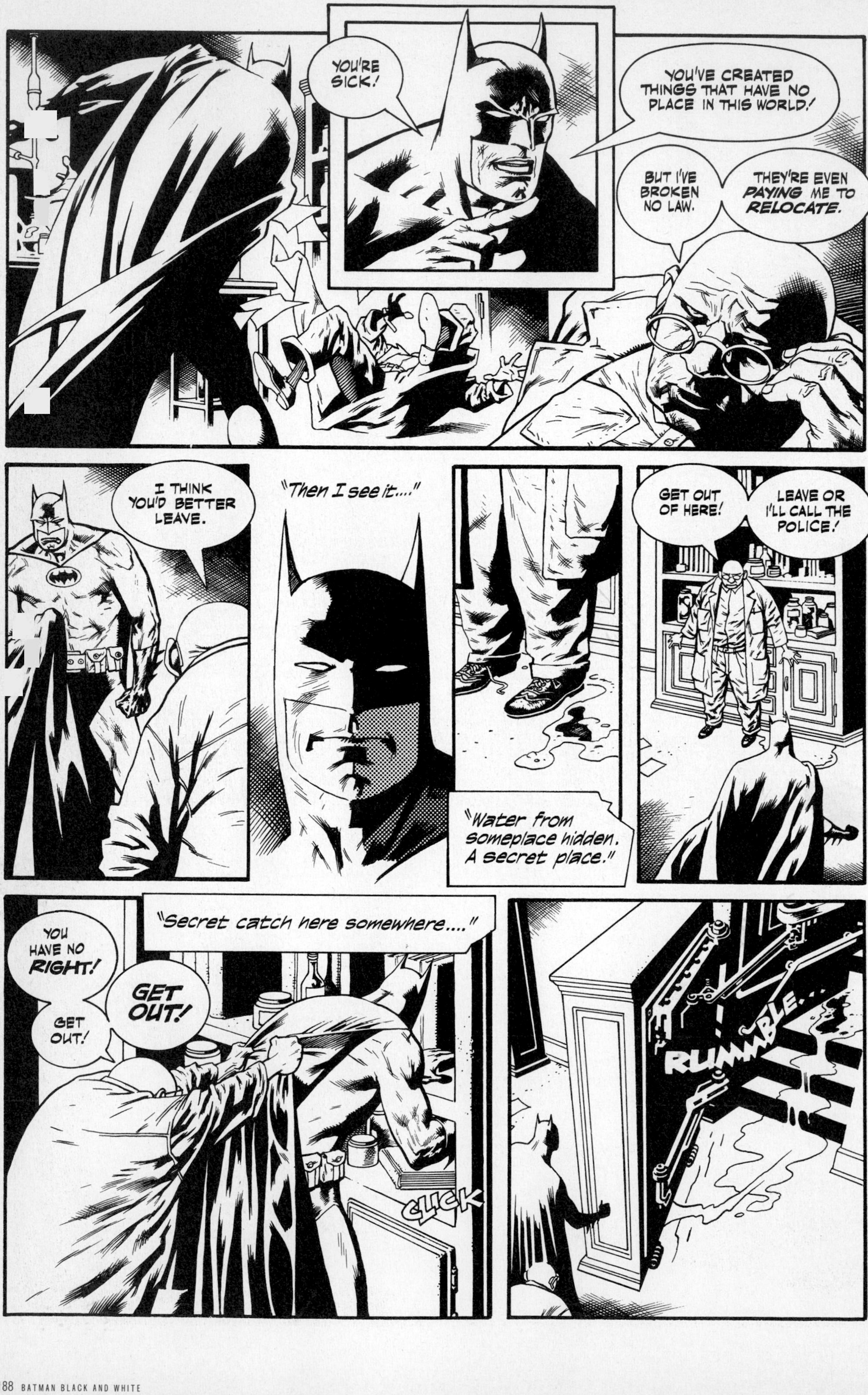

YOU'RE SICK!
YOU'VE CREATED THINGS THAT HAVE NO PLACE IN THIS WORLD!
BUT I'VE BROKEN NO LAW.
THEY'RE EVEN PAYING ME TO RELOCATE.
I THINK YOU'D BETTER LEAVE.
"Then I see it...."
"Water from someplace hidden. A secret place."
GET OUT OF HERE!
LEAVE OR I'LL CALL THE POLICE!
"Secret catch here somewhere...."
YOU HAVE NO RIGHT!
GET OUT!
GET OUT!
CLICK
RUMMMBLE...

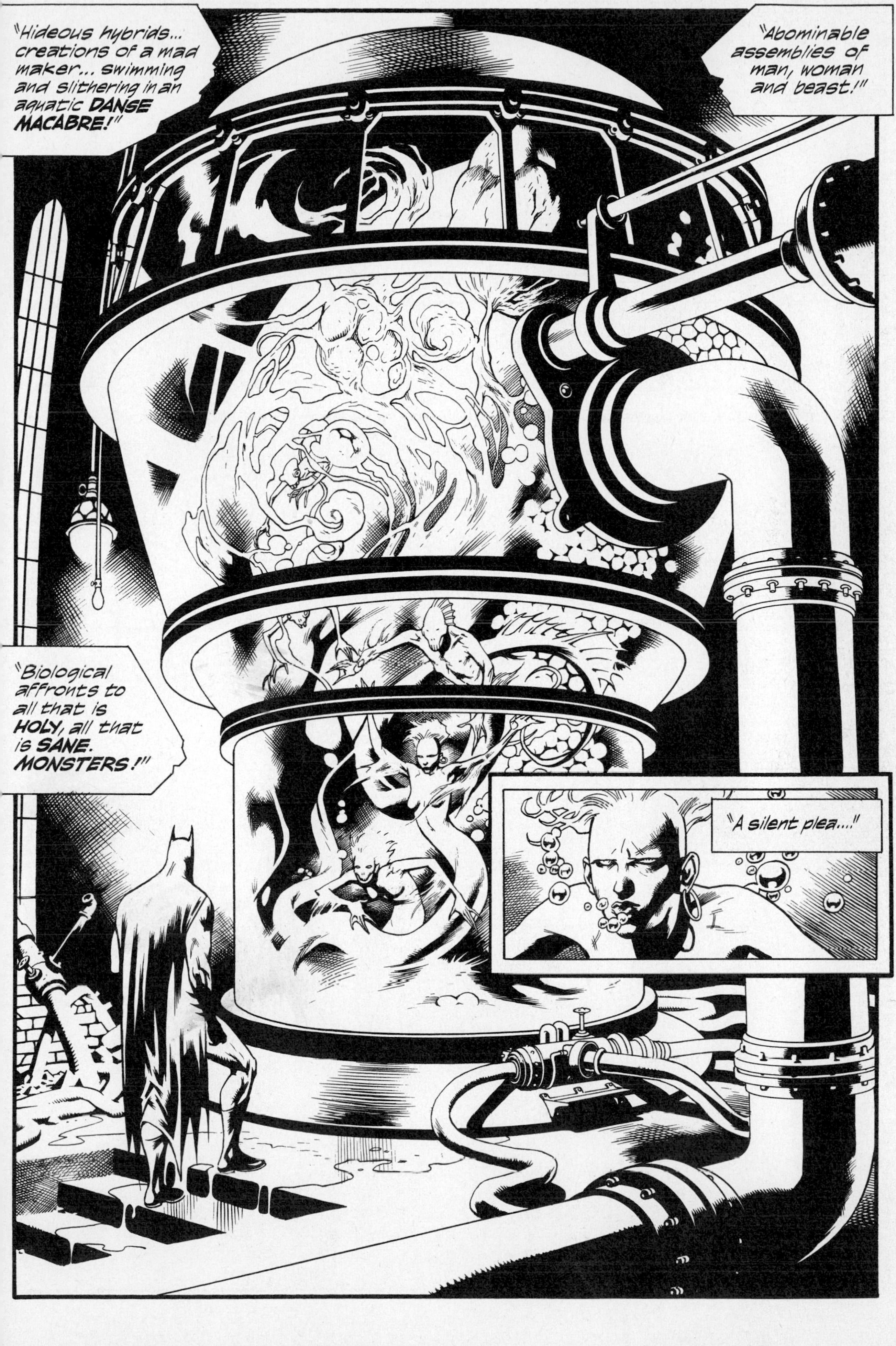
"Hideous hybrids... creations of a mad maker... swimming and slithering in an aquatic DANSE MACABRE!"
"Abominable assemblies of man, woman and beast!"
"Biological affronts to all that is HOLY, all that is SANE. MONSTERS!"
"A silent plea...!"

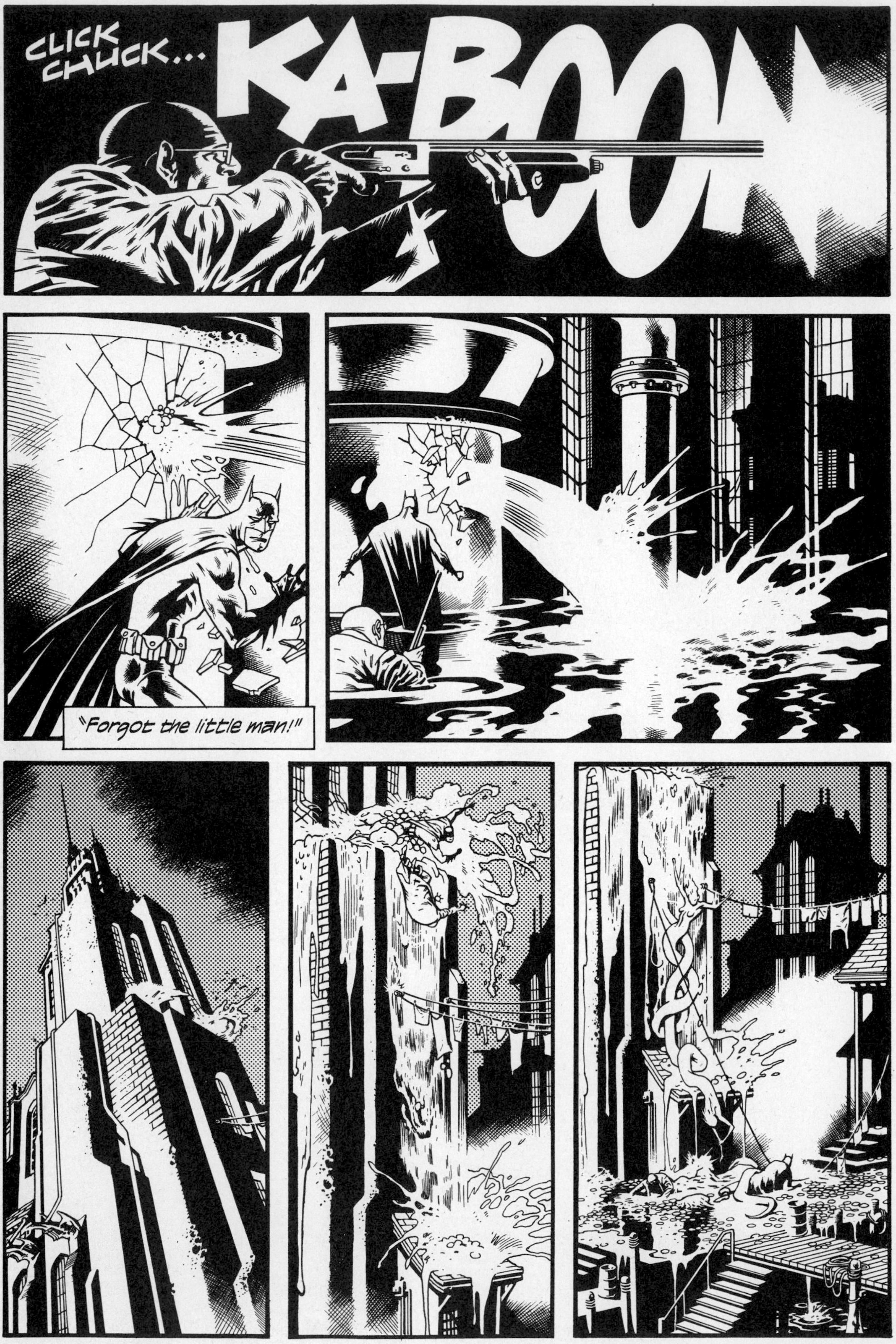
CLICK CHUCK...
KA-BOOM
"Forgot the little man!"

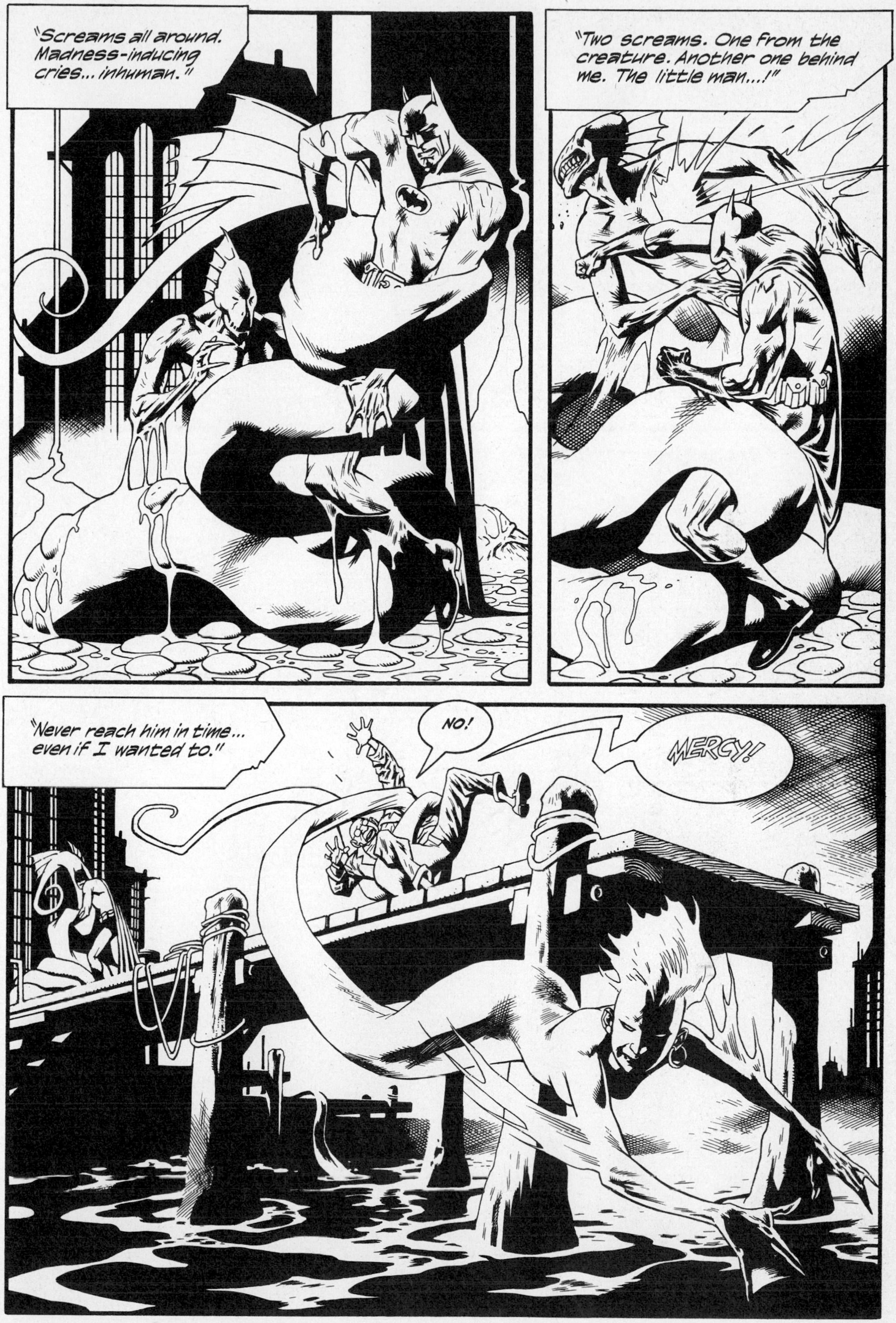
"Screams all around. Madness-inducing cries... inhuman."
"Two screams. One from the creature. Another one behind me. The little man...!"
"Never reach him in time... even if I wanted to."
NO!
MERCY!

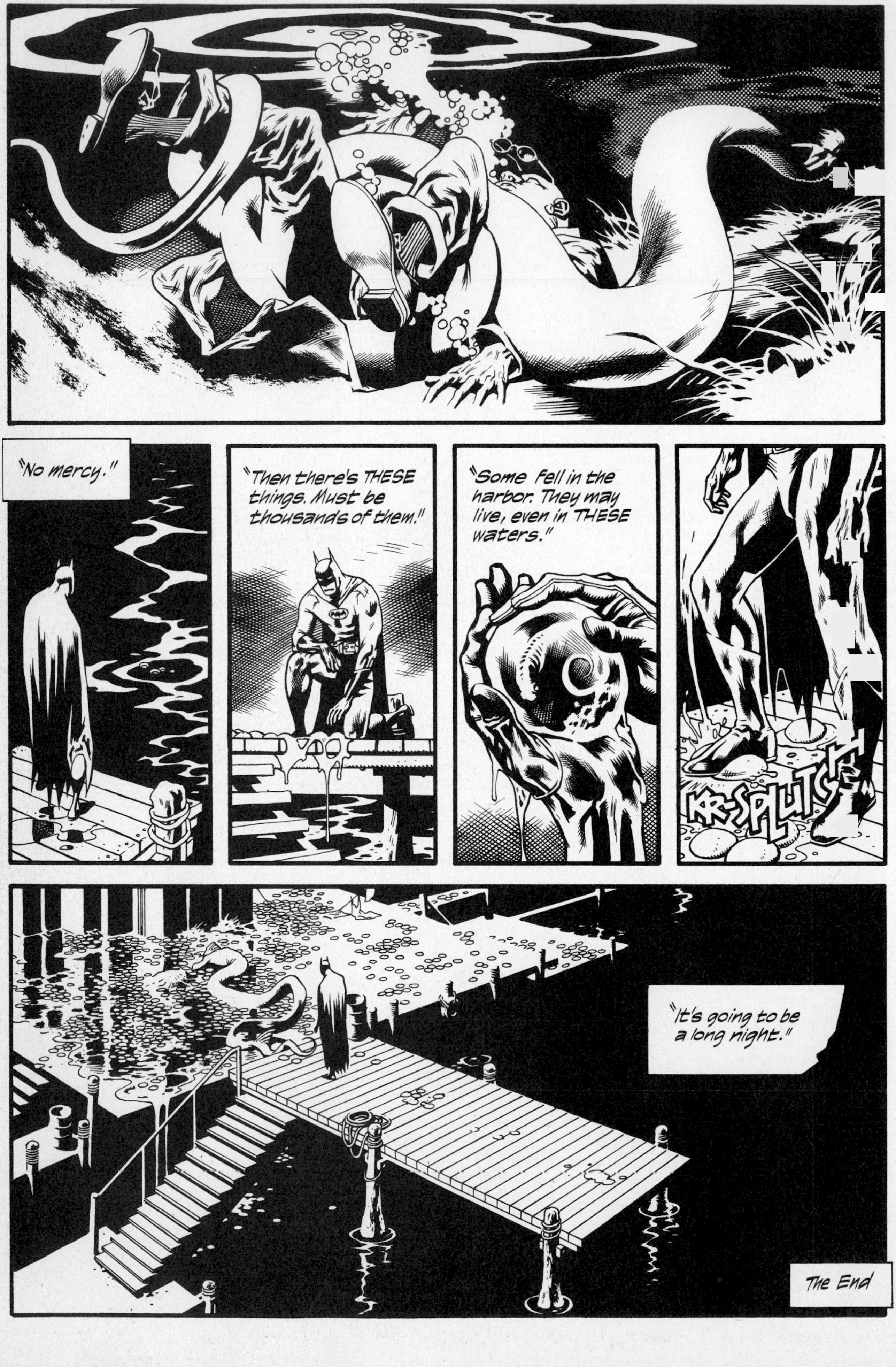
"No mercy."
"Then there's THESE things. Must be thousands of them."
"Some fell in the harbor. They may live, even in THESE waters."
KR-SPLUTSH
"It's going to be a long night."
The End

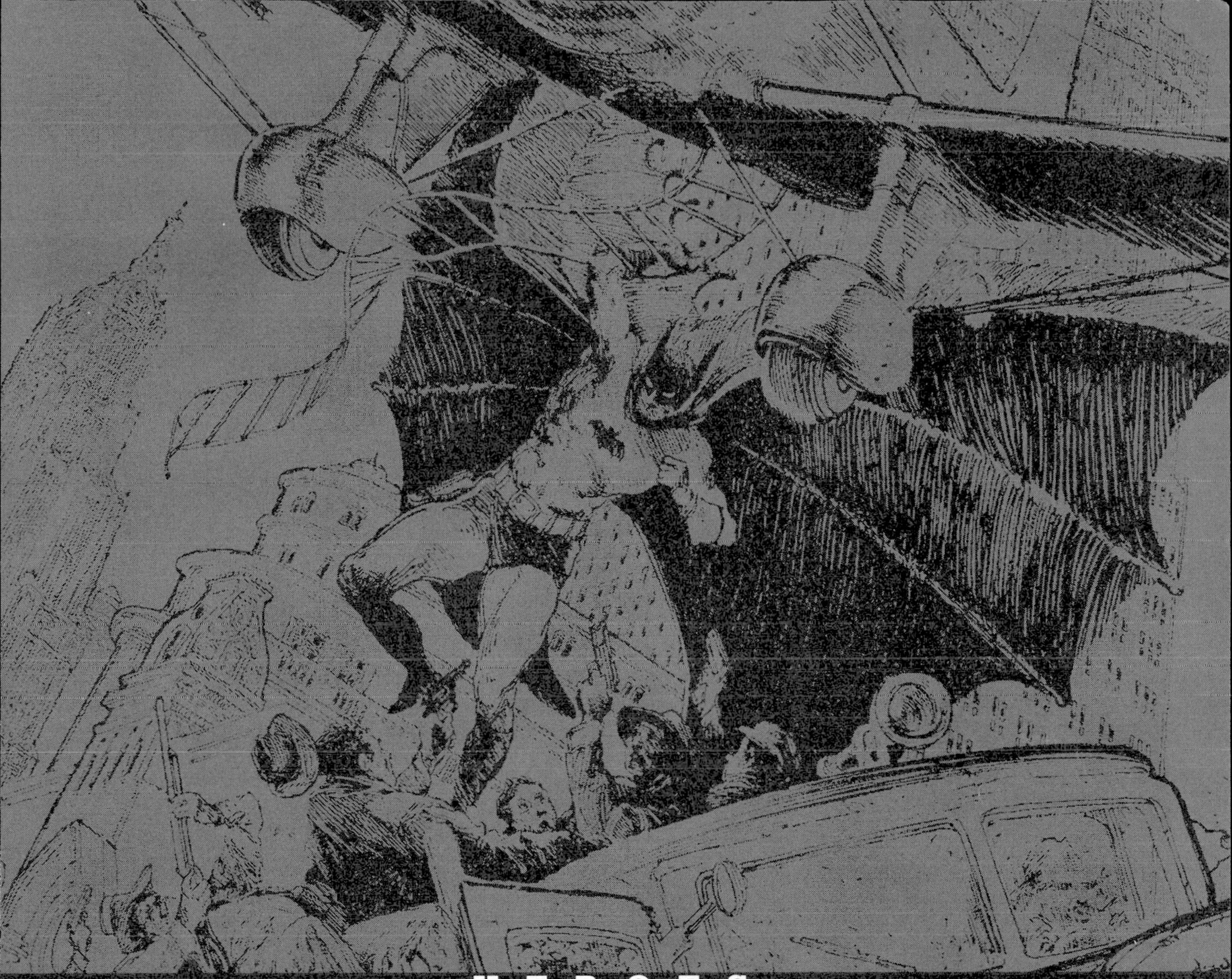

HEROES

GARY **GIANNI**

Gary Gianni's luscious artwork stirs up memories of a time long gone. Taking a cue from penwork masters of the past, like Joseph Clement Coll and Franklin Booth, Gary's approach to comic-book art is as sophisticated as it is enticing. With this Batman story, Gianni adds DC's classic American pulp hero to an already long list of others he's drawn, including The Shadow, Doc Savage and Indiana Jones.

ARCHIE **GOODWIN**

Often hailed as the most respected writer in the industry, Archie Goodwin is a thirty-year veteran in the comics field.

He has written most major characters for DC and Marvel, has written syndicated newspaper strips such as *Star Wars* and *Tarzan*, and was once Editor-in-Chief at Marvel Comics.

Goodwin's astounding writing and editing stints on *Creepy*, *Eerie* and *Blazing Combat* are a creative feat that is still held in awe.
He is currently a group editor at DC Comics.

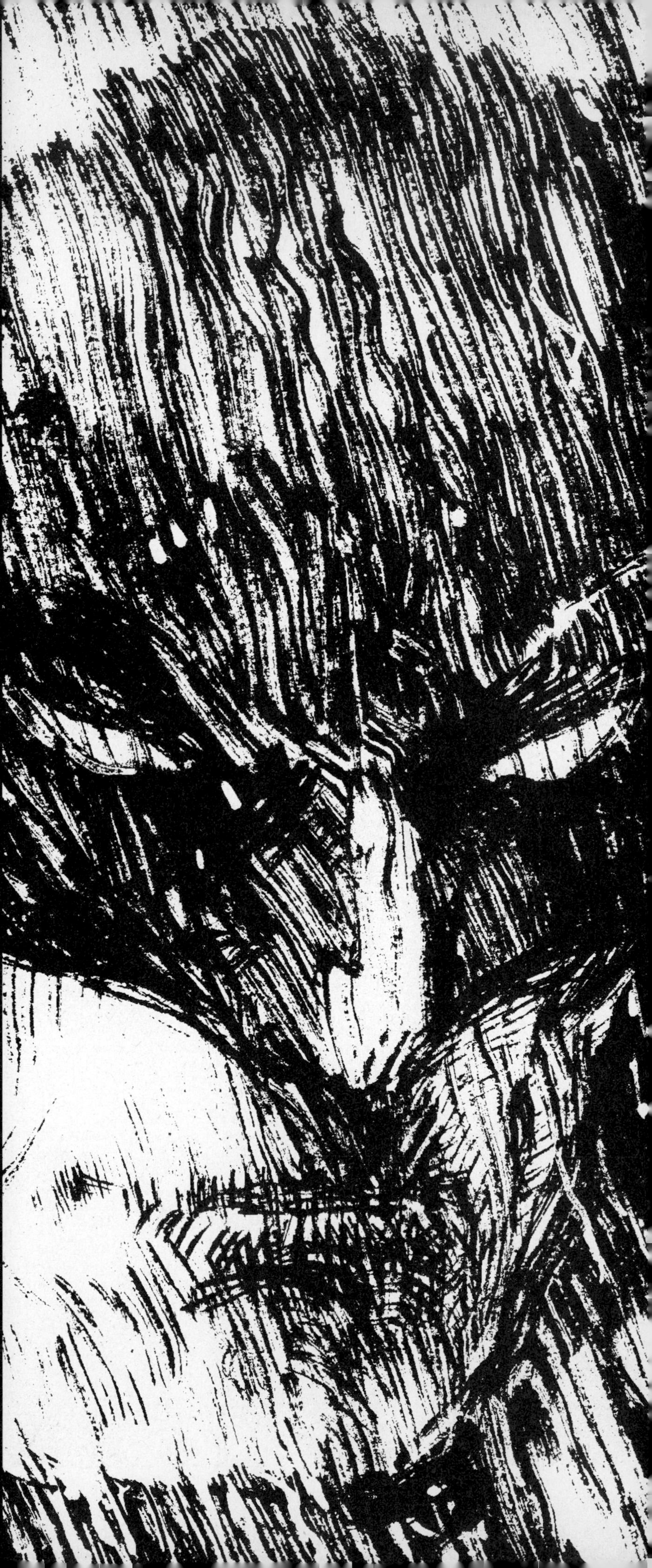

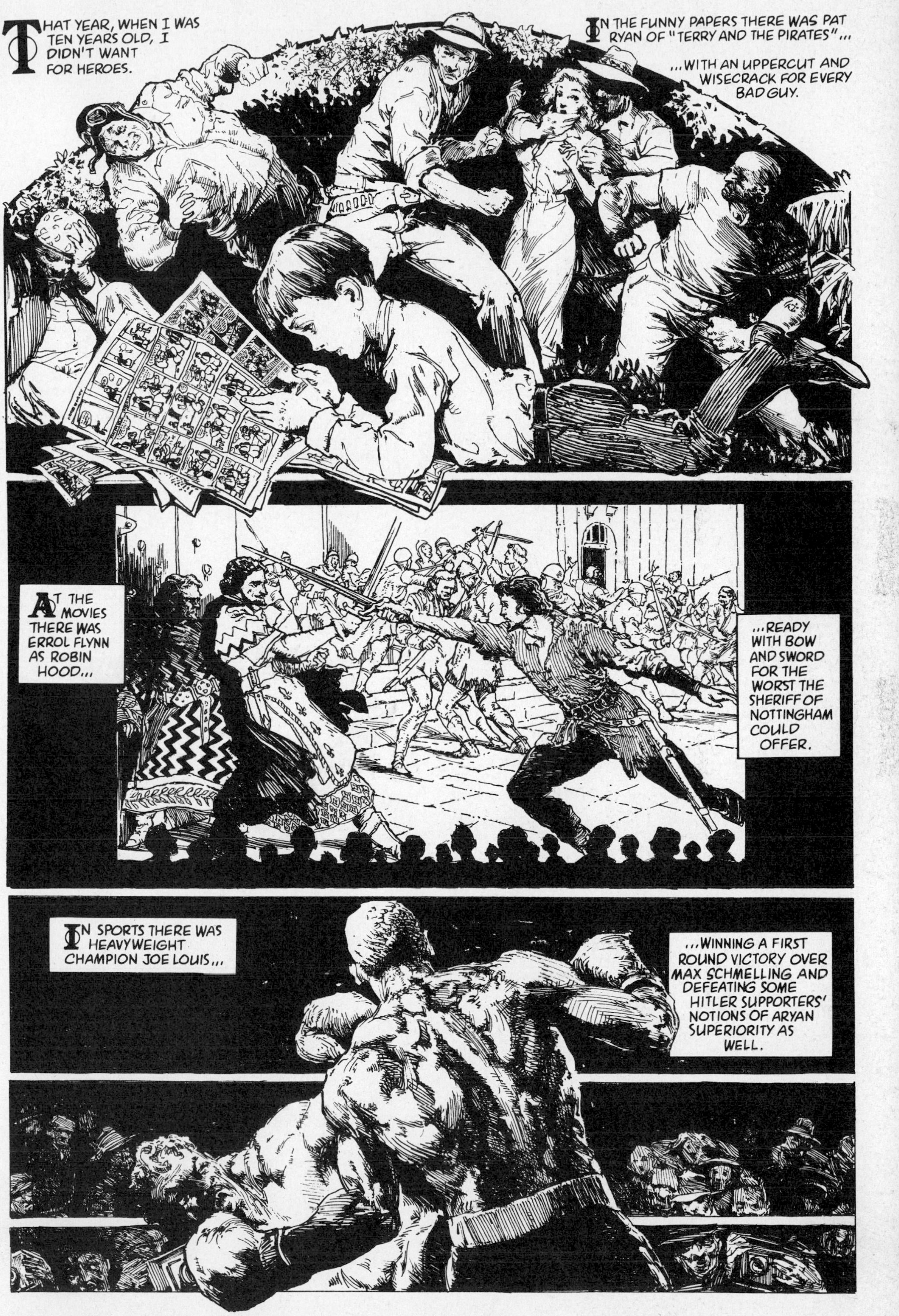
THAT YEAR, WHEN I WAS TEN YEARS OLD, I DIDN'T WANT FOR HEROES.
IN THE FUNNY PAPERS THERE WAS PAT RYAN OF "TERRY AND THE PIRATES"...
...WITH AN UPPERCUT AND WISECRACK FOR EVERY BAD GUY.
AT THE MOVIES THERE WAS ERROL FLYNN AS ROBIN HOOD...
...READY WITH BOW AND SWORD FOR THE WORST THE SHERIFF OF NOTTINGHAM COULD OFFER.
IN SPORTS THERE WAS HEAVYWEIGHT CHAMPION JOE LOUIS...
...WINNING A FIRST ROUND VICTORY OVER MAX SCHMELLING AND DEFEATING SOME HITLER SUPPORTERS' NOTIONS OF ARYAN SUPERIORITY AS WELL.

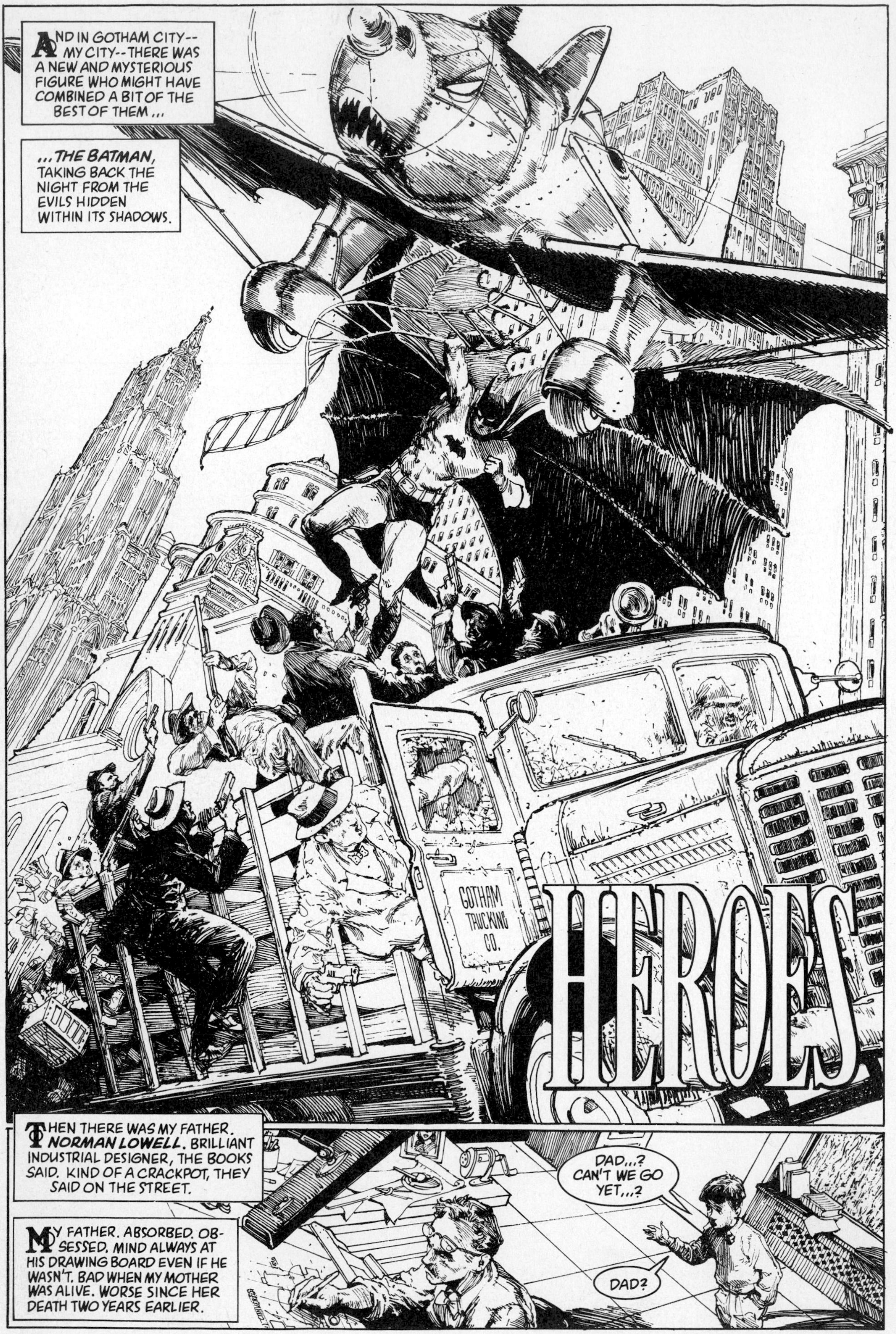
AND IN GOTHAM CITY-- MY CITY--THERE WAS A NEW AND MYSTERIOUS FIGURE WHO MIGHT HAVE COMBINED A BIT OF THE BEST OF THEM ...
...THE BATMAN, TAKING BACK THE NIGHT FROM THE EVILS HIDDEN WITHIN ITS SHADOWS.
GOTHAM TRUCKING CO.
HEROES
THEN THERE WAS MY FATHER. NORMAN LOWELL. BRILLIANT INDUSTRIAL DESIGNER, THE BOOKS SAID. KIND OF A CRACKPOT, THEY SAID ON THE STREET.
MY FATHER. ABSORBED. OBSESSED. MIND ALWAYS AT HIS DRAWING BOARD EVEN IF HE WASN'T. BAD WHEN MY MOTHER WAS ALIVE. WORSE SINCE HER DEATH TWO YEARS EARLIER.
DAD...? CAN'T WE GO YET...?
DAD?

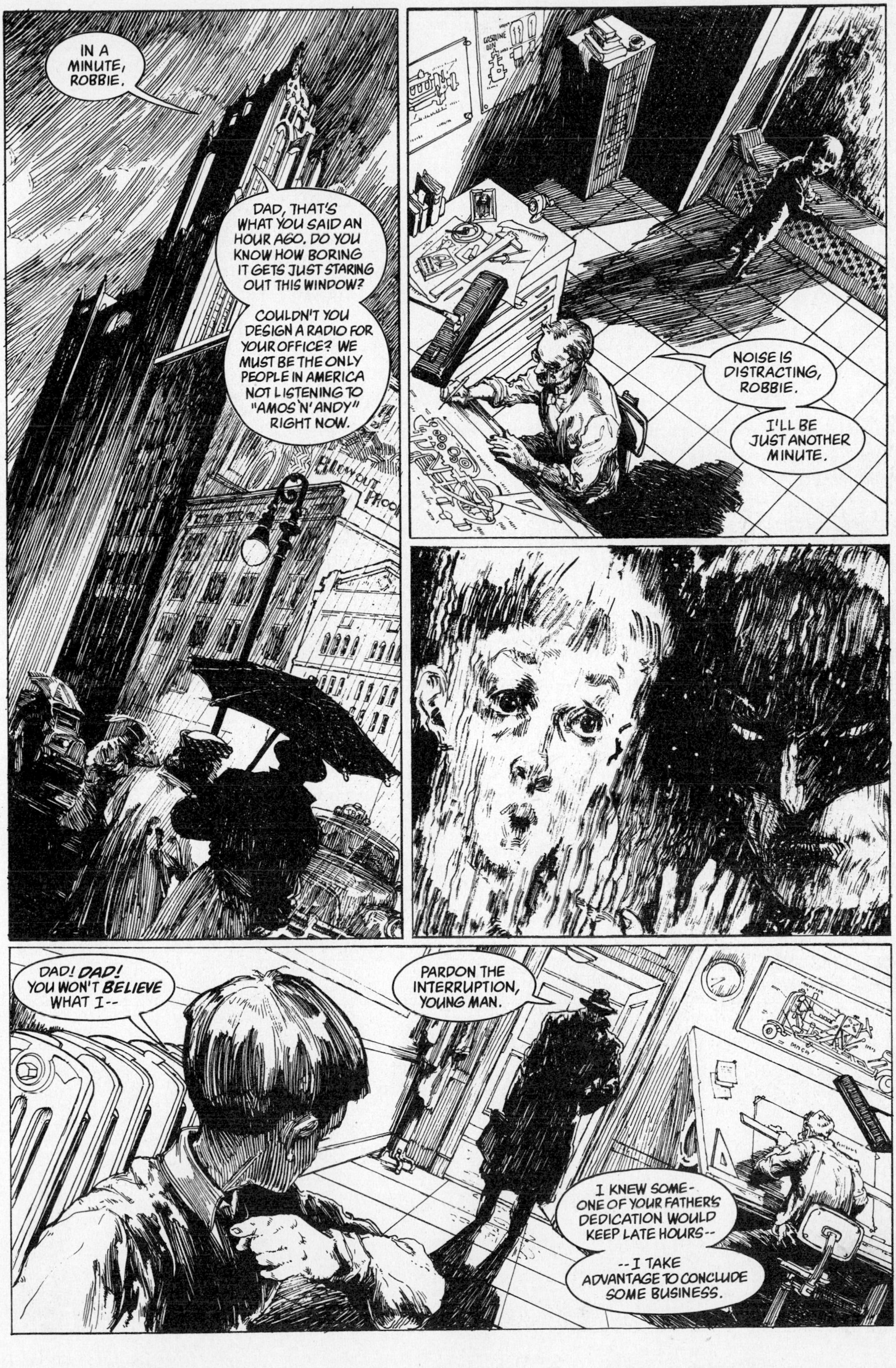
IN A MINUTE, ROBBIE.
DAD, THAT'S WHAT YOU SAID AN HOUR AGO. DO YOU KNOW HOW BORING IT GETS JUST STARING OUT THIS WINDOW?
COULDN'T YOU DESIGN A RADIO FOR YOUR OFFICE? WE MUST BE THE ONLY PEOPLE IN AMERICA NOT LISTENING TO "AMOS 'N' ANDY" RIGHT NOW.
NOISE IS DISTRACTING, ROBBIE.
I'LL BE JUST ANOTHER MINUTE.
DAD! DAD! YOU WON'T BELIEVE WHAT I--
PARDON THE INTERRUPTION, YOUNG MAN.
I KNEW SOME-ONE OF YOUR FATHER'S DEDICATION WOULD KEEP LATE HOURS--
--I TAKE ADVANTAGE TO CONCLUDE SOME BUSINESS.

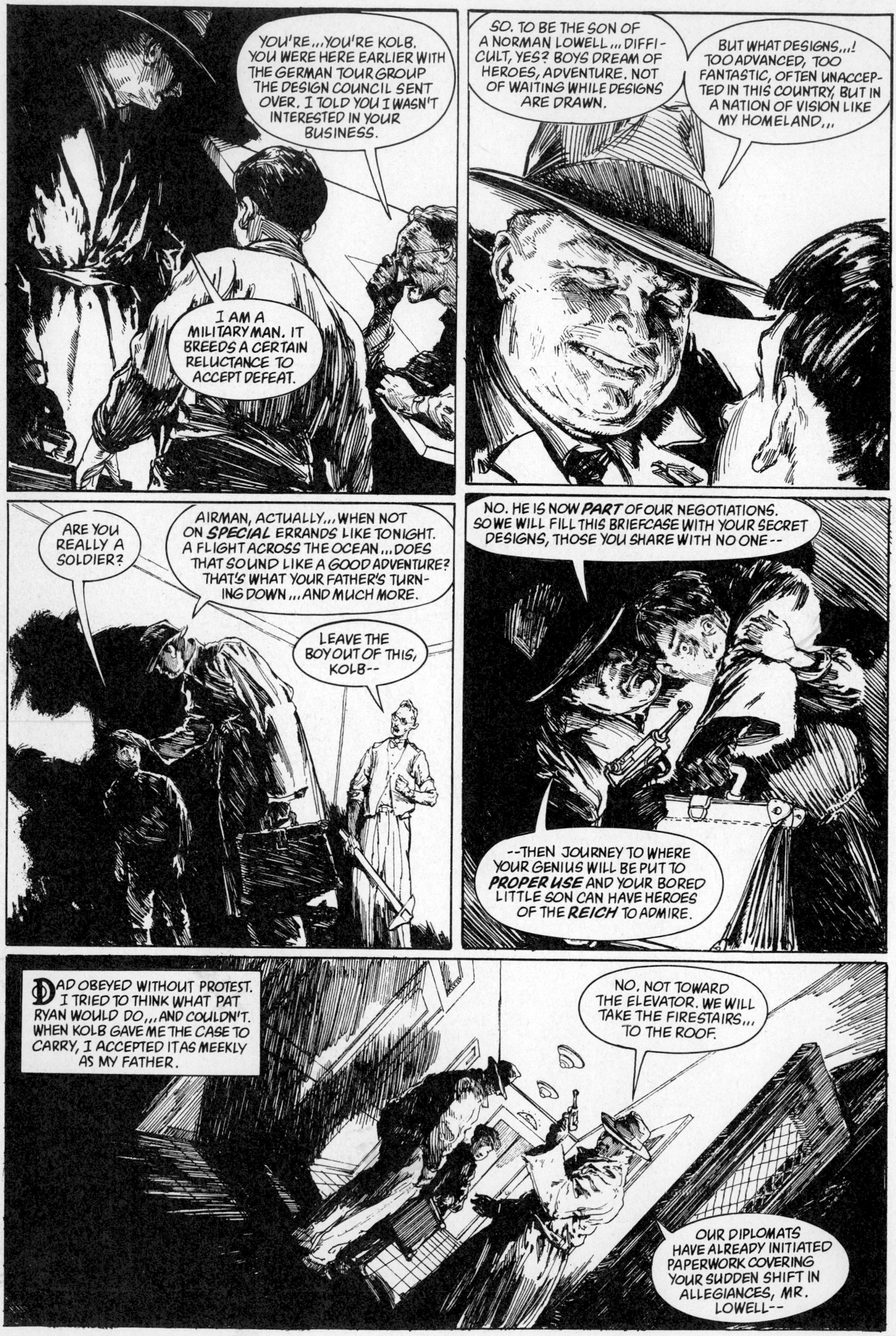
YOU'RE...YOU'RE KOLB. YOU WERE HERE EARLIER WITH THE GERMAN TOUR GROUP THE DESIGN COUNCIL SENT OVER. I TOLD YOU I WASN'T INTERESTED IN YOUR BUSINESS.
I AM A MILITARY MAN. IT BREEDS A CERTAIN RELUCTANCE TO ACCEPT DEFEAT.
SO. TO BE THE SON OF A NORMAN LOWELL... DIFFICULT, YES? BOYS DREAM OF HEROES, ADVENTURE. NOT OF WAITING WHILE DESIGNS ARE DRAWN.
BUT WHAT DESIGNS...! TOO ADVANCED, TOO FANTASTIC, OFTEN UNACCEPTED IN THIS COUNTRY, BUT IN A NATION OF VISION LIKE MY HOMELAND...
ARE YOU REALLY A SOLDIER?
AIRMAN, ACTUALLY... WHEN NOT ON SPECIAL ERRANDS LIKE TONIGHT. A FLIGHT ACROSS THE OCEAN... DOES THAT SOUND LIKE A GOOD ADVENTURE? THAT'S WHAT YOUR FATHER'S TURNING DOWN... AND MUCH MORE.
LEAVE THE BOY OUT OF THIS, KOLB--
NO. HE IS NOW PART OF OUR NEGOTIATIONS. SO WE WILL FILL THIS BRIEFCASE WITH YOUR SECRET DESIGNS, THOSE YOU SHARE WITH NO ONE--
--THEN JOURNEY TO WHERE YOUR GENIUS WILL BE PUT TO PROPER USE AND YOUR BORED LITTLE SON CAN HAVE HEROES OF THE REICH TO ADMIRE.
DAD OBEYED WITHOUT PROTEST. I TRIED TO THINK WHAT PAT RYAN WOULD DO... AND COULDN'T. WHEN KOLB GAVE ME THE CASE TO CARRY, I ACCEPTED IT AS MEEKLY AS MY FATHER.
NO. NOT TOWARD THE ELEVATOR. WE WILL TAKE THE FIRESTAIRS... TO THE ROOF.
OUR DIPLOMATS HAVE ALREADY INITIATED PAPERWORK COVERING YOUR SUDDEN SHIFT IN ALLEGIANCES, MR. LOWELL--

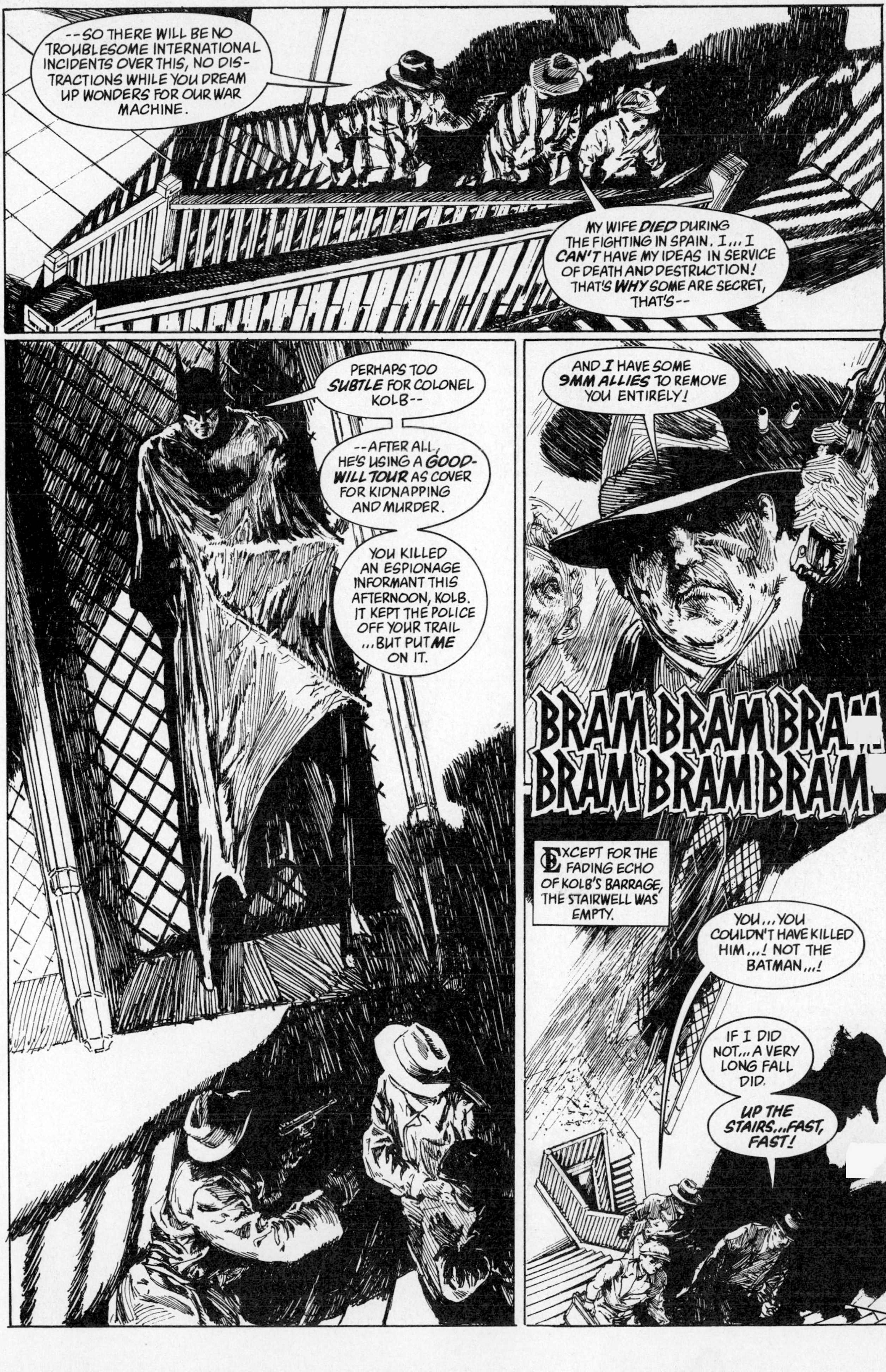
--SO THERE WILL BE NO TROUBLESOME INTERNATIONAL INCIDENTS OVER THIS, NO DISTRACTIONS WHILE YOU DREAM UP WONDERS FOR OUR WAR MACHINE.
MY WIFE DIED DURING THE FIGHTING IN SPAIN. I... I CAN'T HAVE MY IDEAS IN SERVICE OF DEATH AND DESTRUCTION! THAT'S WHY SOME ARE SECRET, THAT'S--
PERHAPS TOO SUBTLE FOR COLONEL KOLB--
--AFTER ALL, HE'S USING A GOOD-WILL TOUR AS COVER FOR KIDNAPPING AND MURDER.
YOU KILLED AN ESPIONAGE INFORMANT THIS AFTERNOON, KOLB. IT KEPT THE POLICE OFF YOUR TRAIL ...BUT PUT ME ON IT.
AND I HAVE SOME 9MM ALLIES TO REMOVE YOU ENTIRELY!
BRAM BRAM BRA
BRAM BRAM BRAM
EXCEPT FOR THE FADING ECHO OF KOLB'S BARRAGE, THE STAIRWELL WAS EMPTY.
YOU... YOU COULDN'T HAVE KILLED HIM...! NOT THE BATMAN...!
IF I DID NOT... A VERY LONG FALL DID.
UP THE STAIRS...FAST, FAST!

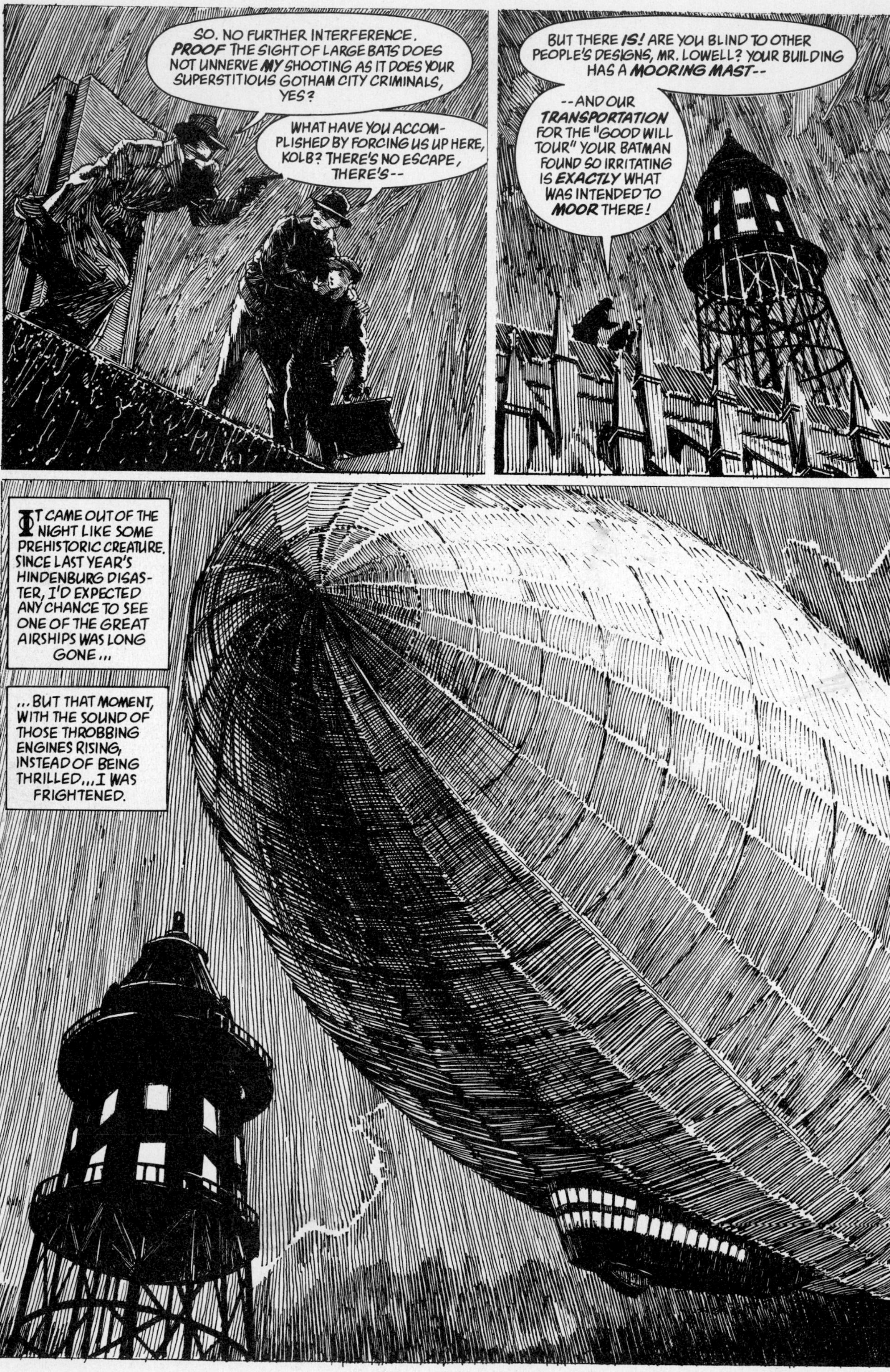
SO. NO FURTHER INTERFERENCE. PROOF THE SIGHT OF LARGE BATS DOES NOT UNNERVE MY SHOOTING AS IT DOES YOUR SUPERSTITIOUS GOTHAM CITY CRIMINALS, YES?
WHAT HAVE YOU ACCOMPLISHED BY FORCING US UP HERE, KOLB? THERE'S NO ESCAPE, THERE'S--
BUT THERE IS! ARE YOU BLIND TO OTHER PEOPLE'S DESIGNS, MR. LOWELL? YOUR BUILDING HAS A MOORING MAST--
--AND OUR TRANSPORTATION FOR THE "GOOD WILL TOUR" YOUR BATMAN FOUND SO IRRITATING IS EXACTLY WHAT WAS INTENDED TO MOOR THERE!
IT CAME OUT OF THE NIGHT LIKE SOME PREHISTORIC CREATURE. SINCE LAST YEAR'S HINDENBURG DISASTER, I'D EXPECTED ANY CHANCE TO SEE ONE OF THE GREAT AIRSHIPS WAS LONG GONE...
...BUT THAT MOMENT, WITH THE SOUND OF THOSE THROBBING ENGINES RISING, INSTEAD OF BEING THRILLED... I WAS FRIGHTENED.

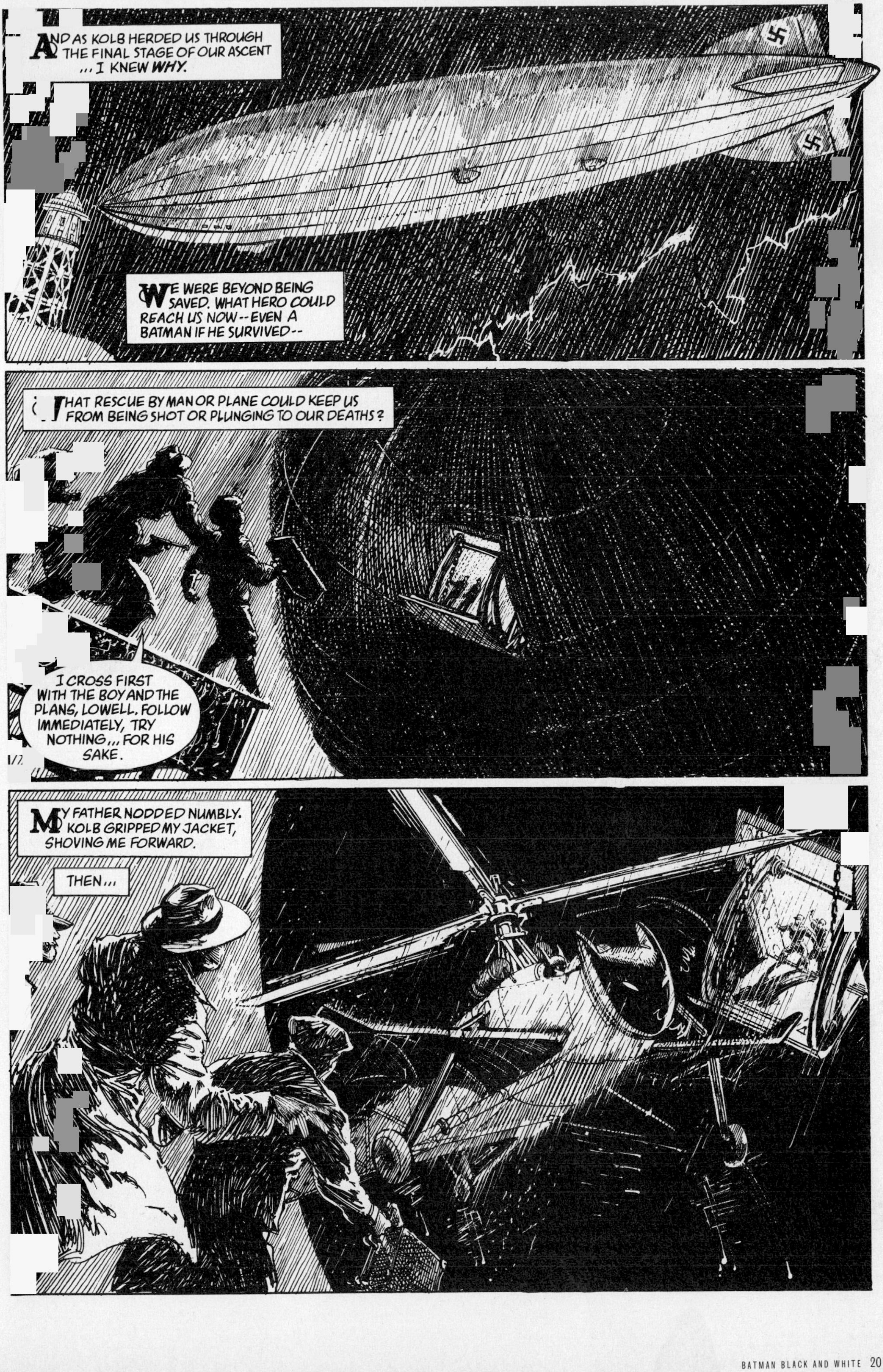
AND AS KOLB HERDED US THROUGH THE FINAL STAGE OF OUR ASCENT ...I KNEW WHY.
WE WERE BEYOND BEING SAVED. WHAT HERO COULD REACH US NOW--EVEN A BATMAN IF HE SURVIVED--
WHAT RESCUE BY MAN OR PLANE COULD KEEP US FROM BEING SHOT OR PLUNGING TO OUR DEATHS?
I CROSS FIRST WITH THE BOY AND THE PLANS, LOWELL. FOLLOW IMMEDIATELY. TRY NOTHING... FOR HIS SAKE.
MY FATHER NODDED NUMBLY. KOLB GRIPPED MY JACKET, SHOVING ME FORWARD.
THEN...

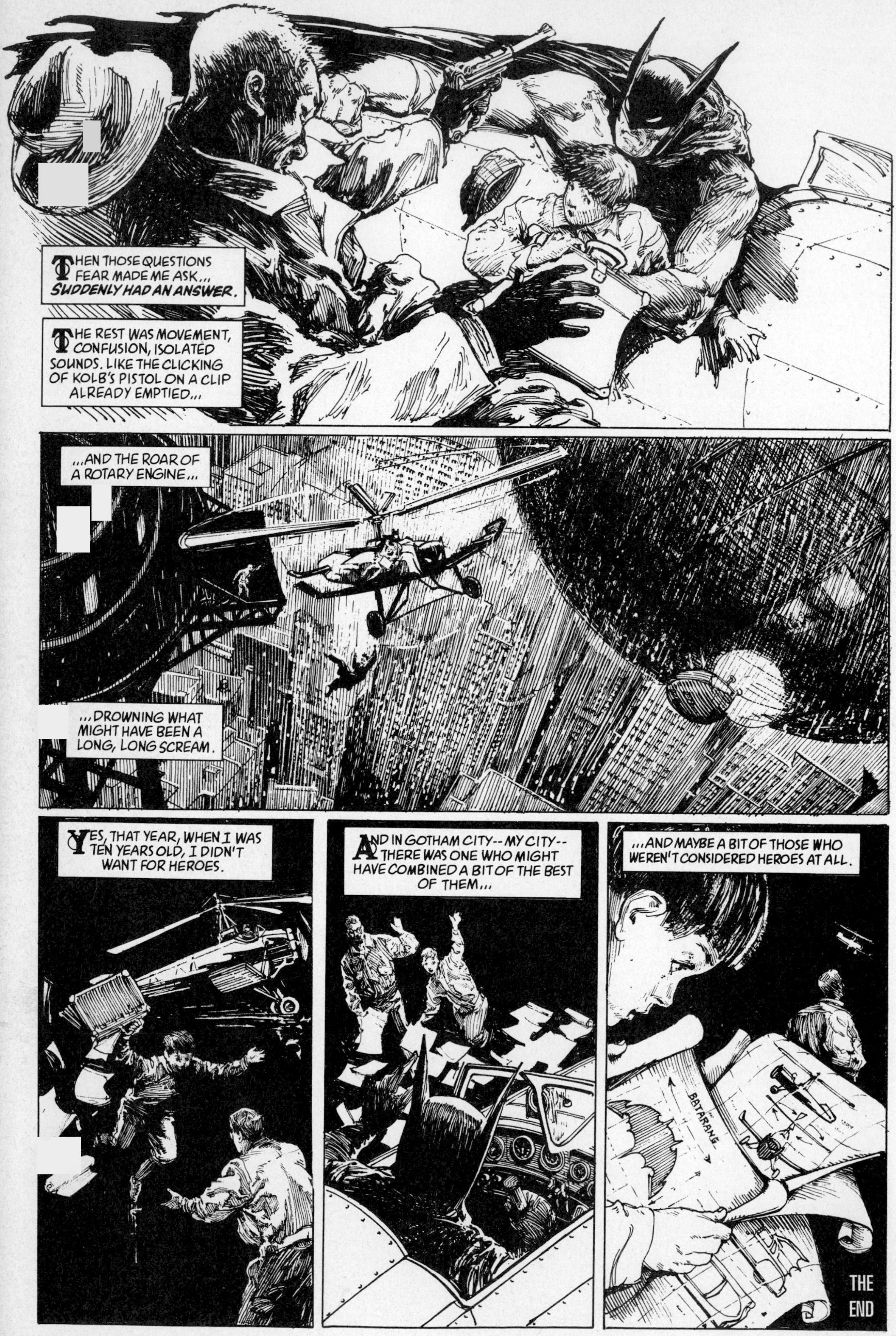
THEN THOSE QUESTIONS FEAR MADE ME ASK... SUDDENLY HAD AN ANSWER.
THE REST WAS MOVEMENT, CONFUSION, ISOLATED SOUNDS. LIKE THE CLICKING OF KOLB'S PISTOL ON A CLIP ALREADY EMPTIED...
...AND THE ROAR OF A ROTARY ENGINE...
...DROWNING WHAT MIGHT HAVE BEEN A LONG, LONG SCREAM.
YES, THAT YEAR, WHEN I WAS TEN YEARS OLD, I DIDN'T WANT FOR HEROES.
AND IN GOTHAM CITY-- MY CITY-- THERE WAS ONE WHO MIGHT HAVE COMBINED A BIT OF THE BEST OF THEM...
...AND MAYBE A BIT OF THOSE WHO WEREN'T CONSIDERED HEROES AT ALL.
BATARANG
THE END

LEAVE**TAKING**

BRIAN**STELFREEZE**

Brian Stelfreeze's art first started making waves in 1988 with *Cycops*, a three-issue
miniseries that introduced the comics world to his stunningly distinctive style, with its
high-contrast look and angular yet slick lines.

Although *Cycops* featured his linework, Brian is best known as a painter. For the past
several years he's concentrated mainly on covers, producing memorable images month after
month, including a four-year run as the cover artist on BATMAN: SHADOW OF THE BAT.
Stelfreeze is now focusing his attention more on interior art, hoping to explore and develop
new directions in storytelling.

DENNIS**O'NEIL**

For over twenty years, Batman editor and writer Dennis O'Neil has put the "dark" in the
Dark Knight and been the guiding force behind the Batman mythos. He has been praised as
a master of the comics form and as the dean of American comics. He prefers to think of
himself as, simply, "a working professional storyteller."

Dennis has written most of Marvel's and DC's major characters including Spider-Man,
Iron Man, Daredevil, Superman, Wonder Woman, and the Justice League of America.
His GREEN LANTERN/GREEN ARROW series in the early '70s is hailed as the first
"relevant" comic book, and his late '80s title, THE QUESTION, is credited with being a
forerunner of "mature reader" comics.

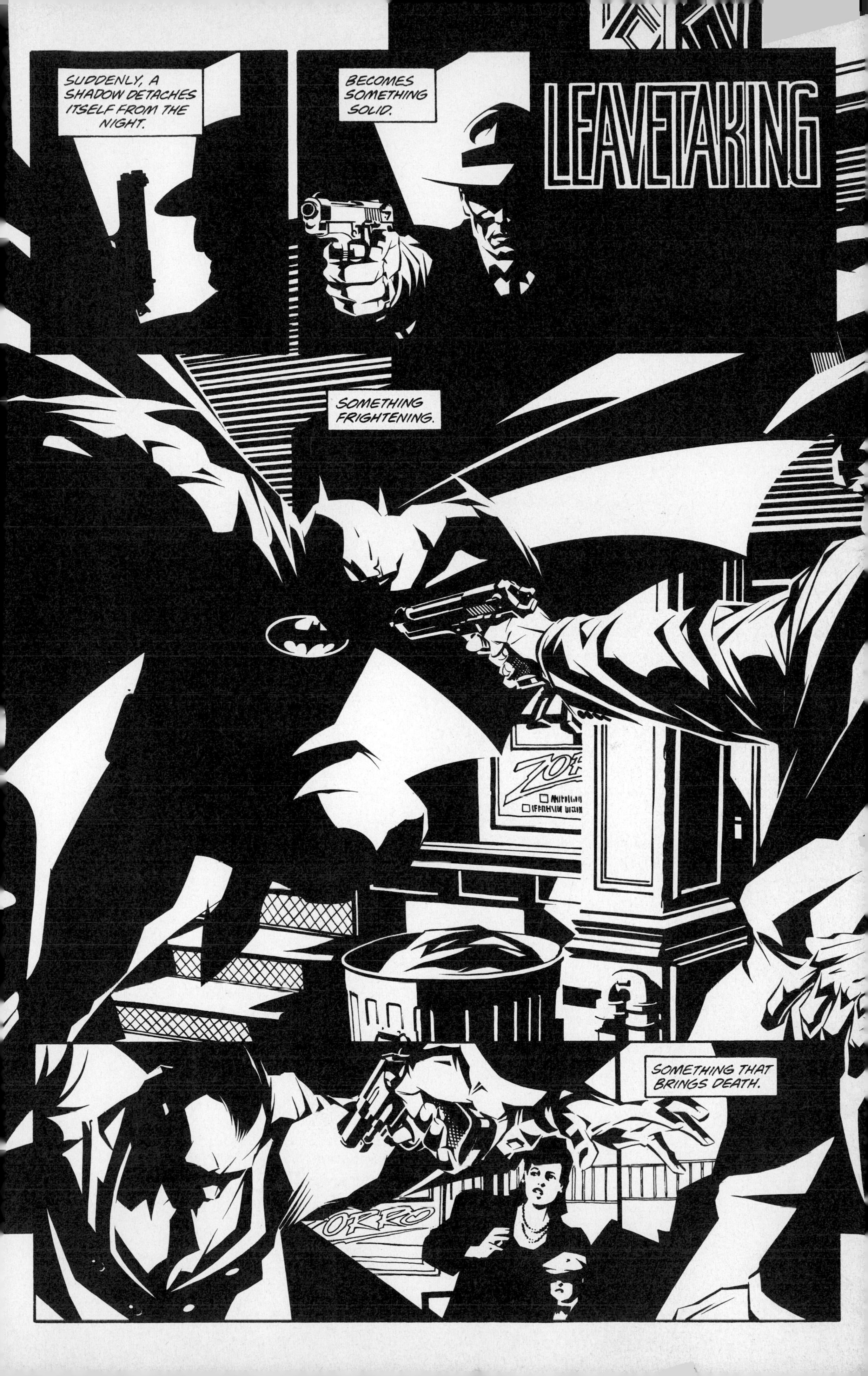
SUDDENLY, A SHADOW DETACHES ITSELF FROM THE NIGHT.
BECOMES SOMETHING SOLID.
LEAVETAKING
SOMETHING FRIGHTENING.
SOMETHING THAT BRINGS DEATH.

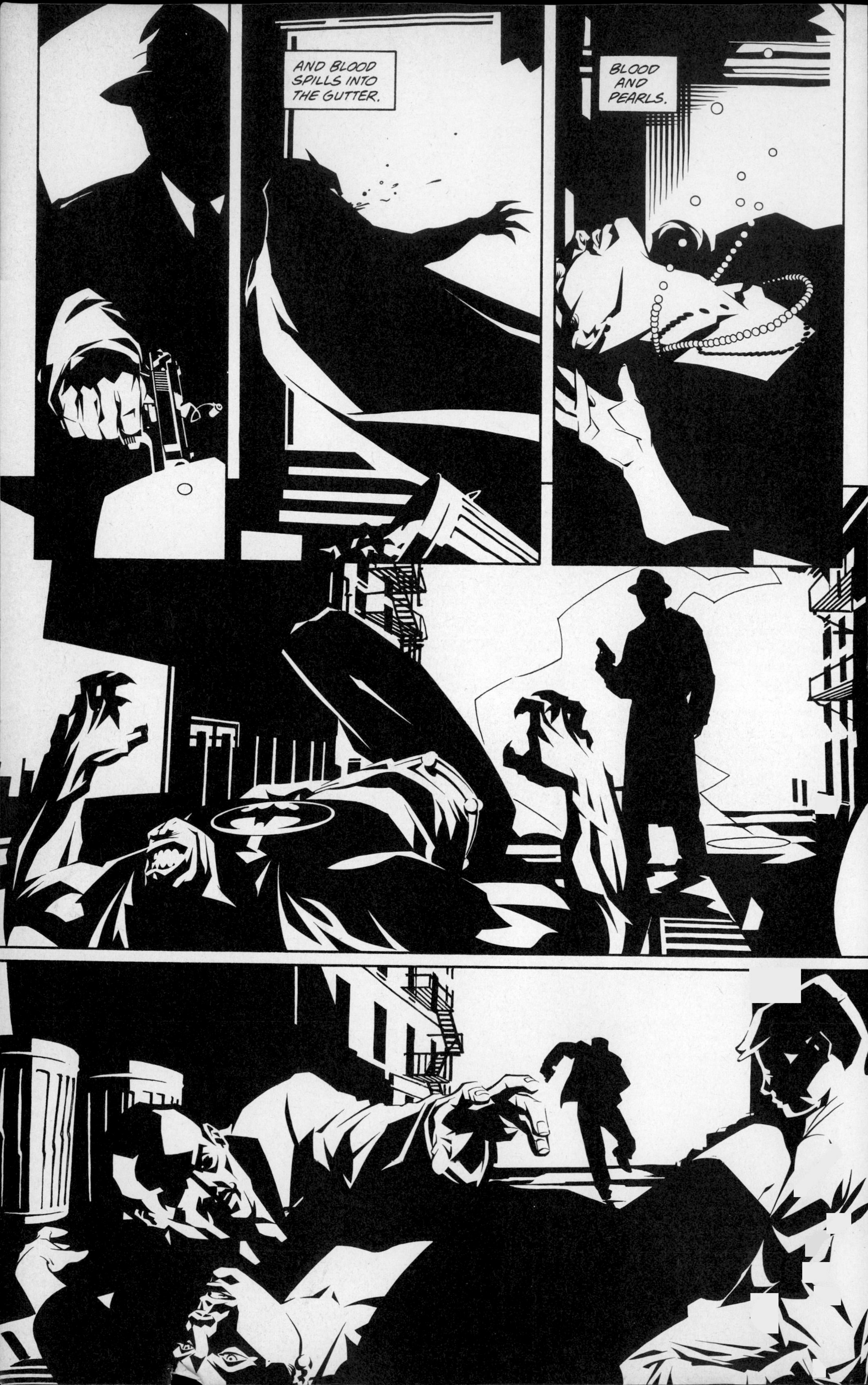
AND BLOOD SPILLS INTO THE GUTTER.
BLOOD AND PEARLS.

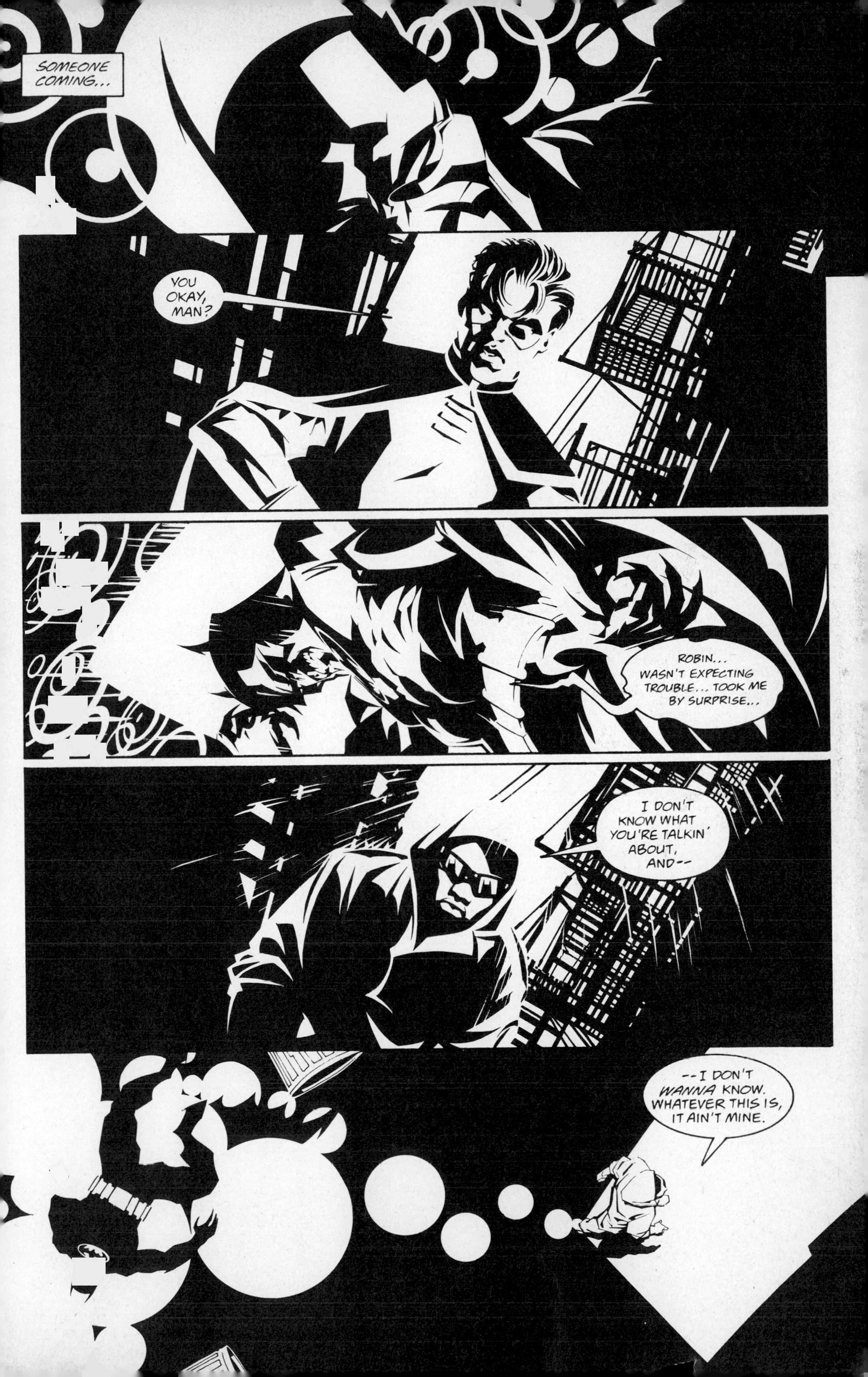
SOMEONE COMING...
YOU OKAY, MAN?
ROBIN... WASN'T EXPECTING TROUBLE... TOOK ME BY SURPRISE...
I DON'T KNOW WHAT YOU'RE TALKIN' ABOUT, AND--
--I DON'T *WANNA* KNOW. WHATEVER THIS IS, IT AIN'T MINE.

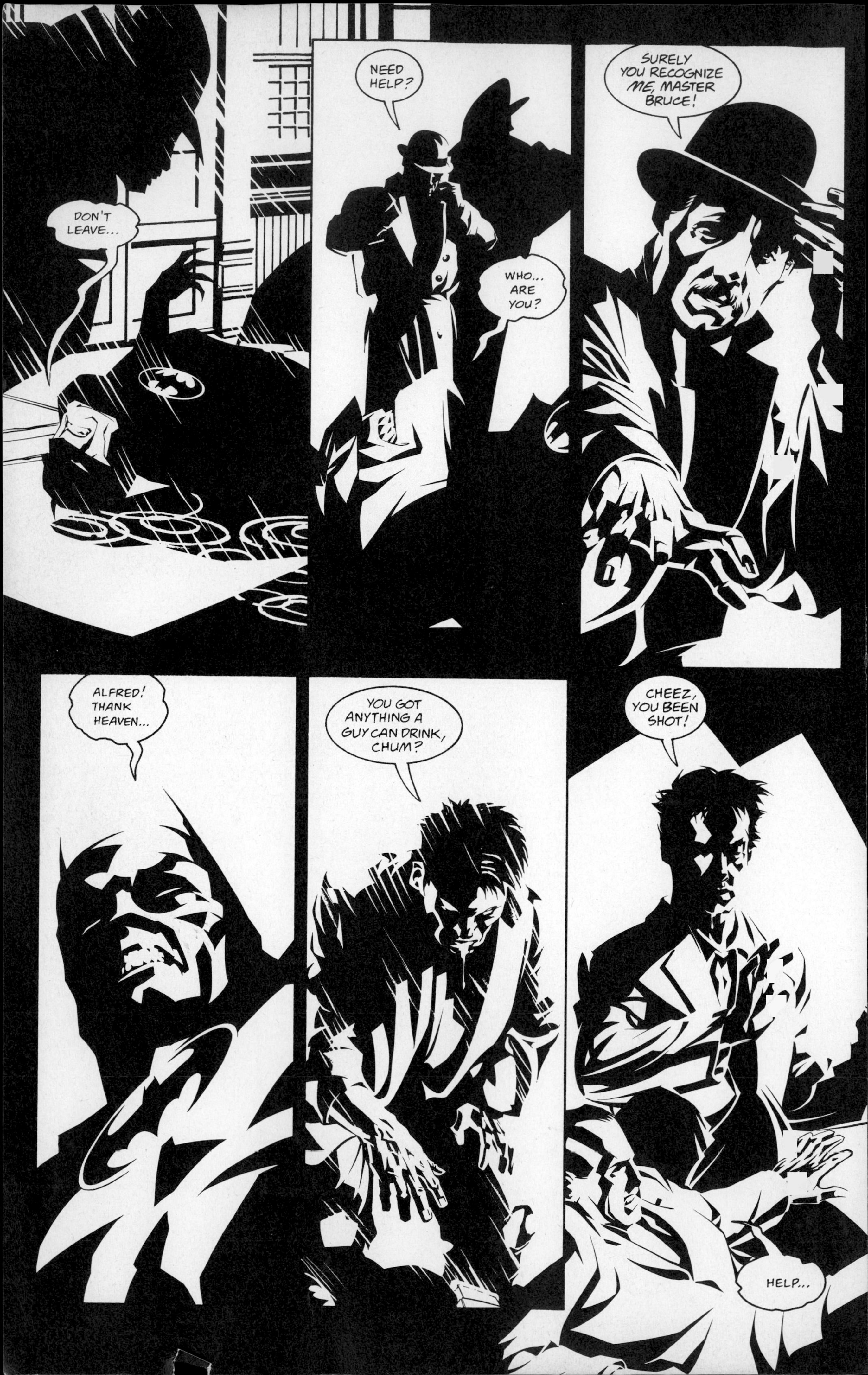
DON'T LEAVE...
NEED HELP?
WHO... ARE YOU?
SURELY YOU RECOGNIZE ME, MASTER BRUCE!
ALFRED! THANK HEAVEN...
YOU GOT ANYTHING A GUY CAN DRINK, CHUM?
CHEEZ, YOU BEEN SHOT!
HELP...

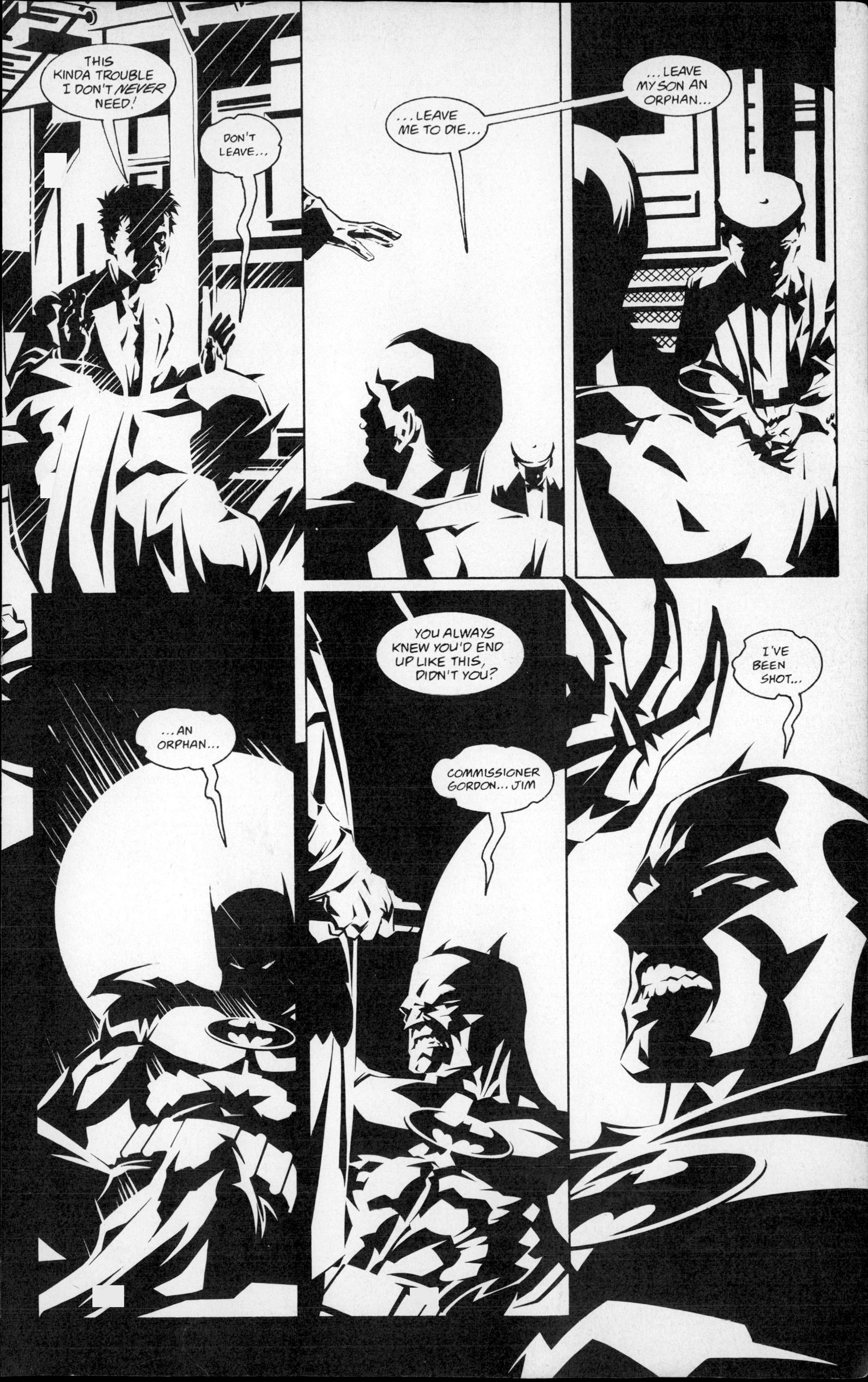
THIS KINDA TROUBLE I DON'T *NEVER* NEED!
DON'T LEAVE...
...LEAVE ME TO DIE...
...LEAVE MY SON AN ORPHAN...
...AN ORPHAN...
YOU ALWAYS KNEW YOU'D END UP LIKE THIS, DIDN'T YOU?
COMMISSIONER GORDON... JIM
I'VE BEEN SHOT...

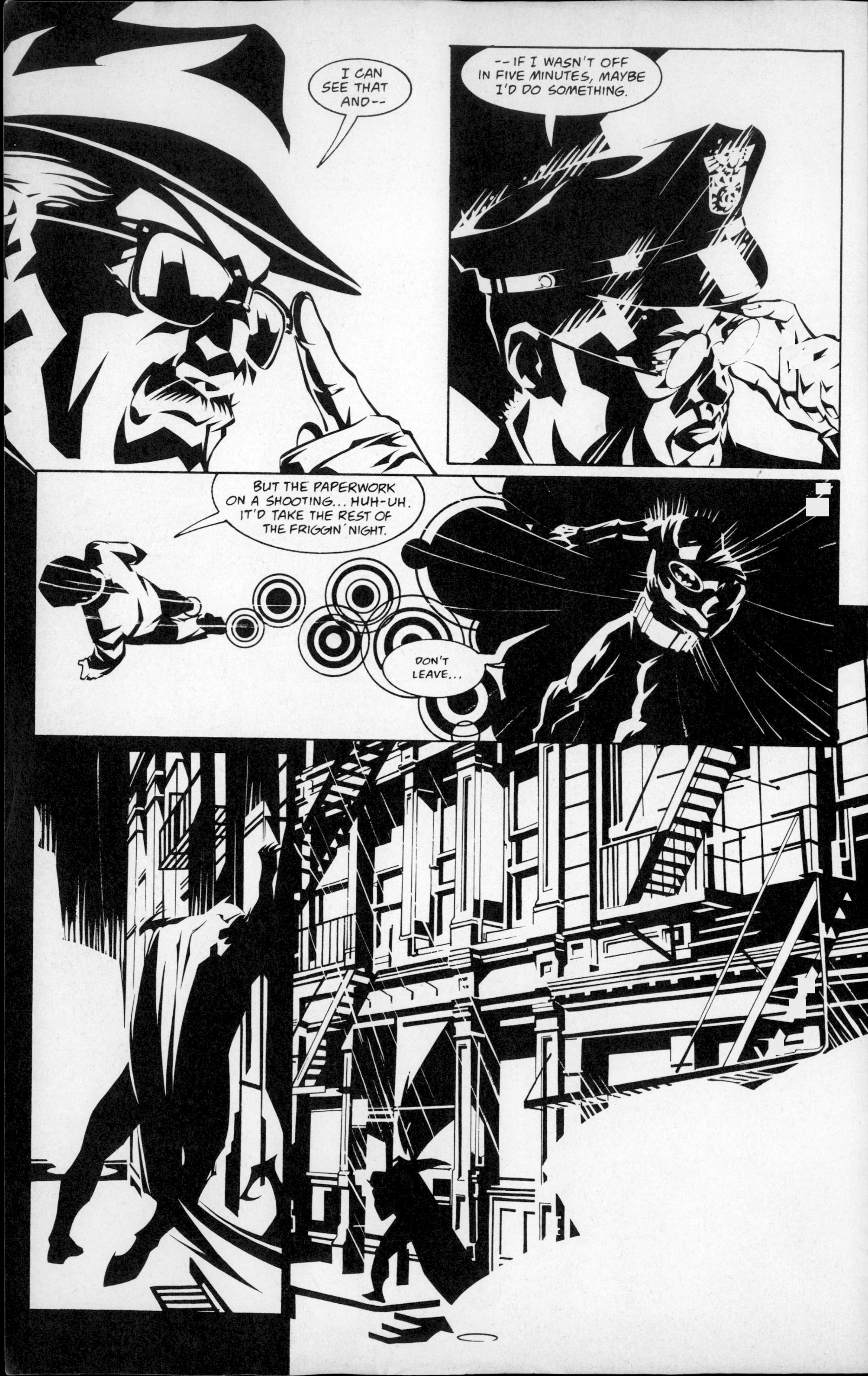
I CAN SEE THAT AND--
--IF I WASN'T OFF IN FIVE MINUTES, MAYBE I'D DO SOMETHING.
BUT THE PAPERWORK ON A SHOOTING... HUH-UH. IT'D TAKE THE REST OF THE FRIGGIN' NIGHT.
DON'T LEAVE...

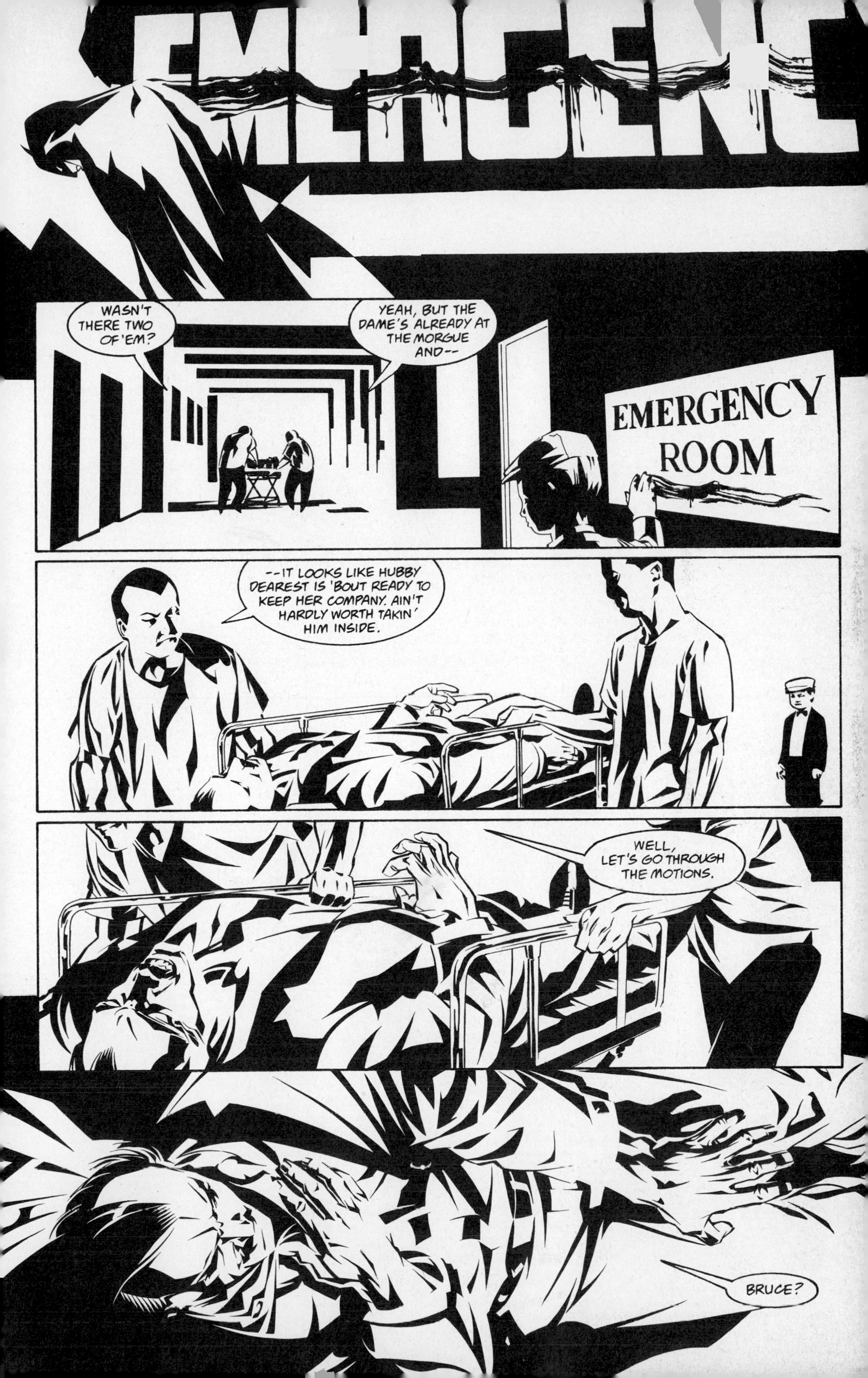
EMERGENCY
WASN'T THERE TWO OF 'EM?
YEAH, BUT THE DAME'S ALREADY AT THE MORGUE AND--
EMERGENCY ROOM
--IT LOOKS LIKE HUBBY DEAREST IS 'BOUT READY TO KEEP HER COMPANY. AIN'T HARDLY WORTH TAKIN' HIM INSIDE.
WELL, LET'S GO THROUGH THE MOTIONS.
BRUCE?

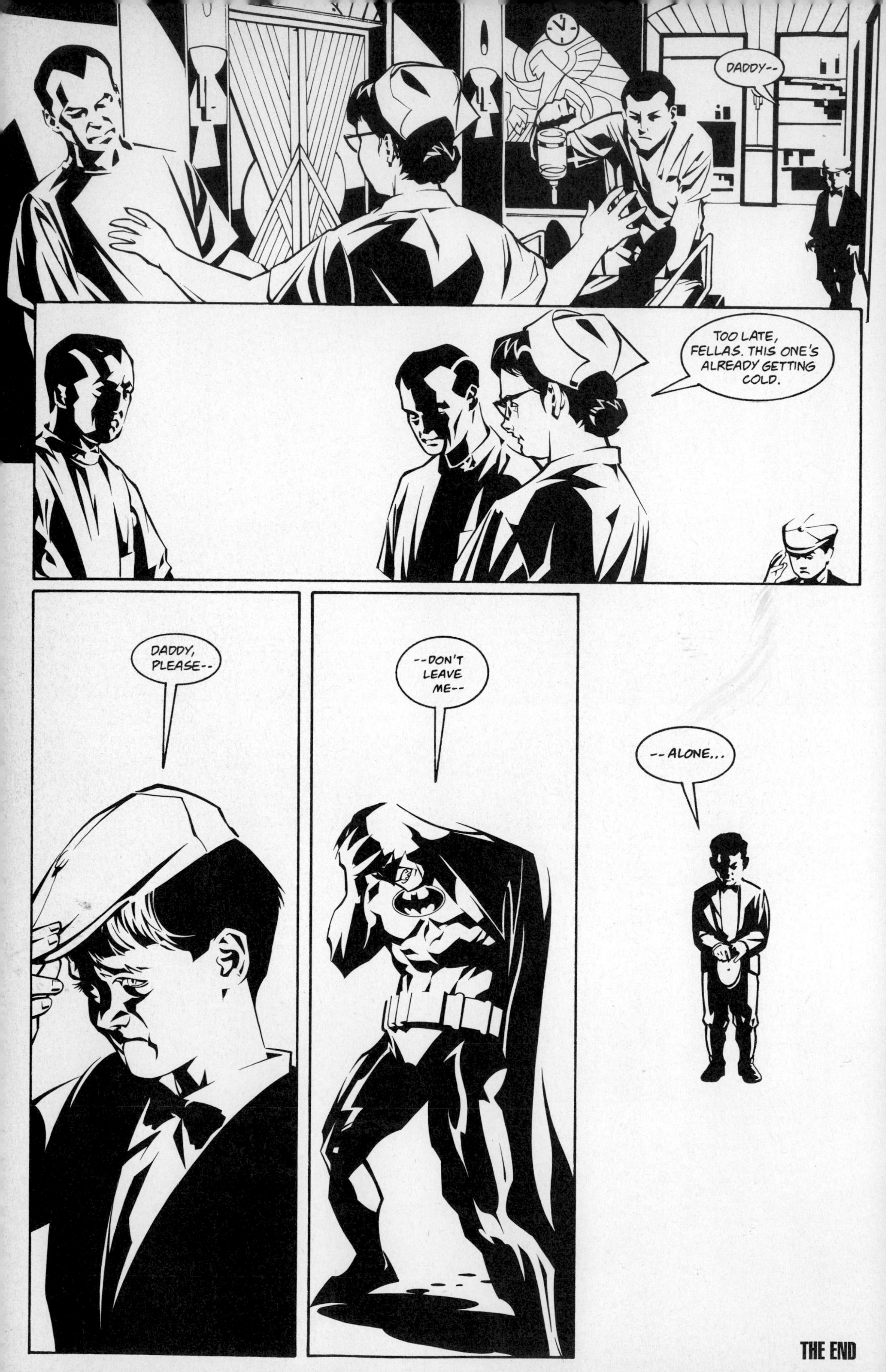
DADDY--
TOO LATE, FELLAS. THIS ONE'S ALREADY GETTING COLD.
DADDY, PLEASE--
--DON'T LEAVE ME--
--ALONE...
THE END

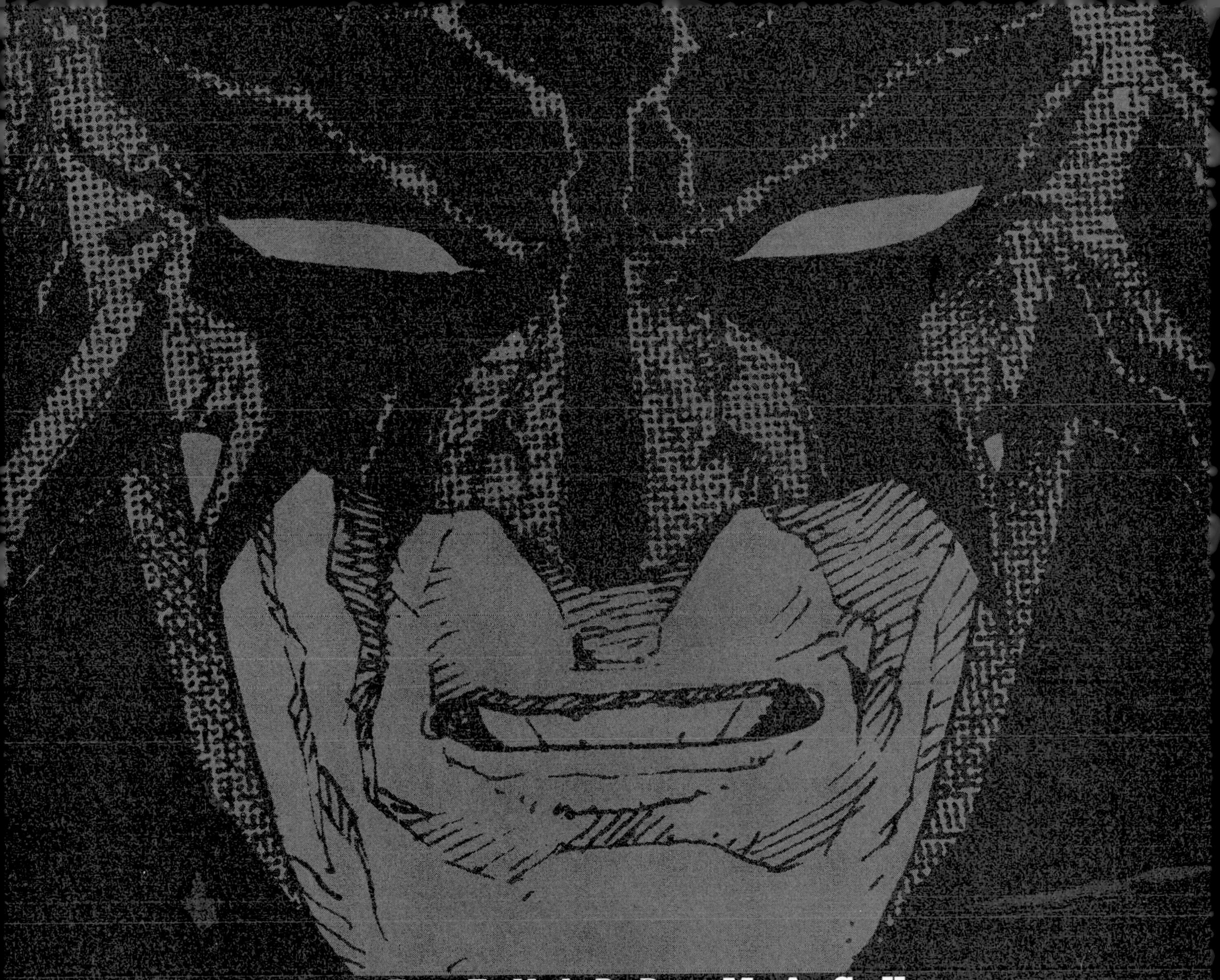

THE THIRD **MASK**

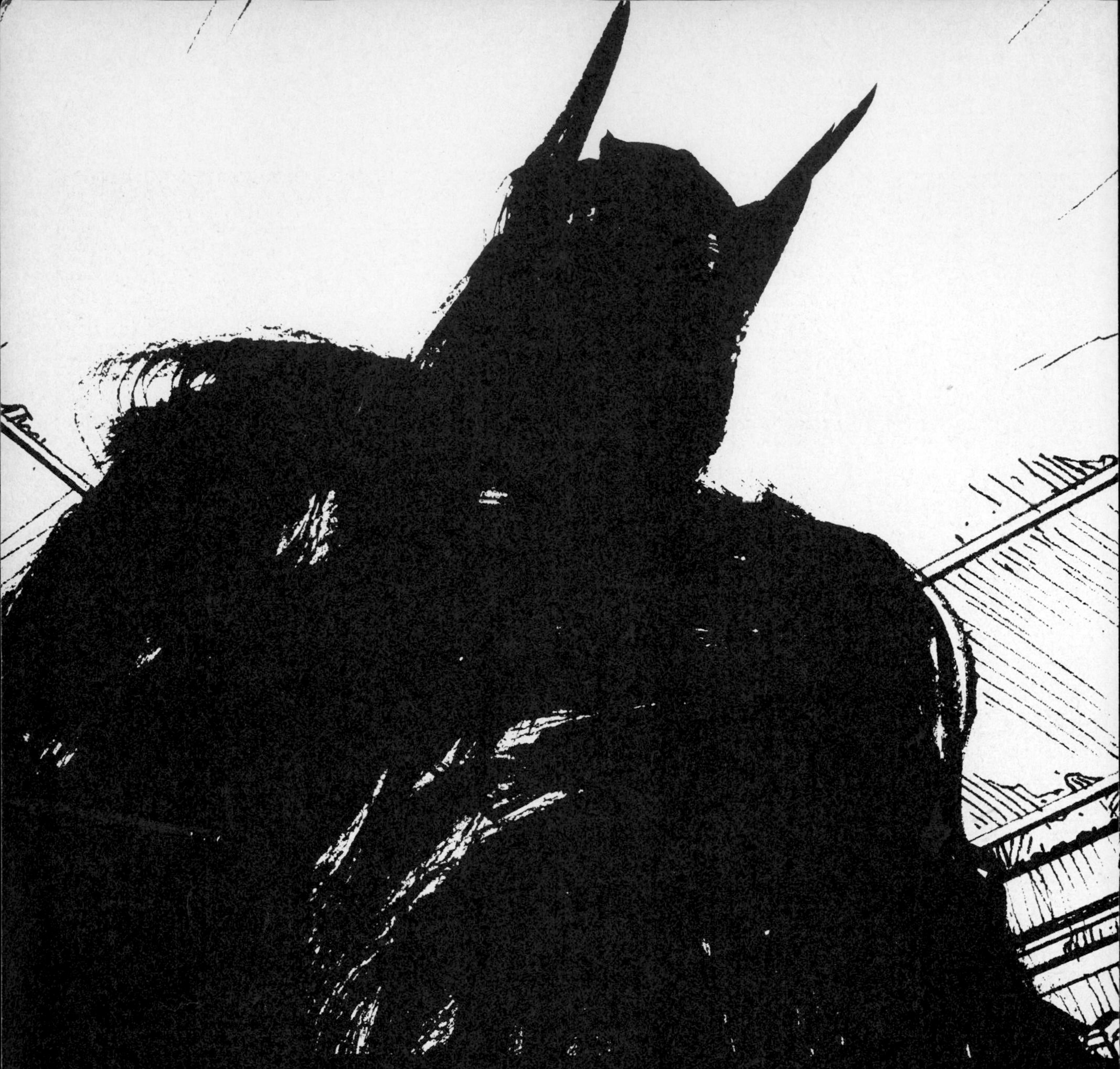

KATSUHIRO **OTOMO**

Comic-book artist and writer Katsuhiro Otomo is a legend on both sides of the Pacific Ocean. His work transcends language on the sheer strength of its creative genius. The phenomenal success of his groundbreaking masterpiece *Akira* sent shock waves throughout the comics and animation world.

Although he is now a famous animator, director, writer and designer, to the legions of Otomo fans he will remain simply one of the greatest comic-book artists in the history of the medium.

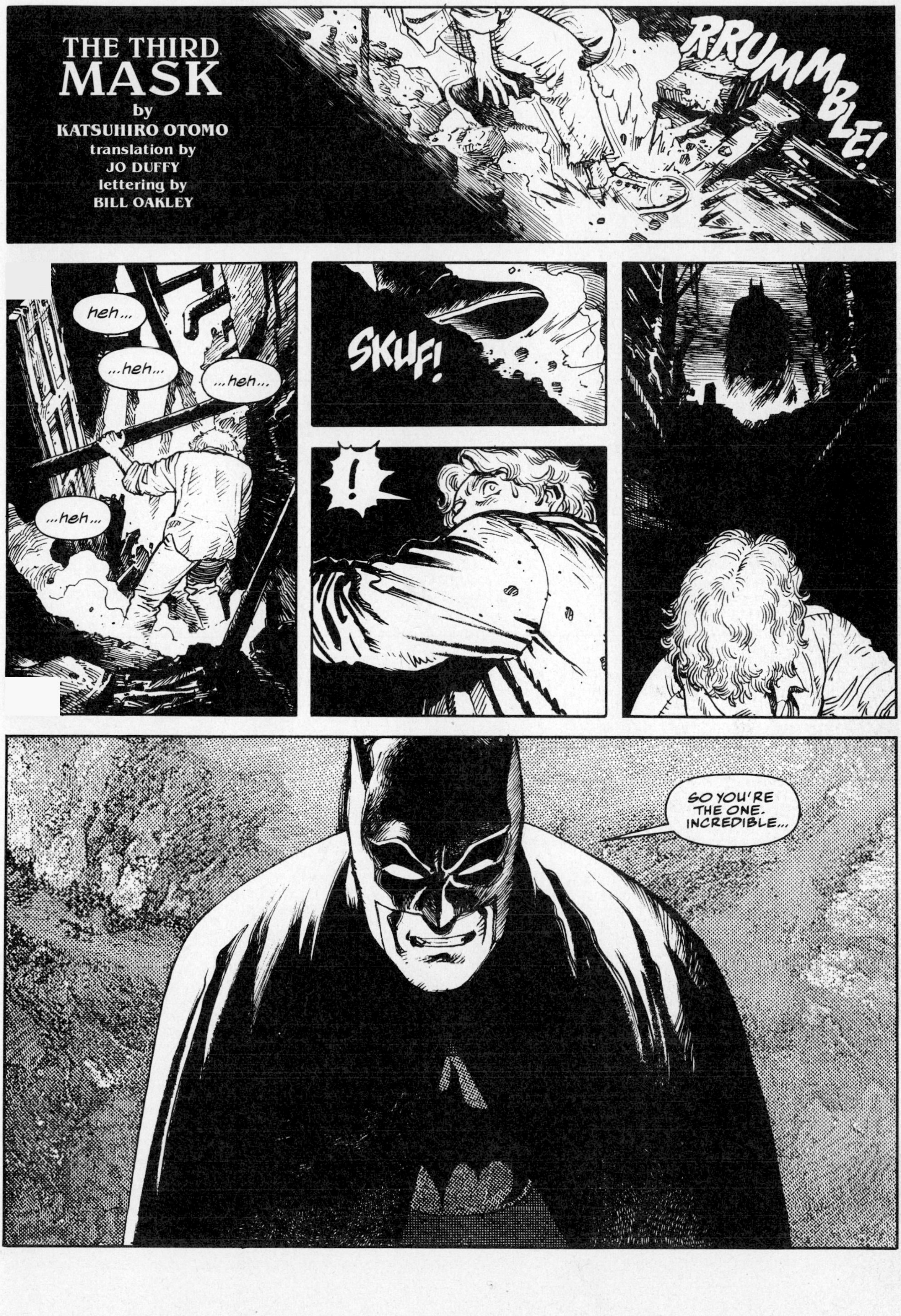
THE THIRD MASK
by
KATSUHIRO OTOMO
translation by
JO DUFFY
lettering by
BILL OAKLEY
RRUMMBLE!
heh...
...heh...
...heh...
...heh...
SKUF!
!
SO YOU'RE THE ONE. INCREDIBLE...

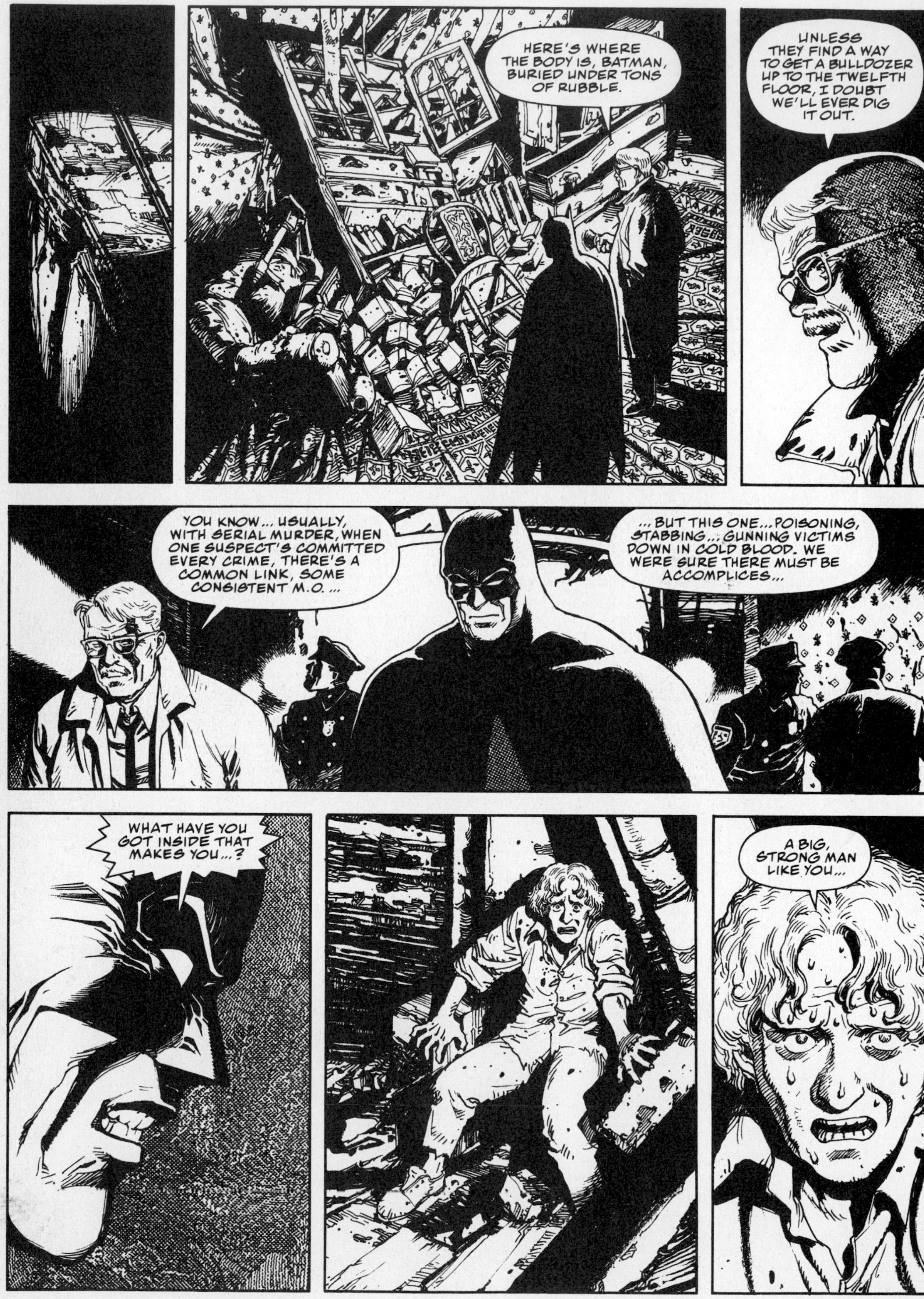
HERE'S WHERE THE BODY IS, BATMAN, BURIED UNDER TONS OF RUBBLE.
UNLESS THEY FIND A WAY TO GET A BULLDOZER UP TO THE TWELFTH FLOOR, I DOUBT WE'LL EVER DIG IT OUT.
YOU KNOW... USUALLY, WITH SERIAL MURDER, WHEN ONE SUSPECT'S COMMITTED EVERY CRIME, THERE'S A COMMON LINK, SOME CONSISTENT M.O. ...
...BUT THIS ONE... POISONING, STABBING... GUNNING VICTIMS DOWN IN COLD BLOOD. WE WERE SURE THERE MUST BE ACCOMPLICES...
WHAT HAVE YOU GOT INSIDE THAT MAKES YOU...?
A BIG, STRONG MAN LIKE YOU...

...SHOULD UNDERSTAND HOW THE HEART CONTRADICTS ITSELF.

TUP!

WHAT...?!

THE GIRLIEST GIRL IS RUTHLESS WHEN IT COMES TO KILLING SPIDERS!

THE SURLIEST BRUTE WILL KEEP A LITTLE PUPPY AS A PET!

GET THE POINT? DO YOU... SWEETHEART?

NOT EXACTLY,

SO MANY VOICES, SO MANY SOULS... BABBLING INSIDE MY HEAD. ALL WITHIN ME!

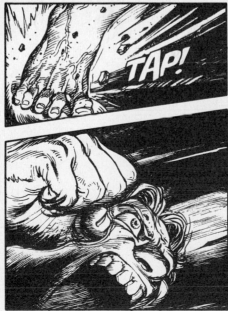

TAP!

POW!

WHOP!

THAK!

KONNG!

BLAST--!

!

WHERE--?!

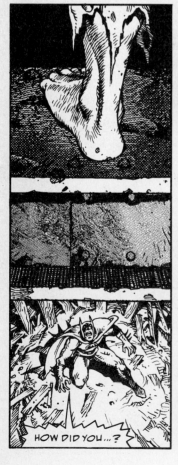

HOW DID YOU...?

YOUR FACE IS CONCEALED BY THE MASK YOU WEAR, BUT THINK ABOUT IT, BATMAN...

THAT DOESN'T HAVE TO BE THE REAL YOU.

WHAT?!

WHY STOP AT TWO? ONCE A PERSONALITY'S BEGUN TO SPLIT... THE POSSIBILITIES ARE... ENDLESS!

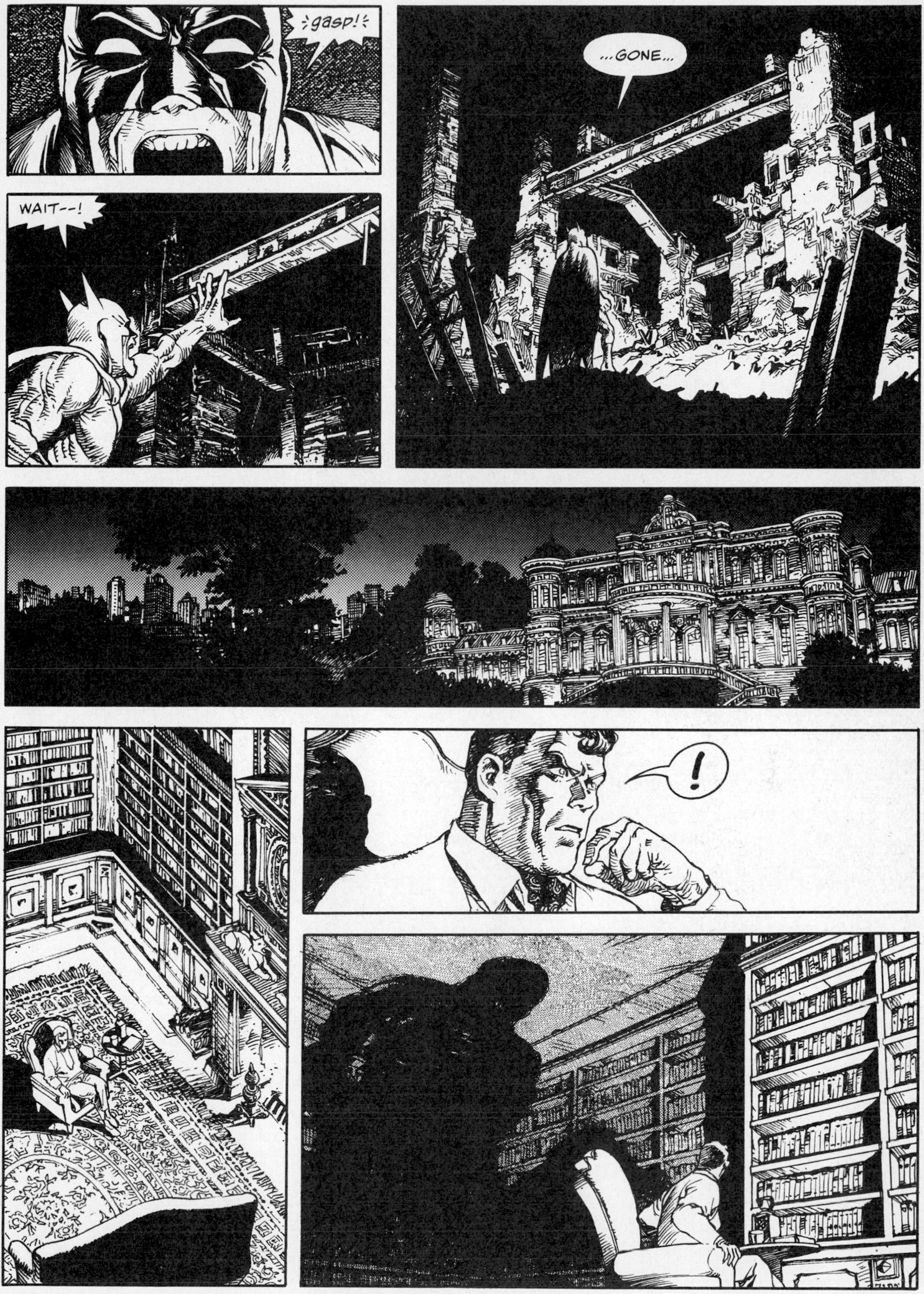
gasp!
WAIT--!
...GONE...
!

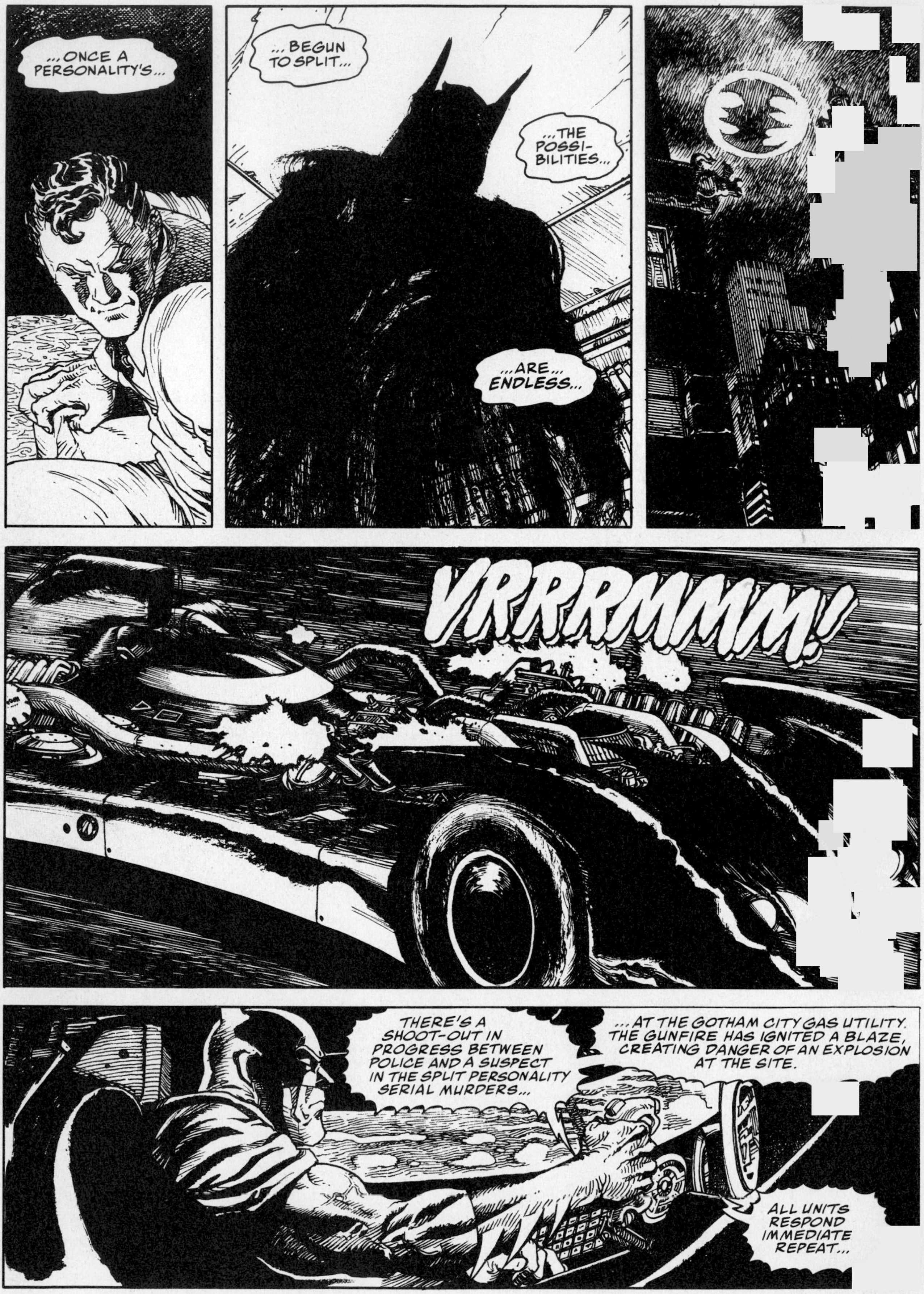
...ONCE A PERSONALITY'S...
...BEGUN TO SPLIT...
...THE POSSI-BILITIES...
...ARE... ENDLESS...
VRRRMMMM!
THERE'S A SHOOT-OUT IN PROGRESS BETWEEN POLICE AND A SUSPECT IN THE SPLIT PERSONALITY SERIAL MURDERS...
...AT THE GOTHAM CITY GAS UTILITY. THE GUNFIRE HAS IGNITED A BLAZE, CREATING DANGER OF AN EXPLOSION AT THE SITE.
ALL UNITS RESPOND IMMEDIATE REPEAT...

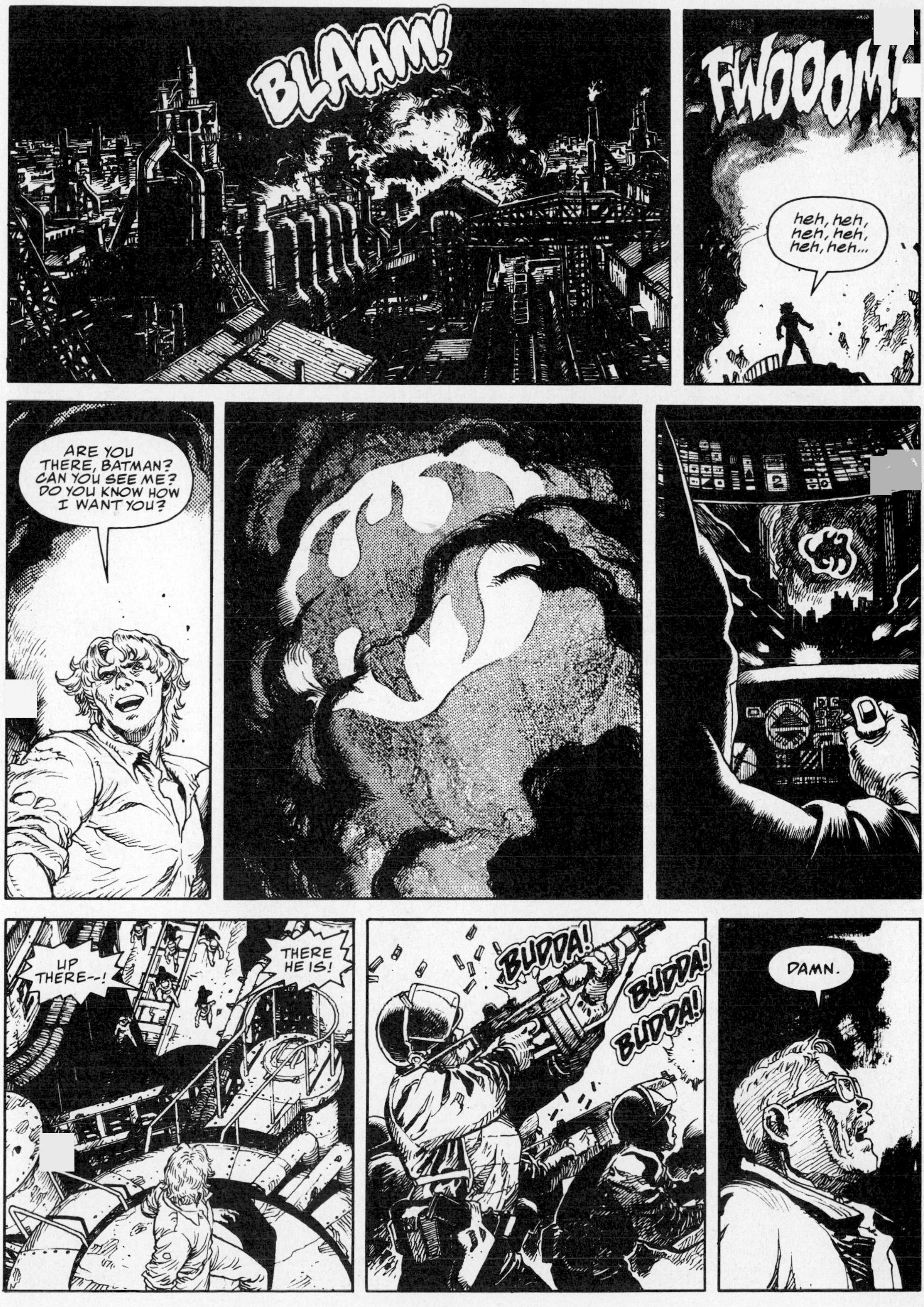
BLAAM!
FWOOOM!
heh, heh, heh, heh, heh, heh...
ARE YOU THERE, BATMAN? CAN YOU SEE ME? DO YOU KNOW HOW I WANT YOU?
UP THERE--!
THERE HE IS!
BUDDA!
BUDDA!
BUDDA!
DAMN.

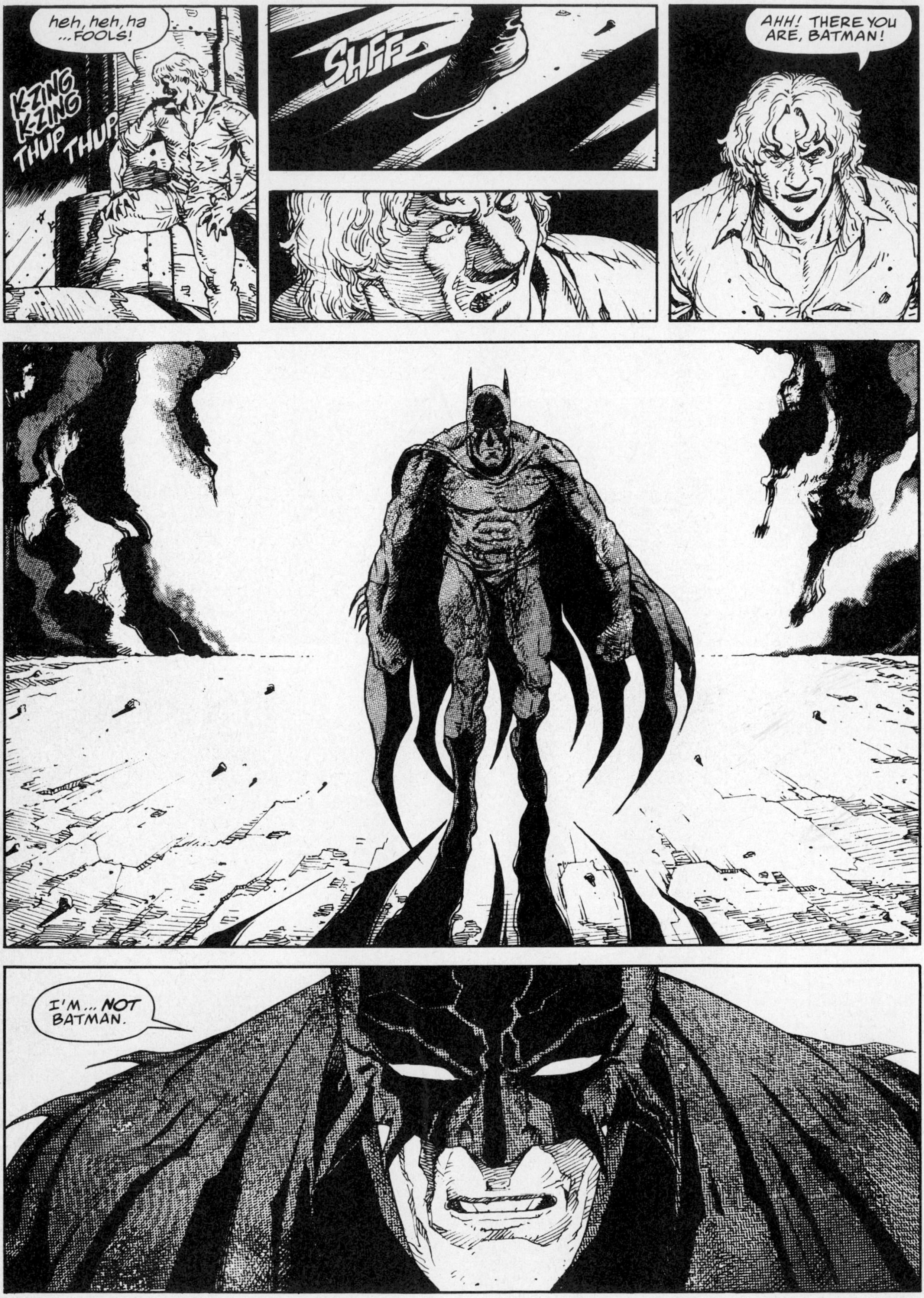
heh, heh, ha ...FOOLS!
K-ZING K-ZING THUP THUP
SHFF
AHH! THERE YOU ARE, BATMAN!
I'M... NOT BATMAN.

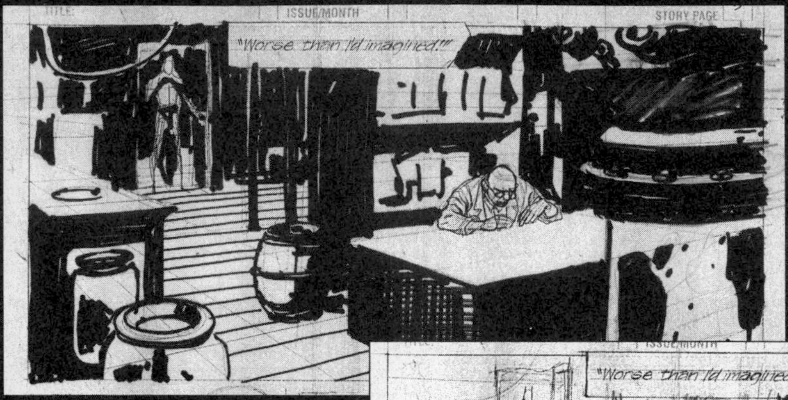
"Worse than I'd imagined!!!"

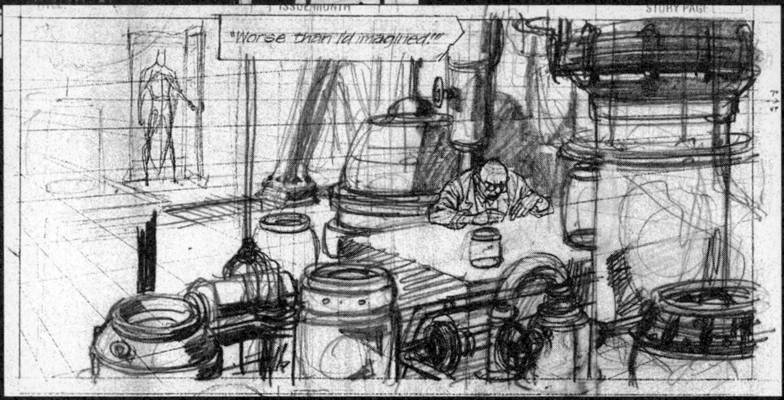
"Worse than I'd imagined!!!"

KEVIN NOWLAN LAYOUTS

There is but a small handful of artists who can truly be called the "artist's artist." Alex Toth, José Luis García-López, Kevin Nowlan are among this very elite group. They're masters at every discipline of comic-book art, from design to draftsmanship to dramatics. When they draw a story or a cover, every artist in the business stops to marvel at their talent. We kid ourselves thinking that if we draw and draw and draw, maybe someday we'll be as good as these guys. Reproduced here are assorted sketches and layouts that give a rare glimpse into Kevin Nowlan's working process.

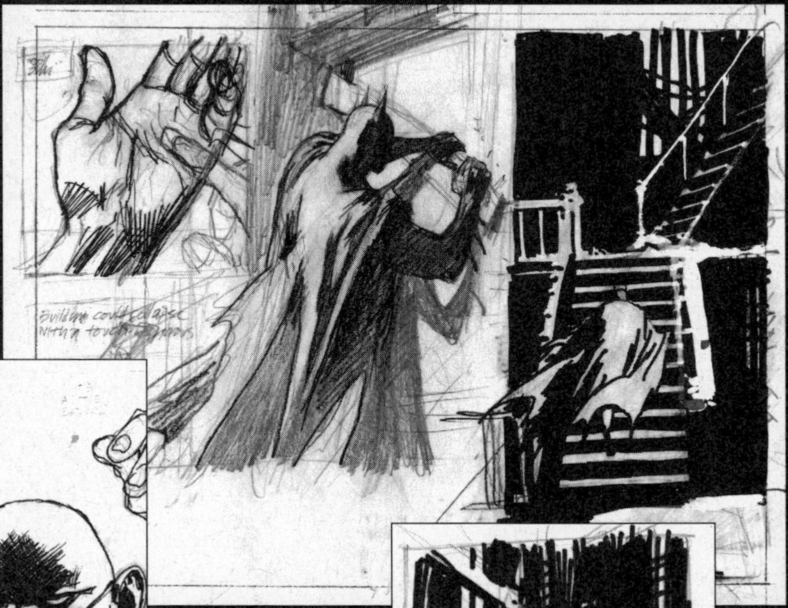

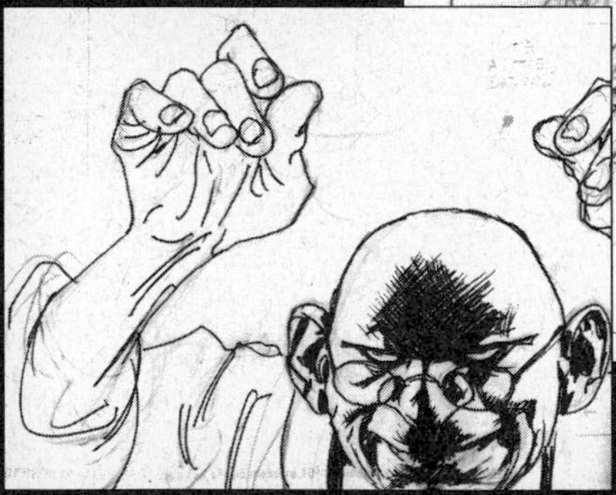

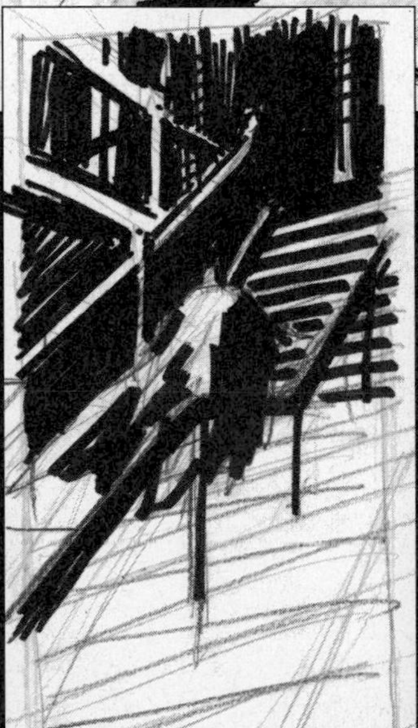

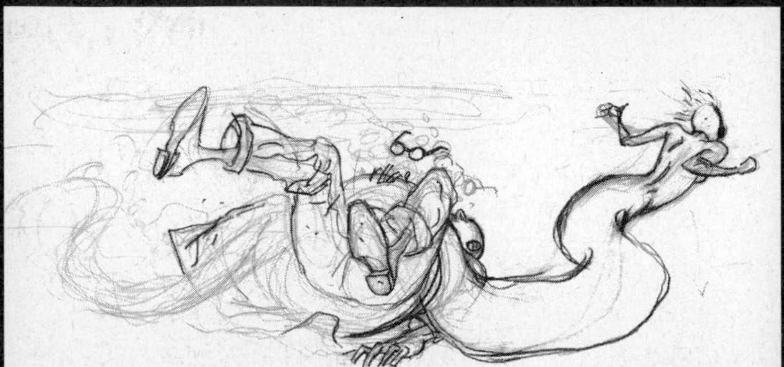

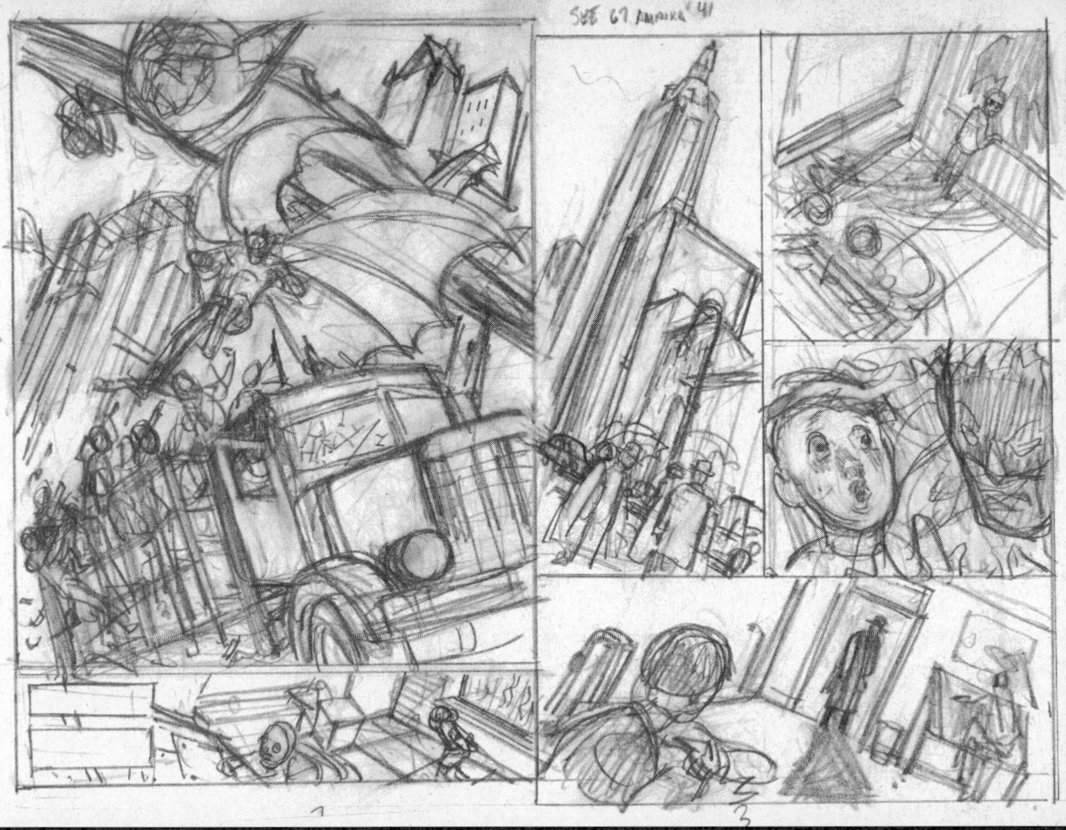

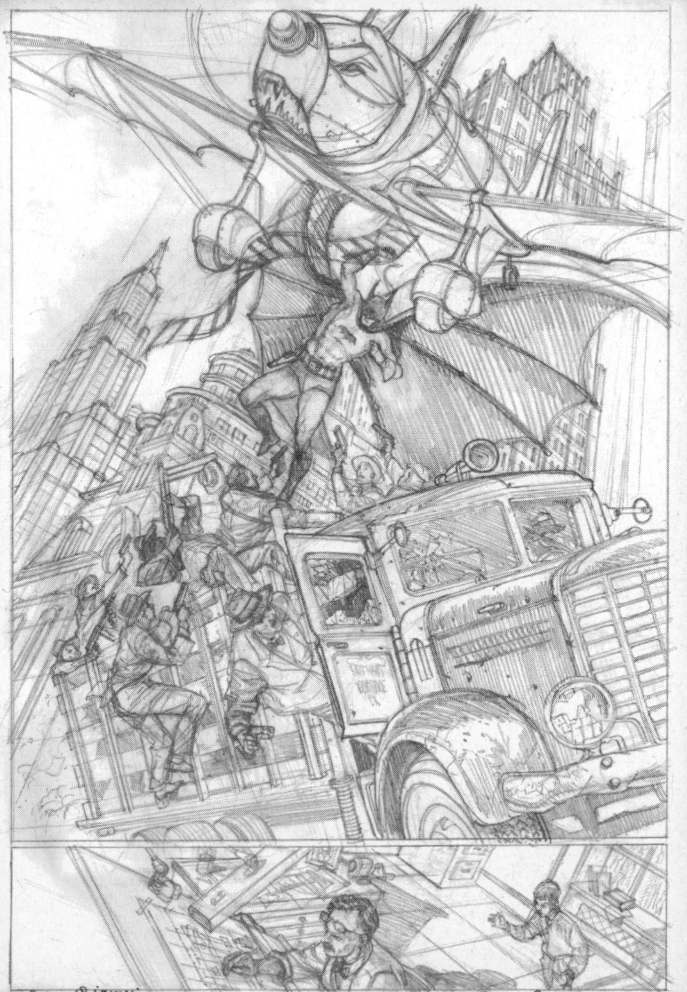

GARY GIANNILAYOUTS

These days, it's very much in vogue to overcrowd comic pages with massive detail and linework. Unfortunately, too many of these hyper-detailed artists get so lost in drawing every nut and bolt that they forget their main objective is to tell a story. It is indeed the rare artist who can lavish the amount of detail that Gary Gianni does on a story without the whole thing looking like an overrendered mess. Gary's ageless inking style makes him one of the true class acts in comics, as evidenced by his work on this 1997 Eisner Award-winning story "Heroes."

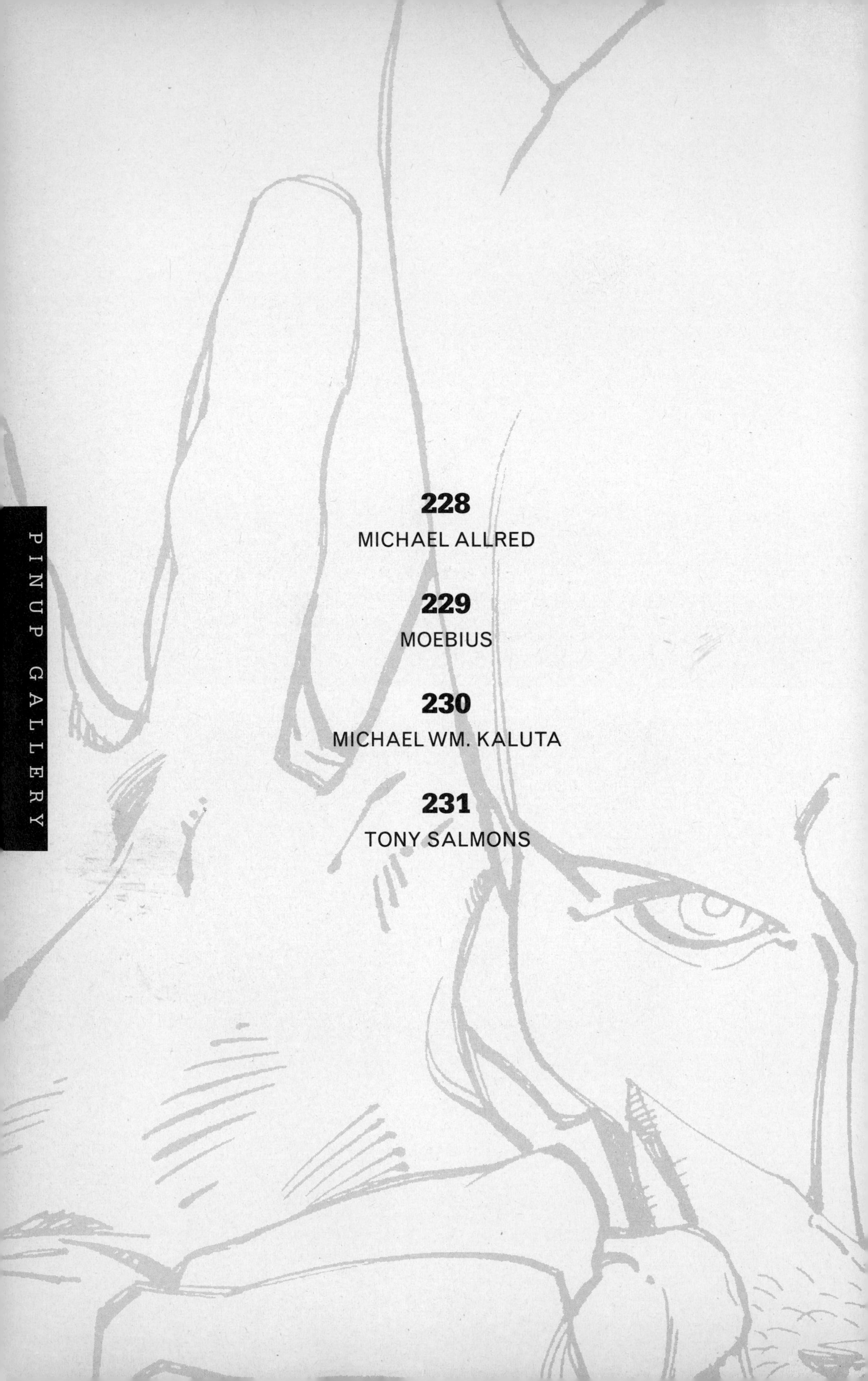

228

MICHAEL ALLRED

229

MOEBIUS

230

MICHAEL WM. KALUTA

231

TONY SALMONS

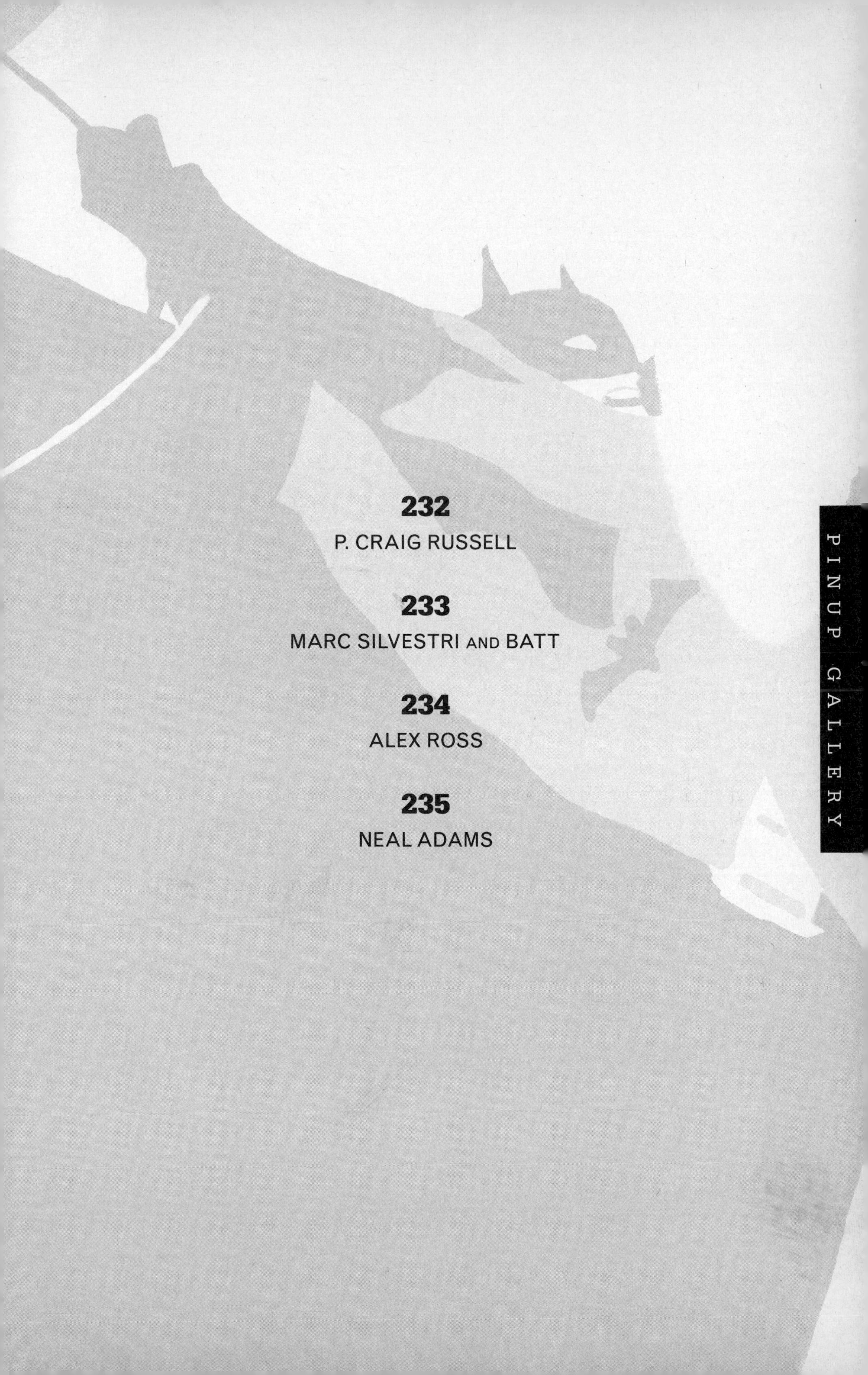

232

P. CRAIG RUSSELL

233

MARC SILVESTRI AND BATT

234

ALEX ROSS

235

NEAL ADAMS

PINUP GALLERY

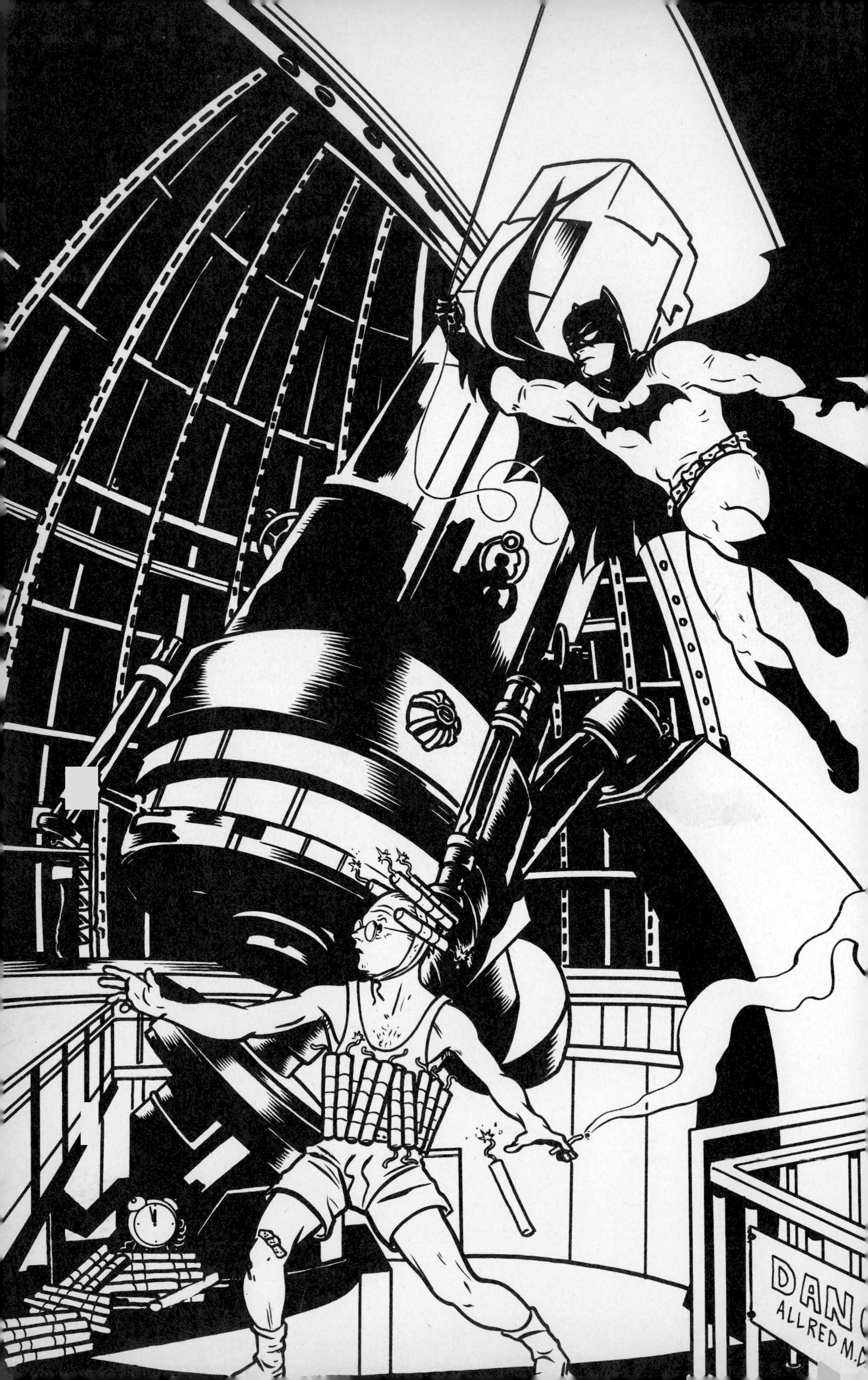
DAN
ALLRED M.

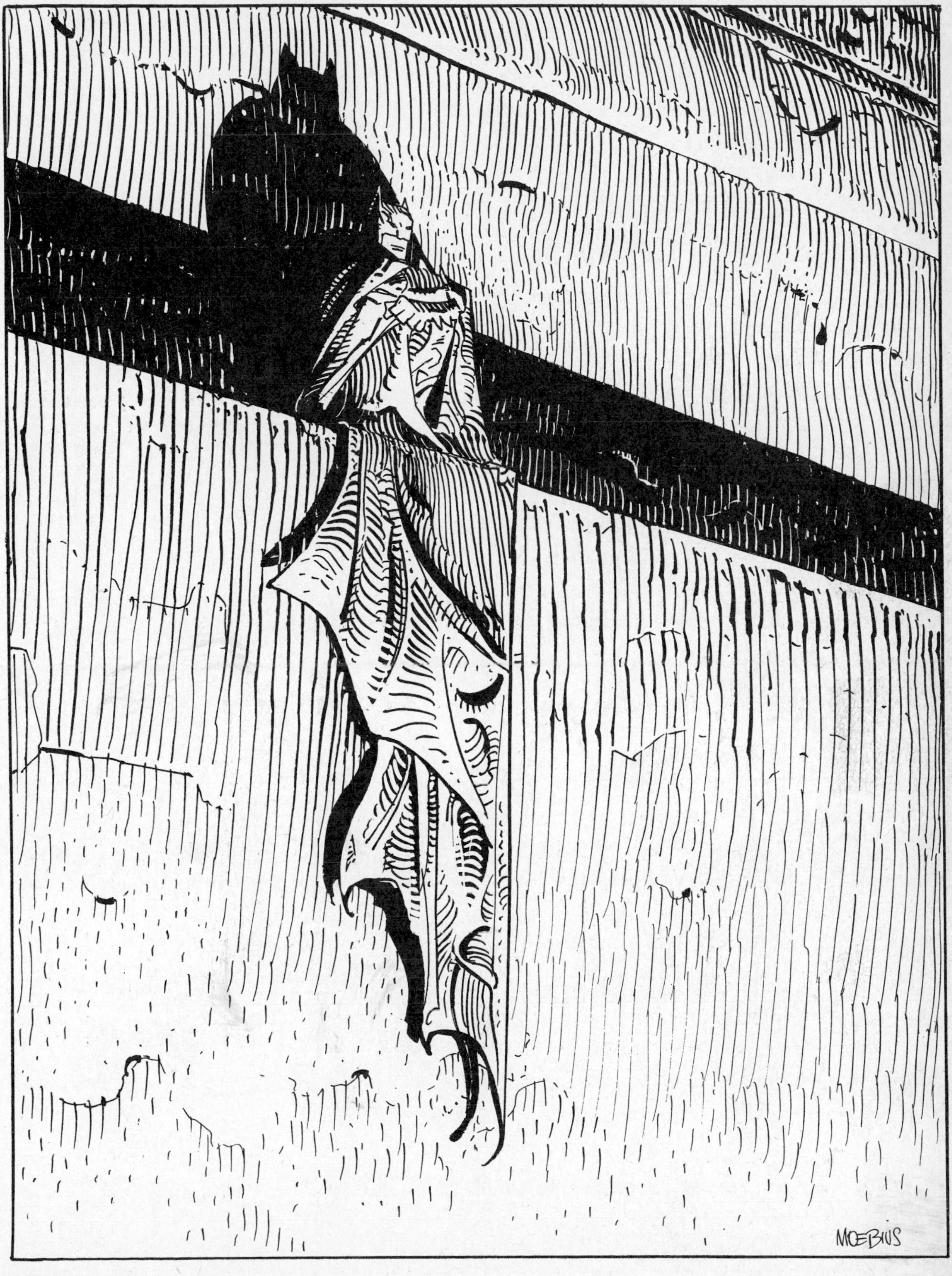
MOEBIUS

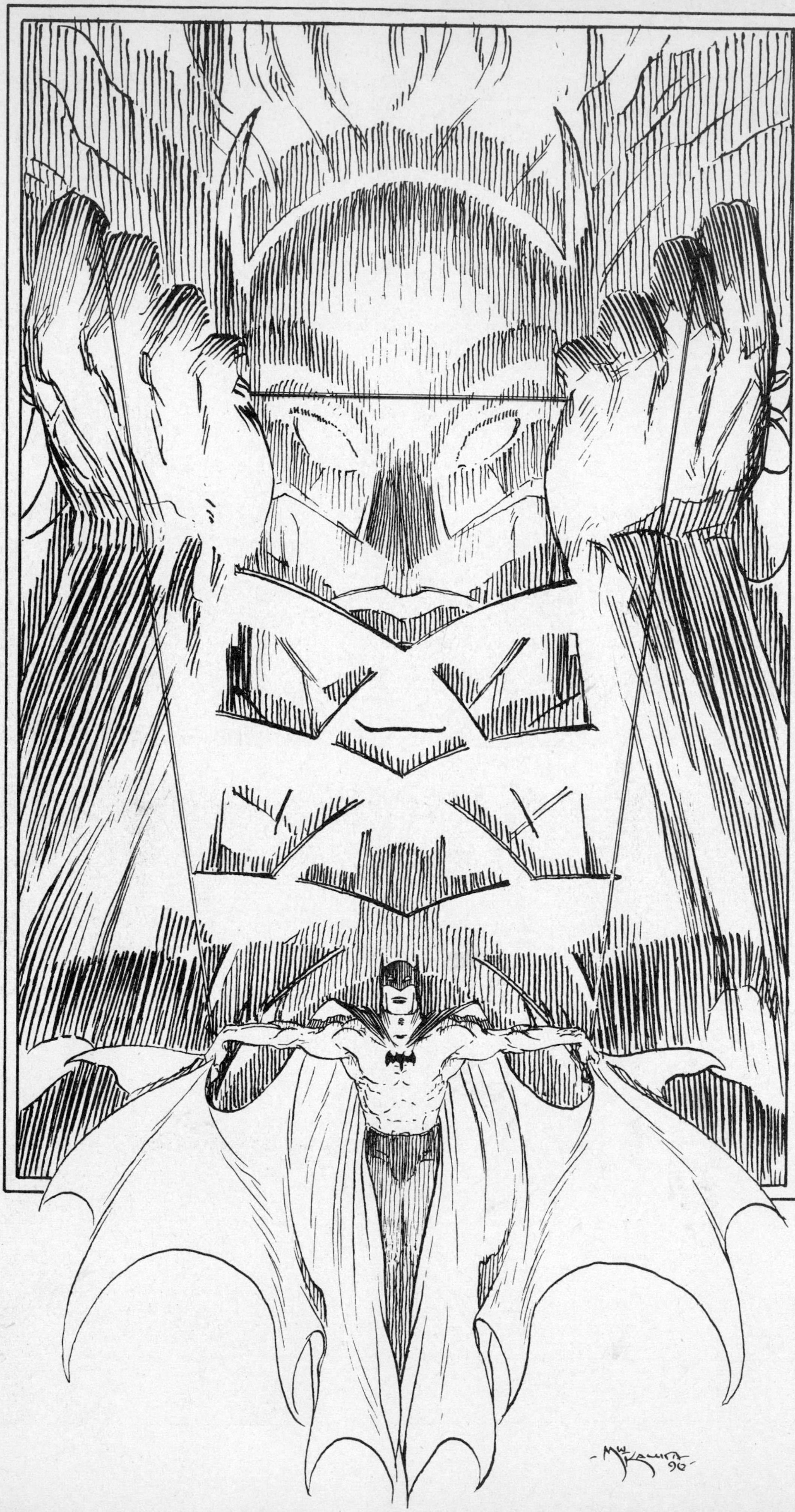

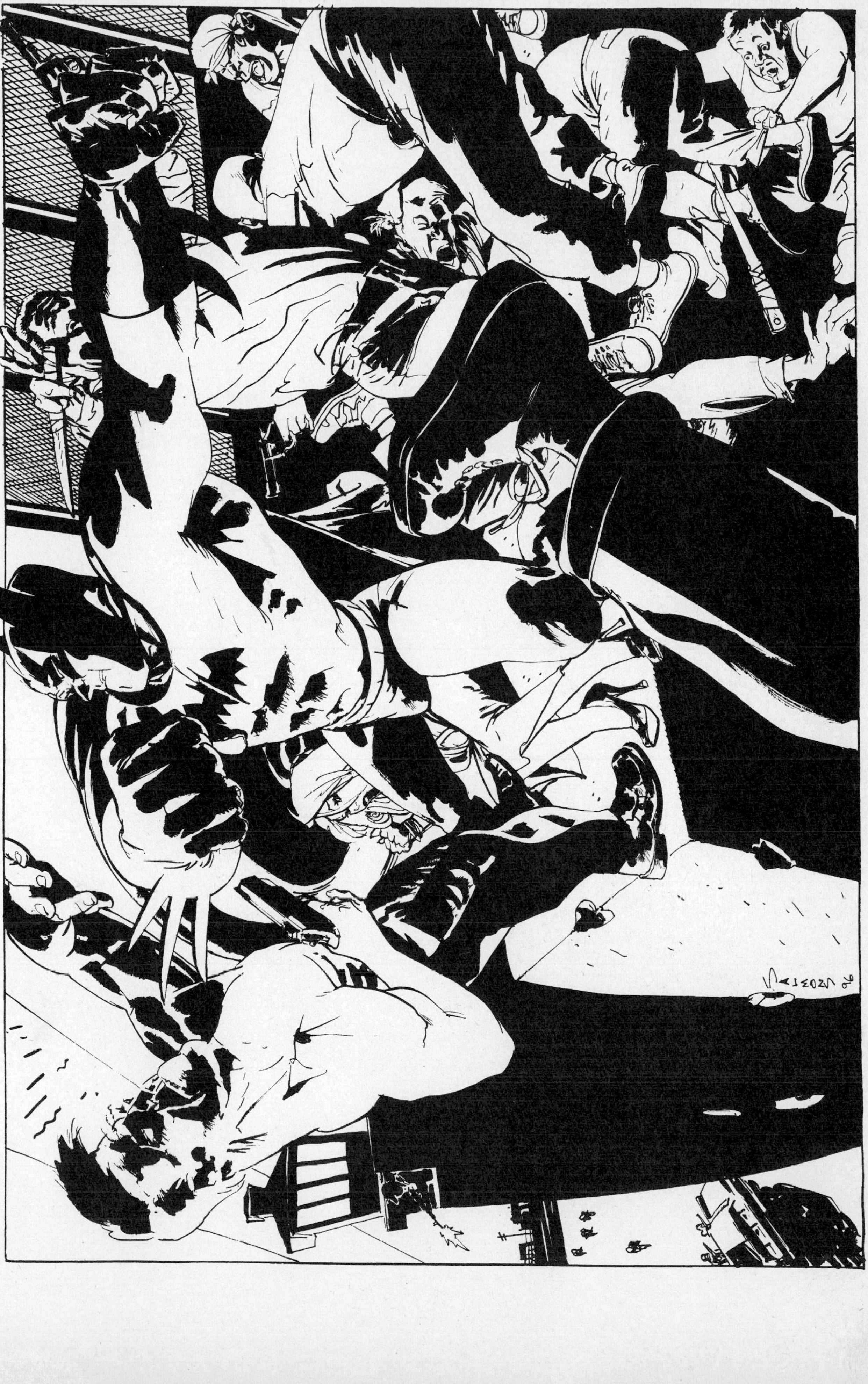

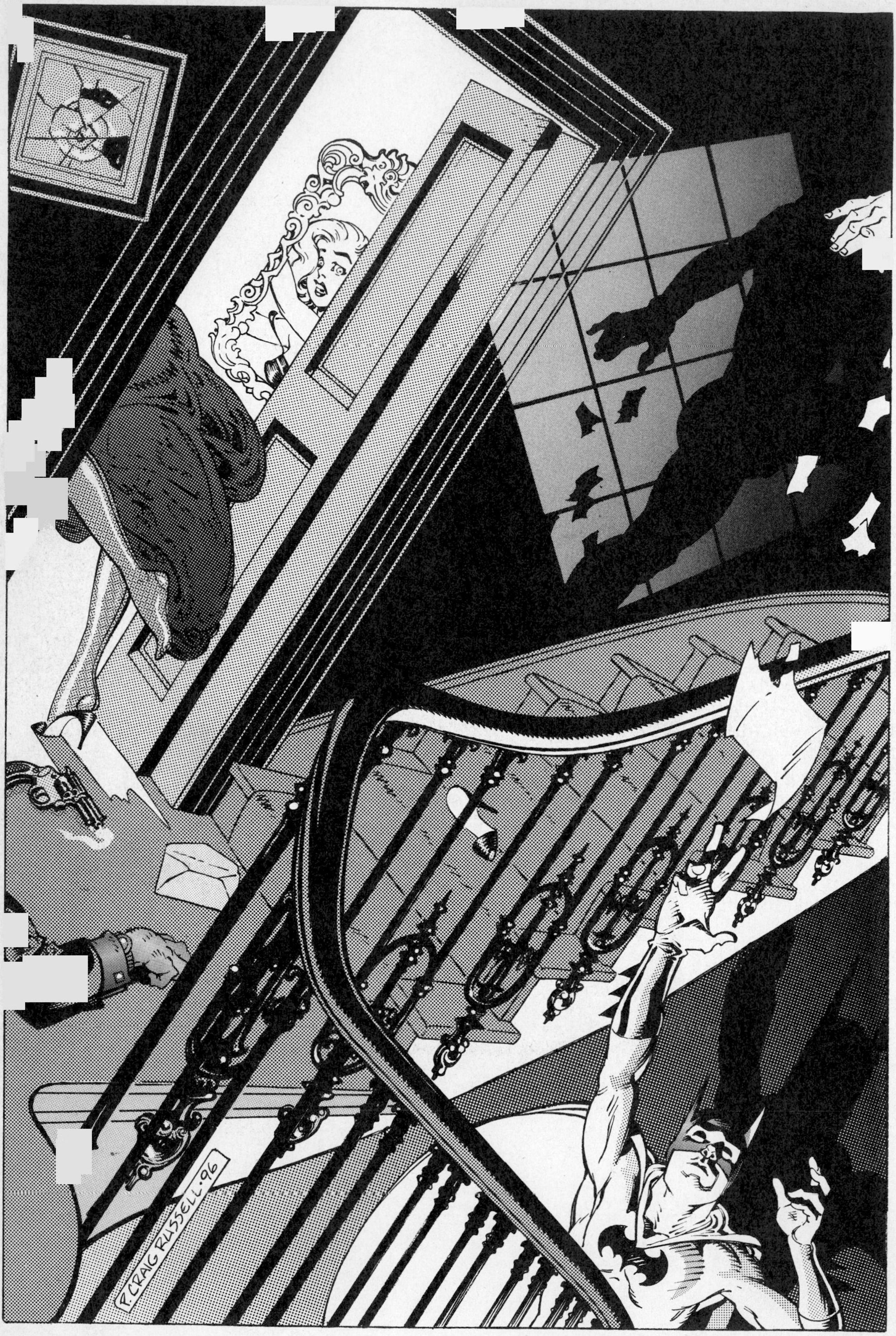
P. CRAIG RUSSELL·96

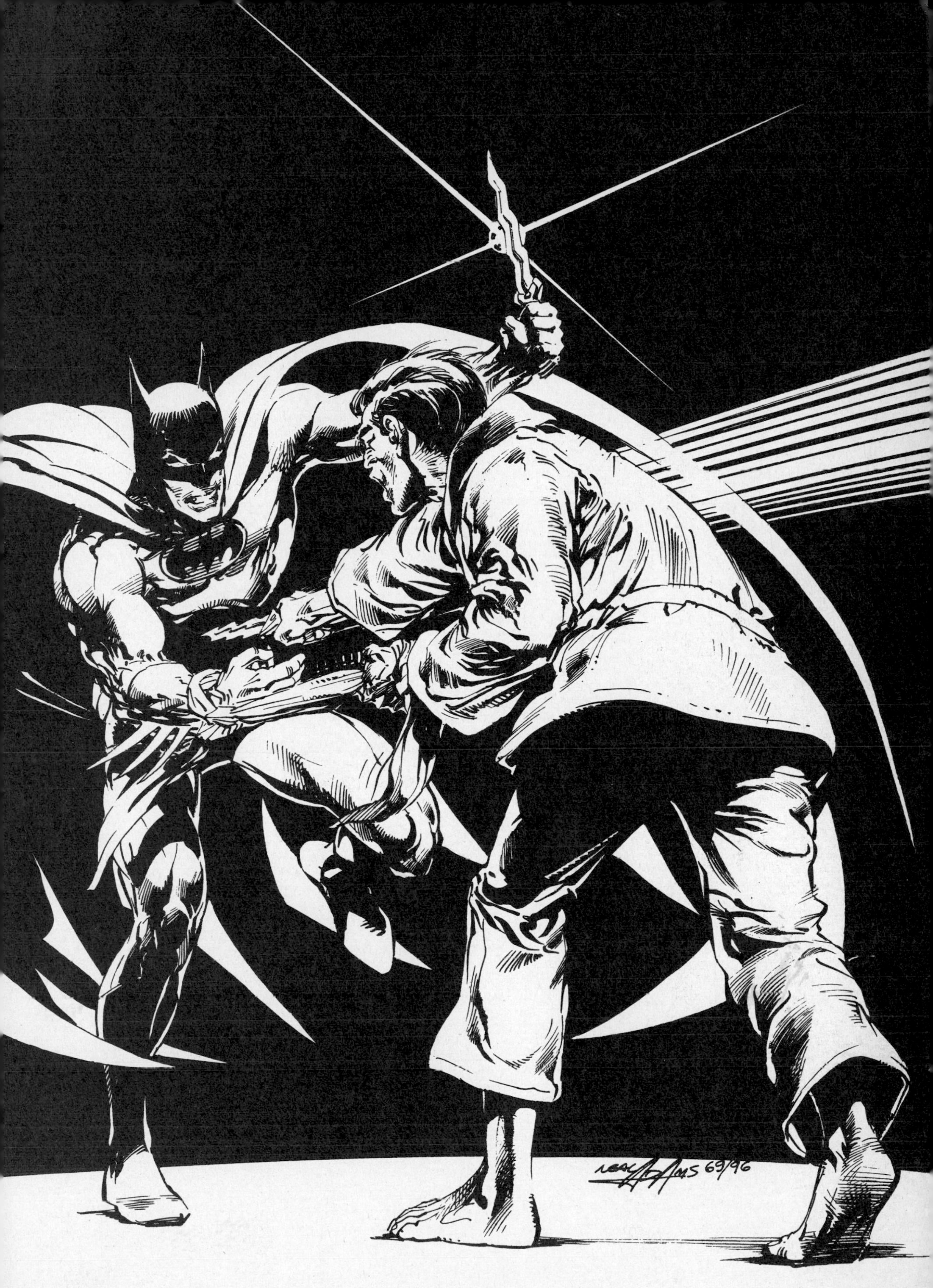

ACKNOWLEDGEMENTS

The editors of this book would like to offer a word of

thanks to the following people for their help and support:

To Klaus Janson and Ted McKeever who both wrote and

drew unusually beautiful stories as well as lent fervent

support during the books' formative days.

To Scott Dunbier who helped deliver a big fish.

To Fershid Bharucha, a man of infinite patience, too.

To Angelo Messina for his usual, but always

appreciated helping hand.

To Jerry Robinson and Bill Finger, whose contribution to

the character's health and well-being can not be overstated.

And, to Alex Toth, whose vision and talent continue to

keep us aiming in the right direction.

THE QUEST FOR JUSTICE CONTINUES IN THESE BOOKS FROM DC:

FOR READERS OF ALL AGES

THE BATMAN ADVENTURES
Puckett/Pasko/Templeton/Rader/Burchett

BATMAN: THE DARK KNIGHT ADVENTURES
Kelley Puckett/Mike Parobeck/Rick Burchett

GRAPHIC NOVELS

BATMAN: ARKHAM ASYLUM
Suggested for mature readers
Grant Morrison/Dave McKean

BATMAN: THE KILLING JOKE
Suggested for mature readers
Alan Moore/Brian Bolland/John Higgins

COLLECTIONS

THE KNIGHTFALL Trilogy
BATMAN: KNIGHTFALL
Part 1: Broken Bat
Various writers and artists

BATMAN: KNIGHTFALL
Part 2: Who Rules the Night
Various writers and artists

BATMAN: KNIGHTSEND
Various writers and artists

BATMAN: YEAR ONE
Frank Miller/David Mazzucchelli

BATMAN: A DEATH IN THE FAMILY
Jim Starlin/Jim Aparo/Mike DeCarlo

BATMAN: A LONELY PLACE OF DYING
Marv Wolfman/George Pérez/various

BATMAN BLACK AND WHITE
Various writers and artists

BATMAN: COLLECTED LEGENDS OF THE
DARK KNIGHT
Robinson/Moore/Grant/Sale/Russell/O'Neil

BATMAN: CONTAGION
Various writers and artists

BATMAN: THE DARK KNIGHT RETURNS
10TH ANNIVERSARY EDITION
Frank Miller/Lynn Varley/Klaus Janson

BATMAN: DARK LEGENDS
Various writers and artists

BATMAN: FACES
Matt Wagner

BATMAN: FEATURING TWO-FACE AND
THE RIDDLER
Various writers and artists

BATMAN: FOUR OF A KIND
Various writers and artists

BATMAN: GOTHIC
Grant Morrison/Klaus Janson

BATMAN: HAUNTED KNIGHT
Jeph Loeb/Tim Sale

BATMAN: THE LAST ARKHAM
Alan Grant/Norm Breyfogle

BATMAN: LEGACY
Various writers and artists

BATMAN: MANBAT
Jamie Delano/John Bolton

BATMAN: OTHER REALMS
Mark Kneece/Bo Hampton/Scott Hampton

BATMAN: PRODIGAL
Various writers and artists

BATMAN: SWORD OF AZRAEL
Dennis O'Neil/Joe Quesada/Kevin Nowlan

BATMAN: TALES OF THE DEMON
Dennis O'Neil/Neal Adams/various

BATMAN: THE MOVIES
Dennis O'Neil/various artists

BATMAN: THRILLKILLER
Howard Chaykin/Dan Brereton

BATMAN: VENOM
Dennis O'Neil/Trevor Von Eeden/various

BATMAN VS. PREDATOR:
THE COLLECTED EDITION
Dave Gibbons/Andy Kubert/Adam Kubert

BATMAN VS. PREDATOR II: BLOODMATCH
Doug Moench/Paul Gulacy/Terry Austin

BATMAN VS. PREDATOR III: BLOOD TIES
Chuck Dixon/Rodolfo Damaggio/
Robert Campanella

THE GREATEST BATMAN STORIES EVER
TOLD Vol. 1
Various writers and artists

THE GREATEST JOKER STORIES
EVER TOLD
Various writers and artists

CATWOMAN: THE CATFILE
Chuck Dixon/Jim Balent/Bob Smith

NIGHTWING: TIES THAT BIND
Dennis O'Neil/Alan Grant/various artists

NIGHTWING: A KNIGHT IN BLÜDHAVEN
Chuck Dixon/Scott McDaniel/Karl Story

ROBIN: A HERO REBORN
Chuck Dixon/Tom Lyle/Bob Smith

ARCHIVE EDITIONS

BATMAN ARCHIVES Vol. 1
(Batman's adventures from DETECTIVE
COMICS 27-50) Bob Kane/Bill Finger/
various

BATMAN ARCHIVES Vol. 2
(Batman's adventures from DETECTIVE
COMICS 51-70) Bob Kane/Bill Finger/
various

BATMAN ARCHIVES Vol. 3
(Batman's adventures from DETECTIVE
COMICS 71-86) Bob Kane/Bill Finger/
various

BATMAN ARCHIVES Vol. 4
(Batman's adventures from DETECTIVE
COMICS 87-102) Bob Kane/Bill Finger/
Dick Sprang/Various

BATMAN: THE DARK KNIGHT ARCHIVES
Vol. 1
(BATMAN 1-4) Bob Kane/Bill Finger/
various

BATMAN: THE DARK KNIGHT ARCHIVES
Vol. 2
(BATMAN 5-8) Bob Kane/Bill Finger/
various

FOR THE NEAREST COMICS SHOP CARRYING COLLECTED EDITIONS AND MONTHLY TITLES FROM DC COMICS,
CALL 1-888-COMIC BOOK.

BM9811